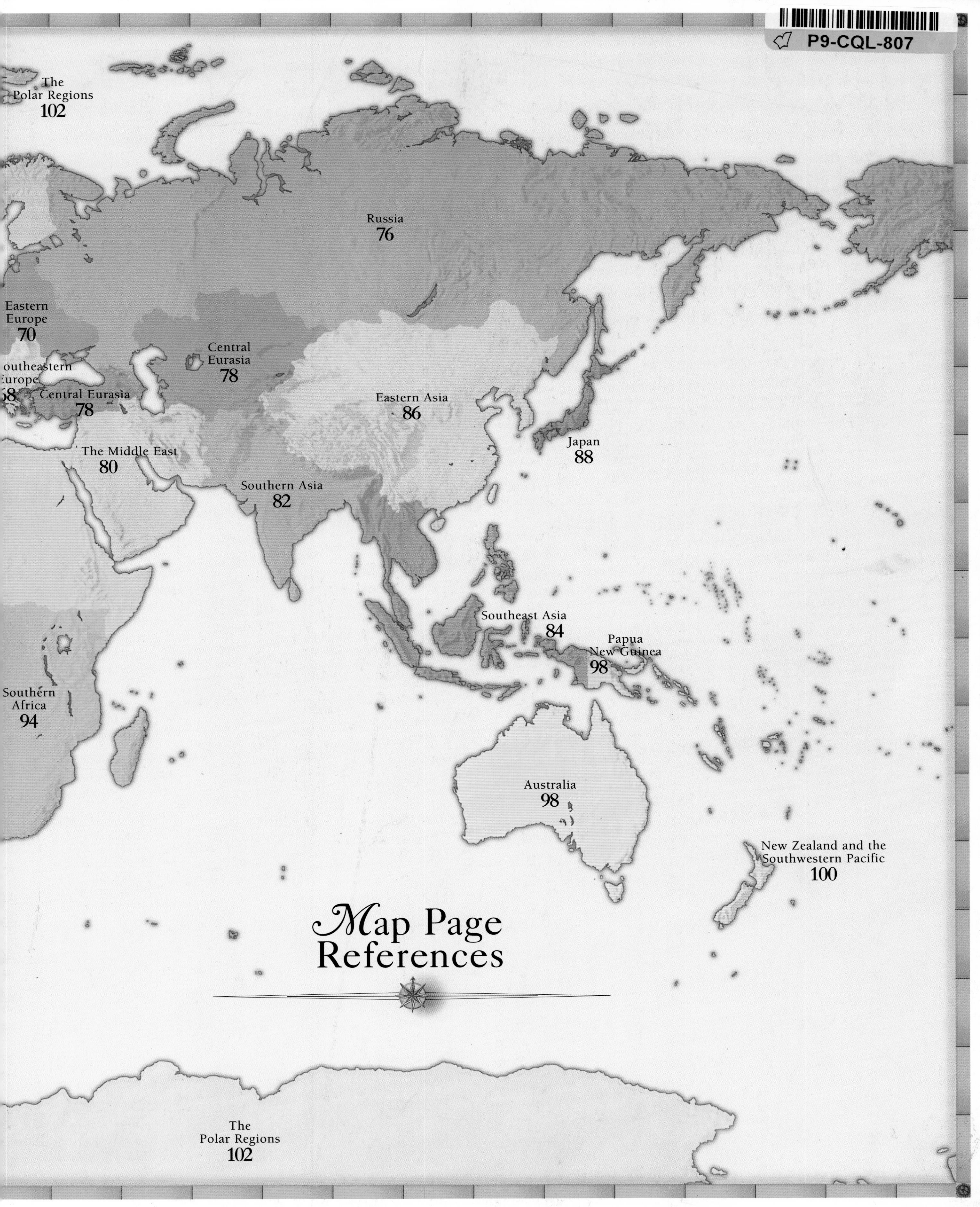

P9-CQL-807
The Polar Regions
102
Russia
76
Eastern Europe
70
Central Eurasia
78
Central Eurasia
78
Eastern Asia
86
Japan
88
The Middle East
80
Southern Asia
82
Southeast Asia
84
Papua New Guinea
98
Southern Africa
94
Australia
98
New Zealand and the Southwestern Pacific
100
Map Page References
The Polar Regions
102

The Reader's Digest

Children's Atlas of the World

The Reader's Digest
Children's Atlas of the World

A Reader's Digest Young Families Book
published by Joshua Morris Publishing, Inc.
355 Riverside Avenue, Westport, CT 06880

Conceived and produced by **Weldon Owen Pty Limited**
43 Victoria Street, McMahons Point, NSW, 2060, Australia
A member of the Weldon Owen Group of Companies
Sydney • San Francisco

READER'S DIGEST YOUNG FAMILIES, INC.
General Manager: Vivian Antonangeli
Creative Consultant: Michael J. Morris
Group Publisher: Rosanna Hansen
U.S. Editor: Sherry Gerstein
Creative Director: Ira Teichberg
Director of Sales and Marketing: Rosanne McManus
Director of U.S. Sales: Lola Valenciano
Marketing Director: Karen Herman
U.S. Consultant: Stephen F. Steiner

WELDON OWEN PTY LTD
Chairman: John Owen
Publisher: Sheena Coupe

Design Concept: John Bull
Managing Editor: Ariana Klepac
Art Director: Sue Burk

Project Editor: Scott Forbes
Consulting Editor: Colin Sale
Editorial Assistant: Anne Ferrier
Text: Scott Forbes

Senior Designer: Hilda Mendham
Designer, Thematic Spreads: Lena Lowe
Pre-press Co-ordinator: Jocelyne Best
Computer Production: Laura Sassin, Amanda Woodward
Computer Graphics: Stuart McVicar
Jacket Design: John Bull
Senior Picture Researcher: Anne Ferrier
Picture Researcher: Peter Barker
Archives: Rita Joseph

Illustrators: Susanna Addario, Andrew Beckett/illustration, André Boos, Anne Bowman, Greg Bridges, Danny Burke, Martin Camm, Fiammetta Dogi, Simone End, Giuliano Fornari, Chris Forsey, John Francis/Bernard Thornton Artists, U.K., Jon Gittoes, Ray Grinaway, Terry Hadler/Bernard Thornton Artists, U.K., Tim Hayward/Bernard Thornton Artists, U.K., David Kirshner, Frank Knight, Mike Lamble, James McKinnon, Peter Mennim, Nicola Oram, Tony Pyrzakowski, Oliver Rennert, Barbara Rodanska, Claudia Saraceni, Michael Saunders, Peter Schouten, Stephen Seymour/Bernard Thornton Artists, U.K., Marco Sparaciari, Sharif Tarabay/illustration, Steve Trevaskis, Thomas Trojer, Genevieve Wallace, Trevor Weekes, Rod Westblade, Ann Winterbotham

Maps: Digital Wisdom Publishing Ltd
Flags: Flag Society of Australia

Production Manager: Caroline Webber
Production Assistant: Kylie Lawson
Vice President International Sales: Stuart Laurence

Library of Congress Cataloging–in–Publication Data

The Reader's digest children's atlas of the world.
p. cm.
Includes bibliographical references and index.
Summary: Includes more than fifty maps; a fact file on each country and territory; illustrations of places, people, landscapes, and wildlife; an introduction to map making and map reading; projects; activities; and quizzes.
ISBN 1–57584–156–8 (trade: alk. paper). — ISBN 1–57584–208–4 (lib. bdg. : alk. paper)
1. Children's atlases. [1. Atlases.] I. Title: Children's atlas of the world.
G1021 R563 1998 97–38041
[<G&M>] CIP
912—DC21 MAPS

Color Reproduction by Colourscan Co Pte Ltd
Printed by Toppan Printing Co, (H.K.) Ltd
Printed in China

A WELDON OWEN PRODUCTION

The Reader's Digest Children's Atlas of the World

Consulting Editor: Colin Sale

Reader's Digest
Young Families®

Westport, Connecticut/Montréal

CONTENTS

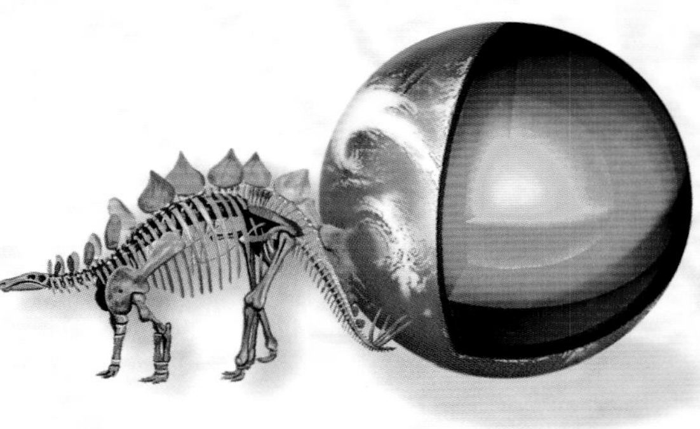

Europe 54

Asia 74

Africa 90

Australia and Oceania 96

How to Use This Atlas

THE READER'S DIGEST CHILDREN'S ATLAS OF THE WORLD takes you on a fascinating tour of our extraordinary world. Before you set off, read the sections called Maps and Mapmaking and How to Read a Map. There you will find out about different kinds of maps and how they are made, and learn how to read and use maps. The remaining introductory pages are a guide to our planet, Earth. They show you where it is located in space, what it is made of, how its landscapes have been shaped, and how weather, wildlife and peoples vary around the world. The atlas maps are divided into seven parts—one for each of the continents of North America, South America, Europe, Asia, Africa, and Australia and Oceania, and one for the polar regions. Each part begins with a continent map that includes country lists and shows the most important features of the landscape. The continent map is followed by a series of illustrated maps which are packed with facts, pictures and activities. The sample maps and notes on these two pages explain the features on both types of map. At the back of the atlas you will find the World Fact File. This provides useful information on all of the world's countries and major territories. Finally, there is a glossary of terms used in this book, as well as a gazetteer—a geographical index that helps you to find places on the maps.

ILLUSTRATED MAP

Country list This is a list of the countries or states on the map, their populations and capital cities.

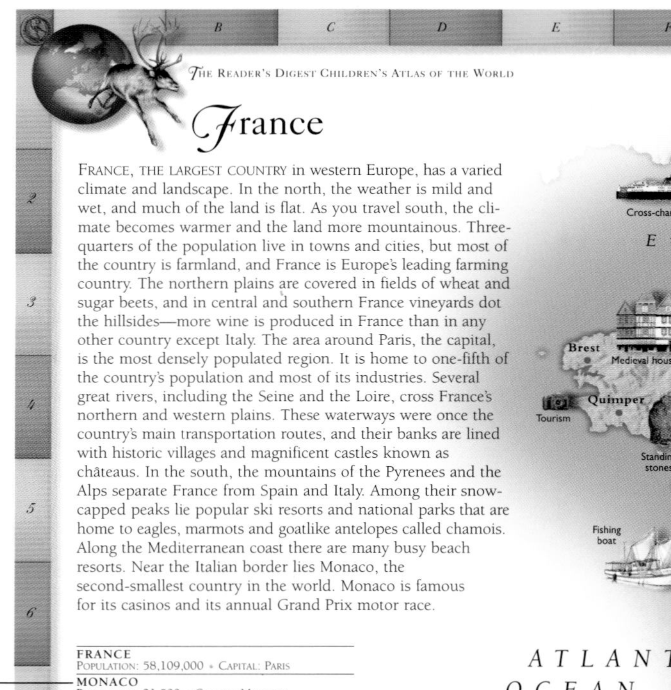
France
FRANCE, THE LARGEST COUNTRY in western Europe, has a varied climate and landscape. In the north, the weather is mild and wet, and much of the land is flat. As you travel south, the climate becomes warmer and the land more mountainous. Three-quarters of the population live in towns and cities, but most of the country is farmland, and France is Europe's leading farming country. The northern plains are covered in fields of wheat and sugar beets, and in central and southern France vineyards dot the hillsides—more wine is produced in France than in any other country except Italy. The area around Paris, the capital, is the most densely populated region. It is home to one-fifth of the country's population and most of its industries. Several great rivers, including the Seine and the Loire, cross France's northern and western plains. These waterways were once the country's main transportation routes, and their banks are lined with historic villages and magnificent castles known as châteaus. In the south, the mountains of the Pyrenees and the Alps separate France from Spain and Italy. Among their snow-capped peaks lie popular ski resorts and national parks that are home to eagles, marmots and goatlike antelopes called chamois. Along the Mediterranean coast there are many busy beach resorts. Near the Italian border lies Monaco, the second-smallest country in the world. Monaco is famous for its casinos and its annual Grand Prix motor race.
FRANCE
POPULATION: 58,109,000 • CAPITAL: PARIS
MONACO
POPULATION: 31,500 • CAPITAL: MONACO
ATLANTIC OCEAN
AMAZING FACT
France is now connected to Great Britain by an undersea rail link known as the Channel Tunnel. The tunnel took seven years to build and includes two rail tracks. Trains take 35 minutes to pass through the tunnel. Travelers can journey from London to Paris in about three hours.
Brest
Quimper
Medieval houses
Tourism
Standing stones
Fishing boat
Cross-channel
Mackerel
BOULES
Boules is a bowling game that is popular in France. It is played with metal balls on a hard dirt surface.
60

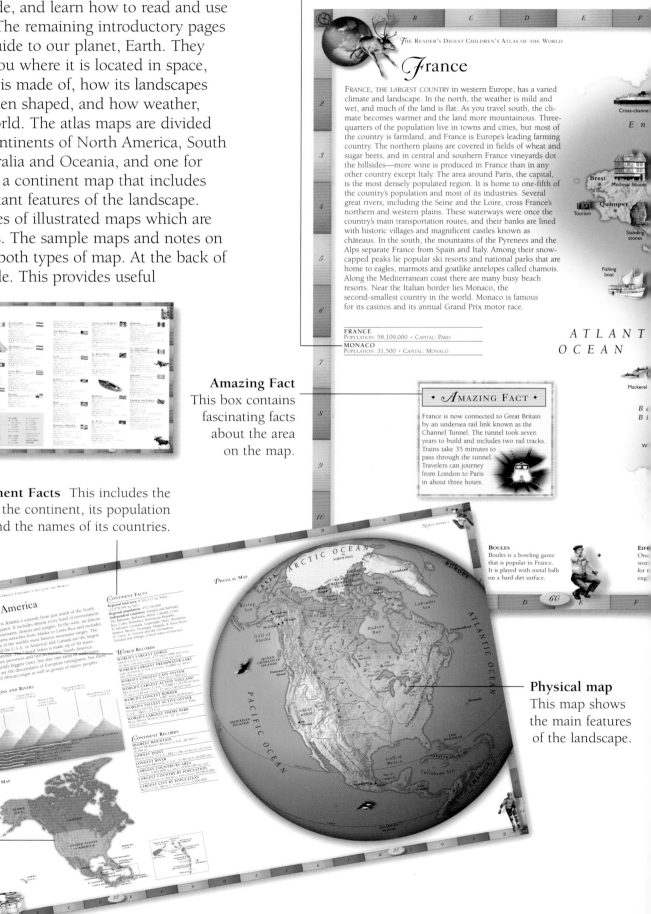

Amazing Fact This box contains fascinating facts about the area on the map.

Continent Facts This includes the size of the continent, its population and the names of its countries.

CONTINENT MAP

Records This is a list of the tallest, longest and largest features of the continent.

Size comparison These pictures show how the continent's most important mountains and rivers would look if you could see them side by side.

Political map This map shows all the countries in the continent.

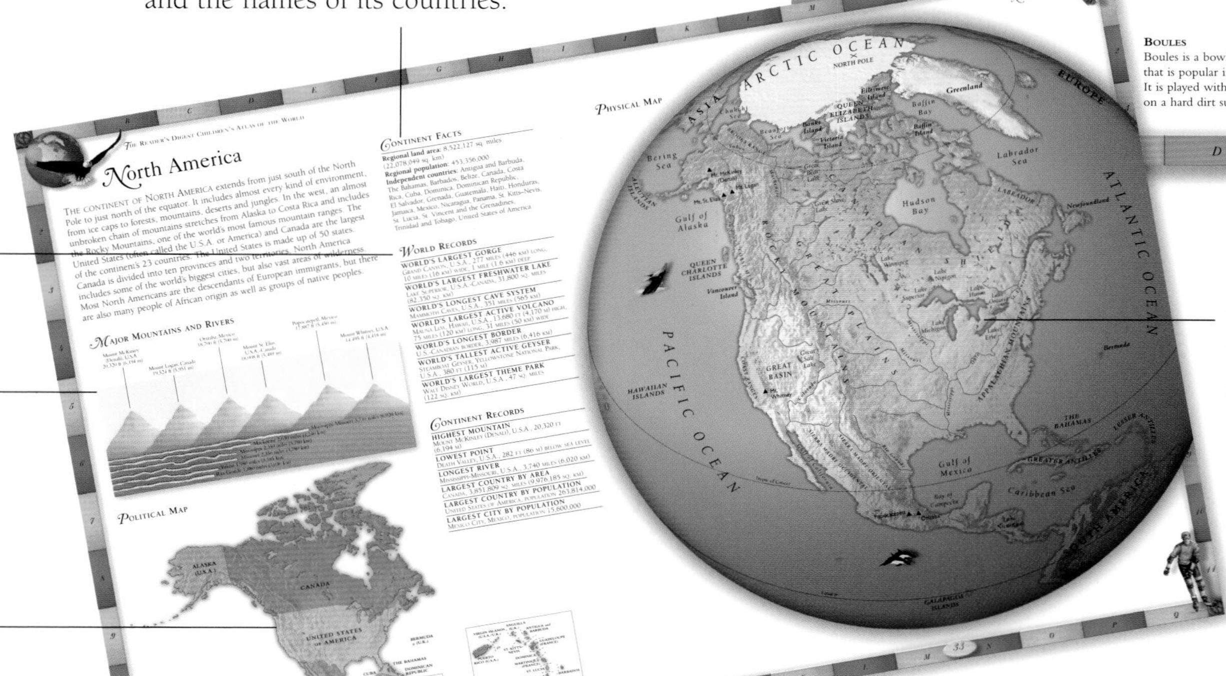
North America
Physical Map
Political Map
ARCTIC OCEAN
ATLANTIC OCEAN
PACIFIC OCEAN

Physical map This map shows the main features of the landscape.

Colored border Each part of the atlas has a different colored border.

Map reader's grid The letters and numbers on the border help you find places on the map. See page 10 to find out how to use the grid.

Projects By trying out these activities and experiments, you can learn more about a topic or a part of the world.

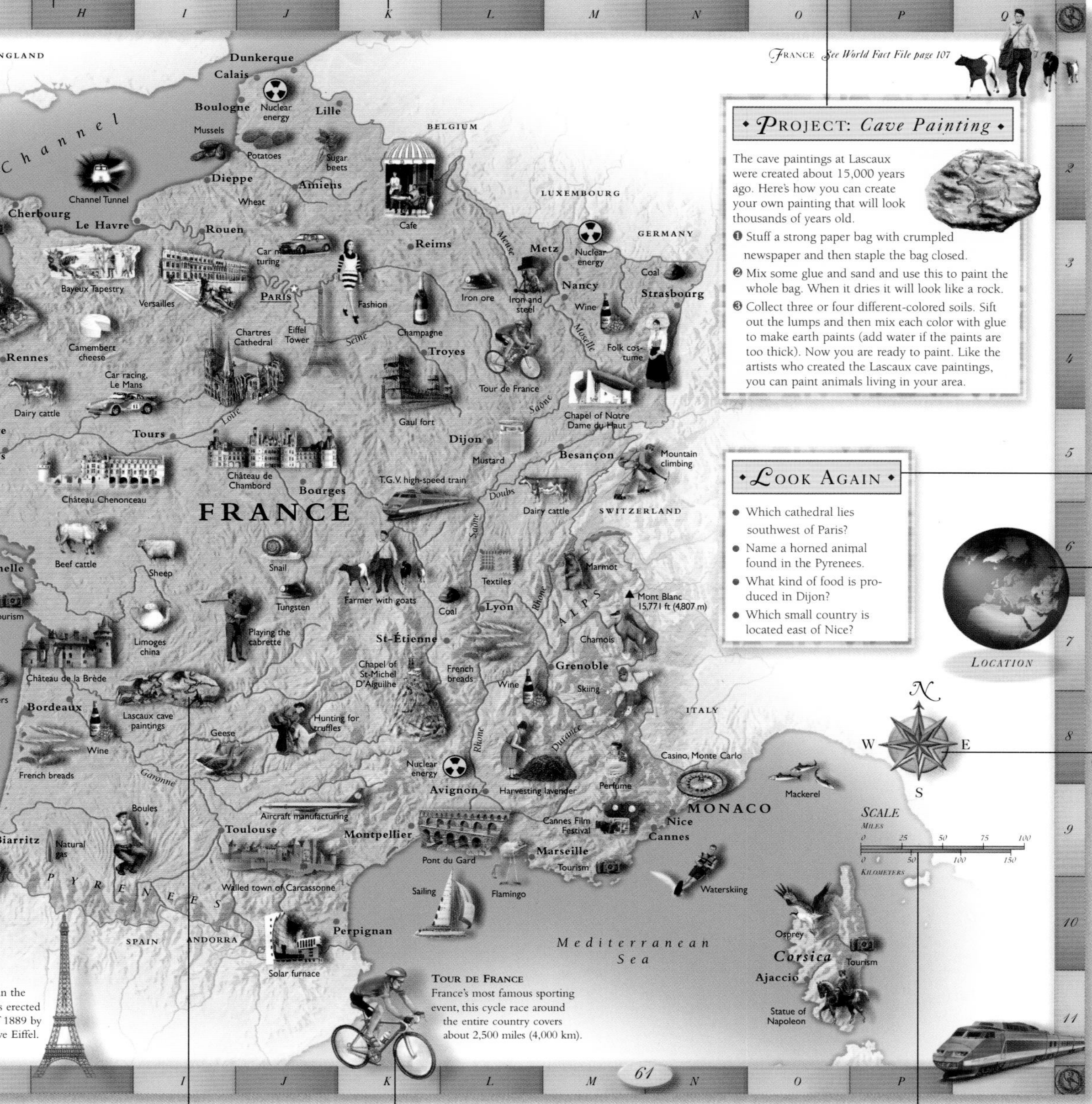

France See World Fact File page 107
PROJECT: Cave Painting
The cave paintings at Lascaux were created about 15,000 years ago. Here's how you can create your own painting that will look thousands of years old.
❶ Stuff a strong paper bag with crumpled newspaper and then staple the bag closed.
❷ Mix some glue and sand and use this to paint the whole bag. When it dries it will look like a rock.
❸ Collect three or four different-colored soils. Sift out the lumps and then mix each color with glue to make earth paints (add water if the paints are too thick). Now you are ready to paint. Like the artists who created the Lascaux cave paintings, you can paint animals living in your area.
LOOK AGAIN
• Which cathedral lies southwest of Paris?
• Name a horned animal found in the Pyrenees.
• What kind of food is produced in Dijon?
• Which small country is located east of Nice?
Location
FRANCE
ENGLAND
BELGIUM
LUXEMBOURG
GERMANY
SWITZERLAND
ITALY
MONACO
SPAIN
ANDORRA
Channel
Mediterranean Sea
Dunkerque
Calais
Boulogne
Lille
Dieppe
Amiens
Cherbourg
Le Havre
Rouen
Reims
Metz
Nancy
Strasbourg
Paris
Rennes
Troyes
Tours
Dijon
Besançon
Bourges
Rochelle
Lyon
St-Étienne
Grenoble
Bordeaux
Avignon
Nice
Cannes
Toulouse
Montpellier
Marseille
Biarritz
Perpignan
Corsica
Ajaccio
Mont Blanc 15,771 ft (4,807 m)
TOUR DE FRANCE
France's most famous sporting event, this cycle race around the entire country covers about 2,500 miles (4,000 km).
Scale
N
W
E
S

Look Again To answer these questions, you'll need to take a close look at the information on the map.

Locator globe This globe shows where the area on the map is located.

Illustrations These show the people, places, wildlife and activities in the area on the map.

Feature illustrations These pullout features provide extra information on some of the map illustrations.

Scale The scale bar helps you to calculate distances on the map. To find out how to do this, see page 10.

Compass The compass helps you find north. To find out how to use the compass, see page 10.

Key to Map Colors

Desert and semidesert

Forest and grassland

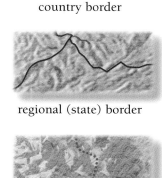

Tundra

Ice cap

Key to Map Symbols

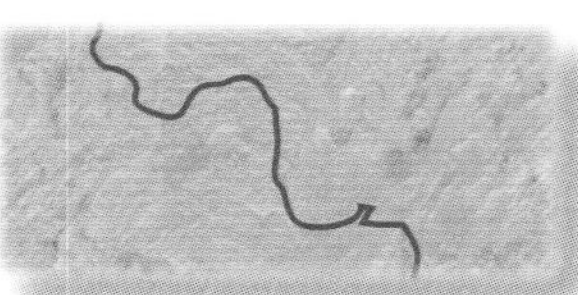

country border

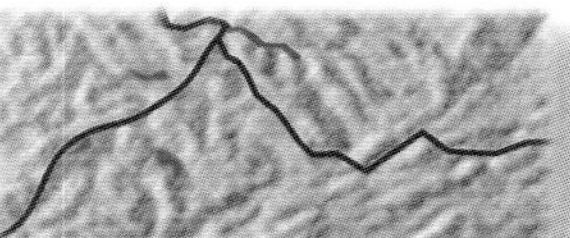

regional (state) border

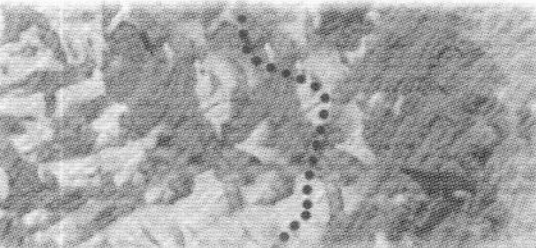

disputed border

MARTINIQUE
(FRANCE)

territory and country to which it belongs

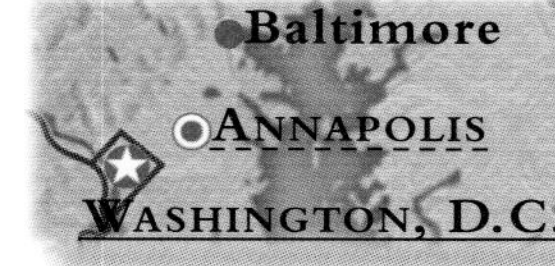

Baltimore
ANNAPOLIS
WASHINGTON, D.C.

✪ national capital
◉ regional capital
● city or town

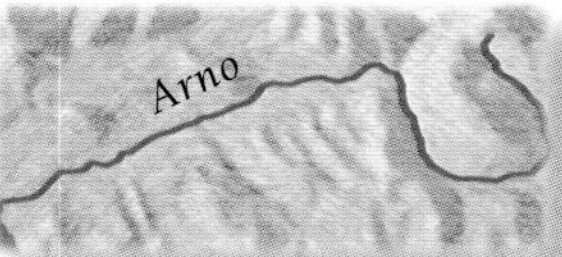

Arno

river

Lake Ontario

lake

▲ Ben Nevis
4,406 ft (1,343 m)

▲ major mountain

Ⓔ African elephants

Ⓔ endangered animal

Maps and Mapmaking

A MAP IS A PICTURE that shows you what an area of land looks like from above. Any area, no matter how large or small, can be drawn as a map. Some maps show small areas such as a town; others show the whole world. Because maps usually show areas that are much larger than the page they are printed on, objects have to be drawn much smaller than they really are. This is called drawing to scale. The bigger the area of a map, the smaller the real objects have to be drawn. Maps that show a small area and a large amount of detail are called large-scale maps. Maps that show a large area and a small amount of detail are called small-scale maps. On most maps, real objects are represented by lines, colors and symbols. For example, on a map of a town, black outlines may indicate streets, and colored shapes may show buildings. On a map of a country, towns may appear as simple black dots, and rivers as blue lines. A book of maps—like the one you are reading now—is called an atlas. An atlas usually contains maps of the whole world as well as maps of countries and continents.

• Amazing Fact •

In Greek mythology, Atlas was a man who led a rebellion against the gods. As a punishment for this act, he was made to support the world on his shoulders. When the first books of maps were published in the 16th century, many had an illustration of Atlas carrying a globe on their covers. As a result, a book of maps soon became known as an atlas.

Mapping the World

Each of these maps shows the location of Riverford School, but each is drawn at a different scale.

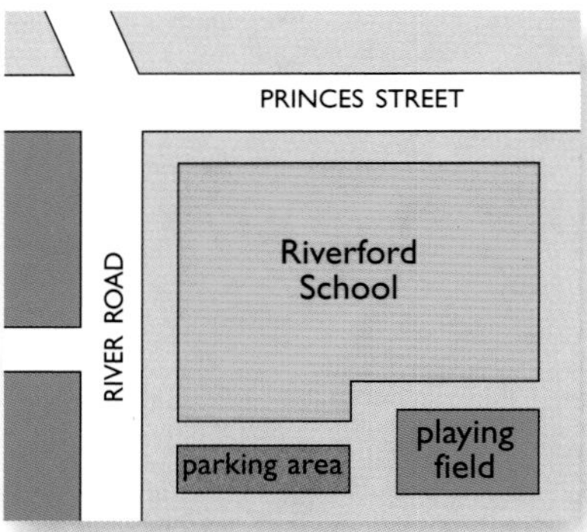
PRINCES STREET
RIVER ROAD
Riverford School
parking area
playing field

In this map of Riverford School, lines, colored shapes and labels are used to show the school, nearby streets and other features. Maps of small areas like this are often called plans.

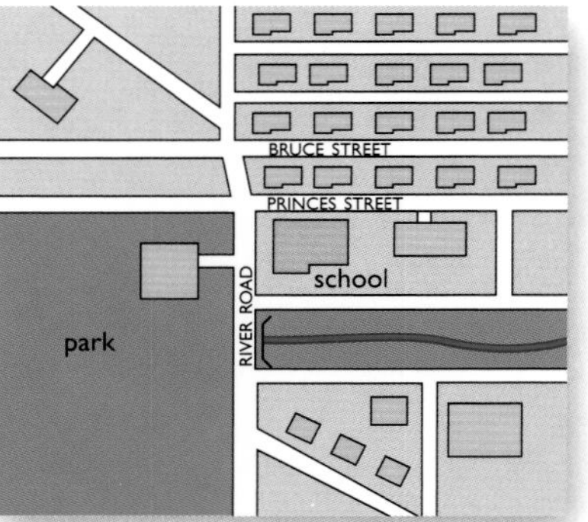
BRUCE STREET
PRINCES STREET
school
RIVER ROAD
park

This is a map of Riverford town. Because the area of the map is larger, less detail can be shown. You can now see that the school is near houses, a park and a river, but you can no longer see the school parking area or playing field.

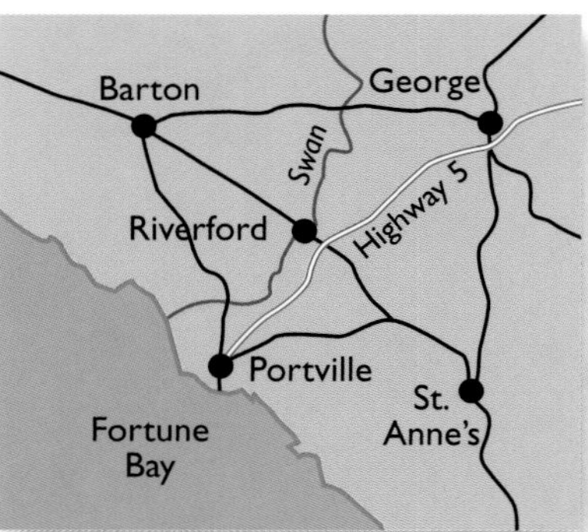
Barton
George
Swan
Riverford
Highway 5
Portville
St. Anne's
Fortune Bay

This map shows the region around Riverford. The town is now represented by a simple black dot, so you can no longer see the school or the streets. But you can see that Riverford is near water, and that it is linked to other towns by major and minor roads.

• Project: *Mapping Your Neighborhood* •

You can draw a map of your neighborhood. To do this you will have to think about where places are, how far apart they are, and what shape they are. You may need to go for a walk and make a list of the things you want to show on your map.

❶ Once you have decided what you are going to include, draw in the streets.

GREEN ST.
RIVER RD.
UNION ST.
MAIN ST.

❷ Then add shapes to represent features such as buildings, parks and rivers. Label the streets.

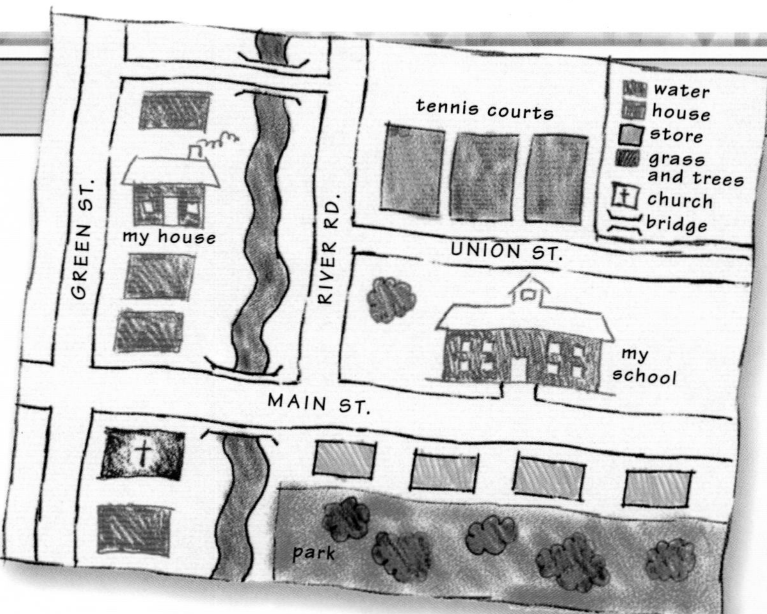
water
house
store
grass and trees
church
bridge
tennis courts
GREEN ST.
my house
RIVER RD.
UNION ST.
my school
MAIN ST.
park

❸ Now color your map. Use one color for houses, one for streets, and so on. Draw a key to show what the colors represent. Finally, add labels for important places such as your home and school.

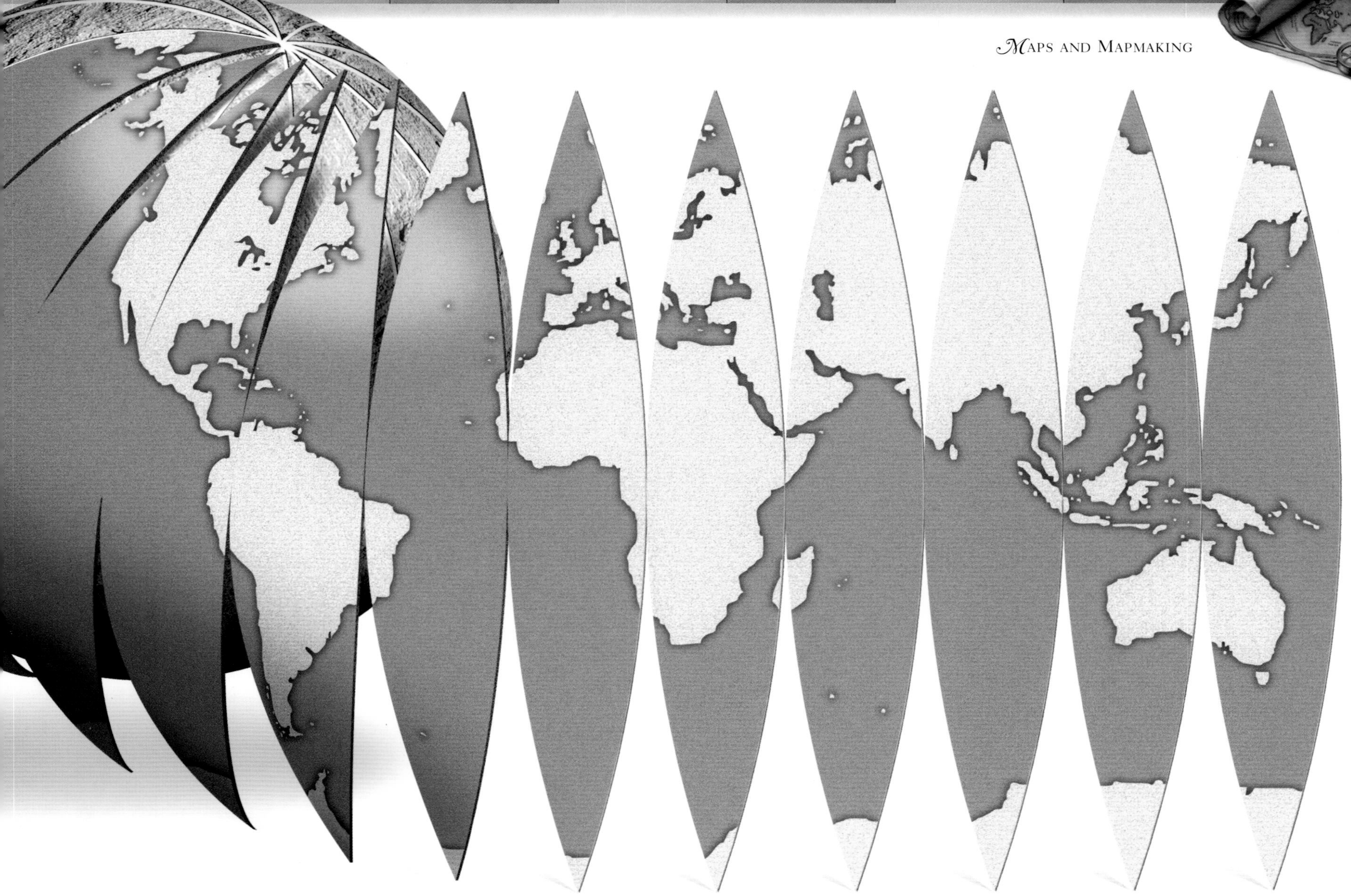

MAKING MAPS

People who make maps are known as mapmakers or cartographers. Before airplanes and spacecraft were invented, mapmakers used information supplied by travelers and explorers to make maps. Nowadays, most maps are based on surveys and on photographs taken by satellites positioned in space, high above Earth. Mapmakers face one major problem: Earth is round, but most maps have to be flat. A globe is the most accurate kind of map because it is the same shape as Earth. But if you tried to create a flat map by simply peeling the surface of a globe, you would end up with a world map made up of pieces, or segments. You can test this for yourself by carefully peeling an orange and trying to flatten out the skin. You will find that it is impossible to make the peel lie flat without breaking it. In order to create a flat map, mapmakers have to stretch and squash the segments of the globe. The different ways in which they do this are known as projections. There are many types of projections, and each creates a slightly different map.

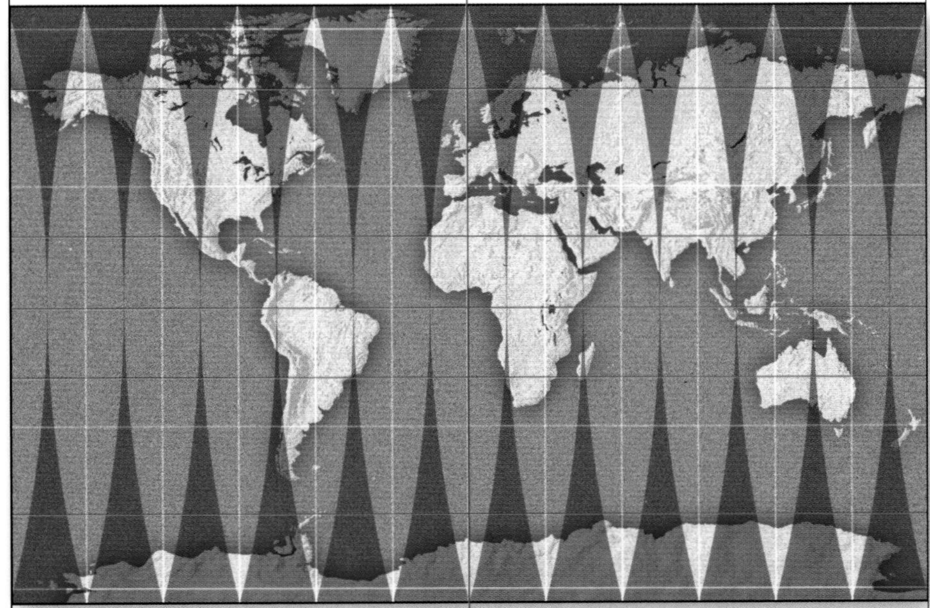
Arctic Circle (66.5°N)
Tropic of Cancer (23.5°N)
Equator (0°)
Tropic of Capricorn (23.5°S)
Antarctic Circle (66.5°S)
180°
Greenwich meridian (0°)
180°

A FLAT EARTH

As shown above, the surface of the globe can be divided into segments. To create a flat, rectangular map like the one on the left, mapmakers must fill in the gaps between the segments. To help them do this and plot locations, mapmakers use lines of latitude (horizontal lines) and longitude (vertical lines).

LINES AROUND THE WORLD

Mapmakers use a grid system to plot locations on the globe. Lines of longitude are drawn between the North Pole and the South Pole and are measured in degrees east or west of the Greenwich meridian (0°). Lines of latitude are drawn in a west-east direction and measured in degrees north or south of the equator (0°). The equator divides the world into the Northern and Southern hemispheres. The Greenwich meridian and the 180° line separate the Eastern and Western hemispheres.

How to Read a Map

MAPS ARE PACKED WITH INFORMATION. They tell you where places are, what size and shape they are, and how far and in what direction they lie from each other. Maps can also tell you about a region's climate, landscape, vegetation, towns and cities, and transportation routes. Once you have learned how to read maps, you can use an atlas to find out many things about countries all around the world.

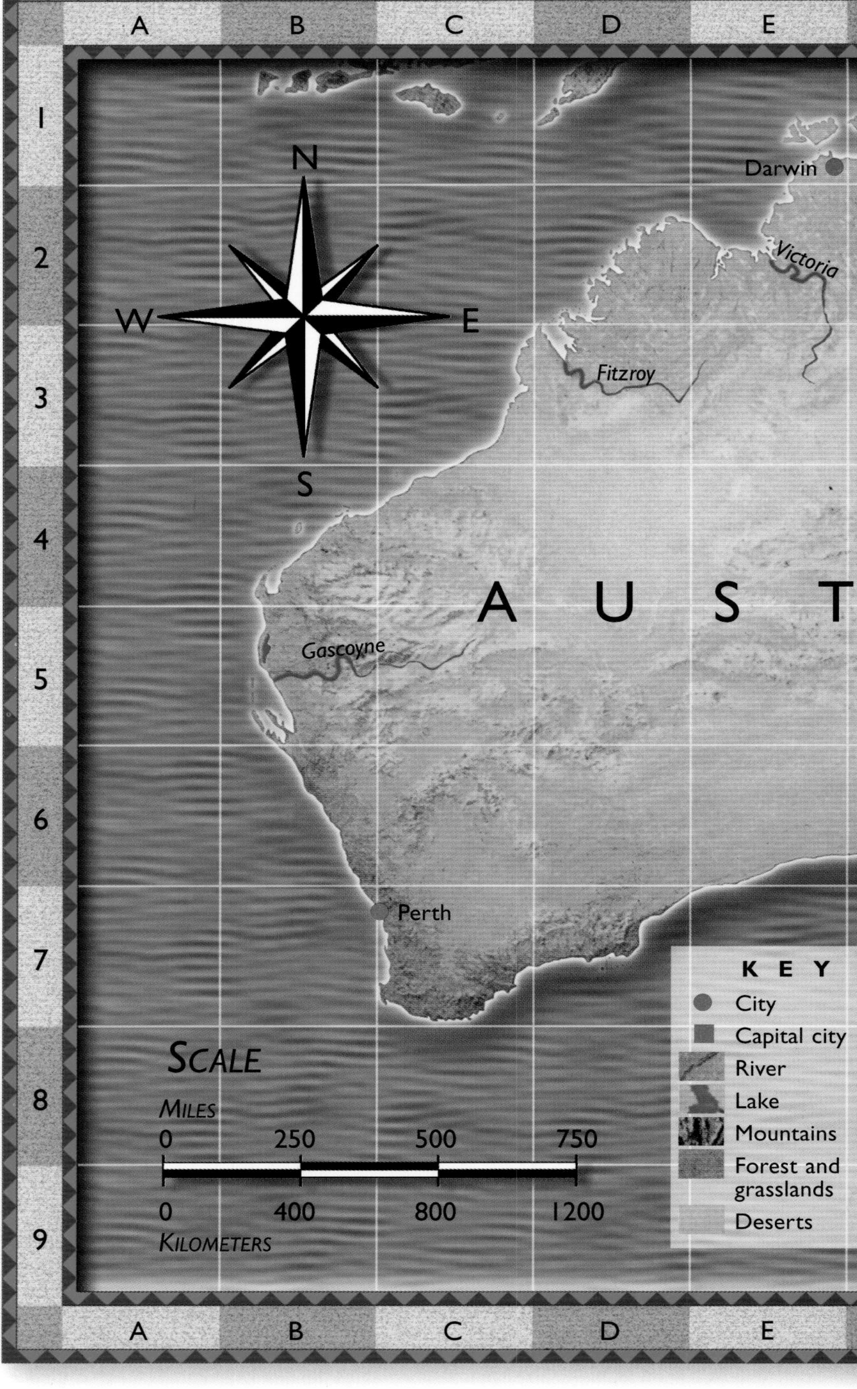

A B C D E
1 2 3 4 5 6 7 8 9
N
S
W
E
Darwin
Victoria
Fitzroy
Gascoyne
Perth
A U S T
SCALE
MILES
0 250 500 750
0 400 800 1200
KILOMETERS
KEY
City
Capital city
River
Lake
Mountains
Forest and grasslands
Deserts

Finding Places

Most maps and atlases use a gazetteer and grid system to help you find places. You look for the place name in the gazetteer—an index of place names which usually appears at the back of the atlas—and then use the grid reference to find the location on the relevant map. Normally, a map grid consists of a series of letters along the top and bottom of the page and a series of numbers down the sides. Take a look at the map of Australia on the right. The grid reference for the city of Melbourne is H8. To find Melbourne, look at the letters on the top or bottom border and find H. Then find 8 on the left- or right-hand border. Imagine a line running down the page between the two Hs and another running across the page between the two 8s. (You can use a ruler to help you line up the numbers.) You will find Melbourne near the intersection of these lines.

Using the Map Grid
In the gazetteer of this book, each place name is followed by a grid reference. The grid reference for the city of Nashville, Tennessee, in the United States is 41 L4. To locate Nashville, turn to page 41 and find L and 4 on the grid. Trace a line down from L and another across from 4. Nashville is near the intersection of the two lines.

Describing Direction

A map usually has a compass symbol, which indicates the direction of north (N) on the map. Sometimes, as on the map above, it also shows the directions of south (S), east (E) and west (W). You can use the points of a compass to describe where places are. For example, on the map above we can say that Sydney is east (E) of Adelaide and that Brisbane is north (N) of Sydney. Brisbane is both north and east of Adelaide, so we can use a combination of compass points and say that Brisbane is northeast (NE) of Adelaide. But Brisbane is farther to the east of Adelaide than it is to the north of it. So, if we want to be even more accurate, we can describe Brisbane as being east-northeast (ENE) of Adelaide. The compass above left shows all the combinations of compass points that you can use to describe direction.

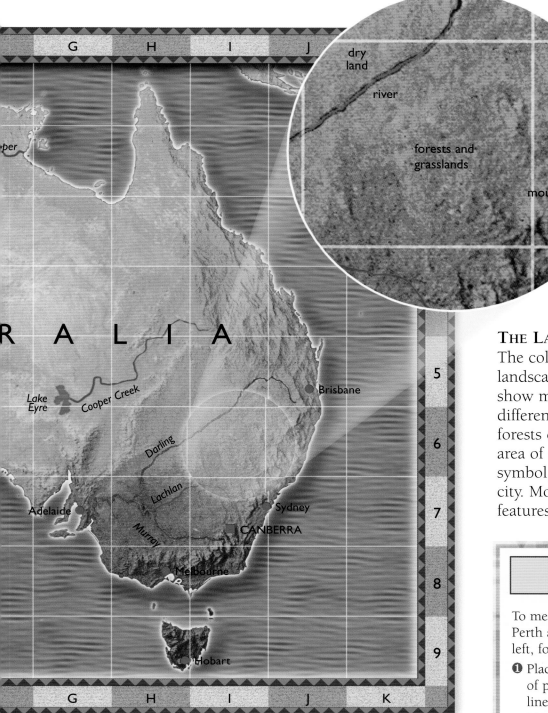

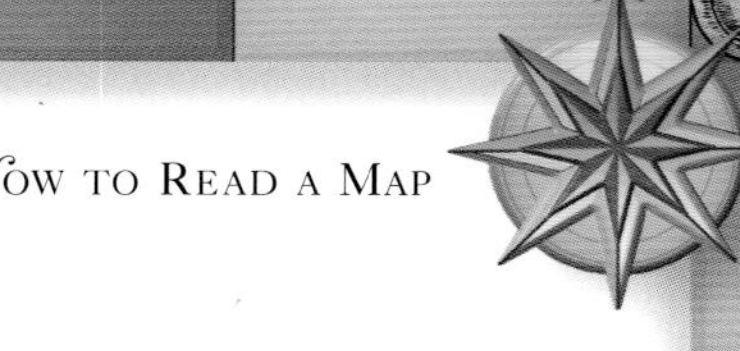

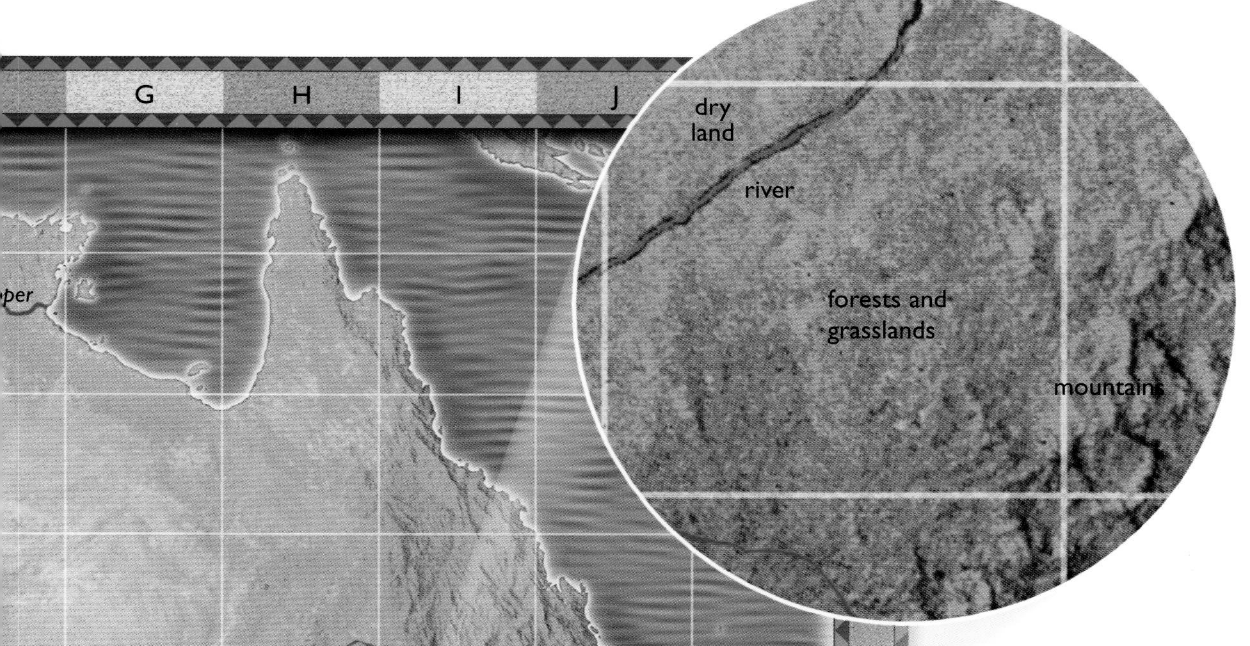
G
H
I
J
K
dry land
river
forests and grasslands
mountains
R A L I A
Lake Eyre
Cooper Creek
Brisbane
Darling
Lachlan
Adelaide
Sydney
Murray
CANBERRA
Melbourne
Hobart
5
6
7
8
9

Color Keys
On this map of Australia, dark shading indicates mountains. Green represents forests and grasslands, and orange shows desert and other dry land. Areas of water such as oceans, lakes and rivers are all colored blue.

The Lay of the Land
The colors of a map may tell you something about a region's landscape, vegetation and climate. Often, shading is used to show mountain ranges, and colors are used to represent different kinds of vegetation. Green normally represents forests or grasslands, while yellow or orange indicates an area of dry land such as desert. On many maps, a special symbol, such as a square or star, is used to indicate a capital city. Most maps and atlases have a key that explains these features. In this atlas, you will find the key on page 7.

Measuring Distance
Most maps have a scale. This shows how distance on the map compares with real distance. Many scales appear as a bar that is divided into sections, as do the ones used in this book. In the scale shown on the map above, each section on the top part of the bar is equal to 250 miles, and each section on the bottom of the bar represents 400 kilometers. The project on this page shows you how to use this type of scale to measure distances on a map. Scales can also be written like this:

1:1,000,000

This shows that the map has been reduced 1,000,000 times. Distances on the ground are therefore 1,000,000 times greater than they are on the map. Thus 1 inch on the map is equal to 1,000,000 inches, or 15¾ miles, and 1 cm on the map is equal to 1,000,000 cm, or 10 km. Other scales are written like this:

1 inch = 10 miles

This shows that 1 inch on the map corresponds to 10 miles in real distance.

◆ Project: *Using a Scale* ◆

To measure the distance between Perth and Sydney on the map at left, follow these steps:

❶ Place the straight edge of a piece of paper on the map so that it lines up the dots of the two cities. Mark their positions on the paper.

❷ Place the paper next to the scale so that one of the dots lines up with zero. The scale is shorter than the distance, so mark the paper where the scale ends and note the distance it represents.

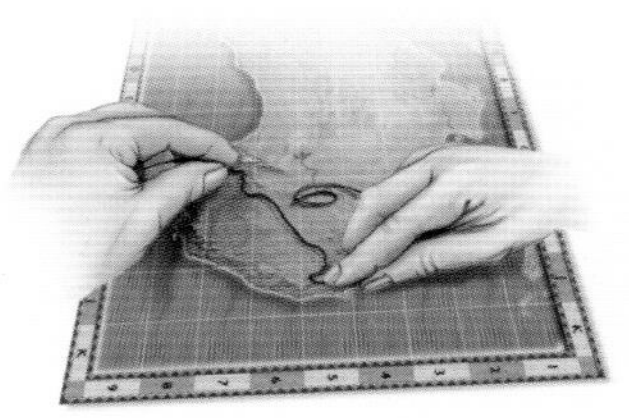

Place the mark back at zero and repeat these steps as often as necessary. Add the figures to calculate the distance between the cities.

You can also use the scale to measure distances along curved lines.

❶ Place a piece of string on the map along the Darling River, bending it to match the course of the river.

❷ Grasp the string at each end of the river, then straighten it out and measure it against the scale. You can then calculate the length of the river.

Planet Earth

We live on a small planet in a tiny part of a vast universe. Our part of the universe is called the solar system. There are nine planets in the solar system, and they move around, or orbit, a star that we call the Sun. Enormous groups of stars are known as galaxies. Our galaxy is called the Milky Way and it is made up of at least 100 billion stars! There are many millions of galaxies in the universe and each one is surrounded by a vast, empty space. The solar system formed about five billion years ago from a large, swirling cloud of dust and gases. The hot, central part of the cloud became the Sun, while farther out, rocks and gases combined to form the planets. Other rock fragments became asteroids, or minor planets.

Amazing Facts

- Our galaxy looks like this. The faint, glowing arms of this galaxy are clouds of stars. Each of these stars is like our Sun and may have its own system of planets.
- It would take a jet aircraft traveling at 500 miles per hour (800 kph) six years to reach Venus and about 1,600 years to reach Pluto!

Round and Round

As each planet orbits the Sun, it also spins, or rotates, on its axis—an imaginary line through its center. Earth rotates once every 24 hours, and takes one year to orbit the Sun. Planets near the Sun orbit more quickly than those farther away. Asteroids also orbit the Sun. Most are located between Mars and Jupiter, in an area known as the asteroid belt. The planets and asteroids are all held in their orbits by gravity, a powerful force that pulls them toward the Sun. Without this force, they would fly off into space.

The Planets in Perspective

The illustration below shows the relative distances between the planets, as well as how long the planet takes to orbit the Sun (a year on that planet) and how long it takes to spin on its axis (a day on that planet).

Sun

Mercury Year: 88 Earth days. Day: 59 Earth days.

Venus Year: 225 Earth days. Day: 243 Earth days.

Earth Year: 365.25 days. Day: 24 hours.

Mars Year: 1.9 Earth years. Day: 24.6 hours.

Asteroid Belt

Jupiter Year: 11.9 Earth years. Day: 9.8 hours.

Saturn Year: 29.5 Earth years. Day: 10.2 hours.

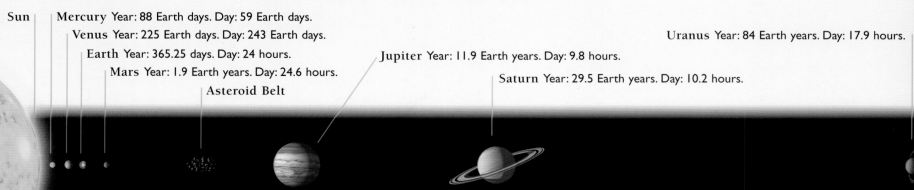

Uranus Year: 84 Earth years. Day: 17.9 hours.

◆ PROJECT: *Space Mobile* ◆

You can make your own mobile of the solar system to hang up in your bedroom or in your classroom at school.

1. First, collect some paper, colored pens, string or cotton thread, scissors and a coat hanger.
2. Draw the Sun and each of the planets and color them. Make sure you copy the colors and relative sizes of the planets as shown in the illustrations on these pages.
3. Carefully cut out each planet using a pair of scissors.
4. Make a small hole in the top of each planet with the point of a pen or pencil and thread a length of string through the hole.
5. Tie the Sun and the planets to the bottom of the coat hanger. Place the Sun in the middle and arrange the planets on either side of it in the order shown in the illustration on these pages. Don't forget that some planets are closer together than others.
6. When all the planets are in place, the mobile is ready to hang.

WORLD IN MOTION

As Earth turns on its axis, we move in and out of the Sun's light. Day begins as we move into the light. As we turn away from the Sun, night falls. Because Earth is tilted at an angle, the amount of sunlight reaching different parts of the world varies throughout the year. When part of Earth is tilted toward the Sun, it is summer there. When it is tilted away from the Sun, it is winter.

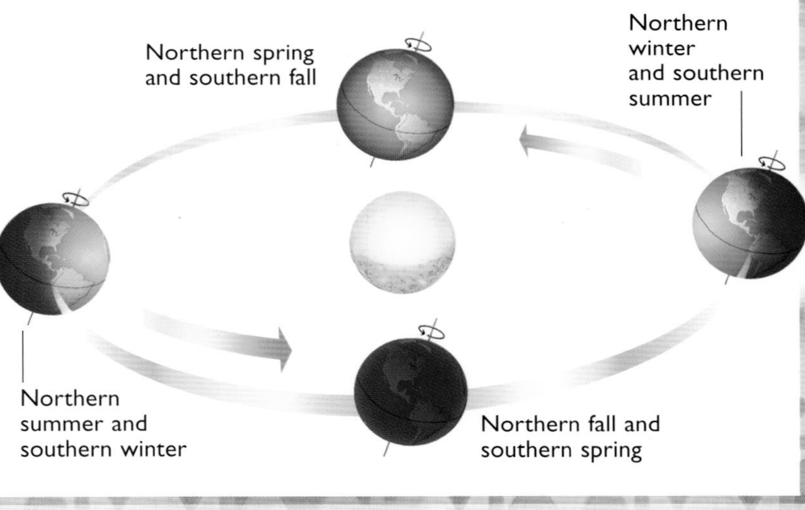
Northern spring and southern fall
Northern winter and southern summer
Northern summer and southern winter
Northern fall and southern spring

FIT FOR LIFE

Some planets are surrounded by a layer of gases called an atmosphere. As far as we know, Earth is the only planet in the solar system with an atmosphere that contains sufficient water and oxygen for life to flourish. Our atmosphere is so thin that if the planet were the size of an apple, the atmosphere would be only as thick as the peel.

Neptune Year: 165 Earth years. Day: 19.2 hours.

Pluto Year: 248 Earth years. Day: 6.4 Earth days.

An Ever-Changing Planet

Earth is shaped like a large ball. Inside are several layers made of different materials. As Earth formed, heavy minerals such as iron and nickel sank to the center, while lighter materials rose to the middle and upper levels. At first, the upper levels consisted entirely of hot, liquid rock, but as Earth cooled, the outside solidified to form a thin, hard crust. This crust broke into several pieces, known as lithospheric plates. These plates float on the liquid, molten rock—or magma—underneath and are constantly moving, although you cannot feel the movement. Energy from Earth's core creates powerful convection currents that force the plates together and apart. This happens extremely slowly, but over millions of years these movements shape and shift the surface of Earth, causing earthquakes and volcanic eruptions and forming mountains and islands.

Inner core
Outer core
Lower mantle
Asthenosphere
Lithosphere
Upper mantle
Ocean crust
Continental crust
Convection currents

Inside Earth

Our planet's solid iron inner core is surrounded by an outer core of liquid iron and nickel. Above this is a layer of solid rock called the lower mantle and a wide band of liquid rock known as the asthenosphere. Earth's outer layer is called the lithosphere. It consists of the solid rock of the upper mantle, and the crust. Crust under the land (continental crust) is usually thicker than crust under the sea (ocean crust). In Earth's core, temperatures reach an amazing 5,400°F (3,000°C). This heat creates strong convection currents that push the crust in different directions.

◆ Projects: *Folding the Crust* ◆

1. Cut a paper plate in half. These halves represent two of Earth's lithospheric plates.
2. Using adhesive tape, attach a sheet of paper to the plate halves. The paper represents Earth's crust.
3. If you slide one half of the plate under the other, the paper buckles. Similarly, when two of Earth's plates collide, their crusts fold, forming mountains.

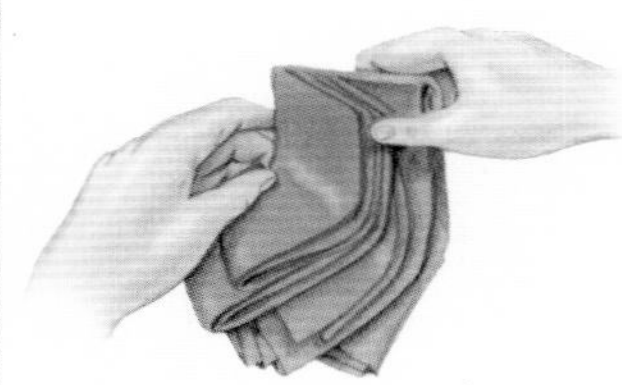

1. Take a sheet of paper, fold it in half and continue to fold it.
2. After six folds, it becomes difficult to fold the paper any further. In the same way, the thicker Earth's crust, the greater the force required to fold it.

Spreading plates
Hot-spot volcanoes
Coastal collisions

Coastal Collisions

When thin ocean crust meets thick continental crust, the thin crust slides under the thicker crust. Magma rises to the surface and forms a line of volcanoes. This process formed Mount St. Helens in the United States.

Hot-Spot Volcanoes

Weaknesses in the middle of plates, known as hot spots, allow magma from the asthenosphere to burst through the crust and form volcanoes. The Hawaiian Islands were created by hot-spot volcanoes.

Spreading Plates

Circulating magma may force plates apart. Where the plates separate, magma rises through the gap and cools and hardens to form a ridge. Normally this happens under the sea, but in Iceland it can be seen on land.

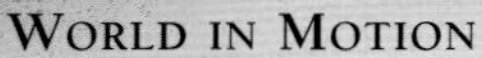

World in Motion

Convection currents cause Earth's plates to collide, separate and slide past each other. The effects of these movements are shown in the illustration above and in the photographs on the right.

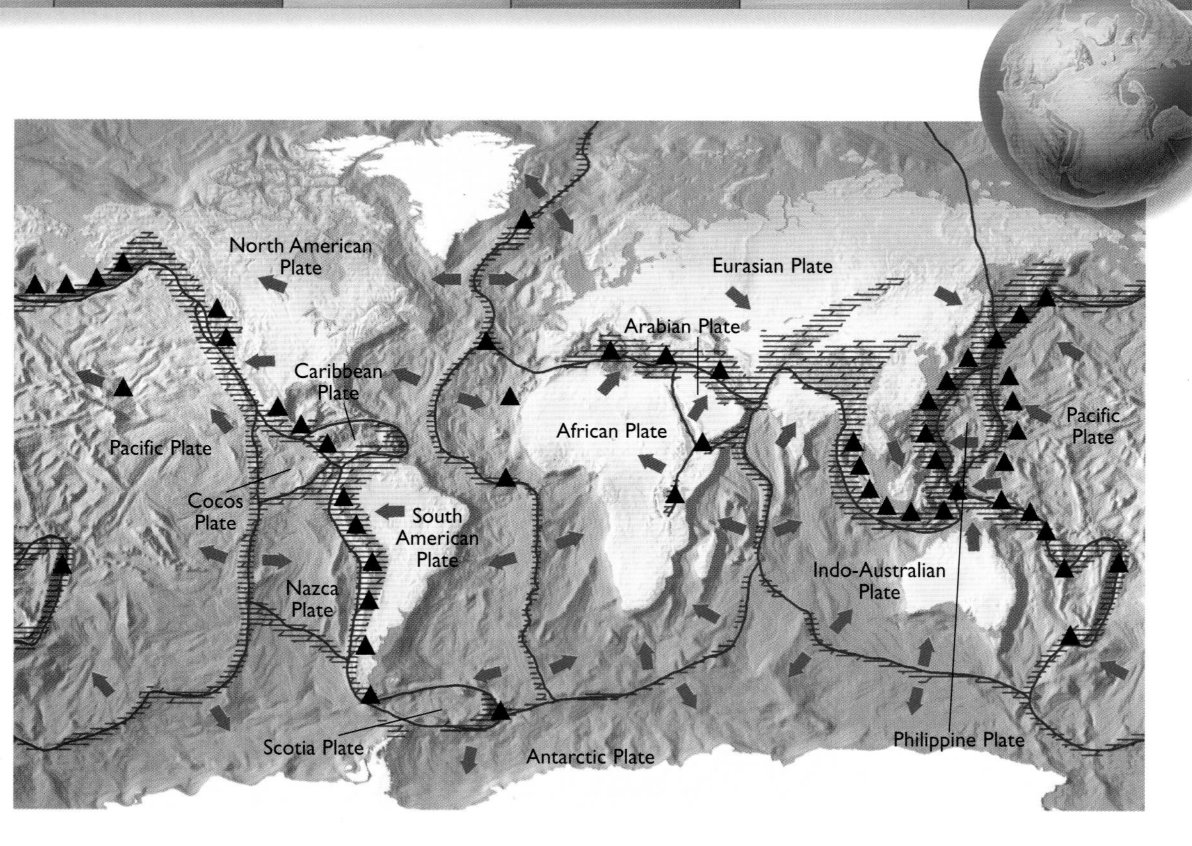
North American Plate
Eurasian Plate
Arabian Plate
Caribbean Plate
Pacific Plate
African Plate
Pacific Plate
Cocos Plate
South American Plate
Nazca Plate
Indo-Australian Plate
Scotia Plate
Antarctic Plate
Philippine Plate

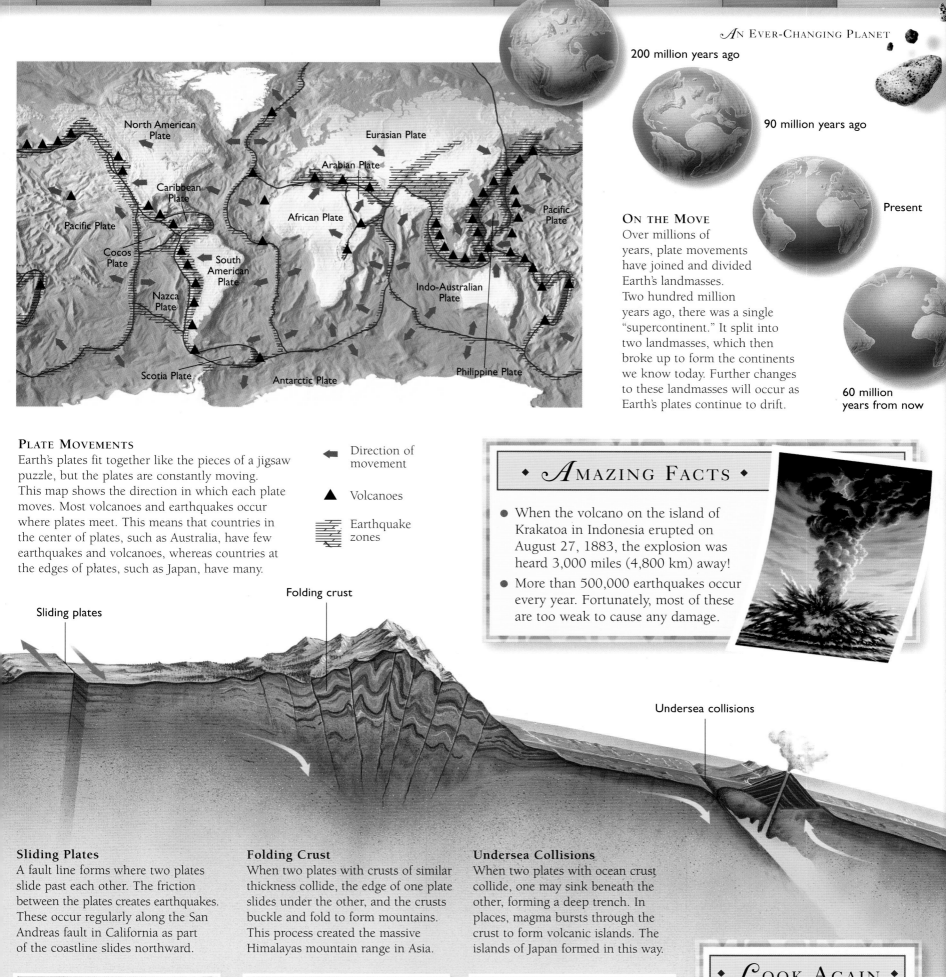

200 million years ago

90 million years ago

Present

60 million years from now

On the Move

Over millions of years, plate movements have joined and divided Earth's landmasses. Two hundred million years ago, there was a single "supercontinent." It split into two landmasses, which then broke up to form the continents we know today. Further changes to these landmasses will occur as Earth's plates continue to drift.

Plate Movements

Earth's plates fit together like the pieces of a jigsaw puzzle, but the plates are constantly moving. This map shows the direction in which each plate moves. Most volcanoes and earthquakes occur where plates meet. This means that countries in the center of plates, such as Australia, have few earthquakes and volcanoes, whereas countries at the edges of plates, such as Japan, have many.

 Direction of movement

 Volcanoes

 Earthquake zones

◆ Amazing Facts ◆

- When the volcano on the island of Krakatoa in Indonesia erupted on August 27, 1883, the explosion was heard 3,000 miles (4,800 km) away!
- More than 500,000 earthquakes occur every year. Fortunately, most of these are too weak to cause any damage.

Sliding plates

Folding crust

Undersea collisions

Sliding Plates

A fault line forms where two plates slide past each other. The friction between the plates creates earthquakes. These occur regularly along the San Andreas fault in California as part of the coastline slides northward.

Folding Crust

When two plates with crusts of similar thickness collide, the edge of one plate slides under the other, and the crusts buckle and fold to form mountains. This process created the massive Himalayas mountain range in Asia.

Undersea Collisions

When two plates with ocean crust collide, one may sink beneath the other, forming a deep trench. In places, magma bursts through the crust to form volcanic islands. The islands of Japan formed in this way.

◆ Look Again ◆

- What is Earth's inner core made of?
- What kind of volcanoes formed the Hawaiian Islands?
- Where are earthquakes most likely to occur?

Weather and Climate

OUR WEATHER MAY CHANGE from day to day, but we usually experience the same kind of weather from year to year. The pattern of weather that occurs in a region over a long period is known as the climate. The climate of an area depends on three main factors: how far north or south of the equator it is (its latitude), how high it is (its altitude), and how close it is to the sea. As a result of Earth's orbit and its round shape, sunlight warms areas near the equator more than areas near the poles. Tropical regions are therefore hot year-round, and the poles are always cold. Areas between the tropics and the poles are temperate. This means that they have warm summers and cool winters. Mountains are colder than lowland areas because as you climb higher the atmosphere becomes thinner and retains less heat. In coastal regions, sea breezes and ocean currents prevent the weather from becoming too hot or too cold, so these areas have a milder climate than inland areas. Where winds blow inland from the sea, they are usually moist and bring high rainfall.

Wind Patterns

Because hot air rises and cold air sinks, the Sun's uneven heating of Earth's surface causes air to circulate as shown in the large diagram below. These patterns of air circulation are deflected by the planet's rotation, and form the major wind systems shown on the globe below right. These winds carry warm or cold, moist or dry air, and are an important influence on Earth's climates.

Air Circulation

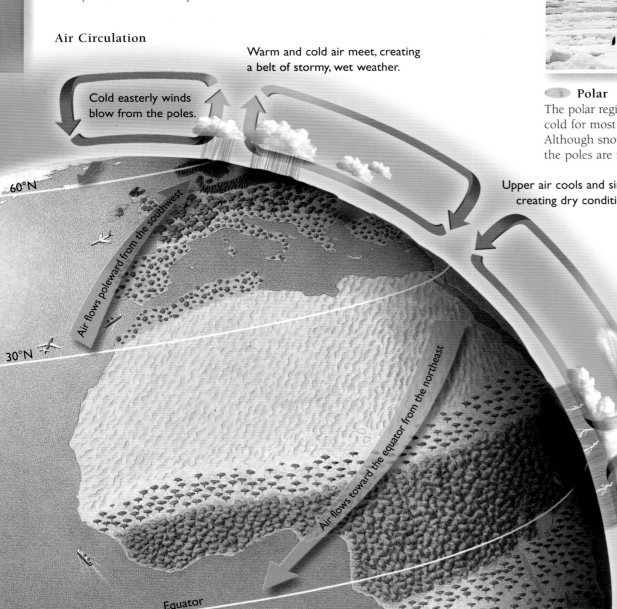

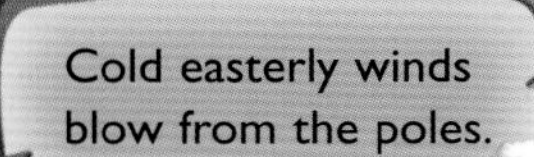
Warm and cold air meet, creating a belt of stormy, wet weather.
Cold easterly winds blow from the poles.
Upper air cools and sinks, creating dry conditions.
60°N
Air flows poleward from the southwest
30°N
Air flows toward the equator from the northeast
Equator

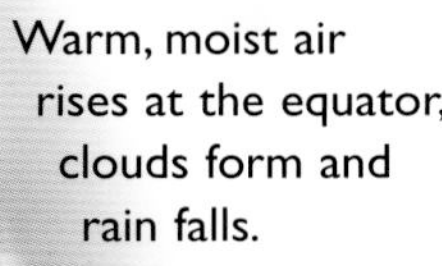
Warm, moist air rises at the equator, clouds form and rain falls.

World Climates

The world can be divided into eight major climate zones, which are shown on this map and described on these pages. Ocean currents influence many of these climates. For example, northwestern Europe has a mild climate as a result of the warm waters of the Gulf Stream.

warm currents
cool currents

Mountain
Mountains are normally colder, wetter and windier than neighboring regions that lie nearer sea level.

Polar
The polar regions are extremely cold for most of the year. Although snow falls regularly, the poles are relatively dry.

Cold Temperate
These regions have long, bitterly cold and snowy winters. Their summers are usually mild and damp.

Wind Systems

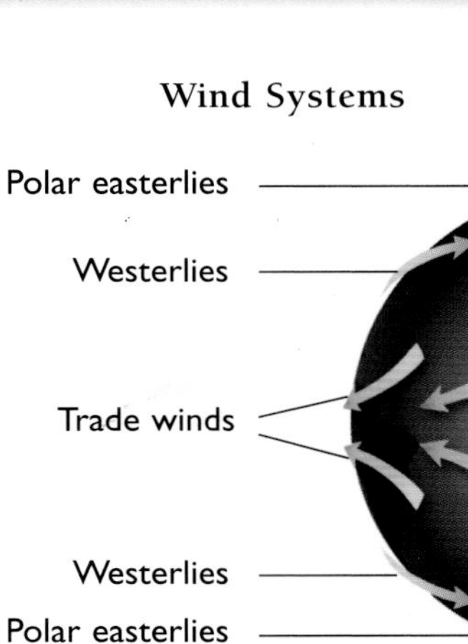
Polar easterlies
Westerlies
Trade winds
Westerlies
Polar easterlies

Wet Temperate
Wet temperate regions have four distinct seasons, with cool, wet winters and warm, wet summers.

Dry Temperate
Rainfall is relatively low in these regions. Most areas have mild, wet winters and hot, dry summers.

Desert and Semidesert
These are dry, barren areas with very low rainfall. They are usually hot by day, but may be cold, or even frosty, at night.

Subtropical
In summer, these regions are hot and wet like tropical areas. In winter, they are dry and mild like deserts.

Tropical
The tropics are hot and wet. In some areas, it rains all year round. In others, most of the rain falls in summer.

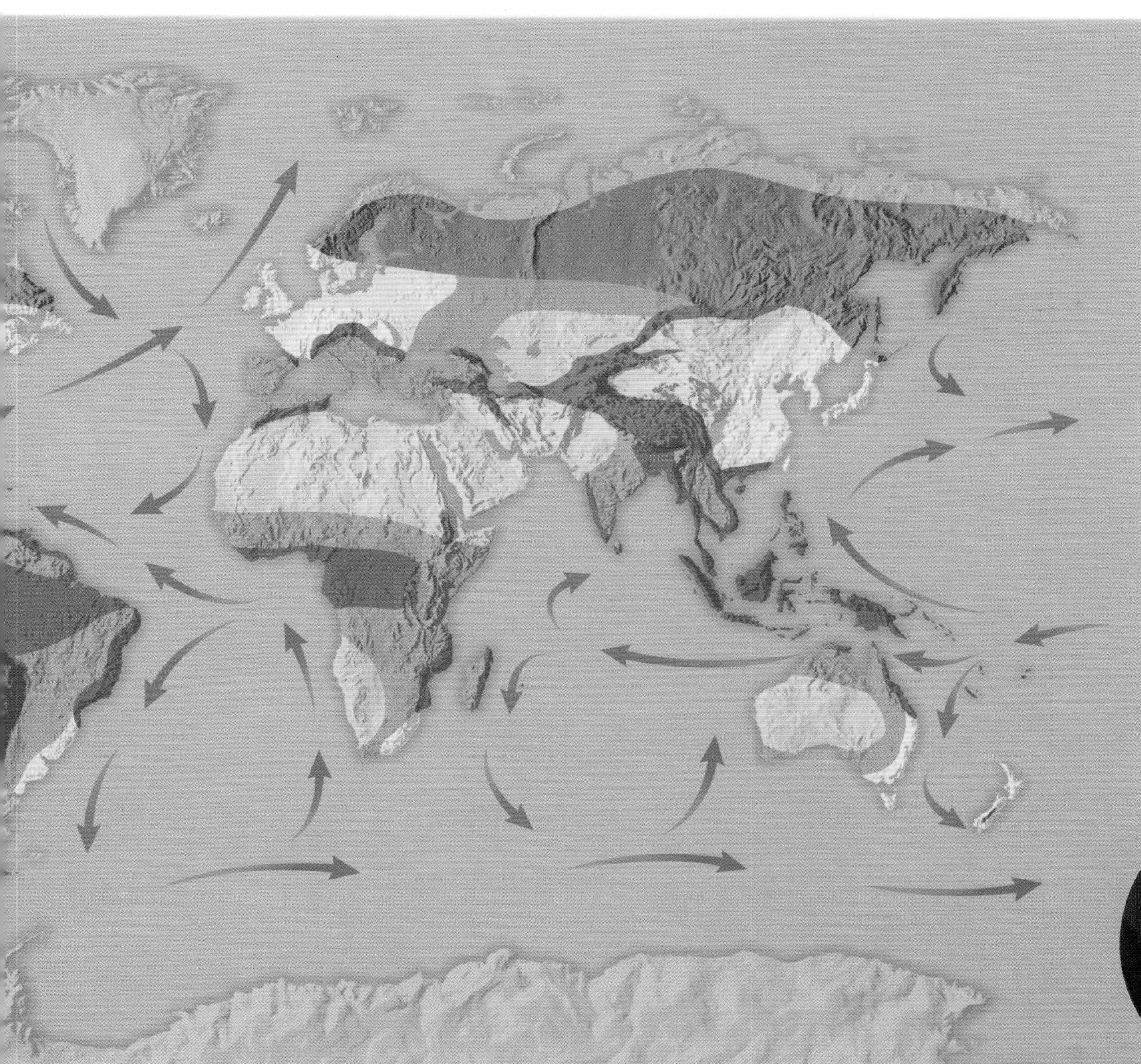

Amazing Fact

Thunderstorms are most common in tropical areas, but occur all over the world. At least 20,000 storms occur each day, and at any one time about 2,000 may be taking place. Lightning from these storms strikes the ground as frequently as 100 times every second.

Energy From the Sun
Because Earth is shaped like a ball, the Sun strikes it more directly near the equator than at the poles. This is why tropical areas are hot and the polar regions are cold.

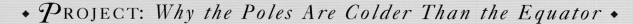

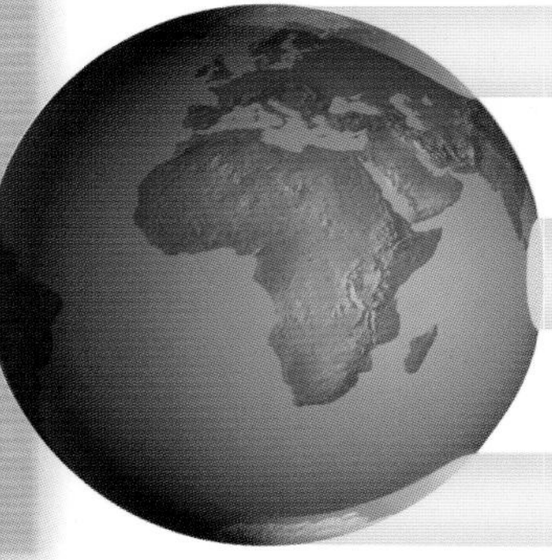

Project: *Why the Poles Are Colder Than the Equator*

❶ In a dark room, hold a lighted flashlight a few inches above, and at right angles to, a flat surface such as a tabletop. Observe the shape and brightness of the patch of light.

❷ Tilt the flashlight and note how the light changes. When the light strikes the surface from directly overhead, the patch of light is small and intense. When the light strikes the table at an angle, the patch is larger and weaker.

In a similar way, sunlight is most intense at the equator, where it strikes the ground from directly overhead. At the poles, the light strikes Earth at an angle and is spread across a wider area, making it much weaker.

The Living World

Almost every part of our planet is inhabited by an amazing variety of living things. So far, scientists have named about two million kinds, or species, of plants and animals, but there may be between 10 and 100 million species on Earth! All living things inhabit the biosphere, which is made up of the land, oceans and atmosphere. Within the biosphere, there are many kinds of environments. Over millions of years, plants and animals have gradually altered their bodies and behavior to suit their particular environments. This process is known as adaptation. Together, an environment and its inhabitants form an ecosystem. The members of each ecosystem depend on each other for food and other resources. For example, vegetation provides food for plant-eating animals (herbivores) which may in turn be eaten by meat-eating animals (carnivores). These close relationships mean that damage to one part of an ecosystem is likely to affect every other part of it.

Global Ecosystems
Each of Earth's environments has its own community of plants and animals. This illustration shows how ecosystems change between the tropical rain forests (far left) and the polar ice caps (far right).

Tropical Rain Forests
The hot, humid weather of the tropics creates dense forests that are home to more species than any other environment. Monkeys and birds live high in the trees, while jaguars and other mammals prowl the forest floor.

Subtropical Savannas
With rain falling only in summer, subtropical areas have few trees. The African savanna grasslands support herds of herbivores such as zebras, which are hunted by lions and other carnivores. Vultures and other scavengers eat the leftovers.

Deserts and Semideserts
Desert species have adapted to drought. Some plants, such as cacti, store water in their stems. Others have long roots that reach water far underground. In hot deserts, many animals come out only at night, when it is cooler.

Oceans
The oceans contain a huge variety of species that have adapted to life under water. Marine plants include many kinds of seaweed. Animals include sea mammals such as seals and whales, coral, and thousands of fish species.

World Environments
Because the weather determines the types of plants that grow, Earth's environments are closely related to its climate zones.

- Tropical rain forests
- Subtropical savannas
- Deserts and semideserts
- Temperate grasslands and shrub woodlands
- Temperate forests
- Coniferous forests
- Mountains
- Polar ice caps and tundra

• Amazing Fact •

The world's largest flower, the rafflesia, is found in the rain forests of southeast Asia and can measure up to three feet (1 m) in diameter. It gives off a smell like rotting flesh which attracts insects.

Mountains
The higher the land, the less vegetation there is and the colder and windier it gets. Thick fur coats keep many mountain animals warm. Some species, such as mountain goats, have special hooves that help them climb rocky slopes.

Polar Ice Caps and Tundra
The ice caps are bitterly cold and offer little shelter. Some animals have fur and a thick layer of fat to keep them warm. Tundra is treeless land that surrounds the Arctic ice cap. Its low shrubs feed hares, lemmings and other herbivores.

Temperate Grasslands and Shrub Woodlands
Moderate rainfall creates grasslands and shrub woodlands. Grasslands attract herbivores such as bison and are ideal hunting grounds for birds of prey. There is little shelter, so some animals live in burrows.

Temperate Forests
Trees grow well in wet temperate regions. In areas with cold winters, most of the trees are deciduous, which means that they shed their leaves in fall. Some animals migrate in winter; others survive on food stored during summer.

Coniferous Forests
Cold temperate regions are covered by forests of evergreen trees called conifers. Shaped so that snow slides off them, these trees are well adapted to the cold winters. Many animals have thick fur, and some hibernate for the winter.

• Look Again •

- Name a plant-eating animal that lives on the African savanna.
- Which plants store water in their stems?
- How have animals adapted to mountain environments?

Our Natural Resources

Earth provides us with everything that we need to live. Its atmosphere, rivers and lakes supply fresh water which, with sunshine and soil, enables plants to grow. In turn, plants produce vital supplies of oxygen and provide us and other animals with food. Animals supply humans with meat, wool and dairy products. Plants also provide timber, fuel, and textiles such as cotton. All these resources—water, plants, crops, animals—are renewable. This means that if we manage them carefully they will never run out. Other resources are nonrenewable. They do not regrow or replenish themselves and will eventually be used up. They include minerals, precious stones and fossil fuels (coal, oil and gas). Minerals—such as clay, chalk and many metals—and precious stones—such as diamonds and emeralds—have a wide range of uses, particularly in industry. Coal, oil and gas supply most of the energy we need for lighting and heating our homes and for fueling our cars. They are known as fossil fuels because they are the remains of animals and plants buried deep underground. Some of these nonrenewable resources may run out within the next 50 years. Because of this, and because burning fossil fuels creates pollution, scientists are trying to find ways of using renewable resources to supply more of the energy we need.

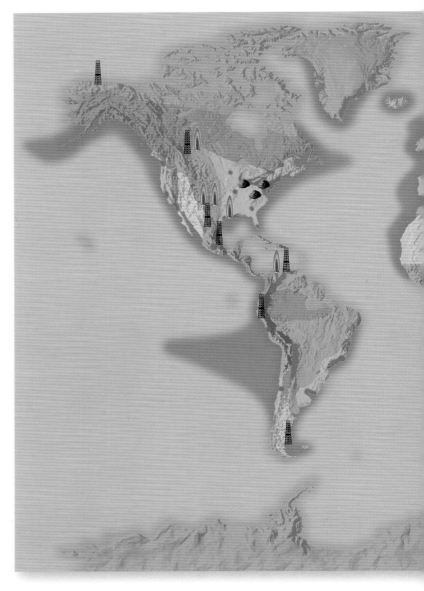

Energy Supplies

The illustration below shows our principal sources of energy. As the chart on the right indicates, coal, oil and gas still supply most of our fuel. But alternative energy supplies such as wind and solar power are being developed in many parts of the world. As reserves of fossil fuels run out, these sources will become increasingly important.

Energy Use

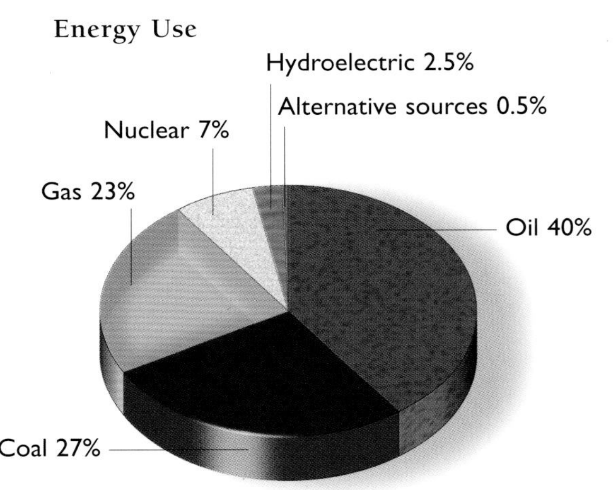
Hydroelectric 2.5%
Alternative sources 0.5%
Nuclear 7%
Gas 23%
Oil 40%
Coal 27%

Earth's Resources

The map above shows how land is used in different parts of the world, and where major fuel reserves are located.

Major gas field

Major coal field

Major oil field

Urban areas: towns, cities and industries

Areas with large farms where people grow crops and raise animals for sale

Oil
Oil and gas are found together in rock layers in Earth's crust. They are extracted by drilling from sea- or land-based rigs.

Coal
Coal is more plentiful than other fossil fuels. It can be collected by digging at the surface or by mining deep underground.

Uranium
Radioactive elements such as uranium emit high-energy particles that are converted into electricity at nuclear power plants.

Geothermal Power
In some parts of the world, ground water is heated by hot volcanic rocks, creating steam that is used to generate power.

Areas with small farms where people grow crops and raise animals mainly for their own use

Deserts, dry grasslands and tundra used for grazing small numbers of animals

Areas that are too cold or dry for farming, but include some mining and hunting

Grassland areas used for grazing large numbers of animals

Forested areas with some farming, hunting and mining

Major fishing grounds

The Water Cycle

A process known as the water cycle provides us with a regular supply of fresh water. Water in oceans, lakes and rivers is constantly evaporating into the air, where it exists as water vapor. The warmer the air, the more water vapor it can hold. When air cools, its ability to hold water decreases, and some of the water vapor turns, or condenses, into tiny water droplets or ice crystals. These droplets or crystals form clouds. If the droplets or crystals combine and become heavy enough, they fall as rain or snow. Water that falls on land drains into rivers, lakes and underground channels. It then flows into the sea, replenishing the oceans and completing the water cycle.

◆ Project: *Create a Water Cycle* ◆

This simple experiment will show you how the water cycle works.

❶ Cool a long, metal spoon or ladle by placing it in a freezer for a few minutes. Choose a spoon with a wooden handle.

❷ Ask an adult to help you boil some water in a kettle or saucepan.

❸ As the water boils, the warm air above the water rises. As it starts to cool, it condenses and forms clouds of steam.

❹ Hold the cold spoon over the steam, being careful not to burn yourself. The cooling effect of the cold metal causes the water vapor to condense more quickly and form droplets of water on the underside of the spoon.

❺ The droplets grow in size until they become heavy enough to fall, just like rain. Some of the droplets may fall back into the kettle or saucepan, replenishing the water supply.

Hydroelectric Power
Hydroelectric power is created when water is passed through electricity-generating turbines at the bottom of a dam.

Wind Power
Windmills convert the power of the wind into electricity. The wind turns the windmills, which drive electrical generators.

Solar Power
Clusters of mirrorlike solar panels reflect the Sun's rays onto a solar furnace, where the intense heat is converted into electricity.

Sea Power
At a tidal dam or barrage, waves pass through narrow tunnels, driving huge turbines that produce power.

The Human Family

OUR PLANET IS HOME to about 5.8 billion people. This population is not spread evenly over Earth's landmasses. Instead, people are concentrated where resources are plentiful, or can be easily obtained by trade. Therefore, few people live in deserts or polar regions, but many live in fertile areas, close to energy sources, and near rivers and coasts. The world's population is now growing more quickly than ever before. In the time it takes you to read this sentence, more than 20 babies will have been born. Since 1950 the number of people on Earth has more than doubled. This growth is the result of a longer life expectancy due to improved medical services, and a high birth rate in some parts of the world. The most rapid population growth occurs in developing countries—poorer countries with little industry or technology. It is difficult for these countries to feed and take care of their growing populations, so many of them are urging their people to have fewer children.

NATIONAL POPULATIONS

This diagram shows the 10 countries with the world's largest populations. China has by far the biggest population—in fact, one in every five people in the world lives in China!

WHERE PEOPLE LIVE

The dots on this map show the world's most densely populated areas.

Developed countries
Developing countries

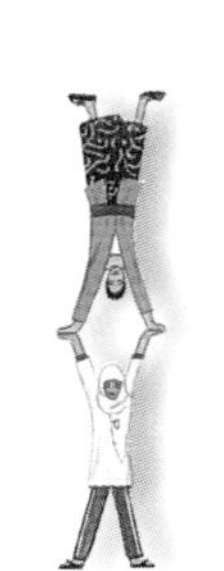

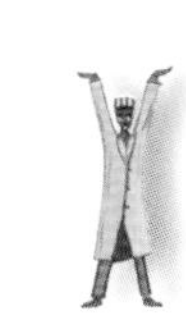

China 1.2 billion
India 937 million
U.S.A. 264 million
Indonesia 204 million
Brazil 161 million
Russia 150 million
Pakistan 132 million
Bangladesh 128 million
Japan 126 million
Nigeria 101 million

CROWDED COUNTRIES

Some countries are densely populated—a large population lives in a small area. Others are sparsely populated—a small population occupies a large area.

The Netherlands:
1,000 people per square mile
(400 per sq. km)

Australia:
6 people per square mile
(2 per sq. km)

GROWING CITIES

As countries develop, people move to cities to look for work in factories and businesses. As shown by this comparison of the populations of Paris, France, and Jakarta, Indonesia, cities in developing countries are now growing more rapidly than those in developed countries.

Paris
Jakarta

	Paris	Jakarta
1970	8.5 million	3.9 million
1990	9.3 million	9.3 million
2010	9.6 million	19.2 million

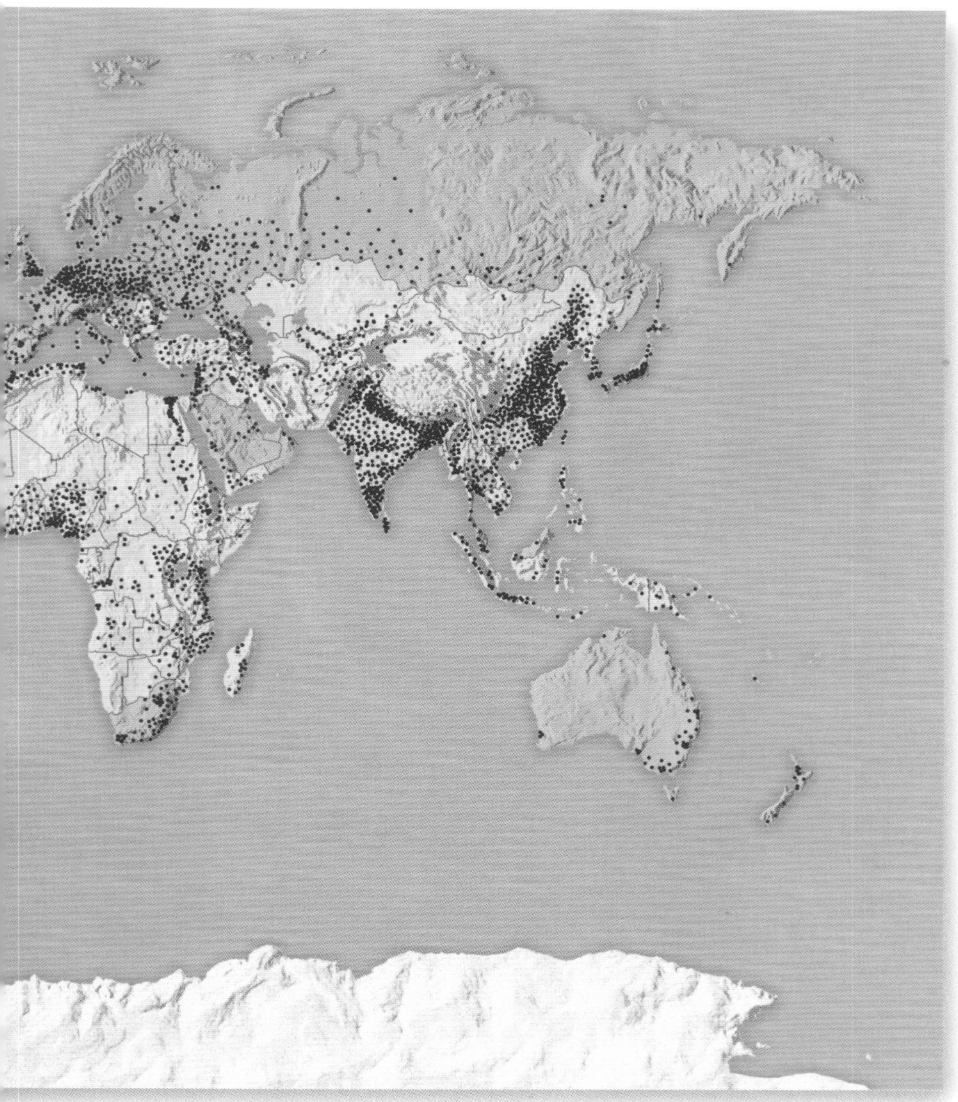

Rich and Poor

Countries with large industries and high levels of technology are called developed countries. People in these parts of the world are generally wealthy and have many possessions. In countries with little industry and technology, people are poorer and have few possessions. These countries are known as developing countries. Although they are home to far fewer people, developed countries are much richer and use a much larger proportion of the world's resources than developing countries.

Developed countries:
make up 20% of the world's population
own 80% of the world's wealth
use 70% of the world's energy

Developing countries:
make up 80% of the world's population
own 20% of the world's wealth
use 30% of the world's energy

◆ Amazing Facts ◆

- Every second, three babies are born.
- If the world's population were spread out evenly over its landmasses, each person would occupy an area larger than four football fields.
- Standing side by side, everyone in the world could fit onto the island of Jamaica.

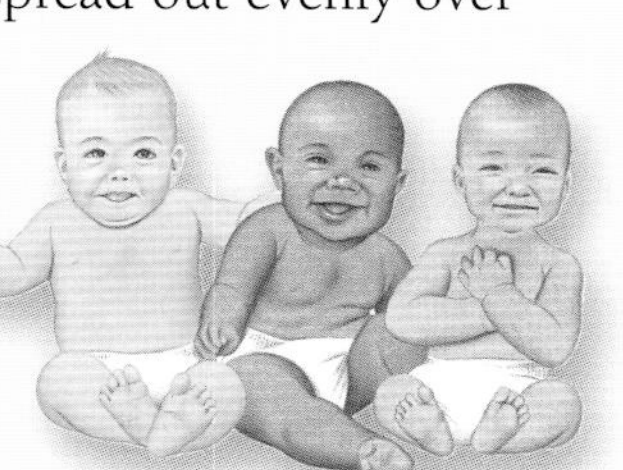

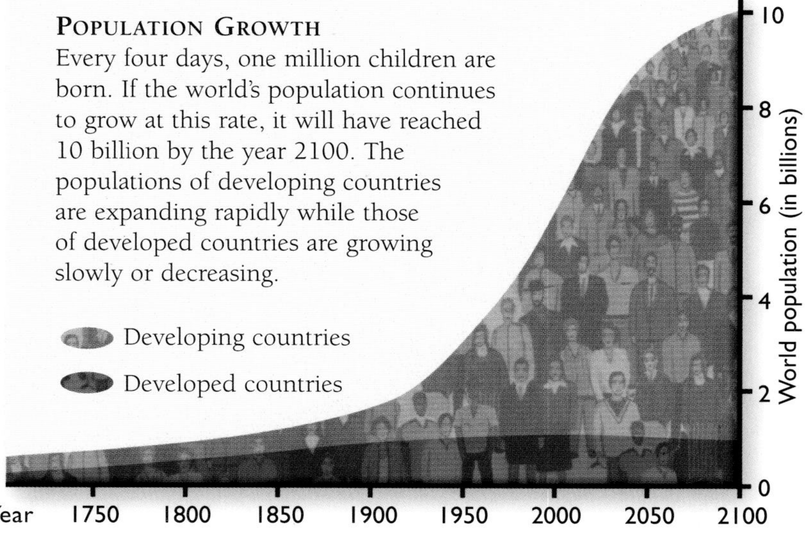
Developing countries
Developed countries
Year
1750
1800
1850
1900
1950
2000
2050
2100
0
2
4
6
8
10
World population (in billions)

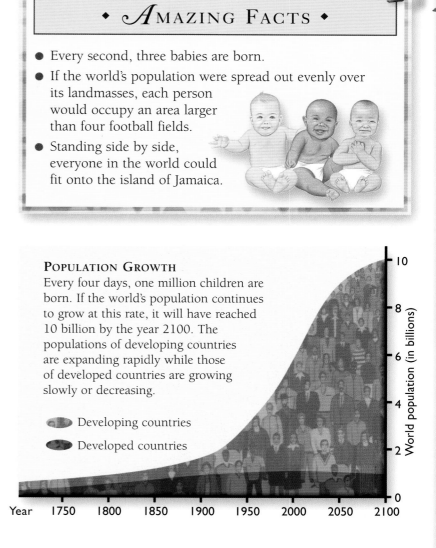

Population Growth

Every four days, one million children are born. If the world's population continues to grow at this rate, it will have reached 10 billion by the year 2100. The populations of developing countries are expanding rapidly while those of developed countries are growing slowly or decreasing.

◆ Project: *Languages* ◆

More than 3,000 languages are spoken around the world, but more than one-third of the world's population speaks one of the following six languages. So you can learn to say "hello" to more than two billion people!

hello
English
(350 million speakers)

你好
ni ***hao***
Chinese
(1 billion speakers)

مرحبا
*mar-ha-**ban***
Arabic
(150 million speakers)

¡hola!
*o-**la***
Spanish
(250 million speakers)

नमस्ते
*na-ma-**stay***
Hindi
(200 million speakers)

привет!
*pree-**vyet***
Russian
(150 million speakers)

A Shrinking World

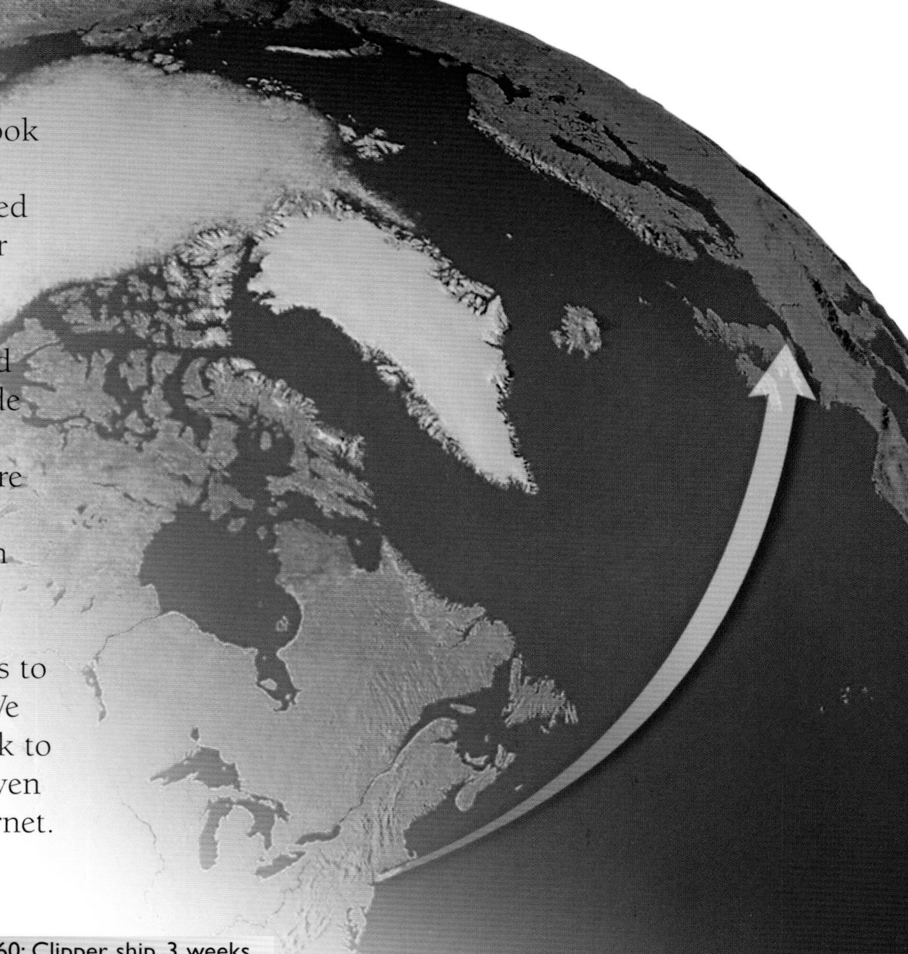

In 1850, the journey between London and New York took about three weeks. Now the same distance can be traveled in just over three hours. This dramatic difference has altered our view of the world. Countries now seem closer together than ever before—the world seems to be shrinking! Faster means of transportation, along with recently developed technologies, have greatly increased international trade and communication. Airplanes can carry goods to the other side of the world within a day. Fresh foods, such as meat, fruit and vegetables, which would previously have spoiled before they reached their destinations, can now be transported over long distances in refrigerated container ships. Modern telecommunications—telephone, fax and electronic mail services—allow businesses to deal directly with customers anywhere in the world. Telecommunications also enable us to increase our understanding of other places and peoples. We can watch television programs about other countries, speak to people on the other side of the world by telephone, and even make new friends on computer networks such as the Internet.

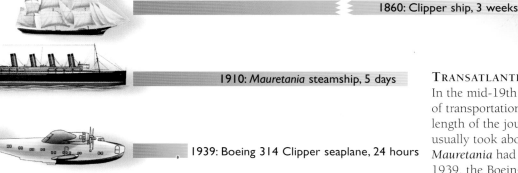

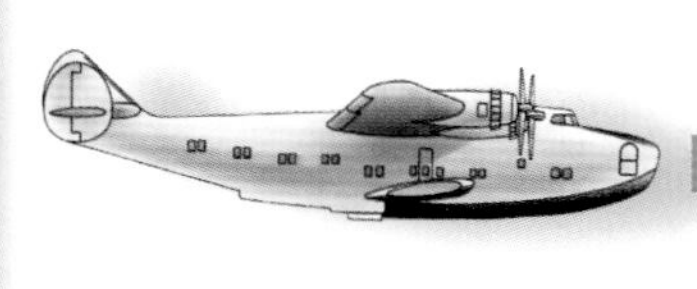

1860: Clipper ship, 3 weeks

1910: *Mauretania* steamship, 5 days

1939: Boeing 314 Clipper seaplane, 24 hours

Today: Concorde supersonic jet, 3½ hours

Transatlantic Transportation

In the mid-19th century, a clipper ship was the fastest means of transportation between New York and London. The exact length of the journey depended on the weather, but the trip usually took about three weeks. By 1910, the steamship *Mauretania* had cut the Atlantic crossing to five days. In 1939, the Boeing 314 Clipper seaplane provided the first passenger aircraft service across the Atlantic, with a flight time of about 24 hours. Today, the Concorde supersonic jet can complete the same trip in three and a half hours.

Oslo
Stockholm
Hamburg
London
Rotterdam
Vancouver
Seattle
Montreal
San Francisco
New York
Marseilles
Istanbul
Piraeus (Athens)
Kuwait
Shanghai
Pusan
Tokyo
Kobe
New Orleans
Honolulu
Bombay
Hong Kong
Manila
Lagos
Colombo
Caracas
Singapore
Dar es Salaam
Jakarta
Rio de Janeiro
Cape Town
Durban
Perth
Sydney
Valparaíso (Santiago)
Buenos Aires
Melbourne
Auckland

Vancouver
London
Moscow
Paris
Frankfurt
Minneapolis
Toronto
Boston
San Francisco
Chicago
New York
Detroit
Denver
Los Angeles
Atlanta
Madrid
Rome
Beijing
Seoul
Tokyo
Dallas
Miami
Delhi
Calcutta
Shanghai
Osaka
Honolulu
Cairo
Hong Kong
Bombay
Mexico City
Bangkok
Caracas
Lagos
Ho Chi Minh City
Nairobi
Singapore
Kinshasa
Lima
Jakarta
Harare
Rio de Janeiro
Johannesburg
Perth
Sydney
Santiago
Buenos Aires
Melbourne
Auckland

Sea Routes

Today, few people travel by sea, but goods of all kinds are transported by container ships and tankers. This map shows the world's most important shipping routes and busiest ports. Rotterdam in the Netherlands handles more cargo than any other seaport.

Air Routes

Flying is now the most popular form of international travel. This map shows the busiest international air routes and airports. Heathrow in London handles more international flights than any other airport, but Chicago's O'Hare Airport is the world's busiest, with more than 2,000 planes landing and taking off each day.

International Trade

The countries of the world exchange a wide variety of goods. Countries that have more raw materials and produce more food and goods than they need export some of those materials to countries that have few resources. Other countries export little because they need all their own resources. In the diagram below, the arrows indicate the direction of trade in three categories of goods: food, raw materials (including minerals, fuels and timber), and manufactured goods (goods that are made in factories, such as cars and electrical equipment). The illustrations show the most important products in each region.

• Look Again •

- If it is midday in England, what is the time in eastern Australia?
- Which is New Zealand's busiest port?
- What kinds of manufactured goods does Japan export?

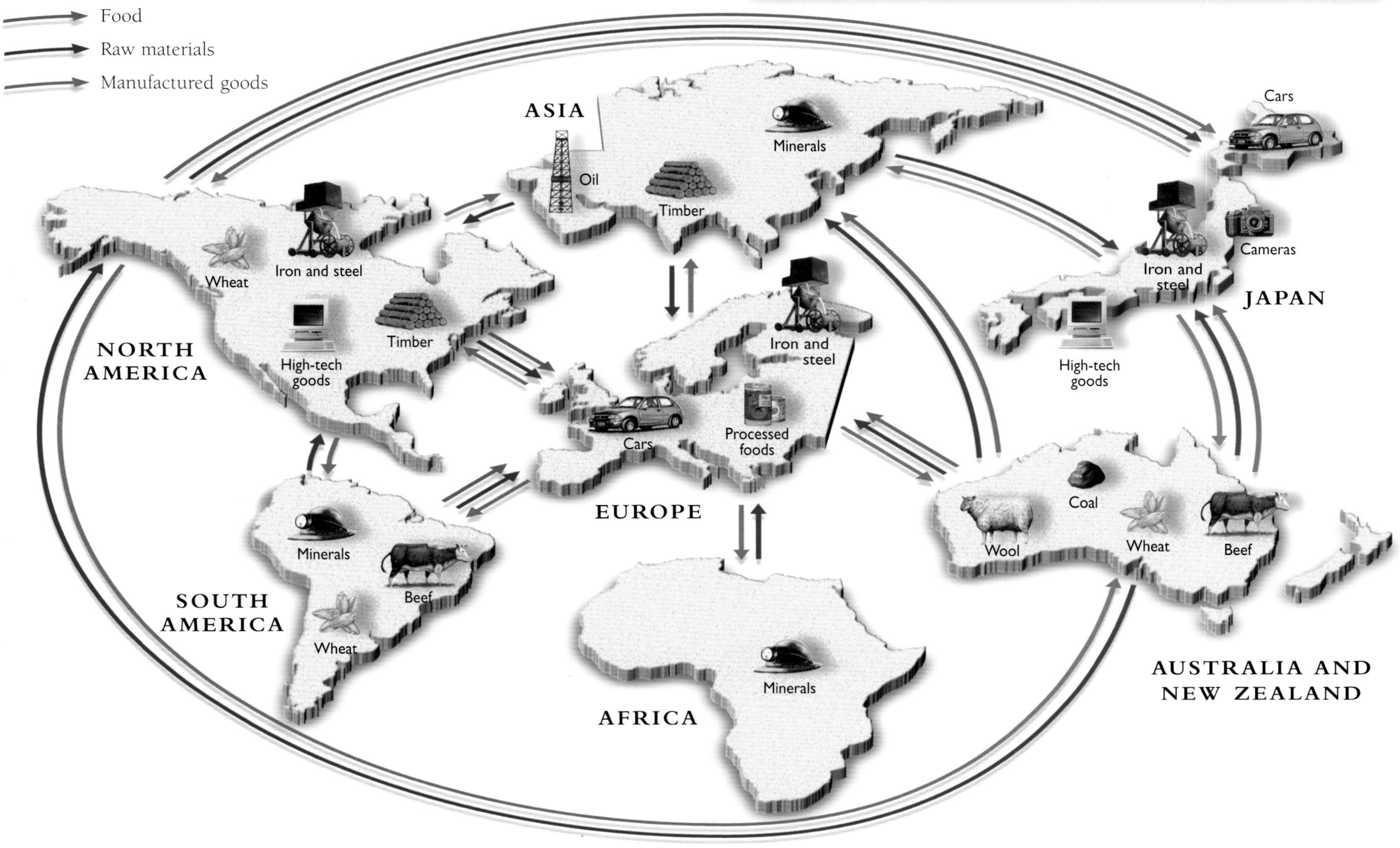

Food
Raw materials
Manufactured goods

ASIA
Oil
Minerals
Timber
Cars
Cameras
Iron and steel
JAPAN
High-tech goods
NORTH AMERICA
Wheat
Iron and steel
High-tech goods
Timber
EUROPE
Iron and steel
Cars
Processed foods
SOUTH AMERICA
Minerals
Beef
Wheat
AFRICA
Minerals
AUSTRALIA AND NEW ZEALAND
Wool
Coal
Wheat
Beef

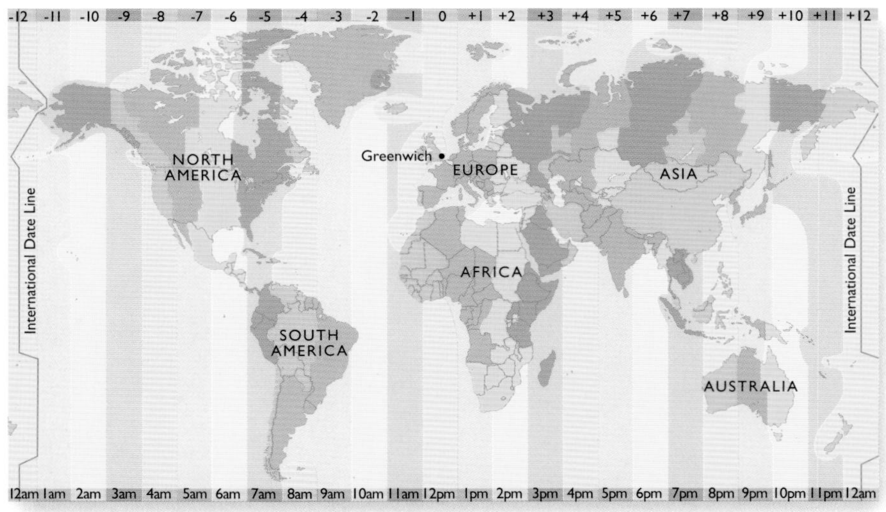
-12 -11 -10 -9 -8 -7 -6 -5 -4 -3 -2 -1 0 +1 +2 +3 +4 +5 +6 +7 +8 +9 +10 +11 +12
NORTH AMERICA
Greenwich
EUROPE
ASIA
AFRICA
SOUTH AMERICA
AUSTRALIA
International Date Line
International Date Line
12am 1am 2am 3am 4am 5am 6am 7am 8am 9am 10am 11am 12pm 1pm 2pm 3pm 4pm 5pm 6pm 7pm 8pm 9pm 10pm 11pm 12am

Time Zones

The world is divided into 24 time zones, and time is measured in hours ahead of or behind the time at Greenwich, England. The time is the same throughout each zone and is usually one hour ahead of or behind the neighboring time zones. The International Date Line marks where one day ends, and another begins.

A Virtual World

Computers are changing the ways in which we work, relax and communicate. You can now send electronic mail (e-mail) and other digital information from one computer to another almost anywhere in the world. You can also read magazines, hear music and even shop using information networks such as the Internet. Some networks allow you to speak directly to other people and even see them on your computer screen. This is called video conferencing. In the future, more and more people are likely to use computers for shopping, entertainment and business.

Planet in Peril

THE FUTURE OF OUR PLANET is at risk, now more than ever before. In the last 200 years, rapid population growth and the development of industry and technology have magnified the effect of our activities on the environment. Supplies of fossil fuels and other nonrenewable resources are running out. We are overusing the soil, forests and fishing grounds, and no longer giving these renewable resources a chance to recover. Waste from our homes and industries is poisoning water supplies, and gases from our cars and factories are polluting the air we breathe. Increasing air pollution may even be changing the climate. Scientists all over the world are trying to find ways to preserve resources and limit the damage we are doing to Earth. Through simple activities such as recycling, using our cars less and buying environmentally friendly products, we can all play a part in protecting Earth and preserving its resources for future generations.

• Amazing Facts •

- An acre (0.4 ha) of Brazilian rain forest is destroyed every nine seconds.
- Every day, more than 50 species become extinct. This is mainly the result of human activities such as forestry and hunting.

A Global Crisis

This map shows that environmental problems affect almost every part of Earth. The most serious problems are described and illustrated on these pages.

- Existing deserts
- Areas at risk of becoming deserts
- Existing rain forest
- Cleared rain forest
- Cities with severe air pollution
- Areas affected by acid rain
- Polluted waterways
- Heavy oil slicks created by shipping
- Light oil slicks created by shipping
-  Major nuclear accidents
-  Major oil tanker disasters
-  Major oil rig explosions

Holding Back the Desert

In dry parts of the world, overgrazing and clearing the land of its natural vegetation can turn fertile areas into desert. To keep deserts from spreading farther, we need to better manage the land we farm and replant trees and shrubs.

Saving the Forests

Vast areas of natural forest are being cleared to supply timber, fuel and paper, and to make way for towns and farms. You can help protect the world's forests and reduce the need for more wood by recycling paper. Replanting trees also helps.

Reducing Air Pollution

Cars and factories fill the air with grime and poisonous gases. Industries and car manufacturers are trying to reduce such pollution. You can also help by walking, cycling or using public transportation instead of traveling by car.

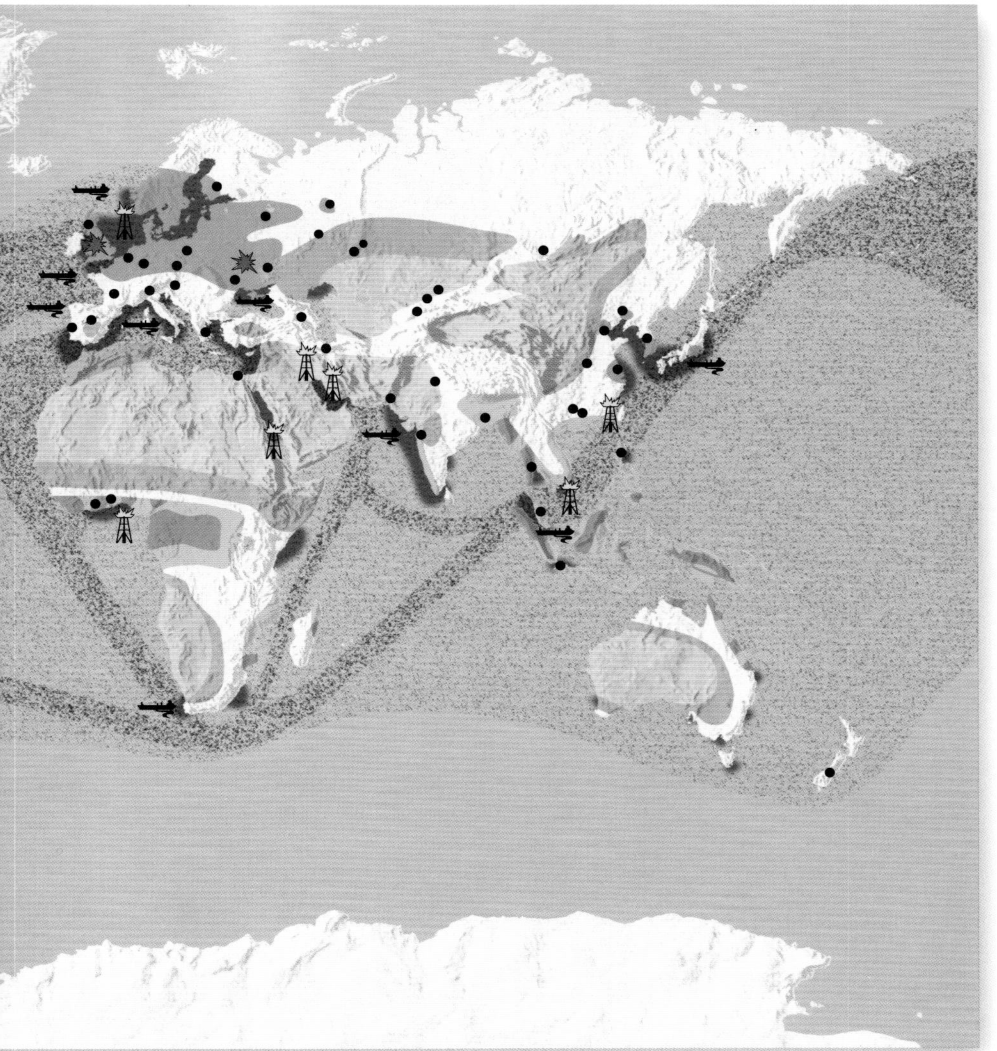

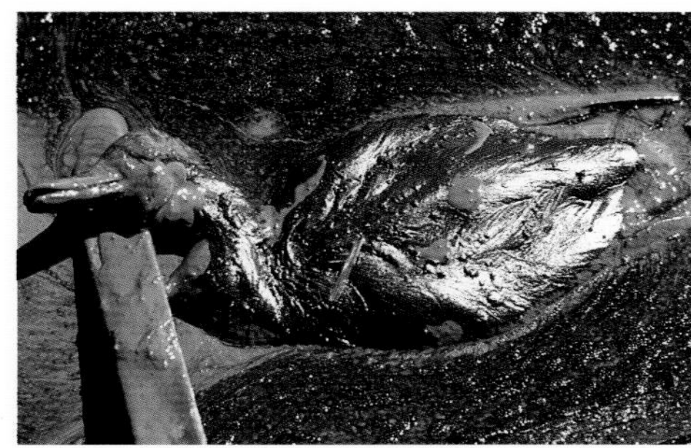

Oil Spills
Oil and other pollutants spilled by ships are a threat to wildlife. In 1989, oil spilled by the tanker *Exxon Valdez* off the coast of Alaska, in the United States, killed thousands of animals, including 350,000 seabirds.

Nuclear Accidents
Nuclear accidents occur rarely but can be devastating. In 1986, an accident at the Chernobyl nuclear power plant in the Ukraine released a cloud of radioactive gas across Europe, poisoning land, crops and people.

Oil Well Explosions
Accidents on oil and gas rigs can cause major environmental problems. During the Gulf War in Kuwait in 1992, hundreds of oil wells were set on fire, causing serious water and air pollution throughout the region.

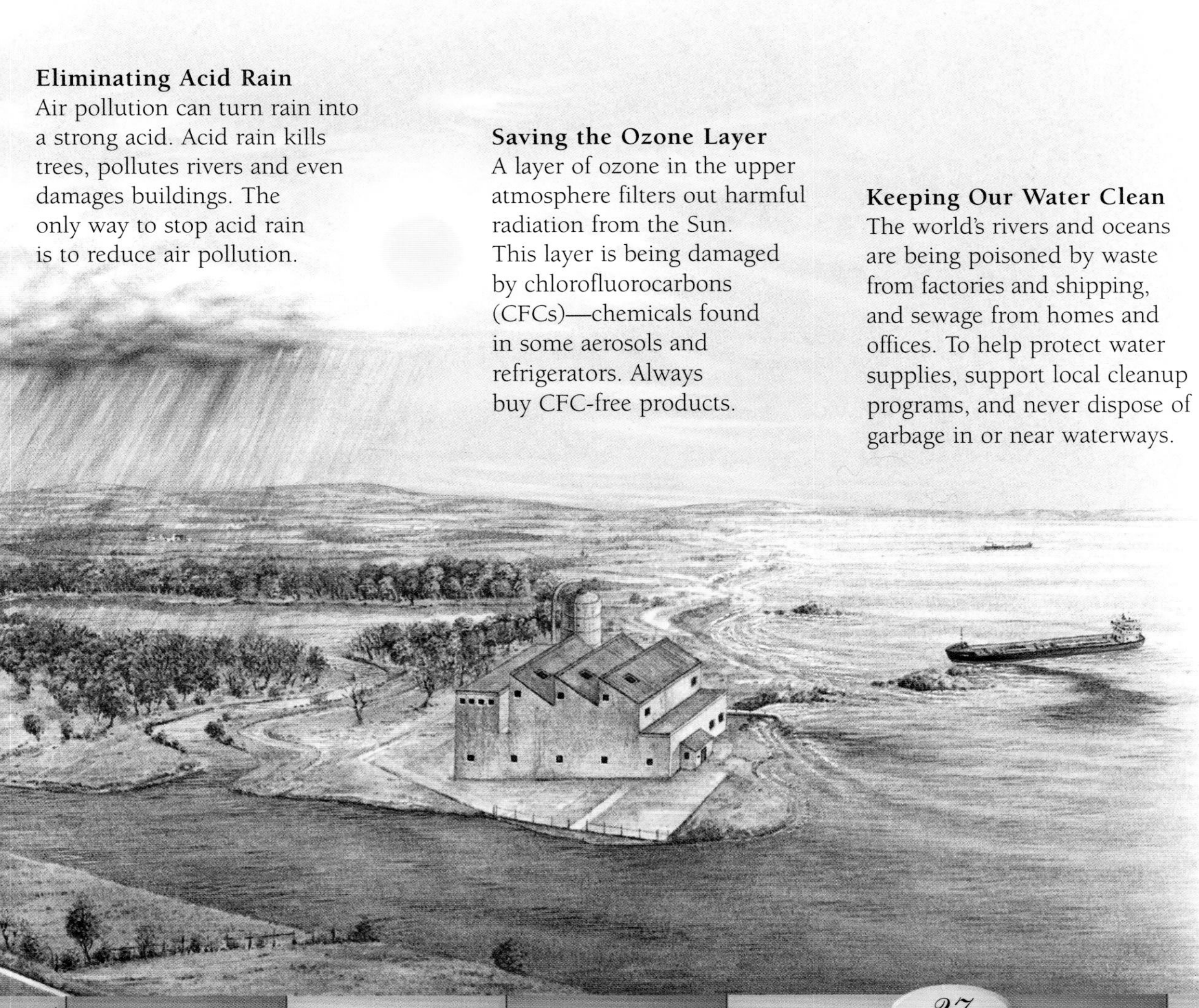

Eliminating Acid Rain
Air pollution can turn rain into a strong acid. Acid rain kills trees, pollutes rivers and even damages buildings. The only way to stop acid rain is to reduce air pollution.

Saving the Ozone Layer
A layer of ozone in the upper atmosphere filters out harmful radiation from the Sun. This layer is being damaged by chlorofluorocarbons (CFCs)—chemicals found in some aerosols and refrigerators. Always buy CFC-free products.

Keeping Our Water Clean
The world's rivers and oceans are being poisoned by waste from factories and shipping, and sewage from homes and offices. To help protect water supplies, support local cleanup programs, and never dispose of garbage in or near waterways.

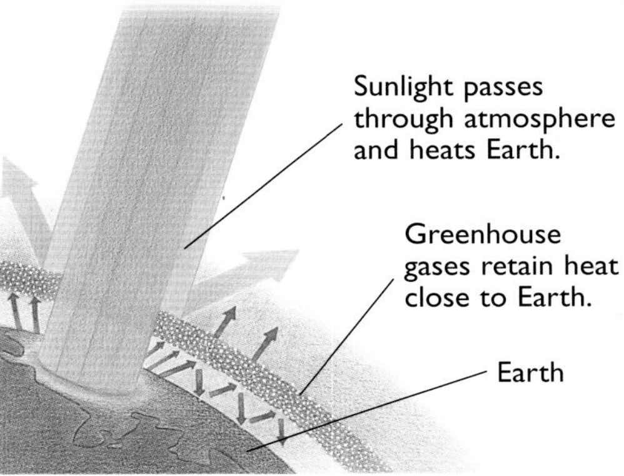
Sunlight passes through atmosphere and heats Earth.
Greenhouse gases retain heat close to Earth.
Earth

GLOBAL WARMING
Gases in the atmosphere, known as greenhouse gases, keep Earth warm by trapping some of the energy that comes from the Sun. But the burning of fossil fuels is raising the levels of these gases, causing the planet to warm too much. If this continues, some fertile land may turn into desert, and ice caps may melt, causing flooding in lowland areas. Most countries are trying to reduce greenhouse gas emissions.

◆ LOOK AGAIN ◆

- How can we prevent acid rain?
- What gases keep Earth warm?
- How can you help protect the ozone layer?

The Physical World

We call our planet Earth, but more than two-thirds of its surface is covered by salt water. Large areas of salt water are called oceans, and smaller areas are known as seas. There are four oceans—the Pacific, Atlantic, Indian and Arctic—and many seas. The Pacific Ocean alone is larger than all of Earth's landmasses combined. Land covers only 29 percent of our planet's surface. Its shape and the kind of soil and vegetation that cover it vary enormously from place to place. Throughout the world there are hills, mountains and areas of flat land called plains. Trees and other plants cover many parts of Earth, but some places have almost no vegetation. Deserts—very dry areas with sparse vegetation—cover about one-fifth of the world's land. The polar regions and many mountaintops are covered in ice and snow. The seas, too, have their mountains and valleys. Deep trenches are found in most oceans, and mountains on many islands are actually the tops of undersea mountains. For instance, Mauna Kea, on the island of Hawaii in the Pacific Ocean, is 33,480 feet (10,205 m) high, measured from the sea floor to its highest point. That's far taller than Mount Everest, the highest mountain on land.

Physical Facts

Circumference of Earth around the equator: 24,902 miles (40,067 km)
Area of sea: 139,782,000 square miles (362,033,000 sq. km)
Area of land above sea level: 57,151,000 square miles (148,021,000 sq. km)
Largest ocean: Pacific Ocean, 64,186,300 square miles (166,241,700 sq. km)
Largest landmass: Eurasia (Europe and Asia), 20,733,000 square miles (53,698,000 sq. km)
Deepest ocean trench: Mariana Trench, Pacific Ocean, 35,797 feet (10,911 m)
Largest island: Greenland, 840,000 square miles (2,175,000 sq. km)

Amazing Fact

Almost all of the water on Earth—97.3 percent—is salt water. Less than 3 percent is fresh water, and two-thirds of this is locked up in icecaps and glaciers. That leaves less than 1 percent in rivers, lakes and underground channels.

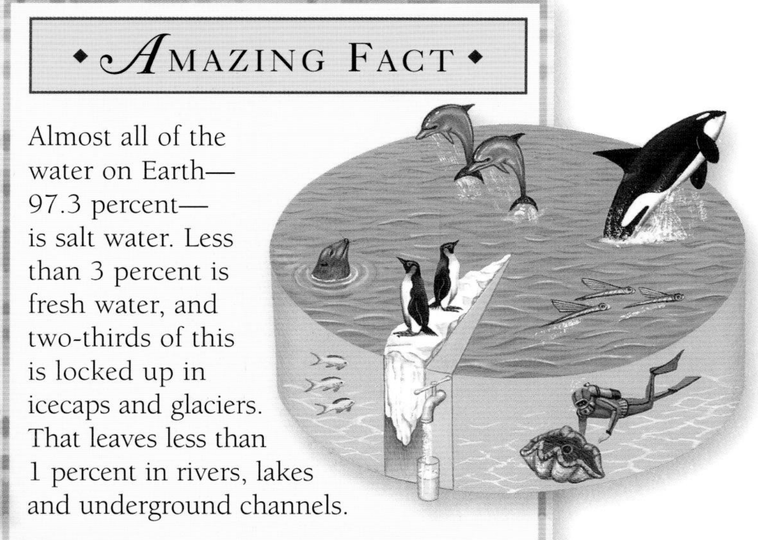

QUEEN ELIZABETH ISLANDS
Ellesmere Island
Greenland
Beaufort Sea
Victoria Island
Baffin Bay
Baffin Island
Davis Strait
BROOKS RANGE
Mackenzie
Great Bear Lake
Yukon
ROCKY MOUNTAINS
Great Slave Lake
Hudson Bay
Gulf of Alaska
CANADIAN SHIELD
Labrador Sea
ALEUTIAN ISLANDS
Lake Winnipeg
Newfoundland
GREAT PLAINS
Missouri
GREAT LAKES
St-Pierre and Miquelon
APPALACHIAN MOUNTAINS
NORTH AMERICA
Colorado
Mississippi
Bermuda
NORTH AMERICAN BASIN
Rio Grande
Gulf of Mexico
THE BAHAMAS
ATLANTIC OCEAN
HAWAIIAN ISLANDS
GREATER ANTILLES
WEST INDIES
MIDDLE AMERICA TRENCH
Caribbean Sea
LESSER ANTILLES
Clipperton Island
PACIFIC OCEAN
LLANOS
Orinoco
GUIANA BASIN
LINE ISLANDS
GUIANA HIGHLANDS
GALÁPAGOS ISLANDS
Amazon
POLYNESIA
AMAZON BASIN
SOUTH AMERICA
SELVAS
TUAMOTU ARCHIPELAGO
PERU-CHILE TRENCH
ANDES
BRAZILIAN HIGHLANDS
São Francisco
GRAN CHACO
Paraná
COOK ISLANDS
SOCIETY ISLANDS
Uruguay
EAST PACIFIC RISE
Easter Island
PAMPAS
SOUTHWEST PACIFIC BASIN
JUAN FERNÁNDEZ ISLANDS
PATAGONIA
ARGENTINE BASIN
FALKLAND ISLANDS
SOUTHEAST PACIFIC BASIN
CAPE HORN
South Georgia
ANTARCTIC PENINSULA
Weddell Sea

J K L M N O P Q

2 3 4 5 6 7 8 9 10

ARCTIC OCEAN
Spitsbergen
SVALBARD
FRANZ JOSEF LAND
SEVERNAYA ZEMLYA
NOVAYA ZEMLYA
Greenland Sea
Barents Sea
Kara Sea
Laptev Sea
NEW SIBERIAN ISLANDS
East Siberian Sea
Chukchi Sea
Jan Mayen Island
Iceland
Norwegian Sea
FAEROE ISLANDS
SCANDINAVIA
Dvina
URAL MOUNTAINS
Ob'
WESTERN SIBERIAN PLAIN
Yenisey
CENTRAL SIBERIAN PLATEAU
Lena
Bering Strait
North Sea
BRITISH ISLES
Ireland
EUROPEAN PLAIN
Volga
EUROPE
Angara
SIBERIA
Lake Baikal
Sea of Okhotsk
Bering Sea
ALEUTIAN ISLANDS
ALEUTIAN TRENCH
Irtysh
ASIA
Amur
CHANNEL ISLANDS
Dnieper
CARPATHIAN MTS.
Danube
ALPS
KIRGIZ STEPPE
Lake Balkhash
KURIL ISLANDS
KURIL TRENCH
Black Sea
Caspian Sea
Aral Sea
GOBI DESERT
TIAN MTS.
AZORES
Mediterranean Sea
Tigris
Euphrates
ZAGROS MTS.
HINDU KUSH
KUNLUN MTS.
Huang (Yellow)
Sea of Japan
Hokkaidō
Honshū
NORTHWEST PACIFIC BASIN
PACIFIC
MADEIRA
ATLAS MTS.
PLATEAU OF TIBET
HIMALAYAS
Chang (Yangtze)
Indus
CANARY ISLANDS
Nile
Red Sea
ARABIAN PENINSULA
Ganges
East China Sea
Taiwan
MIDWAY ISLANDS
MID-PACIFIC MOUNTAINS
MARIANA TRENCH
SAHARA DESERT
NUBIAN DESERT
PHILIPPINE BASIN
MARIANA ISLANDS
Wake Island
OCEAN
CAPE VERDE ISLANDS
Arabian Sea
DECCAN
Bay of Bengal
Luzon
PHILIPPINE TRENCH
PHILIPPINE ISLANDS
Mekong
Niger
SAHEL
AFRICA
LACCADIVE ISLANDS
ANDAMAN ISLANDS
South China Sea
Philippine Sea
Guam
MICRONESIA
CENTRAL PACIFIC BASIN
Johnston Atoll
MARSHALL ISLANDS
Palau
NICOBAR ISLANDS
Sri Lanka
MALDIVES
MID-INDIAN RIDGE
NINETYEAST RIDGE
SUNDA ISLANDS
Gulf of Guinea
Ubangi
Uele
Congo
GREAT RIFT VALLEY
CONGO BASIN
Kasai
Lake Victoria
CAROLINE ISLANDS
MELANESIA
Sumatra
Borneo
Nauru
GILBERT ISLANDS
OCEANIA
MID-ATLANTIC RIDGE
Ascension
SEYCHELLES
MID-INDIAN BASIN
Java
JAVA TRENCH
New Guinea
SOLOMON ISLANDS
Tuvalu
Tokelau
COMOROS ISLANDS
Mayotte
Christmas Island
COCOS (KEELING) ISLANDS
INDIAN OCEAN
SAMOA ISLANDS
St. Helena
Zambezi
Madagascar
Mauritius
Réunion
WHARTON BASIN
Coral Sea
Vanuatu
FIJI ISLANDS
Niue
Tonga
MARTIN VAZ ISLANDS
NAMIB DESERT
KALAHARI DESERT
GREAT SANDY DESERT
SIMPSON DESERT
GREAT DIVIDING RANGE
New Caledonia
TONGA TRENCH
WALVIS RIDGE
Orange
AUSTRALIA
Lake Eyre
GREAT VICTORIAN DESERT
Norfolk Island
KERMADEC ISLANDS
Darling
KERMADEC TRENCH
Murray
CAPE OF GOOD HOPE
Tristan da Cunha
Gough Island
SOUTHWEST INDIAN RIDGE
SOUTHEAST INDIAN RIDGE
Amsterdam Island
St. Paul Island
Great Australian Bight
Tasmania
Tasman Sea
NEW ZEALAND
North Island
South Island
CHATHAM ISLANDS
CROZET ISLANDS
PRINCE EDWARD ISLANDS
KERGUÉLEN ISLANDS
HEARD AND McDONALD ISLANDS
AUCKLAND ISLANDS
SOUTH SANDWICH ISLANDS
Bouvet Island
ATLANTIC-INDIAN BASIN
Macquarie Island
SOUTH INDIAN BASIN
ANTARCTICA
Ross Sea

J K L M N O P

Countries of the World

APART FROM ANTARCTICA, which has no permanent population, all the land on Earth is divided into countries. There are almost 200 countries in the world, and each country has its own government and its own laws. The world's smallest country, the Vatican City, measures only one-fifth of a square mile (0.44 sq. km). That's about the size of 100 football fields. The largest country in the world, Russia, is 39 million times bigger! The lines that separate countries are called borders. On this world map, the countries are shown in different colors so that you can see the borders clearly. Borders may be straight or curved. Some are formed by rivers or mountain ranges; others cross lakes or seas. The sizes of countries and the shapes of their borders often change. Sometimes a large country divides into smaller countries because groups of people want to form separate countries. Neighboring countries often disagree about where a border ought to be. Such disputes have led to wars in many parts of the world. In this atlas, disputed borders are shown by a dotted line. Many countries govern areas of land in other parts of the world. These are called territories. On a map, the name of the governing country usually appears in parentheses after the name of the territory.

Political Facts

Number of countries: 194
Number of territories: 65
Largest countries:
Russia, 6,592,812 square miles (17,075,383 sq. km)
Canada, 3,851,809 square miles (9,976,185 sq. km)
China, 3,700,000 square miles (9,583,000 sq. km)
Smallest country: Vatican City, 0.17 square miles (0.44 sq. km)
Longest border: U.S.-Canada, 3,987 miles (6,416 km)

• Look Again •

The following shapes represent countries shown on the world map on the right. Can you find and name them?

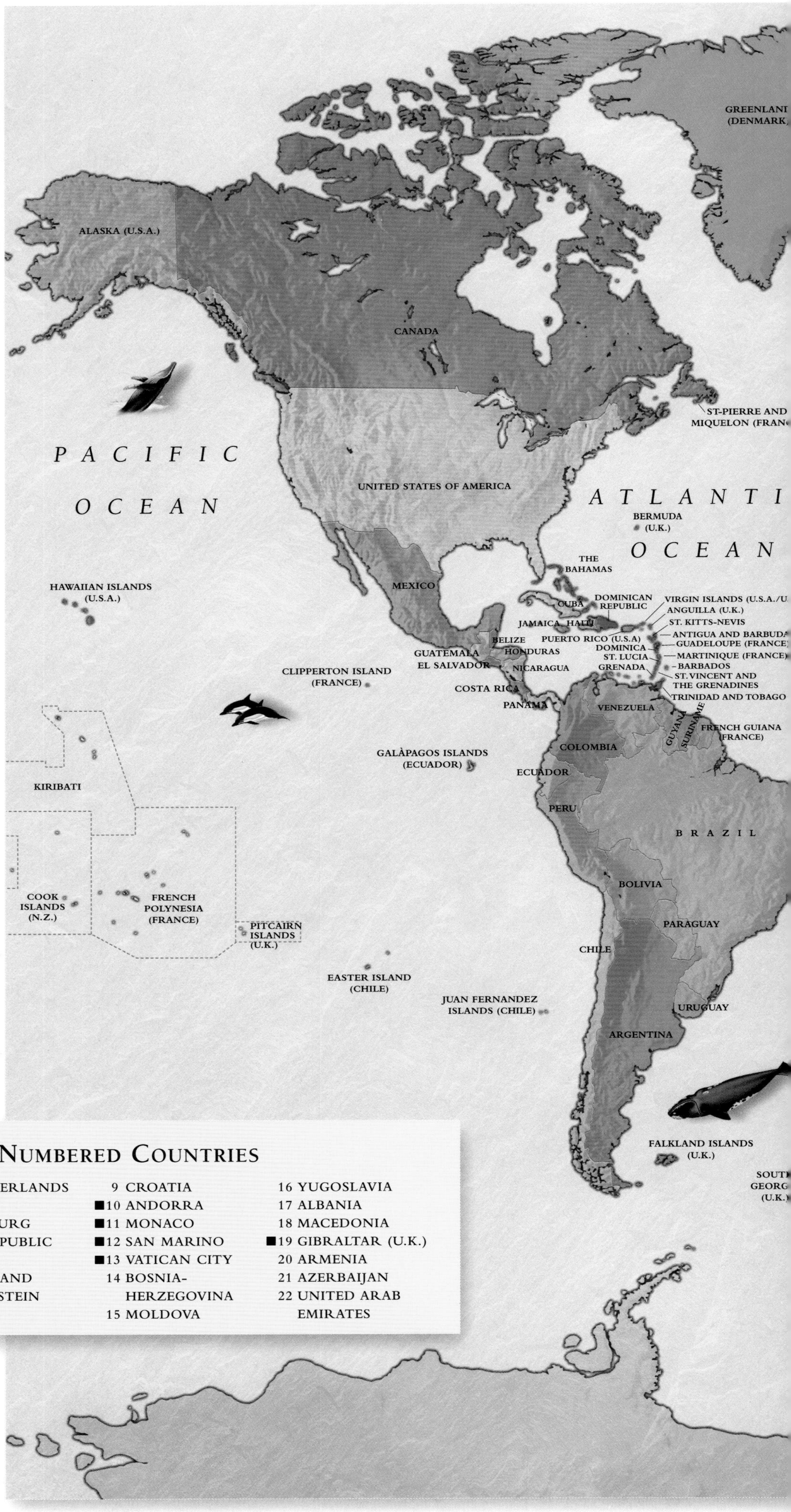

ALASKA (U.S.A.)
CANADA
GREENLAND (DENMARK)
ST-PIERRE AND MIQUELON (FRANCE)
UNITED STATES OF AMERICA
PACIFIC OCEAN
ATLANTIC OCEAN
BERMUDA (U.K.)
THE BAHAMAS
HAWAIIAN ISLANDS (U.S.A.)
MEXICO
CUBA
DOMINICAN REPUBLIC
JAMAICA
HAITI
BELIZE
PUERTO RICO (U.S.A)
HONDURAS
GUATEMALA
EL SALVADOR
NICARAGUA
COSTA RICA
PANAMA
VIRGIN ISLANDS (U.S.A./U.K.)
ANGUILLA (U.K.)
ST. KITTS-NEVIS
ANTIGUA AND BARBUDA
GUADELOUPE (FRANCE)
DOMINICA
MARTINIQUE (FRANCE)
ST. LUCIA
BARBADOS
GRENADA
ST. VINCENT AND THE GRENADINES
TRINIDAD AND TOBAGO
CLIPPERTON ISLAND (FRANCE)
VENEZUELA
GUYANA
SURINAME
FRENCH GUIANA (FRANCE)
COLOMBIA
GALÁPAGOS ISLANDS (ECUADOR)
ECUADOR
PERU
BRAZIL
KIRIBATI
BOLIVIA
COOK ISLANDS (N.Z.)
FRENCH POLYNESIA (FRANCE)
PITCAIRN ISLANDS (U.K.)
PARAGUAY
CHILE
EASTER ISLAND (CHILE)
JUAN FERNANDEZ ISLANDS (CHILE)
URUGUAY
ARGENTINA
FALKLAND ISLANDS (U.K.)
SOUTH GEORGIA (U.K.)

Key to Numbered Countries

1 THE NETHERLANDS
2 BELGIUM
■3 LUXEMBOURG
4 CZECH REPUBLIC
5 SLOVAKIA
6 SWITZERLAND
■7 LIECHTENSTEIN
8 SLOVENIA
9 CROATIA
■10 ANDORRA
■11 MONACO
■12 SAN MARINO
■13 VATICAN CITY
14 BOSNIA-HERZEGOVINA
15 MOLDOVA
16 YUGOSLAVIA
17 ALBANIA
18 MACEDONIA
■19 GIBRALTAR (U.K.)
20 ARMENIA
21 AZERBAIJAN
22 UNITED ARAB EMIRATES

J K L M N O P Q

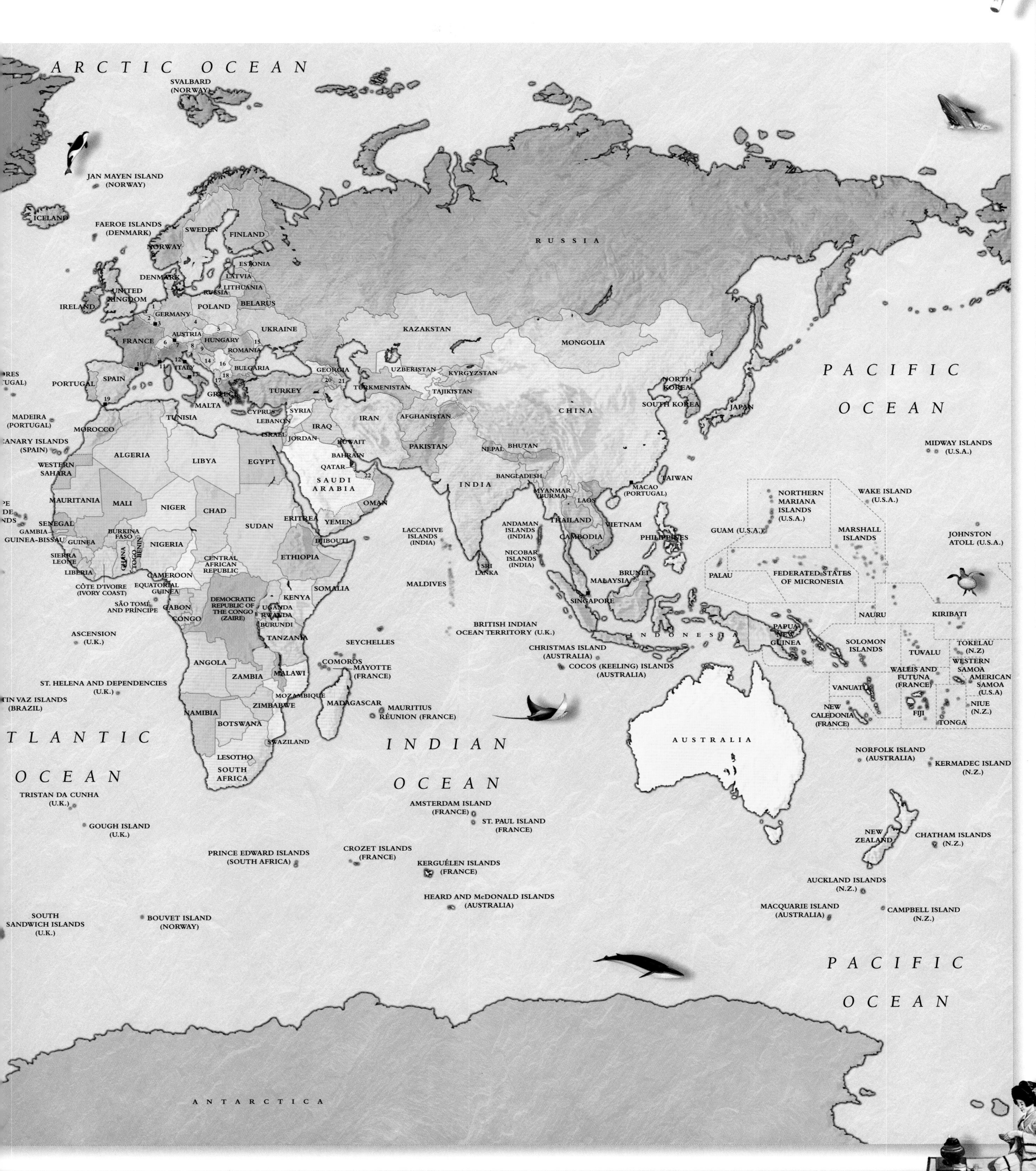
ARCTIC OCEAN
SVALBARD (NORWAY)
JAN MAYEN ISLAND (NORWAY)
ICELAND
FAEROE ISLANDS (DENMARK)
SWEDEN
FINLAND
NORWAY
ESTONIA
DENMARK
LATVIA
LITHUANIA
UNITED KINGDOM
RUSSIA
BELARUS
IRELAND
POLAND
GERMANY
UKRAINE
AUSTRIA
HUNGARY
FRANCE
ROMANIA
BULGARIA
ITALY
SPAIN
PORTUGAL
GREECE
TURKEY
GEORGIA
MALTA
CYPRUS
SYRIA
LEBANON
ISRAEL
JORDAN
IRAQ
IRAN
KUWAIT
BAHRAIN
QATAR
SAUDI ARABIA
OMAN
YEMEN
TUNISIA
MOROCCO
ALGERIA
LIBYA
EGYPT
MADEIRA (PORTUGAL)
CANARY ISLANDS (SPAIN)
WESTERN SAHARA
MAURITANIA
MALI
NIGER
CHAD
SUDAN
ERITREA
DJIBOUTI
ETHIOPIA
SOMALIA
SENEGAL
GAMBIA
GUINEA-BISSAU
GUINEA
BURKINA FASO
NIGERIA
SIERRA LEONE
LIBERIA
GHANA
TOGO
BENIN
CÔTE D'IVOIRE (IVORY COAST)
CAMEROON
CENTRAL AFRICAN REPUBLIC
EQUATORIAL GUINEA
SÃO TOMÉ AND PRÍNCIPE
GABON
CONGO
DEMOCRATIC REPUBLIC OF THE CONGO (ZAIRE)
UGANDA
RWANDA
BURUNDI
KENYA
TANZANIA
ASCENSION (U.K.)
SEYCHELLES
COMOROS
MAYOTTE (FRANCE)
ANGOLA
ZAMBIA
MALAWI
MOZAMBIQUE
ZIMBABWE
NAMIBIA
BOTSWANA
MADAGASCAR
MAURITIUS
RÉUNION (FRANCE)
SWAZILAND
LESOTHO
SOUTH AFRICA
ST. HELENA AND DEPENDENCIES (U.K.)
TRINDADE AND MARTIN VAZ ISLANDS (BRAZIL)
ATLANTIC OCEAN
TRISTAN DA CUNHA (U.K.)
GOUGH ISLAND (U.K.)
PRINCE EDWARD ISLANDS (SOUTH AFRICA)
CROZET ISLANDS (FRANCE)
KERGUÉLEN ISLANDS (FRANCE)
HEARD AND McDONALD ISLANDS (AUSTRALIA)
AMSTERDAM ISLAND (FRANCE)
ST. PAUL ISLAND (FRANCE)
SOUTH SANDWICH ISLANDS (U.K.)
BOUVET ISLAND (NORWAY)
INDIAN OCEAN
RUSSIA
KAZAKSTAN
UZBEKISTAN
KYRGYZSTAN
TURKMENISTAN
TAJIKISTAN
AFGHANISTAN
PAKISTAN
NEPAL
BHUTAN
INDIA
BANGLADESH
MONGOLIA
CHINA
NORTH KOREA
SOUTH KOREA
JAPAN
TAIWAN
MACAO (PORTUGAL)
MYANMAR (BURMA)
LAOS
THAILAND
VIETNAM
CAMBODIA
PHILIPPINES
LACCADIVE ISLANDS (INDIA)
ANDAMAN ISLANDS (INDIA)
NICOBAR ISLANDS (INDIA)
SRI LANKA
MALDIVES
MALAYSIA
BRUNEI
SINGAPORE
INDONESIA
BRITISH INDIAN OCEAN TERRITORY (U.K.)
CHRISTMAS ISLAND (AUSTRALIA)
COCOS (KEELING) ISLANDS (AUSTRALIA)
PAPUA NEW GUINEA
AUSTRALIA
PACIFIC OCEAN
MIDWAY ISLANDS (U.S.A.)
WAKE ISLAND (U.S.A.)
NORTHERN MARIANA ISLANDS (U.S.A.)
GUAM (U.S.A.)
MARSHALL ISLANDS
JOHNSTON ATOLL (U.S.A.)
PALAU
FEDERATED STATES OF MICRONESIA
NAURU
KIRIBATI
SOLOMON ISLANDS
TUVALU
TOKELAU (N.Z)
WESTERN SAMOA
AMERICAN SAMOA (U.S.A)
WALLIS AND FUTUNA (FRANCE)
VANUATU
FIJI
NIUE (N.Z.)
TONGA
NEW CALEDONIA (FRANCE)
NORFOLK ISLAND (AUSTRALIA)
KERMADEC ISLAND (N.Z.)
NEW ZEALAND
CHATHAM ISLANDS (N.Z.)
AUCKLAND ISLANDS (N.Z.)
MACQUARIE ISLAND (AUSTRALIA)
CAMPBELL ISLAND (N.Z.)
PACIFIC OCEAN
ANTARCTICA
2
3
4
5
6
7
8
9
10
11

J K L M N O P Q

North America

The continent of North America extends from just south of the North Pole to just north of the equator. It includes almost every kind of environment, from ice caps to forests, mountains, deserts and jungles. In the west, an almost unbroken chain of mountains stretches from Alaska to Costa Rica and includes the Rocky Mountains, one of the world's most famous mountain ranges. The United States (often called the U.S.A. or America) and Canada are the largest of the continent's 23 countries. The United States is made up of 50 states. Canada is divided into ten provinces and two territories. North America includes some of the world's biggest cities, but also vast areas of wilderness. Most North Americans are the descendants of European immigrants, but there are also many people of African origin as well as groups of native peoples.

Major Mountains and Rivers

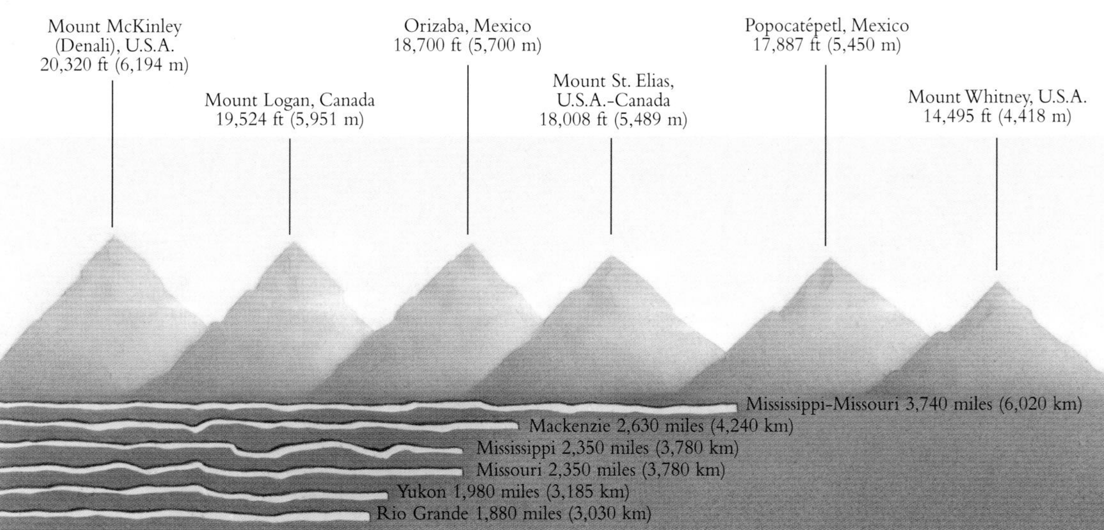
Mount McKinley (Denali), U.S.A. 20,320 ft (6,194 m)
Mount Logan, Canada 19,524 ft (5,951 m)
Orizaba, Mexico 18,700 ft (5,700 m)
Mount St. Elias, U.S.A.-Canada 18,008 ft (5,489 m)
Popocatépetl, Mexico 17,887 ft (5,450 m)
Mount Whitney, U.S.A. 14,495 ft (4,418 m)
Mississippi-Missouri 3,740 miles (6,020 km)
Mackenzie 2,630 miles (4,240 km)
Mississippi 2,350 miles (3,780 km)
Missouri 2,350 miles (3,780 km)
Yukon 1,980 miles (3,185 km)
Rio Grande 1,880 miles (3,030 km)

Political Map

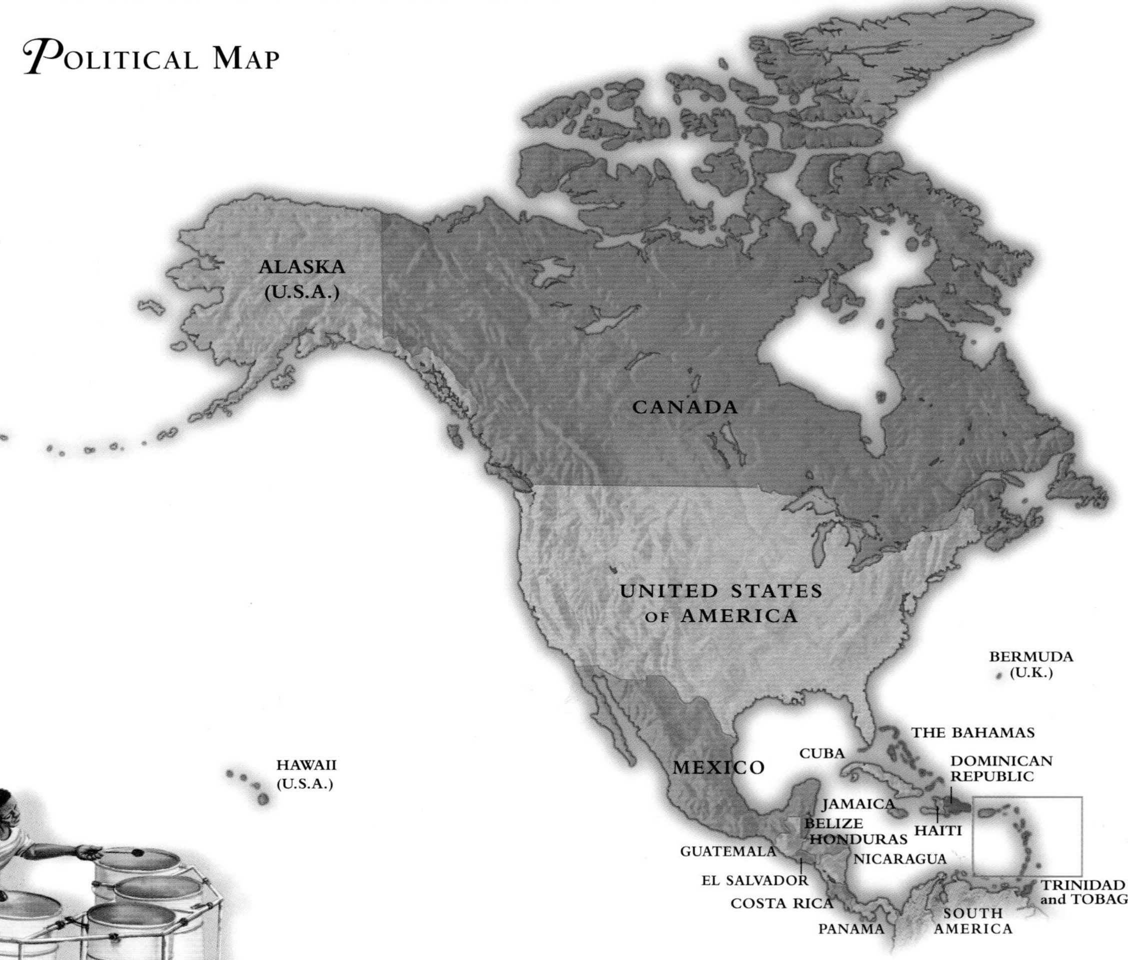
ALASKA (U.S.A.)
CANADA
UNITED STATES OF AMERICA
BERMUDA (U.K.)
THE BAHAMAS
DOMINICAN REPUBLIC
CUBA
MEXICO
HAWAII (U.S.A.)
JAMAICA
BELIZE
HAITI
HONDURAS
GUATEMALA
NICARAGUA
EL SALVADOR
COSTA RICA
PANAMA
SOUTH AMERICA
TRINIDAD and TOBAGO

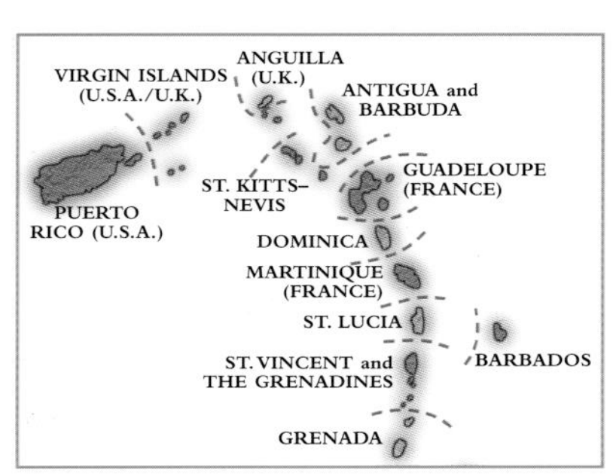
VIRGIN ISLANDS (U.S.A./U.K.)
ANGUILLA (U.K.)
ANTIGUA and BARBUDA
PUERTO RICO (U.S.A.)
ST. KITTS–NEVIS
GUADELOUPE (FRANCE)
DOMINICA
MARTINIQUE (FRANCE)
ST. LUCIA
BARBADOS
ST. VINCENT and THE GRENADINES
GRENADA

Continent Facts

Regional land area: 8,522,127 sq. miles (22,078,049 sq. km)
Regional population: 453,356,000
Independent countries: Antigua and Barbuda, The Bahamas, Barbados, Belize, Canada, Costa Rica, Cuba, Dominica, Dominican Republic, El Salvador, Grenada, Guatemala, Haiti, Honduras, Jamaica, Mexico, Nicaragua, Panama, St. Kitts–Nevis, St. Lucia, St. Vincent and the Grenadines, Trinidad and Tobago, United States of America

World Records

WORLD'S LARGEST GORGE
Grand Canyon, U.S.A., 277 miles (446 km) long, 10 miles (16 km) wide, 1 mile (1.6 km) deep

WORLD'S LARGEST FRESHWATER LAKE
Lake Superior, U.S.A.-Canada, 31,800 sq. miles (82,350 sq. km)

WORLD'S LONGEST CAVE SYSTEM
Mammoth Caves, U.S.A., 351 miles (565 km)

WORLD'S LARGEST ACTIVE VOLCANO
Mauna Loa, Hawaii, U.S.A., 13,680 ft (4,170 m) high, 75 miles (120 km) long, 31 miles (50 km) wide

WORLD'S LONGEST BORDER
U.S.-Canadian border, 3,987 miles (6,416 km)

WORLD'S TALLEST ACTIVE GEYSER
Steamboat Geyser, Yellowstone National Park, U.S.A., 380 ft (115 m)

WORLD'S LARGEST THEME PARK
Walt Disney World, U.S.A., 47 sq. miles (122 sq. km)

Continent Records

HIGHEST MOUNTAIN
Mount McKinley (Denali), U.S.A., 20,320 ft (6,194 m)

LOWEST POINT
Death Valley, U.S.A., 282 ft (86 m) below sea level

LONGEST RIVER
Mississippi-Missouri, U.S.A., 3,740 miles (6,020 km)

LARGEST COUNTRY BY AREA
Canada, 3,851,809 sq. miles (9,976,185 sq. km)

LARGEST COUNTRY BY POPULATION
United States of America, population 263,814,000

LARGEST CITY BY POPULATION
Mexico City, Mexico, population 15,600,000

J
K
L
M
N
O
P
Q
Physical Map
ARCTIC OCEAN
NORTH POLE
ASIA
Chukchi Sea
Ellesmere Island
QUEEN ELIZABETH ISLANDS
Greenland
Baffin Bay
EUROPE
Bering Sea
BROOKS RANGE
Yukon
Beaufort Sea
Banks Island
Victoria Island
Baffin Island
ALEUTIAN ISLANDS
Mt. McKinley (Denali)
Mt. Logan
Mt. St. Elias
Mackenzie
Great Bear Lake
Arctic Circle
Labrador Sea
Gulf of Alaska
Great Slave Lake
CANADIAN SHIELD
Hudson Bay
LABRADOR
ATLANTIC OCEAN
QUEEN CHARLOTTE ISLANDS
COAST MTS
ROCKY MOUNTAINS
GREAT PLAINS
Newfoundland
Vancouver Island
Lake Winnipeg
Lake Nipigon
Lake Superior
Missouri
Lake Huron
Lake Ontario
St. Lawrence
PACIFIC OCEAN
Mississippi
Lake Michigan
HAWAIIAN ISLANDS
COAST RANGES
GREAT BASIN
Great Salt Lake
Lake Erie
APPALACHIAN MOUNTAINS
Mt. Whitney
Colorado
Ohio
Bermuda
SIERRA MADRE OCCIDENTAL
SIERRA MADRE ORIENTAL
Gulf of California
Rio Grande
Tropic of Cancer
THE BAHAMAS
LESSER ANTILLES
Gulf of Mexico
GREATER ANTILLES
Bay of Campeche
Caribbean Sea
Popocatépetl
Orizaba
Lake Nicaragua
SOUTH AMERICA
Equator
GALÁPAGOS ISLANDS
2
3
9
10
11

Western Canada and Alaska

Canada, the world's second-largest country, covers more than half of North America. Northern Canada is a vast, chilly wilderness where bears fish icy rivers for salmon and wolves hunt caribou across snow-covered plains. Few people live in this cold environment. The Northwest Territories occupy one-third of Canada, but the province's population of 65,800 could be contained in a large sports stadium. Eighty percent of Canada's residents live within 185 miles (300 km) of the southern border, where the climate is milder and the land is more fertile. The prairie grassland that covers parts of Alberta, Manitoba and Saskatchewan is one of the world's most productive farming regions. These provinces also supply most of Canada's oil and gas. West of the towering Rocky Mountains is the Pacific coastline, a maze of islands and narrow waterways. In the Gulf of Alaska, glaciers creep down the mountains toward the shore, while seals and whales swim in the bays. Alaska is the biggest of the United States, but it is separated from the rest of the country by Canada. More than half of Alaska's lands are wildlife refuges, and the state contains some of North America's largest oil fields.

ALASKA (U.S.A.)
Population: 603,600 * Capital: Juneau

ALBERTA
Population: 2,747,000 * Capital: Edmonton

BRITISH COLUMBIA
Population: 3,766,000 * Capital: Victoria

MANITOBA
Population: 1,137,500 * Capital: Winnipeg

NORTHWEST TERRITORIES
Population: 65,800 * Capital: Yellowknife

SASKATCHEWAN
Population: 1,015,600 * Capital: Regina

YUKON TERRITORY
Population: 30,100 * Capital: Whitehorse

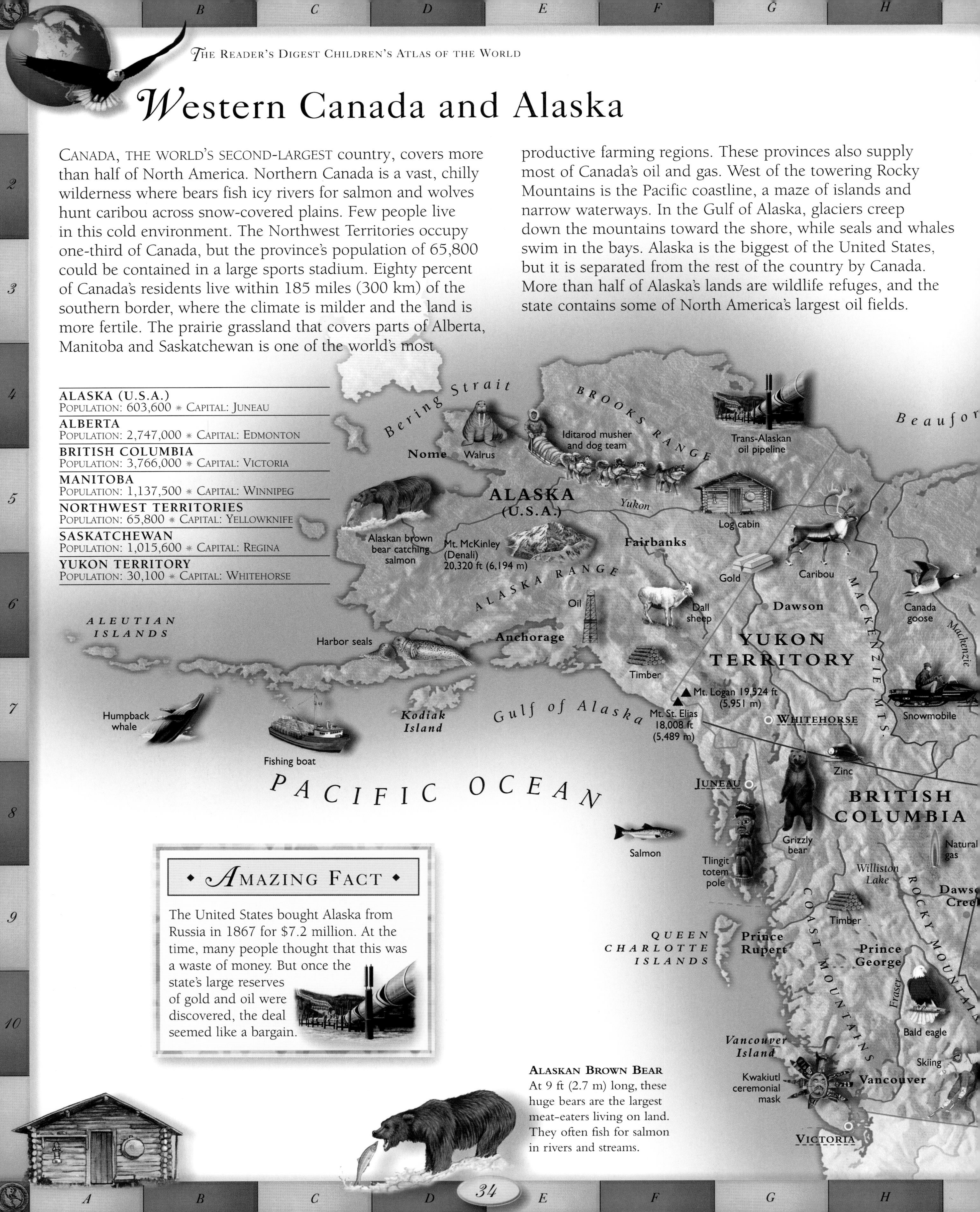

Bering Strait
Brooks Range
Beaufort
Nome
Walrus
Iditarod musher and dog team
Trans-Alaskan oil pipeline
ALASKA (U.S.A.)
Yukon
Log cabin
Alaskan brown bear catching salmon
Mt. McKinley (Denali) 20,320 ft (6,194 m)
Fairbanks
Gold
Caribou
Alaska Range
Oil
Dall sheep
Dawson
Mackenzie Mts.
Canada goose
Mackenzie
Aleutian Islands
Harbor seals
Anchorage
Yukon Territory
Timber
Mt. Logan 19,524 ft (5,951 m)
Humpback whale
Kodiak Island
Gulf of Alaska
Mt. St. Elias 18,008 ft (5,489 m)
Whitehorse
Snowmobile
Fishing boat
Zinc
Pacific Ocean
Juneau
British Columbia
Salmon
Tlingit totem pole
Grizzly bear
Natural gas
Williston Lake
Coast Mountains
Rocky Mountains
Timber
Queen Charlotte Islands
Prince Rupert
Prince George
Fraser
Bald eagle
Vancouver Island
Kwakiutl ceremonial mask
Vancouver
Skiing
Victoria

◆ Amazing Fact ◆

The United States bought Alaska from Russia in 1867 for $7.2 million. At the time, many people thought that this was a waste of money. But once the state's large reserves of gold and oil were discovered, the deal seemed like a bargain.

Alaskan Brown Bear
At 9 ft (2.7 m) long, these huge bears are the largest meat-eaters living on land. They often fish for salmon in rivers and streams.

 See World Fact File page 104

J K L M N O P
1 2 3 4 5 6 7 8 9 10
ARCTIC OCEAN
Narwhal
Ellesmere Island
Musk ox
QUEEN ELIZABETH ISLANDS
Polar bears
Arctic fox
PARRY ISLANDS
Banks Island
Somerset Island
Prince of Wales Island
Snow goose
Arctic hare
Victoria Island
Inuit building igloo
Baffin Bay
GREENLAND
Davis Strait
Baffin Island
Traditional church
Inuit fishing through ice
Kittiwake
Harp seals
Great Bear Lake
Silver
Wolf
Seaplane
Igloo-shaped houses
Southampton Island
Hudson Strait
NORTHWEST TERRITORIES
YELLOWKNIFE
Great Slave Lake
Gold
Gray jay
Moose
CANADA
QUÉBEC
LOCATION
Hudson Bay
Beluga whale
Slave
Zinc and lead
Lake Athabasca
Uranium
Churchill
Churchill
ALBERTA
Reindeer Lake
Peace
Edmontonia dinosaur fossils
Beaver
Nelson
Nickel and copper
N
E
W
S
Mountie
MANITOBA
EDMONTON
SASKATCHEWAN
Gold
ONTARIO
SCALE
MILES
0 100 200 300
0 100 200 300 400 500
KILOMETERS
Oil
Natural gas
Wheat
Saskatchewan
Lake Winnipeg
Saskatoon
Calgary
REGINA
Grain elevators
WINNIPEG
Calgary Stampede
Legislative Building
UNITED STATES OF AMERICA

◆ PROJECT: *Inuit Finger Masks* ◆

In ceremonies and rituals, the Inuit (Eskimos) use tiny finger masks to represent their spirit ancestors. The masks are often carved from wood or stone, but you can make yours out of cardboard.

❶ Cut out a circle about four inches (10 cm) in diameter. Cut two small holes at the bottom of the circle large enough for your fingers to poke through.

❷ Draw a face in the center of the circle and color it. Cut a fringe in the cardboard or glue feathers or beads around the face.

❸ To perform with the mask, move your hand slowly from side to side to the beat of a drum.

ROYAL CANADIAN MOUNTED POLICE (MOUNTIES)
Canada's national police force was founded in 1873 to prevent disputes between native tribes and European traders.

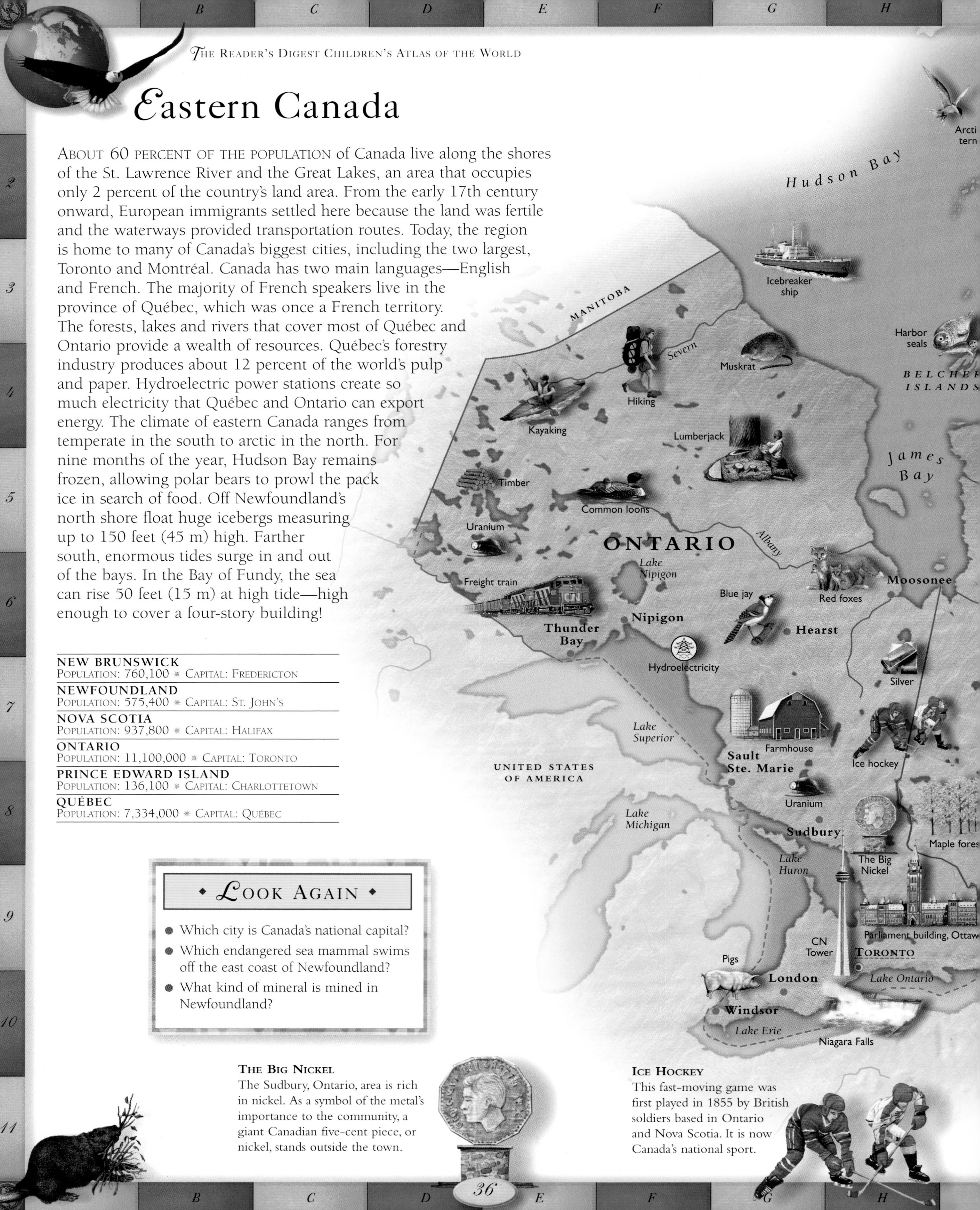
Hudson Bay
Arctic tern
Icebreaker ship
MANITOBA
Severn
Muskrat
Harbor seals
BELCHER ISLANDS
Hiking
Kayaking
Lumberjack
James Bay
Timber
Common loons
Uranium
ONTARIO
Albany
Lake Nipigon
Freight train
Blue jay
Red foxes
Moosonee
Nipigon
Thunder Bay
Hearst
Hydroelectricity
Silver
Lake Superior
Farmhouse
Ice hockey
UNITED STATES OF AMERICA
Sault Ste. Marie
Uranium
Lake Michigan
Sudbury
The Big Nickel
Maple forest
Lake Huron
Parliament building, Ottawa
CN Tower
TORONTO
Pigs
London
Lake Ontario
Windsor
Lake Erie
Niagara Falls

Eastern Canada

ABOUT 60 PERCENT OF THE POPULATION of Canada live along the shores of the St. Lawrence River and the Great Lakes, an area that occupies only 2 percent of the country's land area. From the early 17th century onward, European immigrants settled here because the land was fertile and the waterways provided transportation routes. Today, the region is home to many of Canada's biggest cities, including the two largest, Toronto and Montréal. Canada has two main languages—English and French. The majority of French speakers live in the province of Québec, which was once a French territory. The forests, lakes and rivers that cover most of Québec and Ontario provide a wealth of resources. Québec's forestry industry produces about 12 percent of the world's pulp and paper. Hydroelectric power stations create so much electricity that Québec and Ontario can export energy. The climate of eastern Canada ranges from temperate in the south to arctic in the north. For nine months of the year, Hudson Bay remains frozen, allowing polar bears to prowl the pack ice in search of food. Off Newfoundland's north shore float huge icebergs measuring up to 150 feet (45 m) high. Farther south, enormous tides surge in and out of the bays. In the Bay of Fundy, the sea can rise 50 feet (15 m) at high tide—high enough to cover a four-story building!

NEW BRUNSWICK
POPULATION: 760,100 * CAPITAL: FREDERICTON

NEWFOUNDLAND
POPULATION: 575,400 * CAPITAL: ST. JOHN'S

NOVA SCOTIA
POPULATION: 937,800 * CAPITAL: HALIFAX

ONTARIO
POPULATION: 11,100,000 * CAPITAL: TORONTO

PRINCE EDWARD ISLAND
POPULATION: 136,100 * CAPITAL: CHARLOTTETOWN

QUÉBEC
POPULATION: 7,334,000 * CAPITAL: QUÉBEC

LOOK AGAIN

- Which city is Canada's national capital?
- Which endangered sea mammal swims off the east coast of Newfoundland?
- What kind of mineral is mined in Newfoundland?

THE BIG NICKEL
The Sudbury, Ontario, area is rich in nickel. As a symbol of the metal's importance to the community, a giant Canadian five-cent piece, or nickel, stands outside the town.

ICE HOCKEY
This fast-moving game was first played in 1855 by British soldiers based in Ontario and Nova Scotia. It is now Canada's national sport.

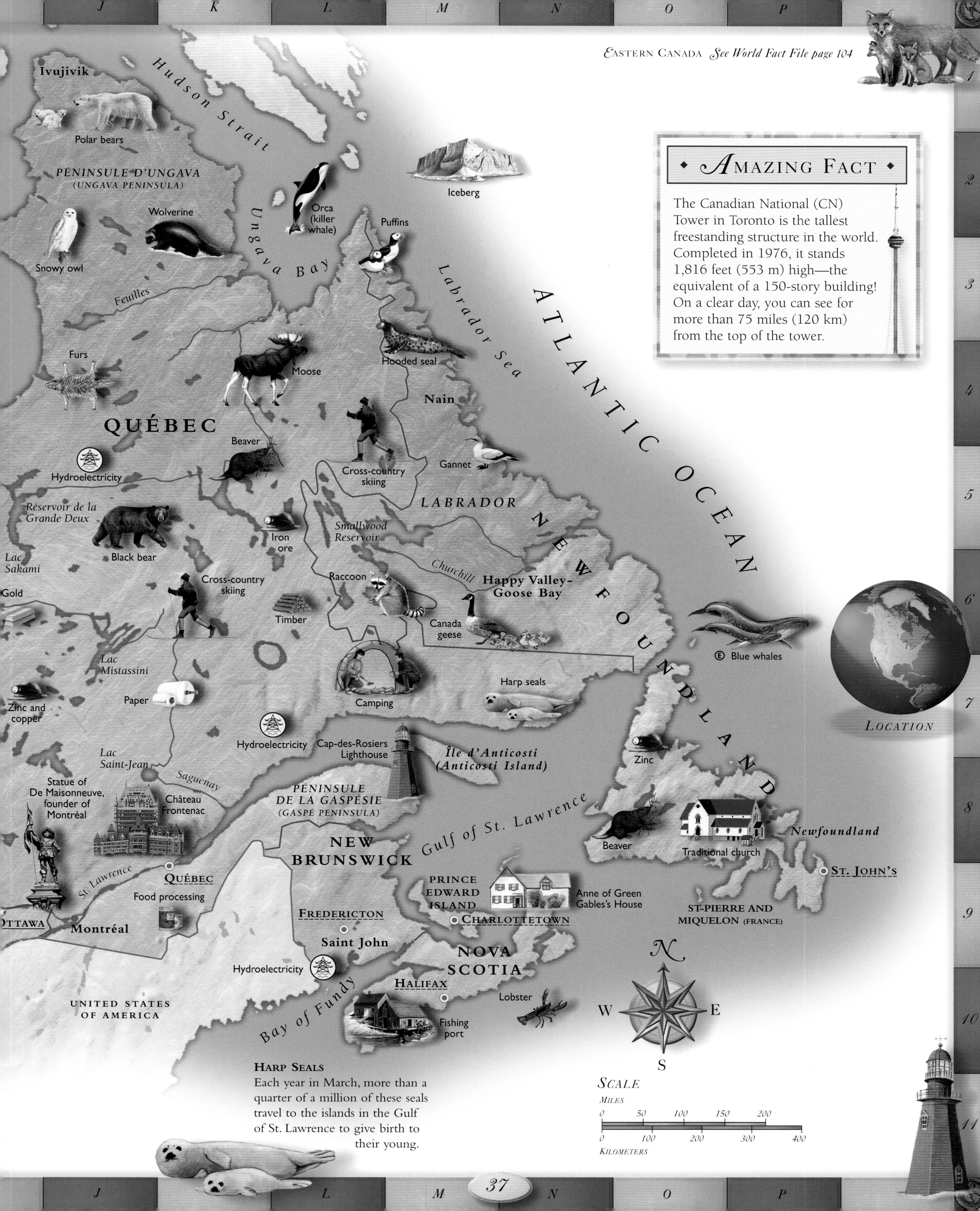

J K L M N O P
1 2 3 4 5 6 7 8 9 10 11
Ivujivik
Hudson Strait
Polar bears
PÉNINSULE D'UNGAVA
(UNGAVA PENINSULA)
Wolverine
Snowy owl
Ungava Bay
Orca (killer whale)
Iceberg
Puffins
Labrador Sea
ATLANTIC OCEAN
Feuilles
Furs
Moose
Hooded seal
Nain
QUÉBEC
Beaver
Hydroelectricity
Cross-country skiing
Gannet
LABRADOR
Réservoir de la Grande Deux
Black bear
Iron ore
Smallwood Reservoir
NEWFOUNDLAND
Lac Sakami
Gold
Cross-country skiing
Timber
Raccoon
Churchill
Happy Valley-Goose Bay
Canada geese
Blue whales
Lac Mistassini
Camping
Harp seals
Paper
Zinc and copper
Hydroelectricity
Cap-des-Rosiers Lighthouse
Île d'Anticosti (Anticosti Island)
Zinc
Lac Saint-Jean
Saguenay
Statue of De Maisonneuve, founder of Montréal
Château Frontenac
PÉNINSULE DE LA GASPÉSIE
(GASPÉ PENINSULA)
Gulf of St. Lawrence
Beaver
Traditional church
Newfoundland
NEW BRUNSWICK
St. Lawrence
QUÉBEC
Food processing
PRINCE EDWARD ISLAND
Anne of Green Gables's House
ST. JOHN'S
ST-PIERRE AND MIQUELON (FRANCE)
OTTAWA
Montréal
FREDERICTON
CHARLOTTETOWN
Saint John
NOVA SCOTIA
Hydroelectricity
HALIFAX
Lobster
Fishing port
UNITED STATES OF AMERICA
Bay of Fundy
N
W
E
S
LOCATION
SCALE
MILES
0 50 100 150 200
0 100 200 300 400
KILOMETERS

AMAZING FACT

The Canadian National (CN) Tower in Toronto is the tallest freestanding structure in the world. Completed in 1976, it stands 1,816 feet (553 m) high—the equivalent of a 150-story building! On a clear day, you can see for more than 75 miles (120 km) from the top of the tower.

HARP SEALS

Each year in March, more than a quarter of a million of these seals travel to the islands in the Gulf of St. Lawrence to give birth to their young.

Northeastern United States

THE NORTHEAST is home to 65 million people—more than one-quarter of the population of the United States. From Boston in the north to Washington, D.C. in the south, a line of great cities stretches for over 400 miles (640 km) along the Atlantic shore. Including its suburbs, New York City is home to more than 16 million people. It is the largest city in the U.S.A. and the third largest in the world. New York is one of the world's leading centers of trade, industry and culture. The heart of the city is the island of Manhattan, where giant skyscrapers, including some of the world's tallest, tower over long, straight streets packed with people and traffic.

The Appalachian Mountains separate the cities of the coast from the Great Lakes and the plains of the interior. They stretch for more than 1,600 miles (2,600 km) from northern Alabama, in the southern United States, to northern Maine. In the south, these mountains are rich in minerals—Kentucky produces more coal than any other state. Farms occupy many Appalachian valleys, but large areas of the mountains are covered by deciduous forests where black bears forage for blueberries and otters swim in the streams. In fall, these forests provide spectacular displays of color, as their leaves change from green to brilliant shades of orange, red and gold.

CONNECTICUT
Population: 3,275,000 * Capital: Hartford

DELAWARE
Population: 717,200 * Capital: Dover

DISTRICT OF COLUMBIA
Population: 554,200 * Capital: Washington, D.C.

KENTUCKY
Population: 3,860,000 * Capital: Frankfort

MAINE
Population: 1,241,000 * Capital: Augusta

MARYLAND
Population: 5,042,000 * Capital: Annapolis

MASSACHUSETTS
Population: 6,074,000 * Capital: Boston

NEW HAMPSHIRE
Population: 1,148,000 * Capital: Concord

NEW JERSEY
Population: 7,945,000 * Capital: Trenton

NEW YORK
Population: 18,136,000 * Capital: Albany

PENNSYLVANIA
Population: 12,072,000 * Capital: Harrisburg

RHODE ISLAND
Population: 989,800 * Capital: Providence

VERMONT
Population: 584,800 * Capital: Montpelier

VIRGINIA
Population: 6,618,000 * Capital: Richmond

WEST VIRGINIA
Population: 1,828,000 * Capital: Charleston

PROJECT: *Iroquois Beads*

According to the custom of the native Iroquois people, a person saying something important must give the listener a gift to confirm the truth of the statement. This gift is often a string of white and purple shell beads known as wampum. Try making your own Iroquois friendship beads. Thread some colored beads onto pieces of string and attach the strings to a length of yarn. Remember to explain the meaning of your gift to the receiver.

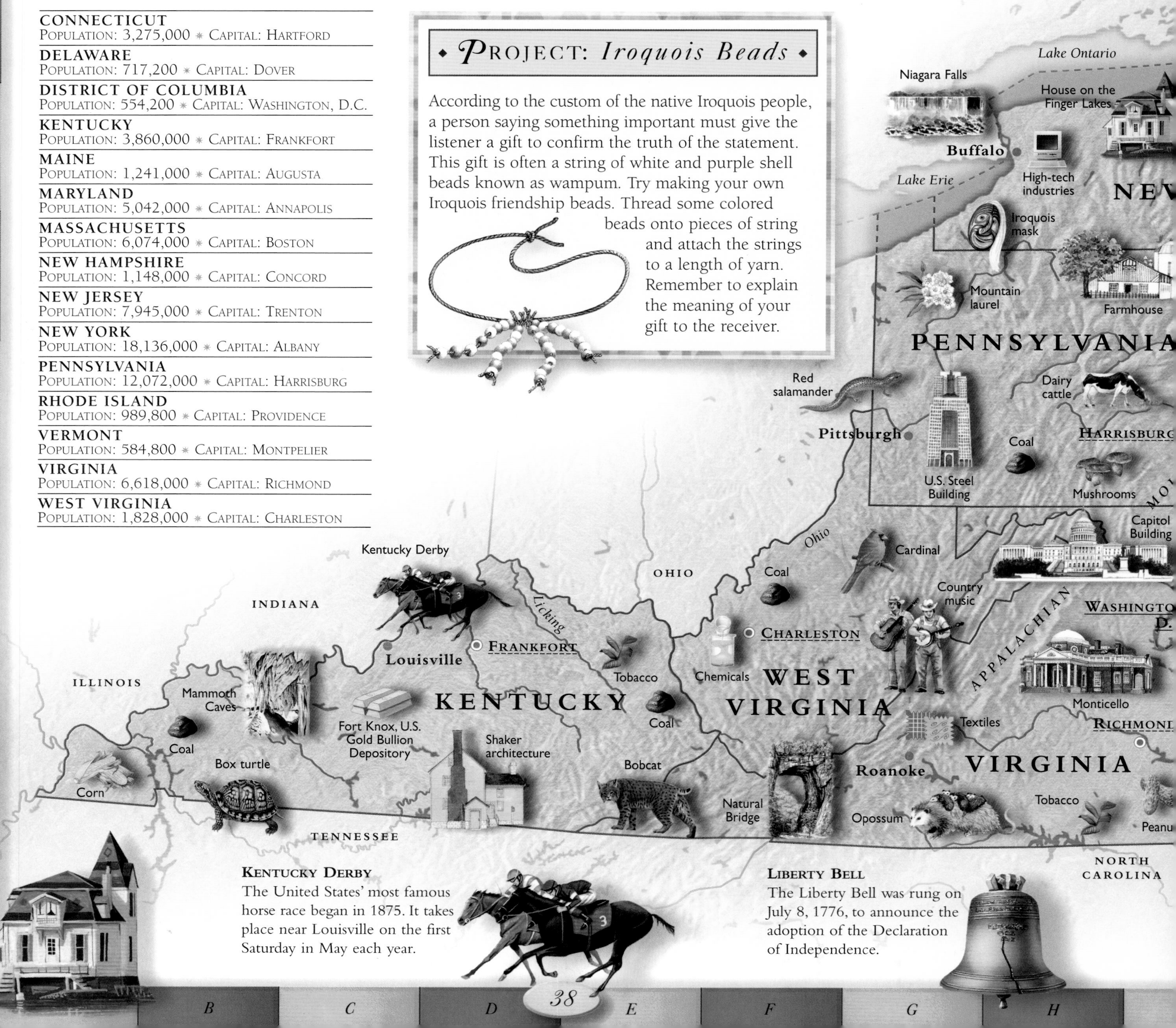

Lake Ontario
Niagara Falls
House on the Finger Lakes
Buffalo
Lake Erie
High-tech industries
NEW
Iroquois mask
Mountain laurel
Farmhouse
PENNSYLVANIA
Red salamander
Dairy cattle
Pittsburgh
Coal
HARRISBURG
U.S. Steel Building
Mushrooms
Capitol Building
Ohio
Cardinal
Kentucky Derby
OHIO
Coal
Country music
WASHINGTON D.C.
INDIANA
Licking
FRANKFORT
Louisville
CHARLESTON
APPALACHIAN
ILLINOIS
Mammoth Caves
Tobacco
Chemicals
WEST VIRGINIA
KENTUCKY
Coal
Monticello
Textiles
RICHMOND
Fort Knox, U.S. Gold Bullion Depository
Shaker architecture
Coal
Box turtle
Bobcat
Roanoke
VIRGINIA
Corn
Natural Bridge
Opossum
Tobacco
TENNESSEE
NORTH CAROLINA

Kentucky Derby
The United States' most famous horse race began in 1875. It takes place near Louisville on the first Saturday in May each year.

Liberty Bell
The Liberty Bell was rung on July 8, 1776, to announce the adoption of the Declaration of Independence.

 See World Fact File page 104

J
K
L
M
N
O
P
Q
1
2
3
4
5
6
7
8
9
10
11
Fort Kent
Potatoes
Chipmunk
Chickadee
Timber
Blueberries
MAINE
Mt. Washington Cog Railway
CANADA
Paper
Lighthouse
VERMONT
Zinc
Apples
MONTPELIER
AUGUSTA
Skiing
Poultry
Dairy cattle
Portland
Bluebird
Fort Ticonderoga
Maple syrup
NEW HAMPSHIRE
CONCORD
Timber
Manchester
Salmon
ALBANY
Connecticut
MASSACHUSETTS
YORK
BOSTON
Baseball Hall of Fame
Basketball Hall of Fame
High-tech industries
Cranberries
Amish people
Hudson
CONNECTICUT
PROVIDENCE
Mayflower
HARTFORD
Chrysler Building
RHODE ISLAND
Rhode Island Red
Minke whale
Tourism
Chocolate
New York
NEW JERSEY
Statue of Liberty
Liberty Bell
TRENTON
Philadelphia
Aircraft carrier
Poultry
Tourism
Baltimore
Atlantic City
DOVER
ANNAPOLIS
DELAWARE
Blue marlin
ATLANTIC OCEAN
Crab
MARYLAND
Norfolk
LOCATION
N
W
E
S
SCALE
MILES
0 25 50 75 100 125
0 50 100 150 200
KILOMETERS

AMAZING FACT

The Statue of Liberty was a gift from the people of France to the people of the United States. It was designed by Frédéric-Auguste Bartholdi and engineered by Alexandre Gustave Eiffel, who built the Eiffel Tower in Paris, France. The statue took nine years to build and was unveiled in 1886. It is made up of 300 copper sheets and stands 151 feet (46 m) tall on a base 154 feet (47 m) high.

CHRYSLER BUILDING
This skyscraper was built by Walter Chrysler, founder of the Chrysler car empire. The steel arches at the top are modeled on car hubcaps.

MAYFLOWER
In 1620 the Mayflower carried the Pilgrims from England to America to establish one of the first permanent colonies.

Southern United States

THE SOUTHERN UNITED STATES is a warm, humid region of plains, rivers, swamps and coastal lagoons. From southern Texas, a broad belt of lowland stretches around the Gulf of Mexico, across Florida and along the shores of the Atlantic Ocean. In the north and west, the coastal plains rise to plateaus and mountain ranges, including the Appalachian Mountains, which formed about 400 million years ago and are North America's oldest mountains. Mixed crop and livestock farms cover the fertile eastern and southern plains. In the west, on the dry Texas grasslands, ranch hands tend huge herds of cattle. Texas is the second-biggest American state after Alaska, and its beef industry and large oil reserves have made it one of the richest parts of the country. Numerous rivers cross the southern United States, including the Mississippi, one of North America's longest rivers and busiest inland waterways. Along the Gulf Coast and in northern Florida, these rivers have formed shallow lakes, muddy deltas and steamy swamps that are home to snakes, turtles and alligators. Florida's sunny climate and sandy beaches make it a popular vacation spot. The Walt Disney World theme park near Orlando is the world's number one tourist attraction, with more than 25 million visitors each year.

Many of the first Europeans to settle in this region came from France and Spain in the 17th century, and their descendants are called Creoles. Other French-speakers known as Cajuns arrived soon afterward from Canada. Florida's large Spanish-speaking population includes immigrants from the island of Cuba, which lies just 135 miles (217 km) south of Key West, the southernmost tip of Florida and the United States.

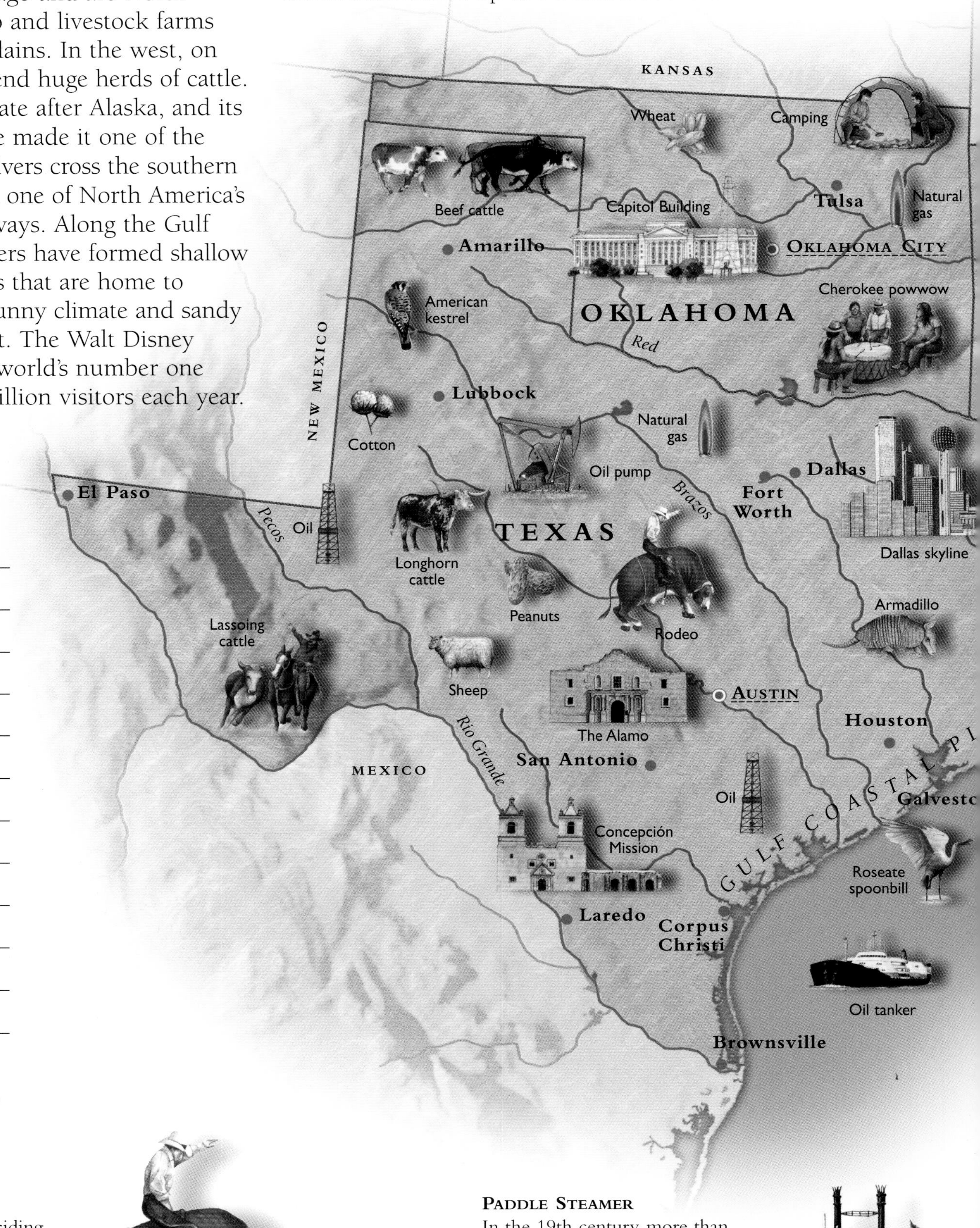

ALABAMA
Population: 4,253,000 * Capital: Montgomery

ARKANSAS
Population: 2,484,000 * Capital: Little Rock

FLORIDA
Population: 14,166,000 * Capital: Tallahassee

GEORGIA
Population: 7,201,000 * Capital: Atlanta

LOUISIANA
Population: 4,342,000 * Capital: Baton Rouge

MISSISSIPPI
Population: 2,697,000 * Capital: Jackson

NORTH CAROLINA
Population: 7,195,000 * Capital: Raleigh

OKLAHOMA
Population: 3,278,000 * Capital: Oklahoma City

SOUTH CAROLINA
Population: 3,673,000 * Capital: Columbia

TENNESSEE
Population: 5,256,000 * Capital: Nashville

TEXAS
Population: 18,724,000 * Capital: Austin

KANSAS
Wheat
Camping
Beef cattle
Capitol Building
Tulsa
Natural gas
Amarillo
OKLAHOMA CITY
American kestrel
OKLAHOMA
Cherokee powwow
Red
NEW MEXICO
Lubbock
Cotton
Natural gas
Oil pump
Dallas
Fort Worth
Brazos
El Paso
Pecos
Oil
Longhorn cattle
TEXAS
Dallas skyline
Peanuts
Rodeo
Armadillo
Lassoing cattle
Sheep
AUSTIN
The Alamo
Houston
MEXICO
Rio Grande
San Antonio
Oil
Concepción Mission
GULF COASTAL PLAIN
Roseate spoonbill
Laredo
Corpus Christi
Oil tanker
Brownsville

Rodeo
Rodeo events test the riding and roping skills of both men and women. In the bull-riding event, riders have to stay on the bucking bull for eight seconds.

Paddle Steamer
In the 19th century, more than 400 of these elegant steamers provided transportation for people and goods along the Mississippi River.

◆ Amazing Fact ◆

The Everglades, the vast wetland that covers southern Florida, is actually an enormous, slow-moving river 50 miles (80 km) wide, 100 miles (160 km) long and, on average, only six inches (15 cm) deep. The water comes from Lake Okeechobee, which overflows during the summer wet season.

◆ Look Again ◆

- What kind of grain is grown in Arkansas?
- In which state is the space shuttle launch site found?
- Which river forms part of the border between the United States and Mexico?

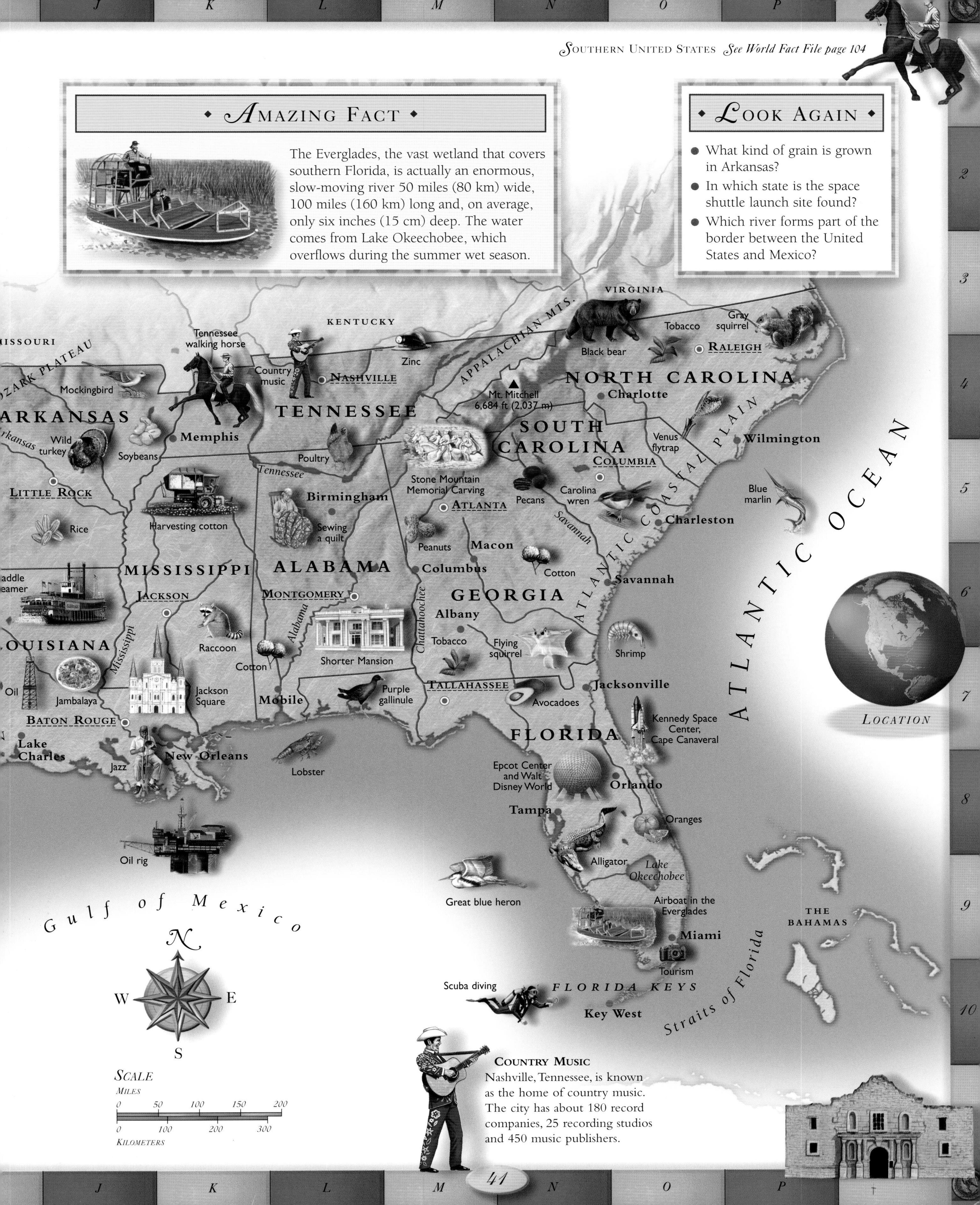
J
K
L
M
N
O
P
2
3
4
5
6
7
8
9
10
VIRGINIA
KENTUCKY
ISSOURI
OZARK PLATEAU
Tennessee walking horse
Country music
NASHVILLE
Zinc
APPALACHIAN MTS.
Black bear
Tobacco
Gray squirrel
RALEIGH
NORTH CAROLINA
Charlotte
Mt. Mitchell 6,684 ft (2,037 m)
Mockingbird
ARKANSAS
Arkansas
Wild turkey
Soybeans
Memphis
TENNESSEE
SOUTH CAROLINA
Venus flytrap
ATLANTIC COASTAL PLAIN
Wilmington
Poultry
Tennessee
Stone Mountain Memorial Carving
COLUMBIA
LITTLE ROCK
Harvesting cotton
Birmingham
ATLANTA
Pecans
Carolina wren
Blue marlin
Savannah
Charleston
Rice
Sewing a quilt
Peanuts
Macon
Cotton
ATLANTIC OCEAN
addle eamer
MISSISSIPPI
ALABAMA
Columbus
Savannah
JACKSON
MONTGOMERY
GEORGIA
Albany
Chattahoochee
Alabama
Mississippi
Raccoon
Shorter Mansion
Tobacco
Flying squirrel
Shrimp
OUISIANA
Cotton
Oil
Jambalaya
Jackson Square
Mobile
Purple gallinule
TALLAHASSEE
Avocadoes
Jacksonville
Kennedy Space Center, Cape Canaveral
LOCATION
BATON ROUGE
FLORIDA
Lake Charles
Jazz
New Orleans
Lobster
Epcot Center and Walt Disney World
Orlando
Tampa
Oranges
Oil rig
Alligator
Lake Okeechobee
Great blue heron
Airboat in the Everglades
THE BAHAMAS
Gulf of Mexico
Miami
Tourism
Straits of Florida
Scuba diving
FLORIDA KEYS
Key West
N
W
E
S
SCALE
MILES
0
50
100
150
200
0
100
200
300
KILOMETERS

Country Music
Nashville, Tennessee, is known as the home of country music. The city has about 180 record companies, 25 recording studios and 450 music publishers.

Central United States

THE CENTRAL UNITED STATES consists of a vast area of lowland known as the Midwest or prairies. In the northeastern part of this region lie the Great Lakes, the largest group of freshwater lakes in the world. Rivers and canals connect the lakes to the Atlantic Ocean and the Gulf of Mexico, forming a major transportation network. This network and the area's many natural resources (including coal and iron ore) have helped turn the Great Lakes region into the industrial heart of the United States. Factories now line the southern shores of Lake Michigan and Lake Erie, and supply most of the country's iron, steel and cars. Unfortunately, these industries create a great deal of waste, and the Great Lakes are now badly polluted. The area south and west of the lakes was once an enormous natural grassland, roamed by millions of bison and deer, and home to Native American tribes such as the Sioux and the Comanche. Now it is one of the world's most important farming regions. Iowa lies at the center of an area known as the Corn Belt because it produces half of the world's corn. Almost all of this corn is used to fatten the region's pigs and cattle, which provide most of the United States' meat. Farther west, on the Great Plains, is a "wheat belt." Here, immense fields of wheat stretch as far as the eye can see.

ILLINOIS
POPULATION: 11,830,000 * CAPITAL: SPRINGFIELD

INDIANA
POPULATION: 5,803,000 * CAPITAL: INDIANAPOLIS

IOWA
POPULATION: 2,842,000 * CAPITAL: DES MOINES

KANSAS
POPULATION: 2,565,000 * CAPITAL: TOPEKA

MICHIGAN
POPULATION: 9,549,000 * CAPITAL: LANSING

MINNESOTA
POPULATION: 4,610,000 * CAPITAL: ST. PAUL

MISSOURI
POPULATION: 5,324,000 * CAPITAL: JEFFERSON CITY

NEBRASKA
POPULATION: 1,637,000 * CAPITAL: LINCOLN

NORTH DAKOTA
POPULATION: 641,400 * CAPITAL: BISMARCK

OHIO
POPULATION: 11,150,000 * CAPITAL: COLUMBUS

SOUTH DAKOTA
POPULATION: 729,000 * CAPITAL: PIERRE

WISCONSIN
POPULATION: 5,123,000 * CAPITAL: MADISON

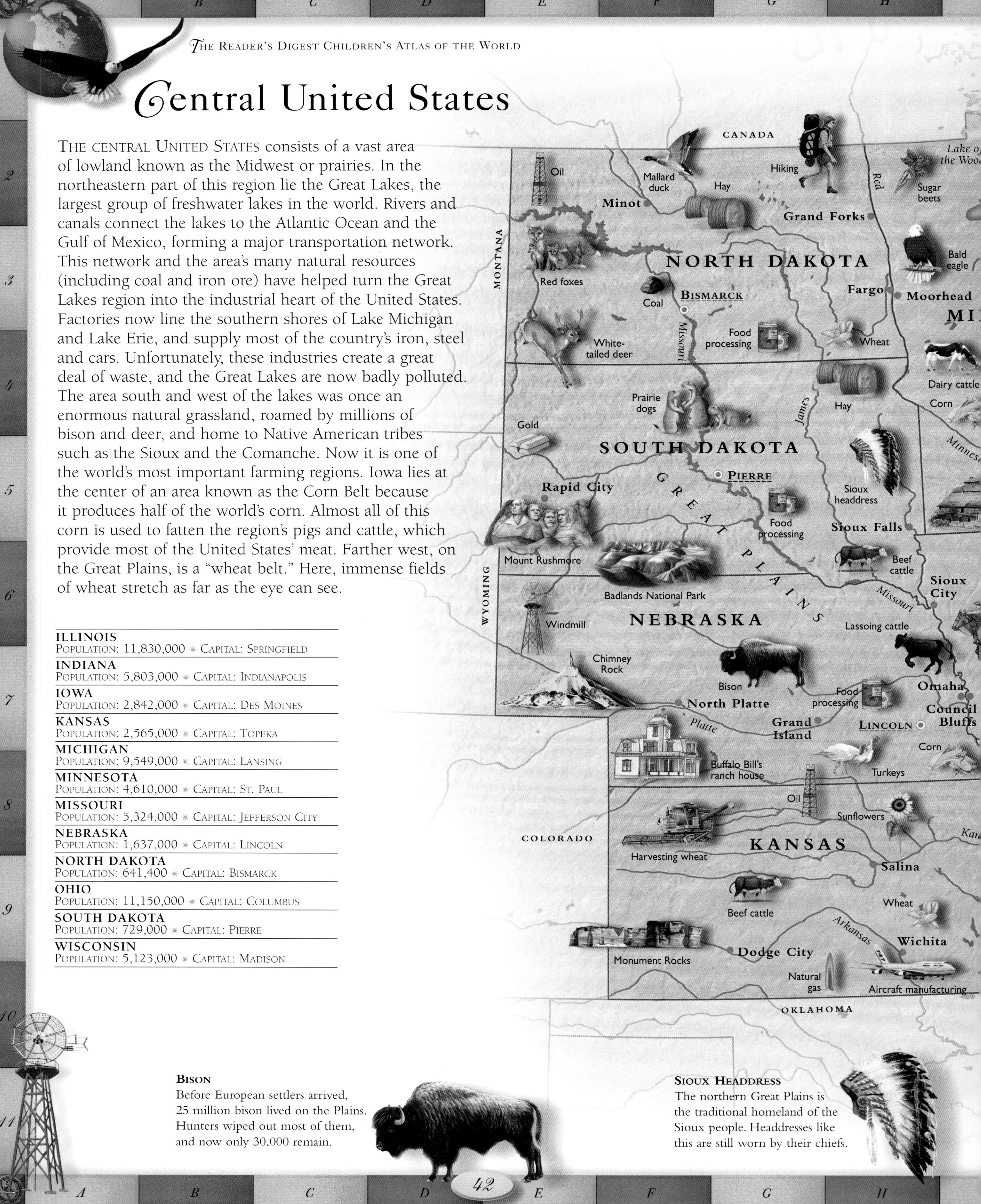
B
C
D
E
F
G
H
2
3
4
5
6
7
8
9
10
11
A
CANADA
MONTANA
WYOMING
COLORADO
OKLAHOMA
NORTH DAKOTA
SOUTH DAKOTA
NEBRASKA
KANSAS
GREAT PLAINS
Oil
Mallard duck
Hiking
Minot
Hay
Grand Forks
Red
Sugar beets
Lake of the Woo
Red foxes
Coal
BISMARCK
Missouri
Food processing
Fargo
Moorhead
Bald eagle
White-tailed deer
Wheat
Prairie dogs
James
Hay
Dairy cattle
Corn
Gold
PIERRE
Minnes
Rapid City
Food processing
Sioux headdress
Sioux Falls
Mount Rushmore
Beef cattle
Badlands National Park
Missouri
Sioux City
Windmill
Lassoing cattle
Chimney Rock
Bison
North Platte
Food processing
Omaha
Council Bluffs
Platte
Grand Island
LINCOLN
Buffalo Bill's ranch house
Corn
Turkeys
Oil
Sunflowers
Harvesting wheat
Salina
Kan
Beef cattle
Wheat
Arkansas
Wichita
Monument Rocks
Dodge City
Natural gas
Aircraft manufacturing

BISON
Before European settlers arrived, 25 million bison lived on the Plains. Hunters wiped out most of them, and now only 30,000 remain.

SIOUX HEADDRESS
The northern Great Plains is the traditional homeland of the Sioux people. Headdresses like this are still worn by their chiefs.

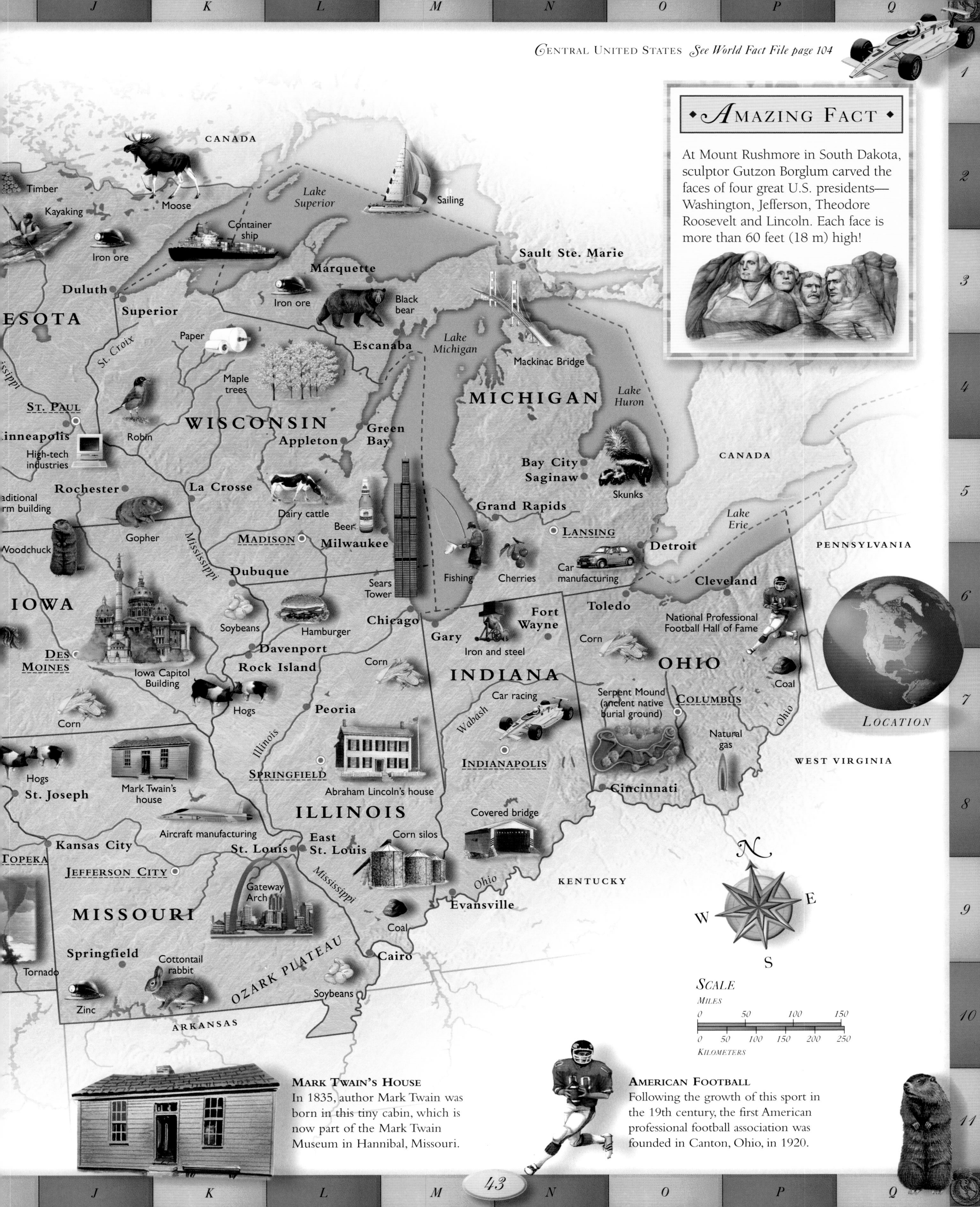
CANADA
Timber
Kayaking
Moose
Iron ore
Duluth
ESOTA
Superior
Container ship
Lake Superior
Sailing
Marquette
Iron ore
Black bear
Sault Ste. Marie
Mackinac Bridge
St. Croix
Paper
Escanaba
Lake Michigan
Maple trees
MICHIGAN
Lake Huron
St. Paul
Robin
WISCONSIN
Green Bay
Appleton
inneapolis
High-tech industries
Bay City
Saginaw
Skunks
CANADA
Rochester
La Crosse
Dairy cattle
Grand Rapids
aditional rm building
Gopher
Beer
Lansing
Lake Erie
Woodchuck
Mississippi
Madison
Milwaukee
Detroit
PENNSYLVANIA
Dubuque
Sears Tower
Fishing
Cherries
Car manufacturing
Cleveland
IOWA
Soybeans
Hamburger
Chicago
Gary
Fort Wayne
Toledo
National Professional Football Hall of Fame
Iron and steel
Corn
Des Moines
Davenport
Rock Island
Iowa Capitol Building
Corn
INDIANA
OHIO
Coal
Hogs
Peoria
Car racing
Serpent Mound (ancient native burial ground)
Columbus
Corn
Wabash
Illinois
Ohio
Location
Natural gas
Hogs
Springfield
Indianapolis
WEST VIRGINIA
St. Joseph
Mark Twain's house
Abraham Lincoln's house
Cincinnati
ILLINOIS
Covered bridge
Aircraft manufacturing
Corn silos
Kansas City
St. Louis
East St. Louis
Topeka
Jefferson City
Gateway Arch
Mississippi
Ohio
KENTUCKY
N
E
W
S
MISSOURI
Evansville
Coal
Springfield
Cottontail rabbit
Cairo
OZARK PLATEAU
Tornado
Zinc
Soybeans
ARKANSAS
SCALE
MILES
0 50 100 150
0 50 100 150 200 250
KILOMETERS

AMAZING FACT

At Mount Rushmore in South Dakota, sculptor Gutzon Borglum carved the faces of four great U.S. presidents—Washington, Jefferson, Theodore Roosevelt and Lincoln. Each face is more than 60 feet (18 m) high!

MARK TWAIN'S HOUSE
In 1835, author Mark Twain was born in this tiny cabin, which is now part of the Mark Twain Museum in Hannibal, Missouri.

AMERICAN FOOTBALL
Following the growth of this sport in the 19th century, the first American professional football association was founded in Canton, Ohio, in 1920.

Western United States

THE COLOSSAL ROCKY MOUNTAINS separate the western United States from the plains of the Midwest. Among the valleys and peaks of this spectacular range, mountain goats bound up steep rock faces and elk feed beside fast-flowing streams. There is little agriculture here, but herds of cattle graze the mountain meadows. West of the Rockies lies a series of dry plateaus, valleys and ranges. The Colorado Plateau has some of the continent's most spectacular scenery, including the world's largest gorge, the Grand Canyon. The states of Washington, Oregon and Idaho are known as the Pacific Northwest. The wet, densely forested western part of this area provides 40 percent of the United States' timber. The largest state in the region, California, is home to more people than any other American state. Most of the population lives in or near the coastal cities of Los Angeles and San Francisco. Inland, between the mountains of the Coast Ranges and the Sierra Nevada, farms form a patchwork of fields across the fertile, irrigated Central Valley. The most westerly state, Hawaii, lies 2,500 miles (4,000 km) off the coast, in the middle of the Pacific Ocean. Hawaii consists of 132 islands, which were formed by undersea volcanoes. Several Hawaiian volcanoes still erupt, including Mauna Loa, the largest active volcano in the world.

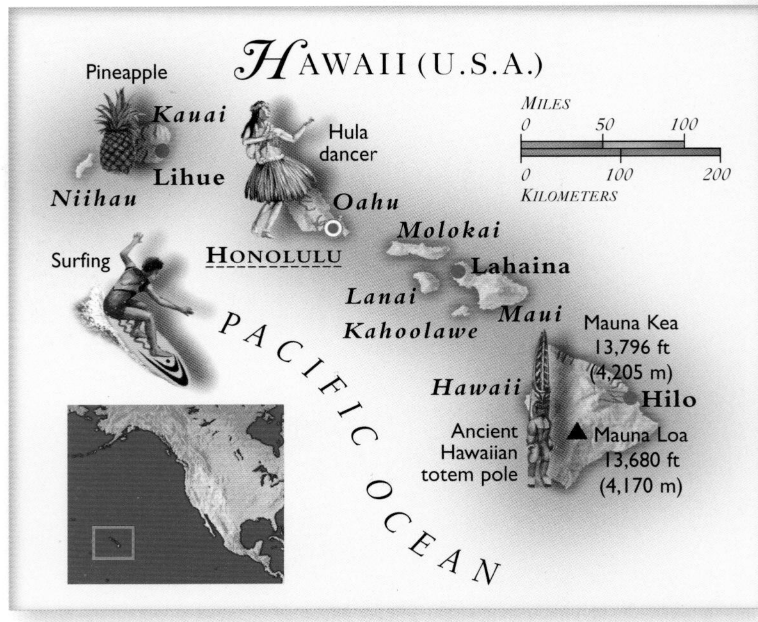
HAWAII (U.S.A.)
MILES
0 50 100
0 100 200
KILOMETERS
Pineapple
Kauai
Lihue
Niihau
Hula dancer
Oahu
HONOLULU
Molokai
Surfing
Lahaina
Lanai
Kahoolawe
Maui
Mauna Kea 13,796 ft (4,205 m)
Hawaii
Hilo
Ancient Hawaiian totem pole
Mauna Loa 13,680 ft (4,170 m)
PACIFIC OCEAN

ARIZONA
POPULATION: 4,218,000 * CAPITAL: PHOENIX

CALIFORNIA
POPULATION: 31,589,000 * CAPITAL: SACRAMENTO

COLORADO
POPULATION: 3,747,000 * CAPITAL: DENVER

HAWAII
POPULATION: 1,187,000 * CAPITAL: HONOLULU

IDAHO
POPULATION: 1,163,000 * CAPITAL: BOISE

MONTANA
POPULATION: 870,300 * CAPITAL: HELENA

NEVADA
POPULATION: 1,530,000 * CAPITAL: CARSON CITY

NEW MEXICO
POPULATION: 1,685,000 * CAPITAL: SANTA FE

OREGON
POPULATION: 3,141,000 * CAPITAL: SALEM

UTAH
POPULATION: 1,951,000 * CAPITAL: SALT LAKE CITY

WASHINGTON
POPULATION: 5,431,000 * CAPITAL: OLYMPIA

WYOMING
POPULATION: 480,200 * CAPITAL: CHEYENNE

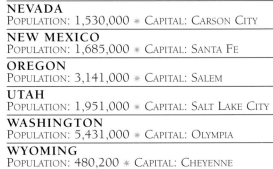

GENERAL SHERMAN TREE
This giant sequoia is the world's largest living thing. It is as tall as a 23-story building and is at least 2,300 years old.

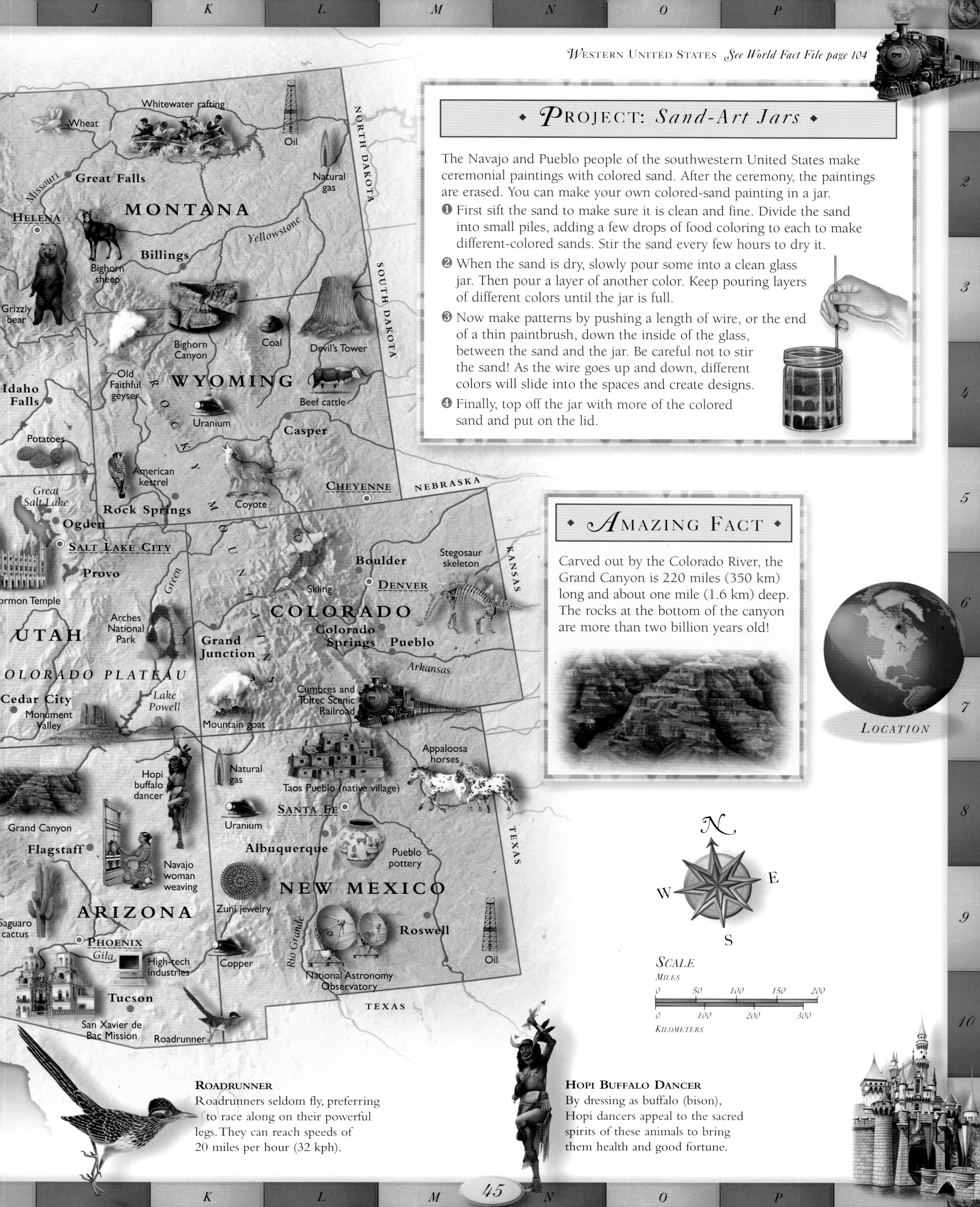

J
K
L
M
N
O
P
Whitewater rafting
Wheat
Oil
Natural gas
Great Falls
Missouri
MONTANA
HELENA
Yellowstone
Billings
Bighorn sheep
Grizzly bear
NORTH DAKOTA
SOUTH DAKOTA
Bighorn Canyon
Coal
Devil's Tower
Old Faithful geyser
WYOMING
ROCKY MOUNTAINS
Idaho Falls
Uranium
Beef cattle
Casper
Potatoes
American kestrel
Coyote
CHEYENNE
NEBRASKA
Great Salt Lake
Rock Springs
Ogden
SALT LAKE CITY
Provo
Green
Boulder
Stegosaur skeleton
KANSAS
Skiing
DENVER
Arches National Park
UTAH
COLORADO
Colorado Springs
Pueblo
Grand Junction
Arkansas
COLORADO PLATEAU
Cedar City
Lake Powell
Monument Valley
Mountain goat
Cumbres and Toltec Scenic Railroad
Hopi buffalo dancer
Natural gas
Taos Pueblo (native village)
Appaloosa horses
SANTA FE
Uranium
Grand Canyon
Flagstaff
Albuquerque
Pueblo pottery
Navajo woman weaving
TEXAS
NEW MEXICO
ARIZONA
Zuni jewelry
Saguaro cactus
Rio Grande
Roswell
PHOENIX
Gila
High-tech industries
Copper
Oil
National Astronomy Observatory
Tucson
TEXAS
San Xavier de Bac Mission
Roadrunner
N
E
W
S
SCALE
MILES
0
50
100
150
200
0
100
200
300
KILOMETERS
LOCATION
2
3
4
5
6
7
8
9
10

◆ Project: *Sand-Art Jars* ◆

The Navajo and Pueblo people of the southwestern United States make ceremonial paintings with colored sand. After the ceremony, the paintings are erased. You can make your own colored-sand painting in a jar.

1. First sift the sand to make sure it is clean and fine. Divide the sand into small piles, adding a few drops of food coloring to each to make different-colored sands. Stir the sand every few hours to dry it.
2. When the sand is dry, slowly pour some into a clean glass jar. Then pour a layer of another color. Keep pouring layers of different colors until the jar is full.
3. Now make patterns by pushing a length of wire, or the end of a thin paintbrush, down the inside of the glass, between the sand and the jar. Be careful not to stir the sand! As the wire goes up and down, different colors will slide into the spaces and create designs.
4. Finally, top off the jar with more of the colored sand and put on the lid.

◆ Amazing Fact ◆

Carved out by the Colorado River, the Grand Canyon is 220 miles (350 km) long and about one mile (1.6 km) deep. The rocks at the bottom of the canyon are more than two billion years old!

Roadrunner
Roadrunners seldom fly, preferring to race along on their powerful legs. They can reach speeds of 20 miles per hour (32 kph).

Hopi Buffalo Dancer
By dressing as buffalo (bison), Hopi dancers appeal to the sacred spirits of these animals to bring them health and good fortune.

Mexico, Central America and the Caribbean

MEXICO AND CENTRAL AMERICA form a land bridge between the United States and South America. At its narrowest point, this strip of land is only 50 miles (80 km) wide and is split by the Panama Canal, an artificial waterway that links the Atlantic and Pacific oceans. Mexico is more than twice the size of the seven Central American countries combined. It is dominated by a large dry plateau, and only 18 percent of the land can be farmed. The narrow plains on the east coast are warm and humid, and contain large oil reserves. Three-quarters of Mexicans live in cities and towns, and Mexico City is one of the largest and fastest-growing cities in the world. Most of Central America is mountainous, and much of the land is covered in rain forests where colorful parrots shriek from the treetops and chattering monkeys swing among branches. Although only a small proportion of Central America can be farmed, about half of the people live in rural areas and many grow their own food on small plots of land. To the east lie the Caribbean Islands, most of which are covered by tropical forests and surrounded by sandy beaches. Spain ruled much of Mexico, Central America and the Caribbean for centuries, and today most of the people speak Spanish. Their ancestors may be settlers from Europe, Native American peoples or Africans who were first brought to the region as slaves.

Tijuana
Mexicali
Tourism
Gila monster
Ciudad Juárez
BAJA CALIFORNIA
Saguaro cactus
Beef cattle
Mexican cowboy
UNITED STATES OF AMERICA
Great white shark
Hermosillo
SIERRA MADRE OCCIDENTAL
Chihuahua
Singing grasshopper mouse
Rio Grande
Gulf of California
Vampire bat
Silver
Natural gas
Leatherback turtle
Elephant seals
Monterrey
Gulf of Mexico
Culiacán
Monarch butterfly
Cotton
Matamoros
La Paz
Torreón
Lobster
Gold
Iron ore
Ancient Toltec stone statue
Mariachi musicians
Snapper
El Castillo, Chichen Itza, Maya city ruins
MEXICO
Tampico
YUCATÁN PENINSULA
Folk dancer
Corn
Metropolitan Cathedral
Oil
Bay of Campeche
Oil
Guadalajara
MEXICO CITY
Jaguar
Common dolphins
Aztec snake carving
Soccer
Orizaba 18,700 ft (5,700 m)
Veracruz
Great Plaza, Tikal
PACIFIC OCEAN
Tourism
Olmec stone carving
Scarlet macaw
BELMOPAN
Acapulco
Thatched corncrib
Folk costume
GUATEMALA
GUATEMALA
SAN SALVADOR
Eagle ray

ANTIGUA AND BARBUDA
POPULATION: 65,200 * CAPITAL: ST. JOHN'S

THE BAHAMAS
POPULATION: 256,600 * CAPITAL: NASSAU

BARBADOS
POPULATION: 256,400 * CAPITAL: BRIDGETOWN

BELIZE
POPULATION: 214,100 * CAPITAL: BELMOPAN

COSTA RICA
POPULATION: 3,419,000 * CAPITAL: SAN JOSÉ

CUBA
POPULATION: 10,938,000 * CAPITAL: HAVANA

DOMINICA
POPULATION: 82,600 * CAPITAL: ROSEAU

DOMINICAN REPUBLIC
POPULATION: 7,511,000 * CAPITAL: SANTO DOMINGO

EL SALVADOR
POPULATION: 5,870,000 * CAPITAL: SAN SALVADOR

GRENADA
POPULATION: 94,500 * CAPITAL: ST. GEORGE'S

GUATEMALA
POPULATION: 10,999,000 * CAPITAL: GUATEMALA

HAITI
POPULATION: 6,540,000 * CAPITAL: PORT-AU-PRINCE

HONDURAS
POPULATION: 5,460,000 * CAPITAL: TEGUCIGALPA

JAMAICA
POPULATION: 2,574,000 * CAPITAL: KINGSTON

MEXICO
POPULATION: 93,986,000 * CAPITAL: MEXICO CITY

NICARAGUA
POPULATION: 4,206,000 * CAPITAL: MANAGUA

PANAMA
POPULATION: 2,681,000 * CAPITAL: PANAMA

ST. KITTS–NEVIS
POPULATION: 41,000 * CAPITAL: BASSETERRE

ST. LUCIA
POPULATION: 156,100 * CAPITAL: CASTRIES

ST. VINCENT AND THE GRENADINES
POPULATION: 117,300 * CAPITAL: KINGSTOWN

TRINIDAD AND TOBAGO
POPULATION: 1,271,000 * CAPITAL: PORT-OF-SPAIN

SINGING GRASSHOPPER MOUSE
This mouse is named for its habit of squeaking or "singing" to warn off rivals. Grasshoppers are its favorite food.

◆ PROJECT: *Make a Mexican Piñata* ◆

A piñata is a pot made from papier-mâché and filled with toys and candy, often shaped like a star or animal. It is a popular part of many celebrations and festivals in Mexico and Central America. Children hang the piñata from the ceiling or a tree branch and take turns trying to break it open. You can make a Mexican piñata for your next party.

❶ Cover a large balloon with strips of newspaper dipped in flour-and-water paste or white glue. Wait for this papier-mâché to dry and then repeat with at least two more layers of newspaper.

❷ When the papier-mâché is completely dry, cut a small hole in the top and fill the piñata with all sorts of goodies. Re-cover the hole with more papier-mâché.

❸ Make star points out of cardboard as shown. Tape them onto the ball using the tabs. Decorate the star with paint and colored tissue paper.

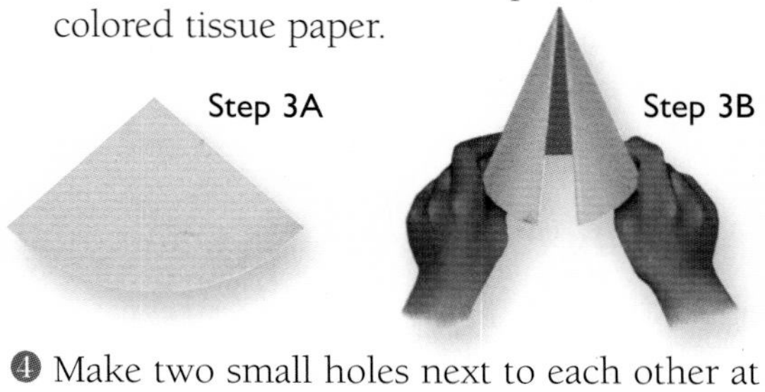

Step 3A

Step 3B

❹ Make two small holes next to each other at the top of the piñata. Thread curved wire through one hole and out the other. Hang up the piñata and have guests take turns hitting it with a stick to open it.

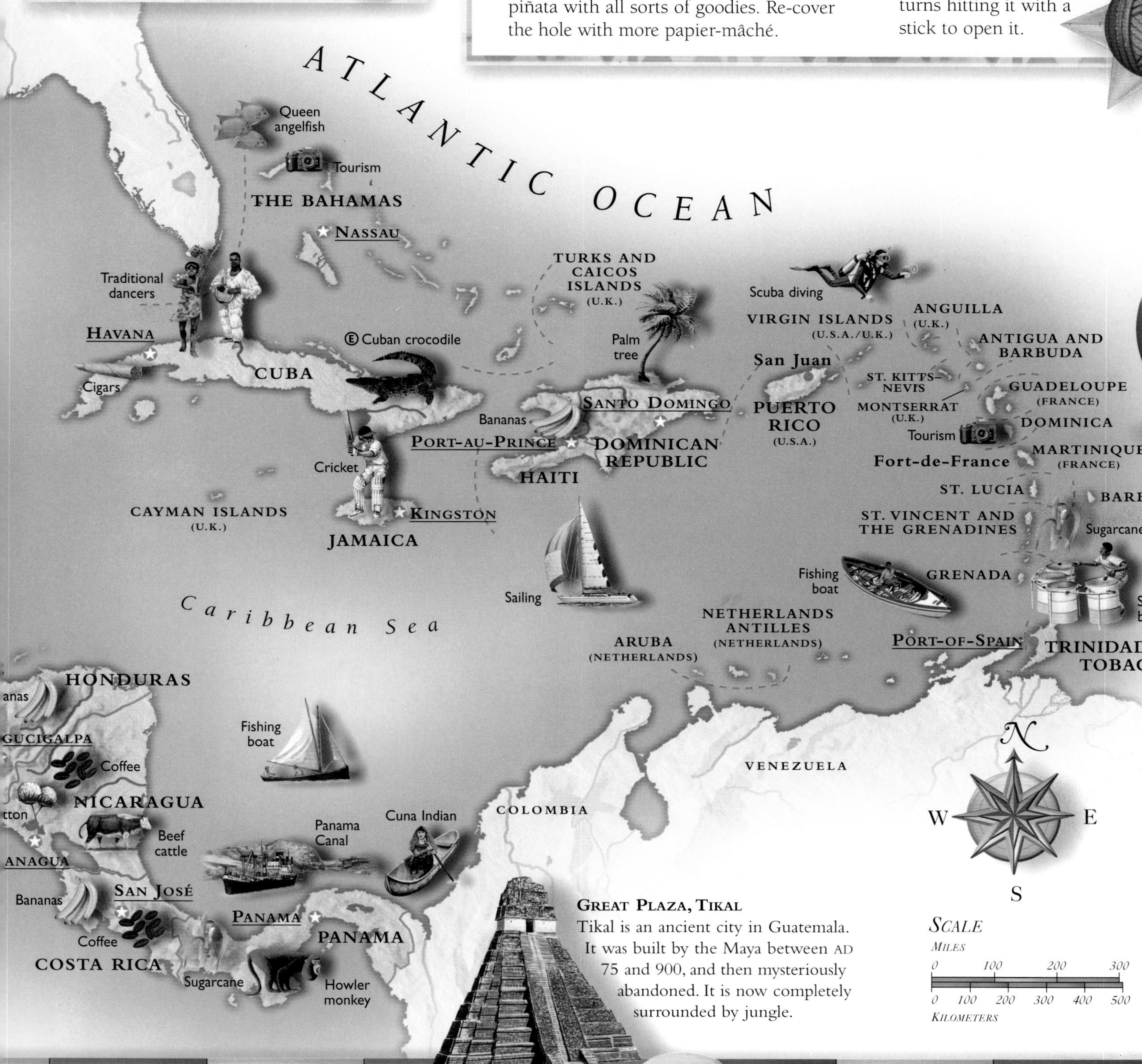

◆ AMAZING FACT ◆

The saguaro cactus is found only in the deserts of northwestern Mexico and the southwestern United States. It grows incredibly slowly, taking 25 years to reach a height of one foot (30 cm). But it can live for 200 years and grow as high as a four-story house. Like other cacti, the saguaro survives on water stored in its stem. A fully grown saguaro may contain enough water to fill 100 bathtubs!

GREAT PLAZA, TIKAL
Tikal is an ancient city in Guatemala. It was built by the Maya between AD 75 and 900, and then mysteriously abandoned. It is now completely surrounded by jungle.

South America

FROM ITS TROPICAL NORTHERN SHORE, South America stretches 4,500 miles (7,240 km) southward to the chilly, storm-battered peninsula of Cape Horn, just 600 miles (1,000 km) from Antarctica. The Andes run the entire length of the continent's west coast, forming the longest mountain chain in the world. In the north, the Amazon River (the world's second-longest river) snakes eastward from the Andes to the Atlantic Ocean, through vast rain forests that once covered more than one-third of the continent. To the south, the forests give way to the grasslands of the Gran Chaco and the Pampas. The southern tip of South America is a dry, windswept plateau known as Patagonia. South America's inhabitants include people of European, native Indian and African origin. Most people speak Spanish, but Portuguese is the official language in Brazil.

MAJOR MOUNTAINS AND RIVERS

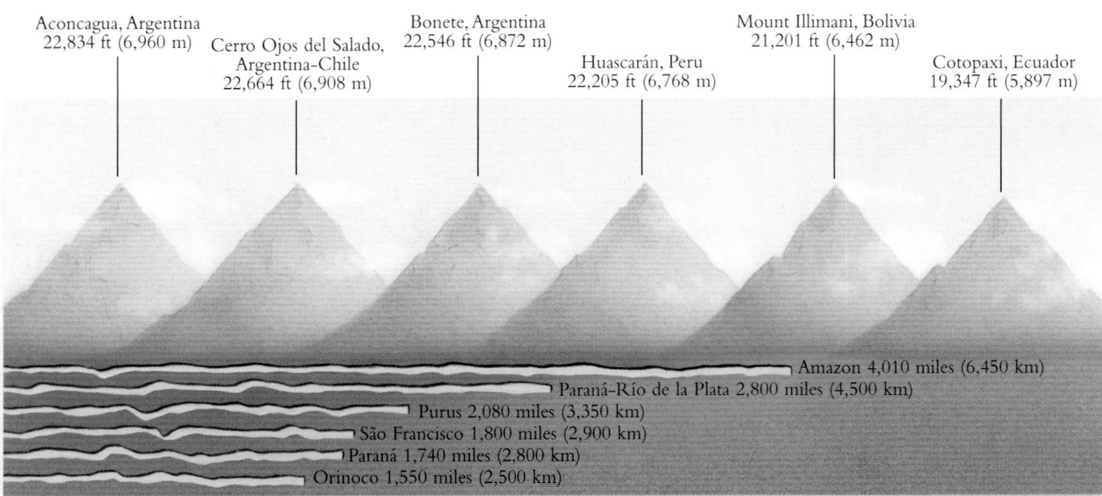
Aconcagua, Argentina 22,834 ft (6,960 m)
Cerro Ojos del Salado, Argentina-Chile 22,664 ft (6,908 m)
Bonete, Argentina 22,546 ft (6,872 m)
Huascarán, Peru 22,205 ft (6,768 m)
Mount Illimani, Bolivia 21,201 ft (6,462 m)
Cotopaxi, Ecuador 19,347 ft (5,897 m)
Amazon 4,010 miles (6,450 km)
Paraná-Río de la Plata 2,800 miles (4,500 km)
Purus 2,080 miles (3,350 km)
São Francisco 1,800 miles (2,900 km)
Paraná 1,740 miles (2,800 km)
Orinoco 1,550 miles (2,500 km)

POLITICAL MAP

VENEZUELA
GUYANA
SURINAME
FRENCH GUIANA (FRANCE)
COLOMBIA
GALÁPAGOS ISLANDS (ECUADOR)
ECUADOR
BRAZIL
PERU
BOLIVIA
MARTIN VAZ ISLANDS (BRAZIL)
PARAGUAY
EASTER ISLAND (CHILE)
CHILE
JUAN FERNANDEZ ISLANDS (CHILE)
URUGUAY
ARGENTINA
FALKLAND ISLANDS (U.K.)
SOUTH GEORGIA (U.K.)

CONTINENT FACTS

Regional land area: 6,877,943 sq. miles (17,818,505 sq. km)
Regional population: 319,153,000
Independent countries: Argentina, Bolivia, Brazil, Chile, Colombia, Ecuador, Guyana, Paraguay, Peru, Suriname, Uruguay, Venezuela

WORLD RECORDS

WORLD'S LONGEST MOUNTAIN CHAIN
ANDES, WESTERN SOUTH AMERICA 4,700 MILES (7,600 KM)

WORLD'S DRIEST PLACE
ATACAMA DESERT, CHILE, AVERAGE ANNUAL RAINFALL LESS THAN 1/250 IN (0.1 MM)

WORLD'S HIGHEST WATERFALL
ANGEL FALLS, VENEZUELA, 3,212 FT (979 M)

WORLD'S HIGHEST CAPITAL CITY
LA PAZ, BOLIVIA, 11,913 FT (3,631 M)

WORLD'S HIGHEST NAVIGABLE LAKE
LAKE TITICACA, PERU-BOLIVIA, 12,500 FT (3,810 M)

WORLD'S LARGEST RIVER BY VOLUME
AMAZON, PERU-BRAZIL, DISCHARGES 7,100,000 CUBIC FEET (200,000 CUBIC M) PER SECOND INTO ATLANTIC OCEAN

WORLD'S LARGEST RIVER BASIN
AMAZON BASIN, NORTHERN SOUTH AMERICA, 2,720,000 SQ. MILES (7,045,000 SQ. KM)

WORLD'S LARGEST LAGOON
LAGOA DOS PATOS, BRAZIL, 3,803 SQ. MILES (9,850 SQ. KM)

CONTINENT RECORDS

HIGHEST MOUNTAIN
ACONCAGUA, ARGENTINA, 22,834 FT (6,960 M)

LOWEST POINT
VALDÉS PENINSULA, ARGENTINA, 131 FT (40 M) BELOW SEA LEVEL

LARGEST LAKE
LAKE TITICACA, PERU-BOLIVIA, 3,200 SQ. MILES (8,288 SQ. KM)

LONGEST RIVER
AMAZON RIVER, PERU-BRAZIL, 4,010 MILES (6,450 KM)

LARGEST COUNTRY BY AREA
BRAZIL, 3,284,426 SQ. MILES (8,506,663 SQ. KM)

LARGEST COUNTRY BY POPULATION
BRAZIL, POPULATION 160,737,000

LARGEST CITY BY POPULATION
SÃO PAULO, BRAZIL, POPULATION 16,400,000

◆ AMAZING FACT ◆

The Atacama Desert in northern Chile is the driest place in the world. Rain showers occur only once or twice a century, and in some parts of the desert rain has never been recorded!

Physical Map

NORTH AMERICA
Tropic of Cancer
Caribbean Sea
Lake Maracaibo
Orinoco
GUIANA HIGHLANDS
Gulf of Panama
LLANOS
Rio Negro
Rio Branco
Amazon Delta
AFRICA
GALÁPAGOS ISLANDS
Cotopaxi
Amazon
Marañon
AMAZON BASIN
Tapajós
Xingu
Gulf of Guayaquil
Equator
ANDES
SELVAS
Purus
Madeira
Tocantins
Huascarán
São Francisco
PACIFIC OCEAN
ATLANTIC OCEAN
MATO GROSSO PLATEAU
BRAZILIAN HIGHLANDS
Lake Titicaca
Mt. Illimani
Lake Poopo
GRAN CHACO
Paraná
ATACAMA DESERT
Paraguay
SERRA DO MAR
Tropic of Capricorn
Cerro Ojos del Salado
Bonete
Uruguay
Lagoa dos Patos
Aconcagua
Easter Island
PAMPAS
Colorado
Rio de la Plata
Blanca Bay
San Matias Gulf
VALDÉS PENINSULA
PATAGONIA
San Jorge Gulf
FALKLAND ISLANDS
Tierra del Fuego
South Georgia
CAPE HORN
Drake Passage
Antarctic Circle
ANTARCTICA

Northern South America

MOST OF NORTHERN SOUTH AMERICA is drained by the world's second-longest river, the Amazon, and its more than 200 tributaries. These waterways flow through lush tropical rain forests that are home to a tenth of all the plants and animals on Earth. Sadly, the rain forests are rapidly disappearing as a growing population clears the land for farming. Every minute, an area of forest the size of five football fields is cut down. More than a quarter of the world's rain forests lie within Brazil, the largest country in South America. Brazil has many resources, including iron ore, oil and gold. It is the continent's most industrialized country and the world's leading producer of coffee, bananas and sugarcane. Northwest of Brazil lies Venezuela, a sparsely populated country that is South America's top oil producer. From Venezuela, the Andes curve southward through Colombia, Ecuador and Peru. At the northern end of this mountain range, the climate is wet, and large coffee and banana plantations cover the hillsides. Farther south, little rain falls and crops can only be grown by using water from mountain streams. On the upper slopes of the Peruvian Andes, farmers grow potatoes and wheat and raise animals, including llamas and alpacas. Six hundred miles (1,000 km) off the coast of Ecuador lie the Galápagos Islands. These volcanic islands are famous for their unusual wildlife, which includes marine iguanas and giant tortoises.

BRAZIL
POPULATION: 160,737,000 * CAPITAL: BRASÍLIA

COLOMBIA
POPULATION: 36,200,000 * CAPITAL: BOGOTÁ

ECUADOR
POPULATION: 10,891,000 * CAPITAL: QUITO

GUYANA
POPULATION: 723,800 * CAPITAL: GEORGETOWN

PERU
POPULATION: 24,087,000 * CAPITAL: LIMA

SURINAME
POPULATION: 429,500 * CAPITAL: PARAMARIBO

VENEZUELA
POPULATION: 21,005,000 * CAPITAL: CARACAS

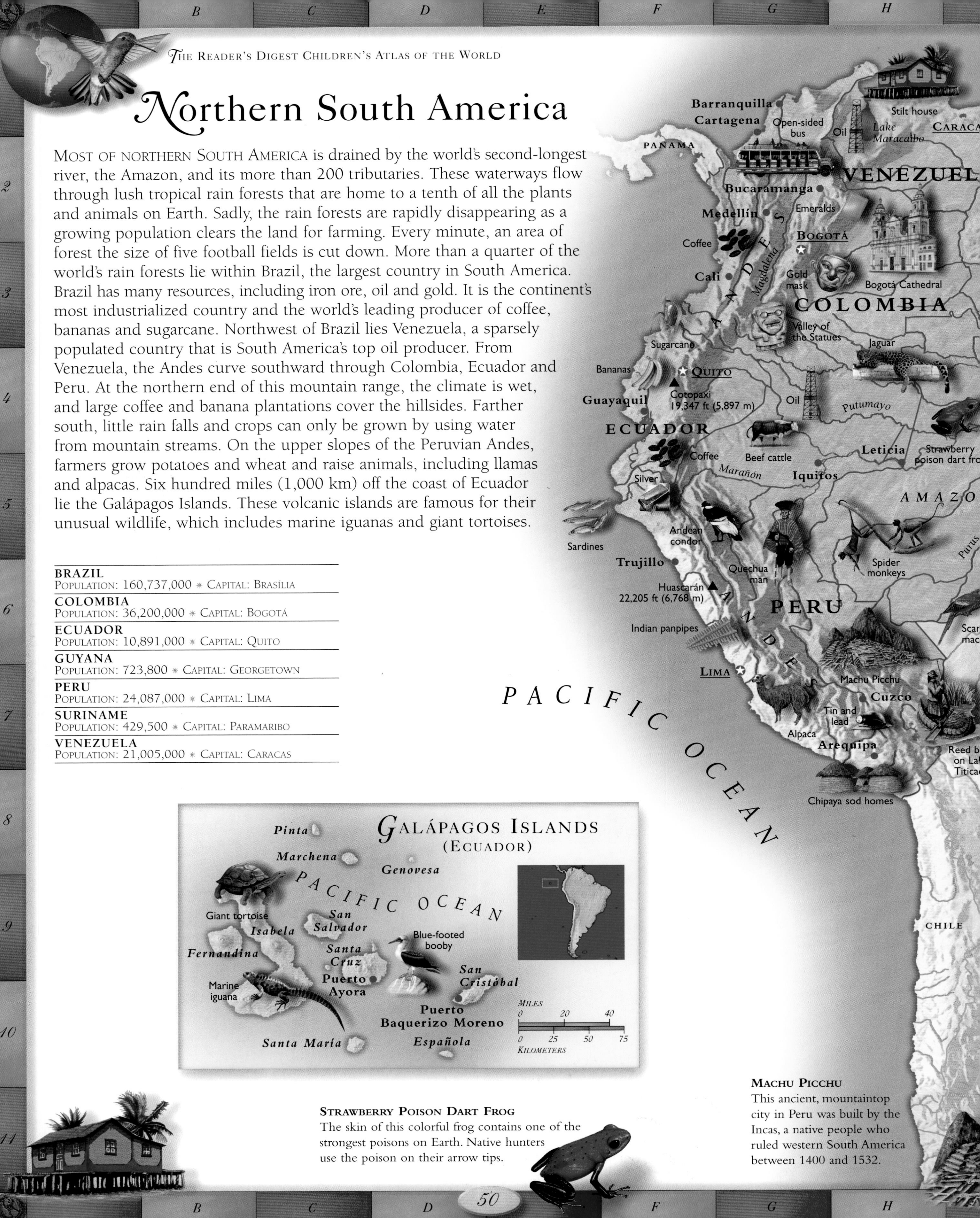
PANAMA
Barranquilla
Cartagena
Open-sided bus
Oil
Stilt house
Lake Maracaibo
CARACA
VENEZUEL
Bucaramanga
Medellín
Emeralds
BOGOTÁ
Coffee
Magdalena
Cali
Gold mask
Bogotá Cathedral
COLOMBIA
ANDES
Valley of the Statues
Sugarcane
Jaguar
Bananas
QUITO
Cotopaxi 19,347 ft (5,897 m)
Guayaquil
Oil
Putumayo
ECUADOR
Coffee
Beef cattle
Leticia
Strawberry poison dart fro
Marañón
Iquitos
Silver
AMAZO
Purus
Sardines
Andean condor
Spider monkeys
Trujillo
Quechua man
Huascarán 22,205 ft (6,768 m)
PERU
Indian panpipes
Scar mac
LIMA
Machu Picchu
Cuzco
PACIFIC OCEAN
Tin and lead
Alpaca
Arequipa
Reed b on La Titica
Chipaya sod homes
CHILE
GALÁPAGOS ISLANDS (ECUADOR)
Pinta
Marchena
Genovesa
PACIFIC OCEAN
Giant tortoise
Isabela
San Salvador
Fernandina
Santa Cruz
Blue-footed booby
Puerto Ayora
San Cristóbal
Marine iguana
Puerto Baquerizo Moreno
Santa María
Española
MILES 0 20 40
0 25 50 75 KILOMETERS

STRAWBERRY POISON DART FROG
The skin of this colorful frog contains one of the strongest poisons on Earth. Native hunters use the poison on their arrow tips.

MACHU PICCHU
This ancient, mountaintop city in Peru was built by the Incas, a native people who ruled western South America between 1400 and 1532.

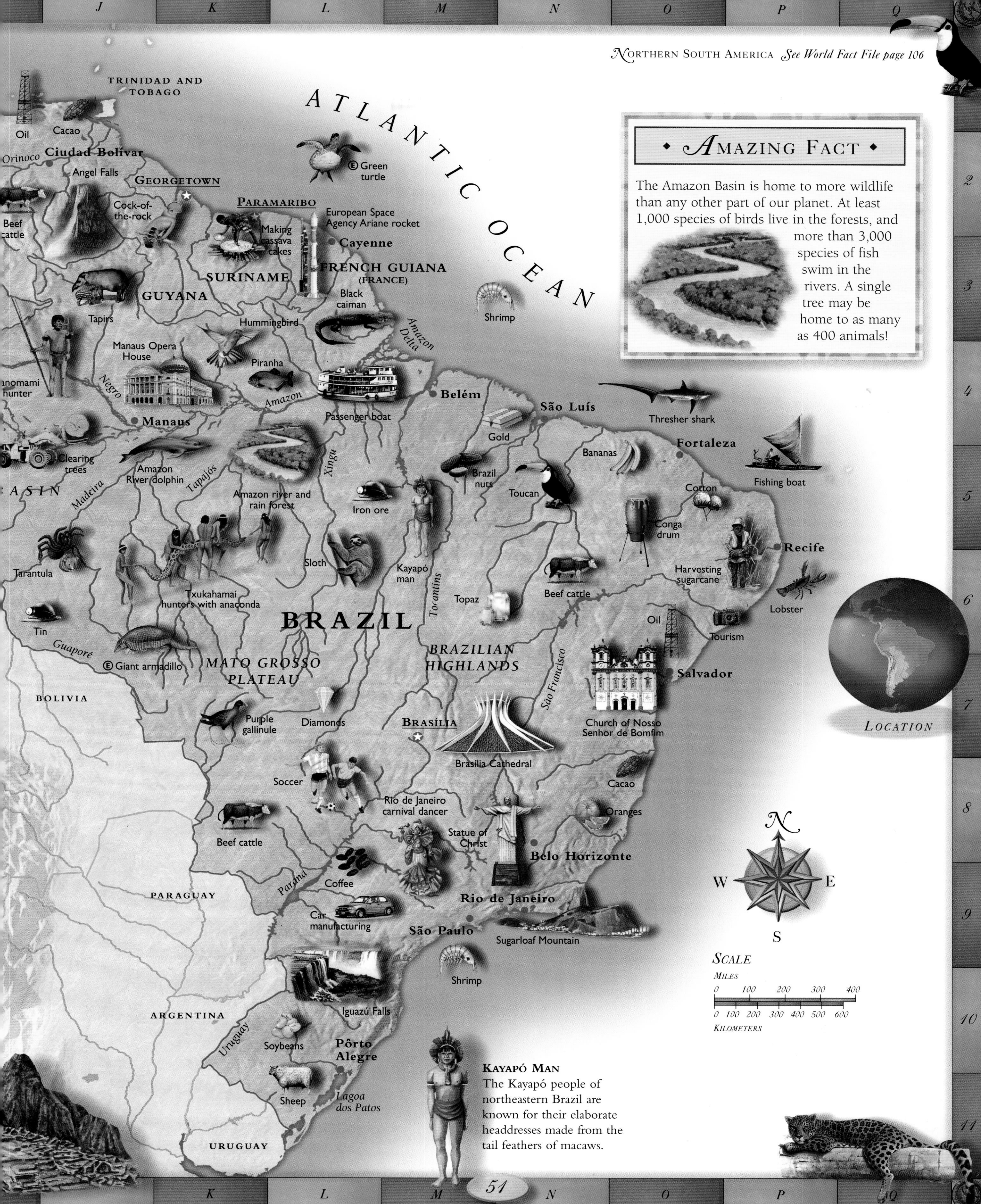
J
K
L
M
N
O
P
Q
TRINIDAD AND TOBAGO
ATLANTIC OCEAN
Oil
Cacao
Orinoco
Ciudad Bolívar
Angel Falls
GEORGETOWN
Green turtle
PARAMARIBO
European Space Agency Ariane rocket
Cock-of-the-rock
Beef cattle
Making cassava cakes
Cayenne
SURINAME
FRENCH GUIANA (FRANCE)
GUYANA
Tapirs
Black caiman
Shrimp
Hummingbird
Amazon Delta
Manaus Opera House
Piranha
anomami hunter
Negro
Amazon
Passenger boat
Belém
São Luís
Thresher shark
Manaus
Gold
Clearing trees
Amazon River dolphin
Tapajós
Xingu
Brazil nuts
Bananas
Fortaleza
Fishing boat
ASIN
Madeira
Amazon river and rain forest
Iron ore
Toucan
Cotton
Conga drum
Recife
Tarantula
Sloth
Kayapó man
Harvesting sugarcane
Tocantins
Topaz
Beef cattle
Lobster
Txukahamai hunters with anaconda
BRAZIL
Oil
Tin
Tourism
Guaporé
Giant armadillo
MATO GROSSO PLATEAU
BRAZILIAN HIGHLANDS
São Francisco
Salvador
BOLIVIA
Purple gallinule
Diamonds
BRASÍLIA
Church of Nosso Senhor de Bomfim
LOCATION
Brasília Cathedral
Cacao
Soccer
Rio de Janeiro carnival dancer
Oranges
Beef cattle
Statue of Christ
Belo Horizonte
N
W
E
S
Paraná
Coffee
PARAGUAY
Rio de Janeiro
Car manufacturing
São Paulo
Sugarloaf Mountain
Shrimp
SCALE
MILES
0 100 200 300 400
0 100 200 300 400 500 600
KILOMETERS
ARGENTINA
Iguazú Falls
Uruguay
Soybeans
Pôrto Alegre
Sheep
Lagoa dos Patos
URUGUAY
2
3
4
5
6
7
8
9
10
11

◆ AMAZING FACT ◆

The Amazon Basin is home to more wildlife than any other part of our planet. At least 1,000 species of birds live in the forests, and more than 3,000 species of fish swim in the rivers. A single tree may be home to as many as 400 animals!

KAYAPÓ MAN

The Kayapó people of northeastern Brazil are known for their elaborate headdresses made from the tail feathers of macaws.

Southern South America

SOUTHERN SOUTH AMERICA IS SHAPED like a long, narrow triangle that tapers to a point on the southern island of Tierra del Fuego. The Andes run down the western side of the region, separating the country of Chile from its neighbors. Twenty times as long as it is wide, Chile has a variety of climates and landscapes. In the cold, wet, sparsely populated south, mountains rise steeply from the ocean, and glaciers snake through valleys. Central Chile has milder weather and many farms, vineyards and orchards. The north is very arid and includes the driest place in the world, the Atacama Desert. East of the Atacama, the Andes spread into Bolivia, one of the poorest countries in South America. From eastern Bolivia, wide plains stretch southward through Paraguay, Uruguay and northern Argentina. Enormous herds of cattle and sheep roam the eastern and southern parts of these plains, tended by ranch hands called gauchos. Argentina has more than 50 million cattle, and beef production is one of its most important industries. The country's most fertile grasslands, the Pampas, surround the capital, Buenos Aires. This city is home to one-third of the Argentinian population. Few people live in southern Argentina, a cold, barren plateau known as Patagonia, but the area is rich in minerals. The seas around Tierra del Fuego in the far south are often stormy. Hundreds of ships have been wrecked attempting to round Cape Horn or navigate the Strait of Magellan.

ARGENTINA
POPULATION: 34,293,000 * CAPITAL: BUENOS AIRES

BOLIVIA
POPULATION: 7,896,000 * CAPITALS: LA PAZ, SUCRE

CHILE
POPULATION: 14,161,000 * CAPITAL: SANTIAGO

PARAGUAY
POPULATION: 5,358,000 * CAPITAL: ASUNCIÓN

URUGUAY
POPULATION: 3,223,000 * CAPITAL: MONTEVIDEO

PROJECT: *Easter Island Moai*

Easter Island is covered with huge statues called "moai." Some are more than 30 ft (9 m) high! The early inhabitants of Easter Island may have built the statues to honor their ancestors. You can make an Easter Island statue, too.

1. Mix equal parts of plaster and vermiculite (both available at hardware stores). Stir as you add enough water to make a thick plaster. Pour the mixture into an old shoe box.
2. When the mixture hardens, tear away the cardboard. Carve the stone using tools such as a plastic knife or an ice pop stick.
3. Alternatively, make your carving out of a block of modeling clay, plaster of Paris or any other modeling material.

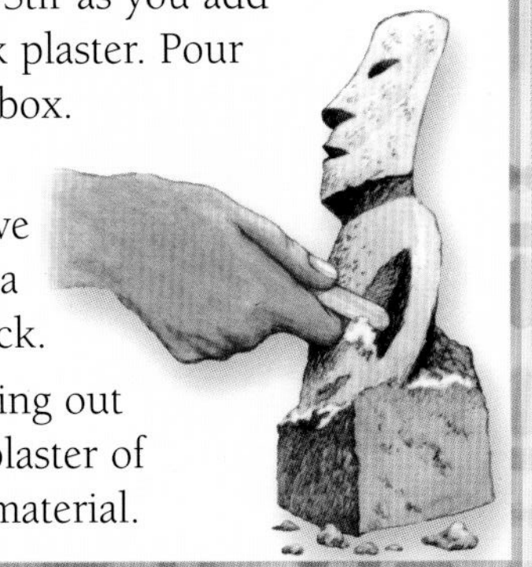

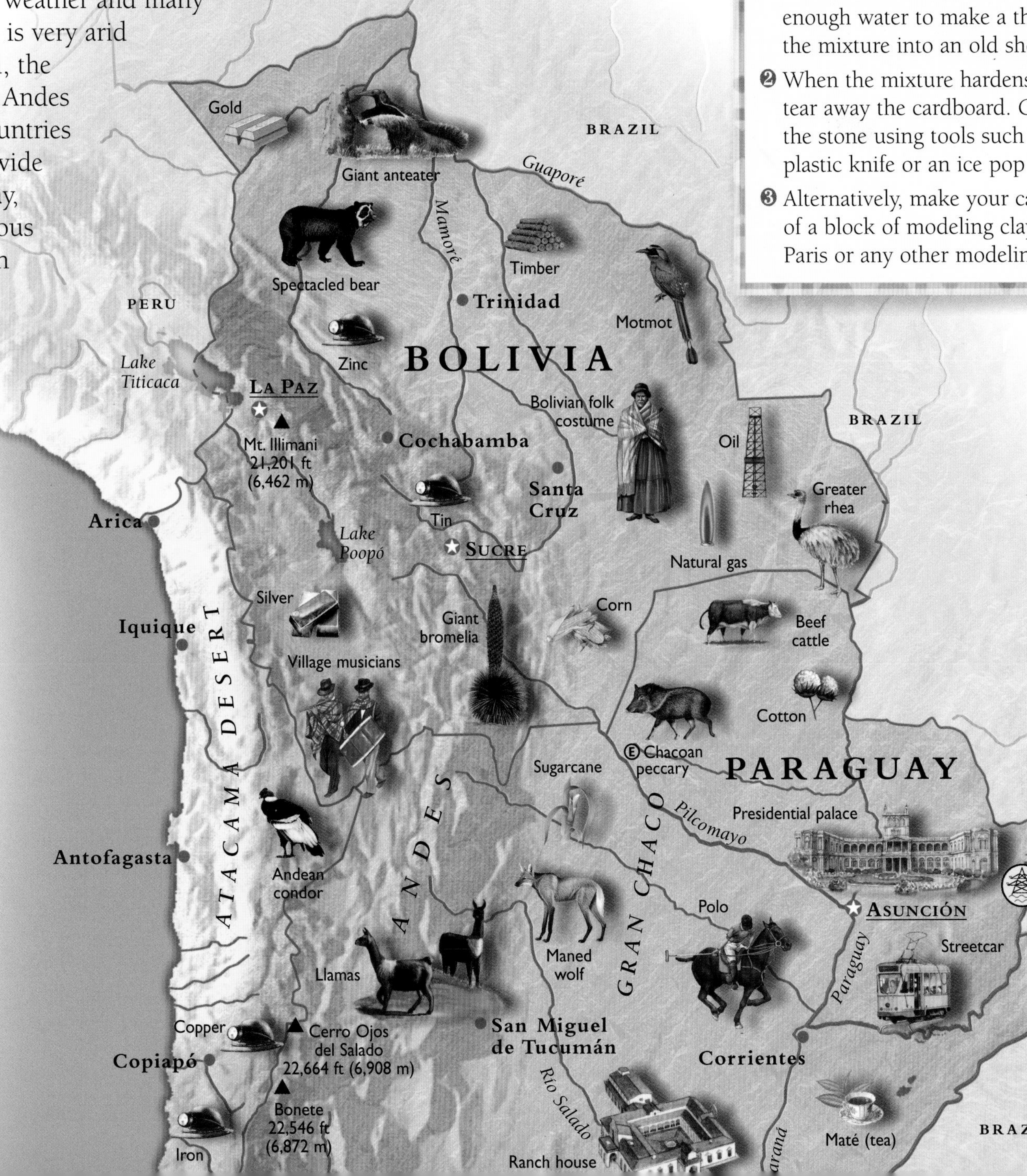

LLAMA
A common domestic animal in South America, the llama is a relative of the camel. It is kept for its wool and is also used for carrying goods through mountainous terrain.

PERU
BRAZIL
BOLIVIA
PARAGUAY
Gold
Giant anteater
Guaporé
Mamoré
Timber
Spectacled bear
Trinidad
Motmot
Zinc
Lake Titicaca
LA PAZ
Mt. Illimani 21,201 ft (6,462 m)
Cochabamba
Bolivian folk costume
Oil
Santa Cruz
Tin
SUCRE
Lake Poopó
Natural gas
Greater rhea
Arica
Silver
Giant bromelia
Corn
Beef cattle
Iquique
Village musicians
Cotton
ATACAMA DESERT
ANDES
Sugarcane
Chacoan peccary
GRAN CHACO
Pilcomayo
Presidential palace
Antofagasta
Andean condor
Polo
ASUNCIÓN
Hydroelectricity
Llamas
Maned wolf
Paraguay
Streetcar
Copper
Cerro Ojos del Salado 22,664 ft (6,908 m)
San Miguel de Tucumán
Copiapó
Corrientes
Río Salado
Bonete 22,546 ft (6,872 m)
Iron
Ranch house
Maté (tea)

La Serena
San Juan
Córdoba
Mendoza
Valparaíso
SANTIAGO
Aconcagua 22,834 ft (6,960 m)
Wine
Oil
Presidential palace
CHILE
ARGENTINA
URUGUAY
PAMPAS
Rosario
BUENOS AIRES
La Plata
MONTEVIDEO
Río de la Plata
Uruguay
Jesuit church
Corn
Beef cattle
Tango dancers
Pampas cat
Soccer
Branding cattle
Wheat
Sheep
Tourism
Bronze whaler shark
Pygmy sperm whale
LOCATION
Concepción
Villarica volcano
ANDES
Colorado
Negro
Viscacha
Mar del Plata
Bahía Blanca
Herding cattle
Iron ore
Skiing
Eoraptor dinosaur fossils
Crested caracara
VALDÉS PENINSULA
Puerto Montt
Sheep
Mara
Southern right whale
Timber
Natural gas
PATAGONIA
Guanacos
Comodoro Rivadavia
Sea lion
Mackerel
Puerto Deseado
Magellan penguin
Moreno Glacier
FALKLAND ISLANDS (U.K.)
Albatross chick
Stanley
Rockhopper penguin
Fur seal
Río Gallegos
Strait of Magellan
Punta Arenas
Tierra del Fuego
Ushuaia
CAPE HORN
PACIFIC OCEAN
ATLANTIC OCEAN
N
W
E
S
SCALE
MILES
0 100 200 300
0 100 200 300 400 500
KILOMETERS
A B C D E F G H I J
10 11 12 13 14 15 16 17

◆ AMAZING FACT ◆

Found only on the slopes of the Bolivian Andes, the giant bromelia is the world's largest herb, and the slowest-flowering plant on Earth. Its single stem can grow to a height of 35 feet (11 m), but the plant doesn't usually bloom until it is between 80 and 150 years old. Each plant may have up to 8,000 white flowers.

EASTER ISLAND (CHILE)

Magnificent frigate bird
Moai statues
Mataveri
PACIFIC OCEAN
MILES
0 5 10 15
0 10 20
KILOMETERS

TANGO DANCERS
The tango is both a style of music, and a dance that involves a series of long, gliding steps and sudden stops. It began in Argentina and is now popular around the world.

BOLIVIAN COSTUME
Native people make up half of Bolivia's population. Many still wear traditional dress including striped ponchos, shawls and bowler hats.

Europe

Europe is a small, densely populated continent made up of many countries, each of which has its own culture and, in most cases, its own language. It is bounded by the Arctic and Atlantic oceans in the north and west, and the Mediterranean Sea in the south. In the east, Russia's Ural Mountains separate Europe from Asia. A series of mountain ranges, including the Pyrenees, the Alps and the Carpathian Mountains, crosses Europe from east to west. South of these ranges, the land is rugged and the climate is warm and dry in summer and mild and wet in winter. To the north, a broad band of flat land known as the European Plain extends from the Atlantic coast to western Russia. Northwestern Europe has a mild, wet climate, but in the east and far north winters can be bitterly cold. At one time, most of Europe was covered in forest, but the trees were gradually cleared to make way for cities, farms and industries.

Continent Facts

Regional land area: 3,997,929 sq. miles (10,354,636 sq. km) (including European Russia)
Regional population: 693,950,000 (including European Russia)
Independent countries: Albania, Andorra, Austria, Belarus, Belgium, Bosnia and Herzegovina, Bulgaria, Croatia, Czech Republic, Denmark, Estonia, Finland, France, Germany, Greece, Hungary, Iceland, Ireland, Italy, Latvia, Liechtenstein, Lithuania, Luxembourg, Macedonia, Malta, Moldova, Monaco, The Netherlands, Norway, Poland, Portugal, Romania, Russia, San Marino, Slovakia, Slovenia, Spain, Sweden, Switzerland, Ukraine, United Kingdom, Vatican City, Yugoslavia

World Records

WORLD'S SMALLEST COUNTRY
Vatican City, 0.17 sq. miles (0.44 sq. km)

WORLD'S TALLEST STALAGMITE
Krásnohorská Cave, Slovakia, 105 ft (32 m)

Major Mountains and Rivers

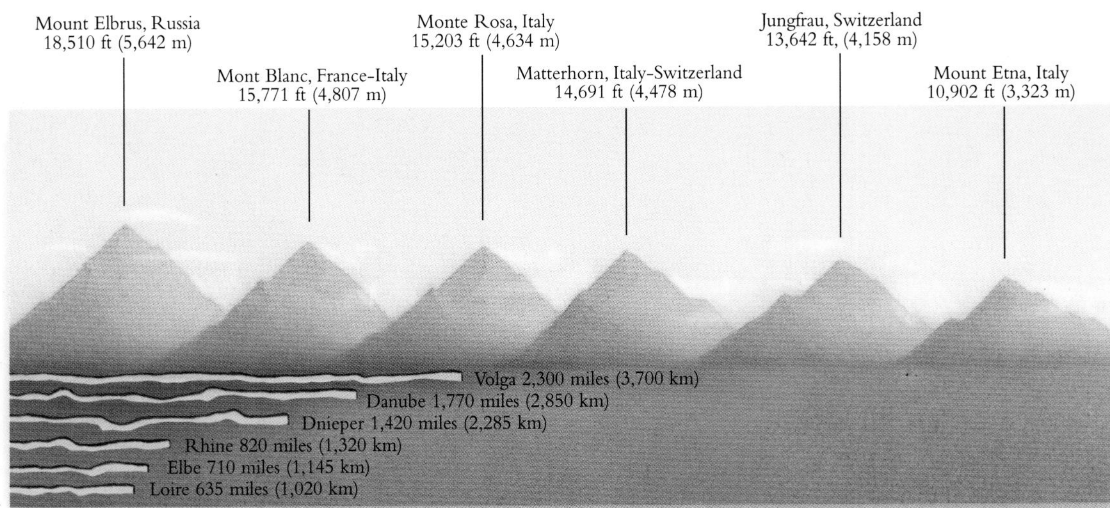
Mount Elbrus, Russia
18,510 ft (5,642 m)
Mont Blanc, France-Italy
15,771 ft (4,807 m)
Monte Rosa, Italy
15,203 ft (4,634 m)
Matterhorn, Italy-Switzerland
14,691 ft (4,478 m)
Jungfrau, Switzerland
13,642 ft, (4,158 m)
Mount Etna, Italy
10,902 ft (3,323 m)
Volga 2,300 miles (3,700 km)
Danube 1,770 miles (2,850 km)
Dnieper 1,420 miles (2,285 km)
Rhine 820 miles (1,320 km)
Elbe 710 miles (1,145 km)
Loire 635 miles (1,020 km)

Continent Records

HIGHEST MOUNTAIN
Mount Elbrus, Russia, 18,510 ft (5,642 m)

LOWEST POINT
Volga River Delta, 92 ft (28 m) below sea level

LARGEST LAKE
Lake Ladoga, Russia, 6,835 sq. miles (17,703 sq. km)

LONGEST RIVER
Volga River, Russia, 2,300 miles (3,700 km)

LARGEST COUNTRY BY AREA
European Russia, 233,089 sq. miles (603,701 sq. km)

LARGEST COUNTRY BY POPULATION
European Russia, population 109,909,000

LARGEST CITY BY POPULATION
Paris, France, population 9,500,000

Political Map

ICELAND
FAEROE ISLANDS (DENMARK)
SWEDEN
FINLAND
NORWAY
ESTONIA
UNITED KINGDOM
LATVIA
RUSSIA
DENMARK
KALININGRAD OBLAST (RUSSIA)
LITHUANIA
IRELAND
THE NETHERLANDS
BELARUS
GERMANY
POLAND
BELGIUM
CZECH REPUBLIC
UKRAINE
LUXEMBOURG
SLOVAKIA
FRANCE
AUSTRIA
SWITZERLAND
HUNGARY
MOLDOVA
SLOVENIA
ROMANIA
CROATIA
YUGOSLAVIA
BOSNIA and HERZEGOVINA
BULGARIA
ALBANIA
MACEDONIA
PORTUGAL
SPAIN
ITALY
GREECE
MALTA
1
2
3
4
5

Key to Numbered Countries

- 1 LIECHTENSTEIN
- 2 ANDORRA
- 3 MONACO
- 4 SAN MARINO
- 5 VATICAN CITY

Physical Map
J K L M N O P Q
1 2 3 9 10
ARCTIC OCEAN
NORTH POLE
NORTH AMERICA
Greenland
Norwegian Sea
Barents Sea
FAEROE ISLANDS
Iceland
Arctic Circle
ATLANTIC OCEAN
ASIA
URAL MOUNTAINS
SCANDINAVIA
Gulf of Bothnia
Lake Onega
Lake Ladoga
Lake Vanern
Volga
Ireland
North Sea
Baltic Sea
EUROPEAN PLAIN
Great Britain
English Channel
Rhine
Elbe
Seine
Loire
Bay of Biscay
Jungfrau
Matterhorn
Mont Blanc
ALPS
Monte Rosa
CARPATHIAN MTS
Dnieper
Don
Mt. Elbrus
CAUCASUS MTS
Caspian Sea
Black Sea
Danube
PYRENEES
IBERIAN PENINSULA
Corsica
BALEARIC IS.
APENNINES
Adriatic Sea
BALKAN PENINSULA
Strait of Gibraltar
Sardinia
Sicily
Mediterranean Sea
Ionian Sea
Mt. Etna
Aegean Sea
Crete
Tropic of Cancer
AFRICA
Equator

 See World Fact File page 107

The United Kingdom and the Republic of Ireland

THE UNITED KINGDOM AND THE REPUBLIC OF IRELAND occupy islands known as the British Isles. The United Kingdom is made up of the countries of England, Wales, Scotland and Northern Ireland, which are ruled by one government based in London but have their own cultures. Scotland and Wales also have their own parliaments, and Scotland has its own legal and educational systems, churches and bank notes. England is a crowded country with many large cities. Almost eight million people live in London, the capital city. London is one of the world's most important centers of trade and finance and is famous for its many historic buildings. Southeastern England is flat and fertile and its farms provide most of the United Kingdom's crops. The country's most important industries are located in central England, an area known as the Midlands, and around the coalfields of the Pennine hills. To the west and north, the countryside is wet and mountainous and is used mainly for grazing animals. In the rugged, sparsely populated Scottish Highlands, red deer and sheep roam the hills and eagles soar overhead. The Republic of Ireland occupies about 85 percent of the island of Ireland. It is a land of green plains surrounded by coastal mountains. Most of the country's industries are located in the capital, Dublin, and the southern city of Cork.

IRELAND
POPULATION: 3,550,000 * CAPITAL: DUBLIN

UNITED KINGDOM
POPULATION: 58,295,000 * CAPITAL: LONDON

ENGLAND
POPULATION: 48,620,000 * CAPITAL: LONDON

NORTHERN IRELAND
POPULATION: 1,640,000 * CAPITAL: BELFAST

SCOTLAND
POPULATION: 5,130,000 * CAPITAL: EDINBURGH

WALES
POPULATION: 2,905,000 * CAPITAL: CARDIFF

• *A*MAZING FACT •

In the 19th century, as a hoax, the name of the Welsh village Llanfairpwllgwyngyll was lengthened to the tongue-twisting Llanfairpwllgwyngyllgogerychwyrn-drobwllllantysiliogogogoch. The name means "St. Mary's church by the pool of white hazel trees, near the rapid whirlpool, by the red cave of the Church of St. Tysilio." In 1988 the village officially returned to using the shorter name. However, the railway station is still called by the 58-letter version.

LLANFAIRPWLLGWYNGYLLGOGERYCHWYRNDROBWLLLLANTYSILIOGOGOGOCH

• *L*OOK AGAIN •

- Which famous railway bridge is located near the capital of Scotland?
- Name a sport that is played in Ireland.
- What is the name of the group of islands near Land's End?

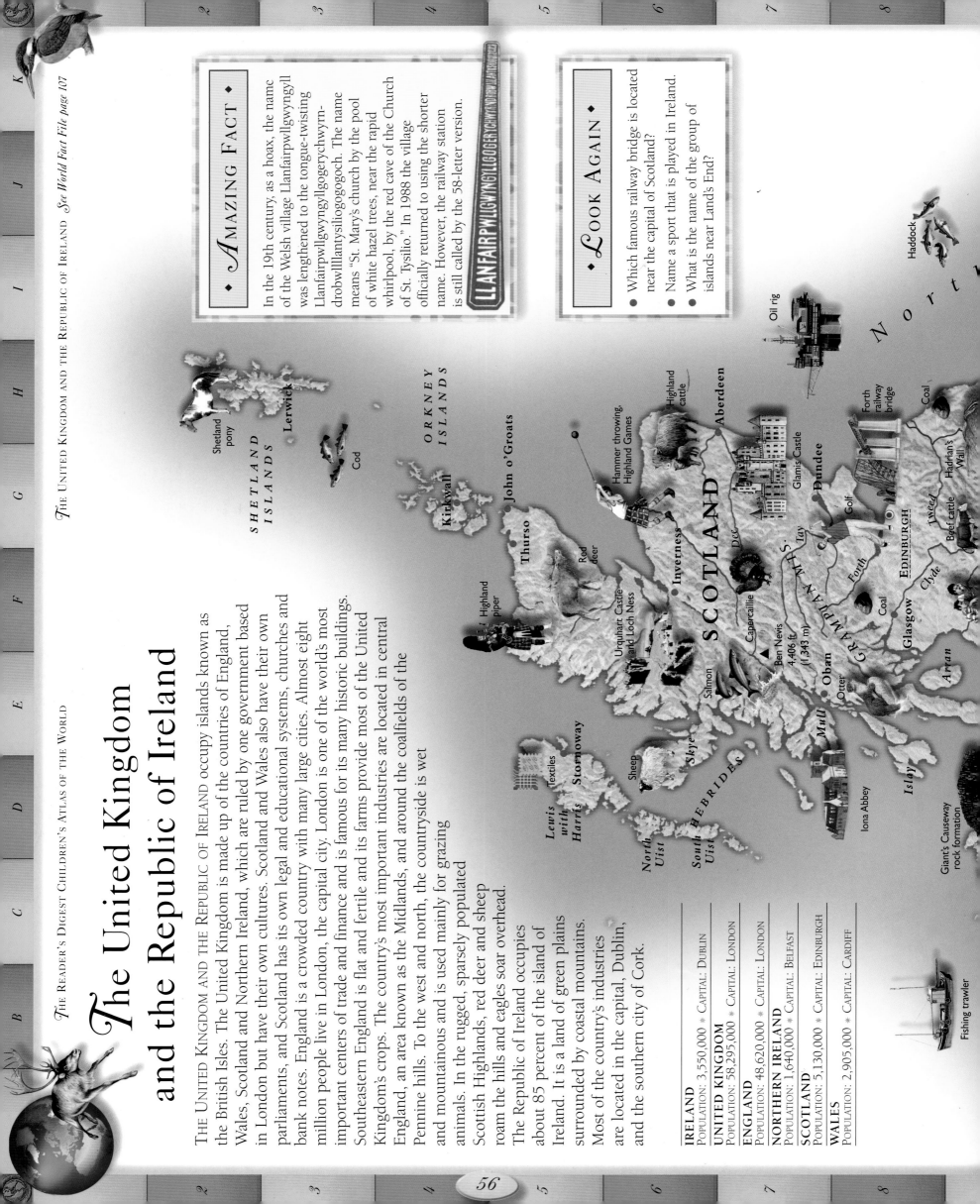

Shetland pony
SHETLAND ISLANDS
Lerwick
Cod
ORKNEY ISLANDS
Kirkwall
John o'Groats
Thurso
Highland piper
Red deer
Lewis with Harris
Textiles
Stornoway
Hammer throwing, Highland Games
Urquhart Castle and Loch Ness
Sheep
North Uist
Inverness
Highland cattle
South Uist
HEBRIDES
Skye
Salmon
SCOTLAND
Aberdeen
Dee
Capercaillie
Ben Nevis 4,406 ft (1,343 m)
GRAMPIAN MTS.
Tay
Glamis Castle
Oil rig
Dundee
Mull
Oban
Otter
Golf
Iona Abbey
Forth
Forth railway bridge
Coal
Glasgow
EDINBURGH
Islay
Clyde
Tweed
Coal
Haddock
Arran
Beef cattle
Hadrian's Wall
Giant's Causeway rock formation
Fishing trawler
North

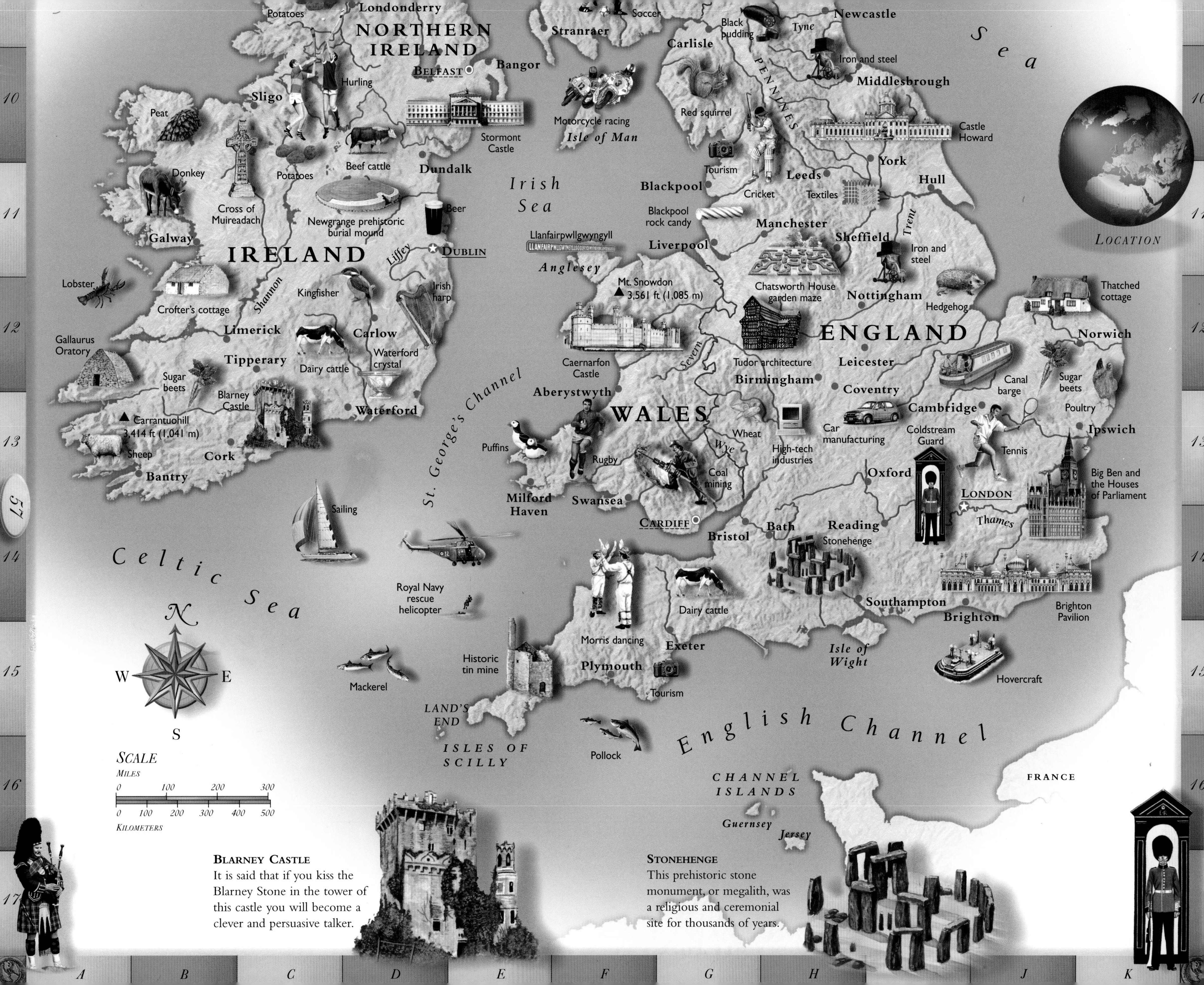
NORTHERN IRELAND
Londonderry
Potatoes
Hurling
Belfast
Bangor
Sligo
Stormont Castle
Peat
Beef cattle
Donkey
Potatoes
Dundalk
Cross of Muireadach
Newgrange prehistoric burial mound
Beer
Galway
IRELAND
Dublin
Liffey
Lobster
Shannon
Kingfisher
Irish harp
Crofter's cottage
Limerick
Carlow
Gallaurus Oratory
Tipperary
Dairy cattle
Waterford crystal
Sugar beets
Blarney Castle
Waterford
Carrantuohill 3,414 ft (1,041 m)
Sheep
Cork
Bantry
Sailing
Celtic Sea
Stranraer
Soccer
Motorcycle racing
Isle of Man
Irish Sea
Llanfairpwllgwyngyll
Anglesey
Mt. Snowdon 3,561 ft (1,085 m)
Caernarfon Castle
Aberystwyth
St. George's Channel
WALES
Puffins
Rugby
Milford Haven
Swansea
Cardiff
Coal mining
Wye
Severn
Royal Navy rescue helicopter
Mackerel
Historic tin mine
Land's End
Isles of Scilly
Carlisle
Black pudding
Tyne
Newcastle
Iron and steel
Middlesbrough
PENNINES
Red squirrel
Castle Howard
Tourism
York
Blackpool
Cricket
Leeds
Hull
Textiles
Blackpool rock candy
Manchester
Trent
Sheffield
Liverpool
Iron and steel
Chatsworth House garden maze
Nottingham
Hedgehog
Thatched cottage
ENGLAND
Tudor architecture
Leicester
Norwich
Birmingham
Coventry
Canal barge
Sugar beets
Poultry
Wheat
High-tech industries
Car manufacturing
Cambridge
Ipswich
Coldstream Guard
Tennis
Oxford
London
Thames
Big Ben and the Houses of Parliament
Bath
Reading
Bristol
Stonehenge
Dairy cattle
Southampton
Brighton
Brighton Pavilion
Morris dancing
Exeter
Plymouth
Tourism
Isle of Wight
Hovercraft
Pollock
English Channel
Channel Islands
Guernsey
Jersey
France
Sea
Location
N
W
E
S
Scale
Miles
0
100
200
300
0
100
200
300
400
500
Kilometers
A
B
C
D
E
F
G
H
J
K
10
11
12
13
14
15
16
17

Blarney Castle
It is said that if you kiss the Blarney Stone in the tower of this castle you will become a clever and persuasive talker.

Stonehenge
This prehistoric stone monument, or megalith, was a religious and ceremonial site for thousands of years.

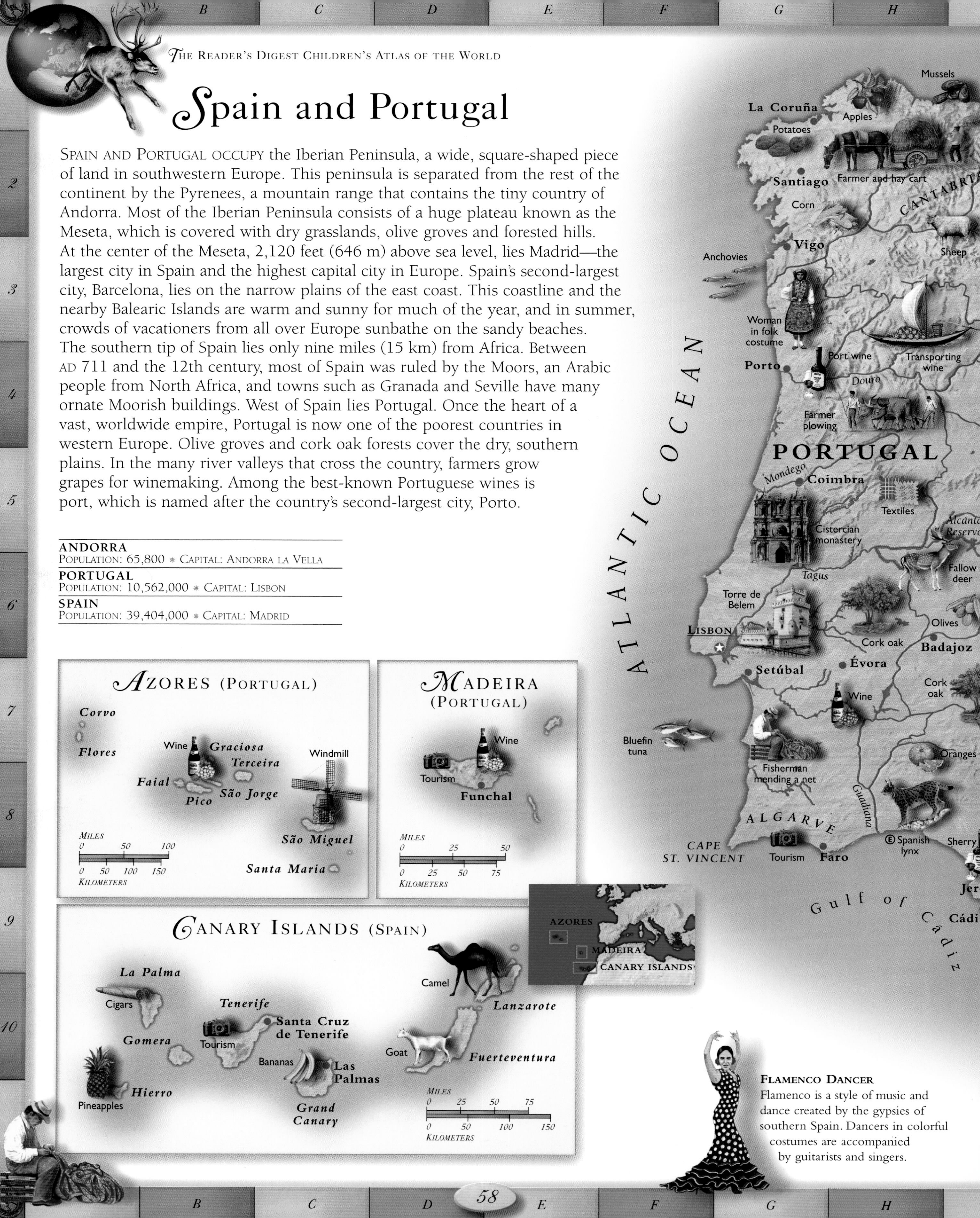

Spain and Portugal

SPAIN AND PORTUGAL OCCUPY the Iberian Peninsula, a wide, square-shaped piece of land in southwestern Europe. This peninsula is separated from the rest of the continent by the Pyrenees, a mountain range that contains the tiny country of Andorra. Most of the Iberian Peninsula consists of a huge plateau known as the Meseta, which is covered with dry grasslands, olive groves and forested hills. At the center of the Meseta, 2,120 feet (646 m) above sea level, lies Madrid—the largest city in Spain and the highest capital city in Europe. Spain's second-largest city, Barcelona, lies on the narrow plains of the east coast. This coastline and the nearby Balearic Islands are warm and sunny for much of the year, and in summer, crowds of vacationers from all over Europe sunbathe on the sandy beaches. The southern tip of Spain lies only nine miles (15 km) from Africa. Between AD 711 and the 12th century, most of Spain was ruled by the Moors, an Arabic people from North Africa, and towns such as Granada and Seville have many ornate Moorish buildings. West of Spain lies Portugal. Once the heart of a vast, worldwide empire, Portugal is now one of the poorest countries in western Europe. Olive groves and cork oak forests cover the dry, southern plains. In the many river valleys that cross the country, farmers grow grapes for winemaking. Among the best-known Portuguese wines is port, which is named after the country's second-largest city, Porto.

ANDORRA
POPULATION: 65,800 * CAPITAL: ANDORRA LA VELLA

PORTUGAL
POPULATION: 10,562,000 * CAPITAL: LISBON

SPAIN
POPULATION: 39,404,000 * CAPITAL: MADRID

B
C
D
E
F
G
H
2
3
4
5
6
7
8
9
10
La Coruña
Potatoes
Apples
Mussels
Farmer and hay cart
Santiago
Corn
CANTABRIA
Sheep
Vigo
Anchovies
Woman in folk costume
Port wine
Transporting wine
Porto
Douro
Farmer plowing
ATLANTIC OCEAN
PORTUGAL
Mondego
Coimbra
Textiles
Cistercian monastery
Alcántara Reservoir
Fallow deer
Tagus
Torre de Belem
Olives
LISBON
Cork oak
Badajoz
Setúbal
Évora
Cork oak
Wine
Bluefin tuna
Oranges
Fisherman mending a net
Guadiana
ALGARVE
Spanish lynx
Sherry
CAPE ST. VINCENT
Tourism
Faro
Jere
Gulf of Cádiz
Cádiz
AZORES (PORTUGAL)
Corvo
Flores
Wine
Graciosa
Terceira
Windmill
Faial
São Jorge
Pico
São Miguel
Santa Maria
MILES
0
50
100
0
50
100
150
KILOMETERS
MADEIRA (PORTUGAL)
Wine
Tourism
Funchal
MILES
0
25
50
0
25
50
75
KILOMETERS
AZORES
MADEIRA
CANARY ISLANDS
CANARY ISLANDS (SPAIN)
La Palma
Camel
Cigars
Tenerife
Lanzarote
Santa Cruz de Tenerife
Gomera
Tourism
Goat
Fuerteventura
Bananas
Las Palmas
Hierro
Pineapples
Grand Canary
MILES
0
25
50
75
0
50
100
150
KILOMETERS

FLAMENCO DANCER
Flamenco is a style of music and dance created by the gypsies of southern Spain. Dancers in colorful costumes are accompanied by guitarists and singers.

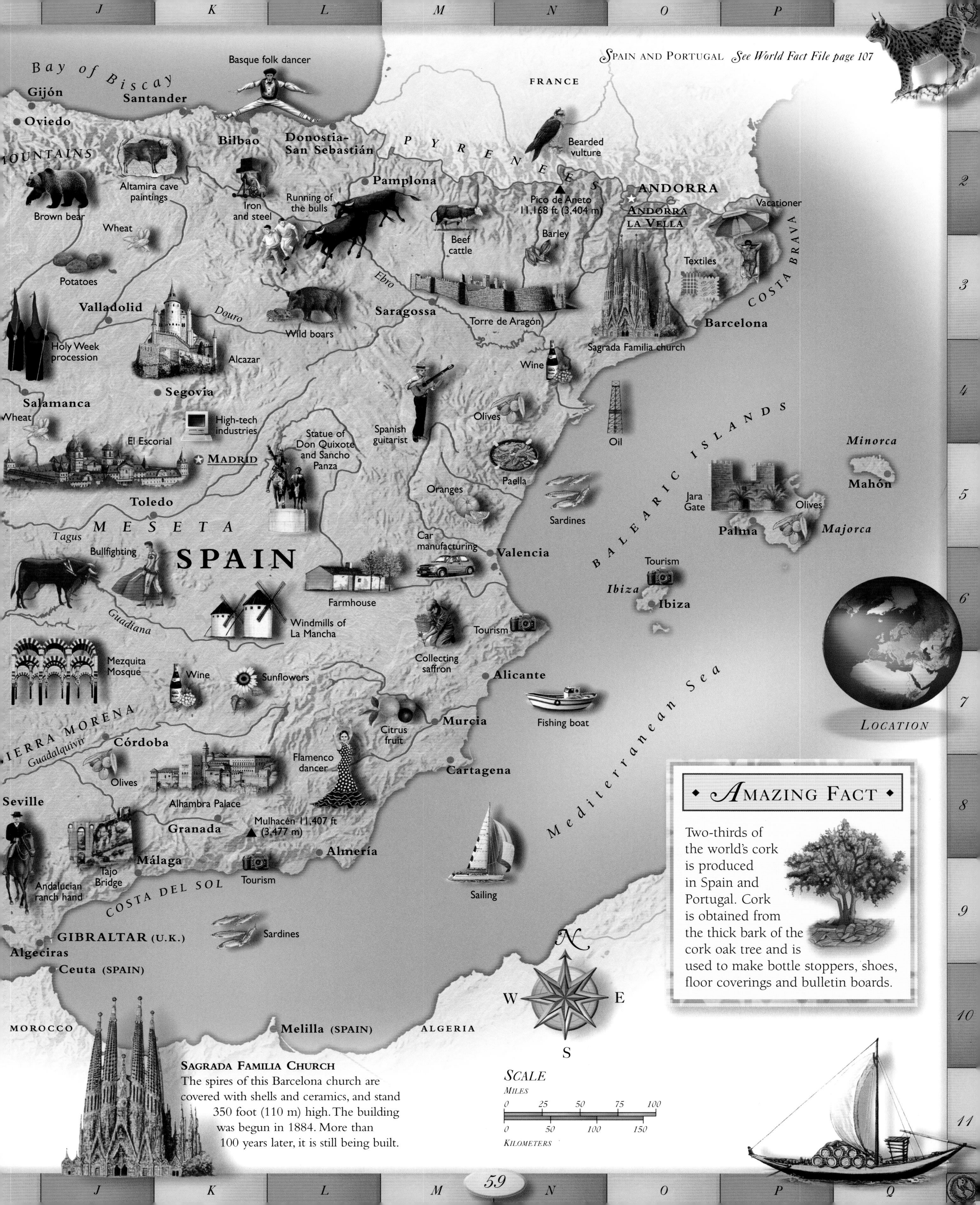
J
K
L
M
N
O
P
Bay of Biscay
Basque folk dancer
FRANCE
Gijón
Santander
Oviedo
Bilbao
Donostia-San Sebastián
PYRENEES
Bearded vulture
MOUNTAINS
Altamira cave paintings
Iron and steel
Pamplona
Running of the bulls
Pico de Aneto 11,168 ft (3,404 m)
ANDORRA
ANDORRA LA VELLA
Vacationer
Brown bear
Wheat
Beef cattle
Barley
Potatoes
Ebro
Textiles
COSTA BRAVA
Valladolid
Douro
Saragossa
Torre de Aragón
Barcelona
Wild boars
Sagrada Familia church
Holy Week procession
Alcazar
Wine
Segovia
Salamanca
Wheat
High-tech industries
Oil
Spanish guitarist
Olives
BALEARIC ISLANDS
Minorca
El Escorial
MADRID
Statue of Don Quixote and Sancho Panza
Paella
Mahón
Oranges
Jara Gate
Olives
Toledo
Sardines
Palma
Majorca
MESETA
Tagus
Car manufacturing
Valencia
Bullfighting
SPAIN
Tourism
Ibiza
Ibiza
Farmhouse
Guadiana
Windmills of La Mancha
Tourism
Mezquita Mosque
Collecting saffron
Wine
Sunflowers
Alicante
Mediterranean Sea
SIERRA MORENA
Citrus fruit
Murcia
Fishing boat
LOCATION
Córdoba
Guadalquivir
Flamenco dancer
Cartagena
Olives
Seville
Alhambra Palace
Mulhacén 11,407 ft (3,477 m)
Granada
Almería
Tajo Bridge
Málaga
Tourism
Sailing
Andalucian ranch hand
COSTA DEL SOL
Sardines
GIBRALTAR (U.K.)
Algeciras
Ceuta (SPAIN)
N
W
E
S
MOROCCO
Melilla (SPAIN)
ALGERIA
SCALE
MILES
0 25 50 75 100
0 50 100 150
KILOMETERS
2
3
4
5
6
7
8
9
10
11
Q

Amazing Fact

Two-thirds of the world's cork is produced in Spain and Portugal. Cork is obtained from the thick bark of the cork oak tree and is used to make bottle stoppers, shoes, floor coverings and bulletin boards.

Sagrada Familia Church
The spires of this Barcelona church are covered with shells and ceramics, and stand 350 foot (110 m) high. The building was begun in 1884. More than 100 years later, it is still being built.

France

France, the largest country in western Europe, has a varied climate and landscape. In the north, the weather is mild and wet, and much of the land is flat. As you travel south, the climate becomes warmer and the land more mountainous. Three-quarters of the population live in towns and cities, but most of the country is farmland, and France is Europe's leading farming country. The northern plains are covered in fields of wheat and sugar beets, and in central and southern France vineyards dot the hillsides—more wine is produced in France than in any other country except Italy. The area around Paris, the capital, is the most densely populated region. It is home to one-fifth of the country's population and most of its industries. Several great rivers, including the Seine and the Loire, cross France's northern and western plains. These waterways were once the country's main transportation routes, and their banks are lined with historic villages and magnificent castles known as châteaus. In the south, the mountains of the Pyrenees and the Alps separate France from Spain and Italy. Among their snow-capped peaks lie popular ski resorts and national parks that are home to eagles, marmots and goatlike antelopes called chamois. Along the Mediterranean coast there are many busy beach resorts. Near the Italian border lies Monaco, the second-smallest country in the world. Monaco is famous for its casinos and its annual Grand Prix motor race.

FRANCE
Population: 58,109,000 * Capital: Paris

MONACO
Population: 31,500 * Capital: Monaco

Amazing Fact

France is now connected to Great Britain by an undersea rail link known as the Channel Tunnel. The tunnel took seven years to build and includes two rail tracks. Trains take 35 minutes to pass through the tunnel. Travelers can journey from London to Paris in about three hours.

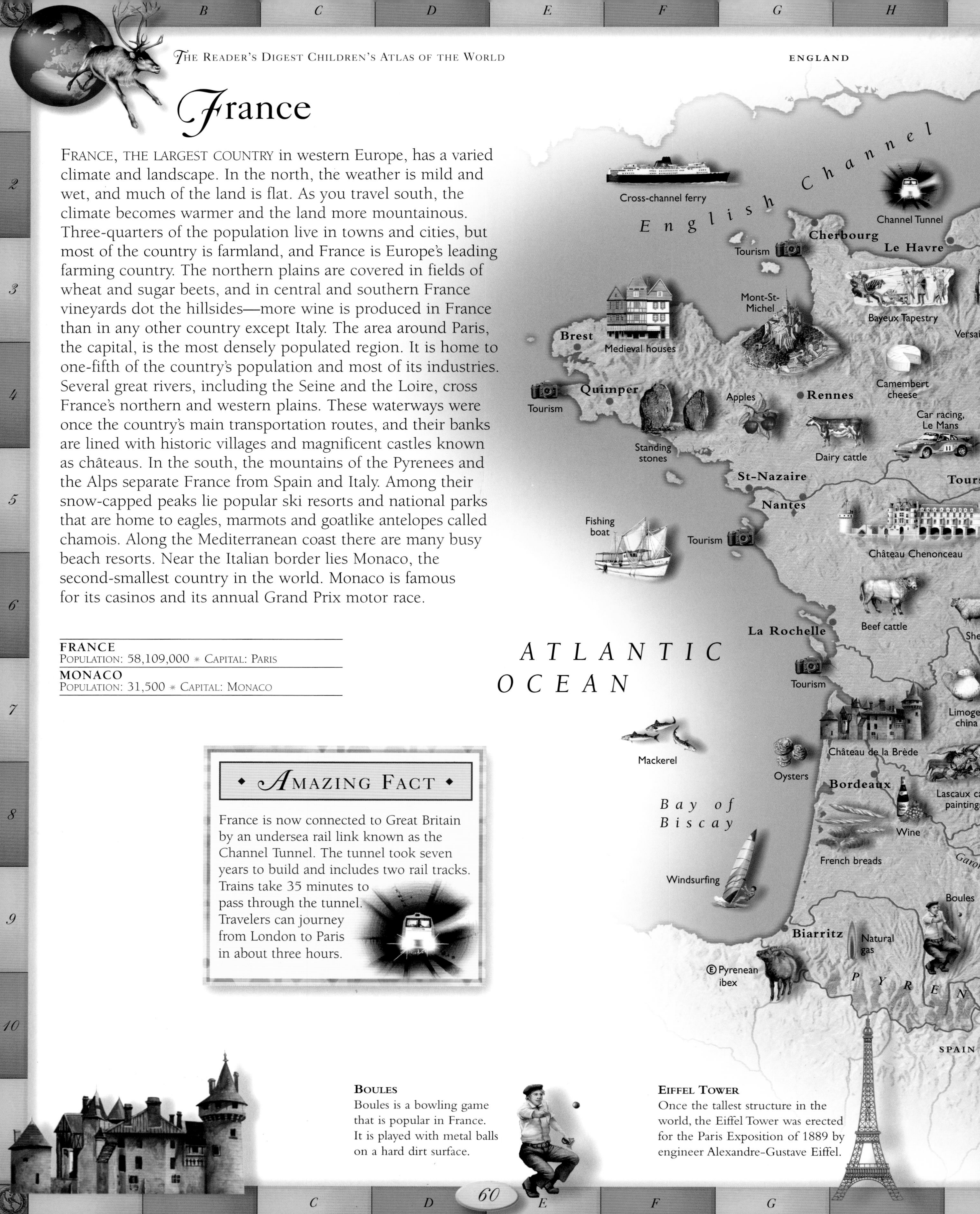

ENGLAND
English Channel
Cross-channel ferry
Channel Tunnel
Cherbourg
Le Havre
Tourism
Mont-St-Michel
Bayeux Tapestry
Versai
Brest
Medieval houses
Camembert cheese
Quimper
Tourism
Apples
Rennes
Car racing, Le Mans
Standing stones
Dairy cattle
St-Nazaire
Tours
Nantes
Fishing boat
Tourism
Château Chenonceau
Beef cattle
La Rochelle
She
ATLANTIC OCEAN
Tourism
Limoge china
Mackerel
Château de la Brède
Oysters
Bordeaux
Lascaux ca paintings
Bay of Biscay
Wine
French breads
Garon
Windsurfing
Boules
Biarritz
Natural gas
Ⓔ Pyrenean ibex
PYREN
SPAIN

Boules
Boules is a bowling game that is popular in France. It is played with metal balls on a hard dirt surface.

Eiffel Tower
Once the tallest structure in the world, the Eiffel Tower was erected for the Paris Exposition of 1889 by engineer Alexandre-Gustave Eiffel.

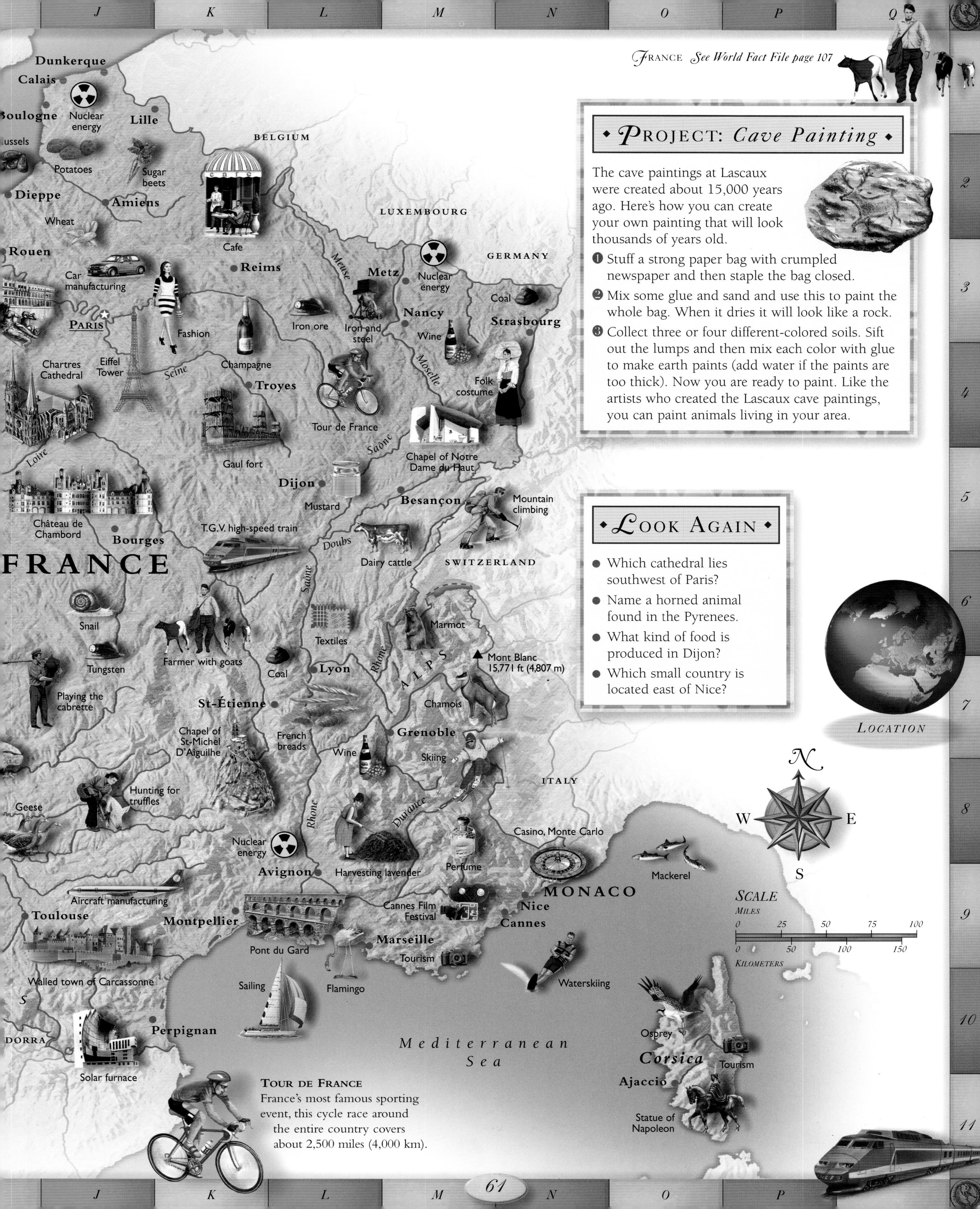

J
K
L
M
N
O
P
Q
Dunkerque
Calais
Boulogne
Nuclear energy
Lille
BELGIUM
Potatoes
Sugar beets
Dieppe
Amiens
Wheat
LUXEMBOURG
Rouen
Cafe
Reims
GERMANY
Car manufacturing
Meuse
Metz
Nuclear energy
Coal
PARIS
Fashion
Iron ore
Iron and steel
Nancy
Strasbourg
Wine
Chartres Cathedral
Eiffel Tower
Seine
Champagne
Troyes
Moselle
Folk costume
Loire
Tour de France
Saône
Gaul fort
Chapel of Notre Dame du Haut
Dijon
Mustard
Besançon
Mountain climbing
Château de Chambord
Bourges
T.G.V. high-speed train
Doubs
Dairy cattle
SWITZERLAND
FRANCE
Saône
Snail
Textiles
Marmot
Farmer with goats
Tungsten
Rhone
Mont Blanc 15,771 ft (4,807 m)
Coal
Lyon
ALPS
Playing the cabrette
St-Étienne
Chamois
Chapel of St-Michel D'Aiguilhe
French breads
Grenoble
Wine
Skiing
ITALY
Hunting for truffles
Geese
Rhone
Durance
Casino, Monte Carlo
Nuclear energy
Avignon
Harvesting lavender
Perfume
Mackerel
MONACO
Aircraft manufacturing
Cannes Film Festival
Nice
Toulouse
Montpellier
Cannes
Pont du Gard
Marseille
Tourism
Walled town of Carcassonne
Sailing
Flamingo
Waterskiing
Perpignan
Mediterranean Sea
Osprey
Corsica
Tourism
Solar furnace
Ajaccio
Statue of Napoleon
N
W
E
S
SCALE
MILES
0
25
50
75
100
0
50
100
150
KILOMETERS
LOCATION
2
3
4
5
6
7
8
9
10
11

◆ PROJECT: *Cave Painting* ◆

The cave paintings at Lascaux were created about 15,000 years ago. Here's how you can create your own painting that will look thousands of years old.

1. Stuff a strong paper bag with crumpled newspaper and then staple the bag closed.
2. Mix some glue and sand and use this to paint the whole bag. When it dries it will look like a rock.
3. Collect three or four different-colored soils. Sift out the lumps and then mix each color with glue to make earth paints (add water if the paints are too thick). Now you are ready to paint. Like the artists who created the Lascaux cave paintings, you can paint animals living in your area.

◆ LOOK AGAIN ◆

- Which cathedral lies southwest of Paris?
- Name a horned animal found in the Pyrenees.
- What kind of food is produced in Dijon?
- Which small country is located east of Nice?

TOUR DE FRANCE
France's most famous sporting event, this cycle race around the entire country covers about 2,500 miles (4,000 km).

The Low Countries

THE DENSELY POPULATED COUNTRIES OF the Netherlands (also called Holland), Belgium and Luxembourg are known as the Low Countries because they have no high mountains and few hills. Much of the land, including one-third of the Netherlands, actually lies below sea level. Over the centuries, local people have built large barriers known as dikes to keep the sea out, pumped water out of the marshes behind the dikes to create areas of new land called polders, and constructed thousands of miles of canals. Throughout the region, barges chug along these waterways, past windmills, dairy farms and colorful fields of tulips—both Belgium and the Netherlands export flowers and bulbs all over the world. The capital of the Netherlands, Amsterdam, has more than 150 canals, many of which are lined with tall, narrow, 17th-century buildings. In Belgium, canals link the country's ports to the historic cities of Bruges and Ghent, and to Brussels, the capital. Brussels is often referred to as the capital of Europe because it is the headquarters of the European Union (EU). Southeast of Brussels lies the only high part of the Low Countries, the Ardennes. This range of forest-covered hills spreads across the northern half of Luxembourg, one of Europe's smallest countries but also one of its most important financial centers.

BELGIUM
POPULATION: 10,082,000 * CAPITAL: BRUSSELS

LUXEMBOURG
POPULATION: 404,700 * CAPITAL: LUXEMBOURG

THE NETHERLANDS
POPULATION: 15,453,000 * CAPITALS: AMSTERDAM, THE HAGUE

EUROPEAN UNION FORMER HEADQUARTERS
The European Union, or EU, consists of a group of European countries that have developed close trade and political links in order to encourage the free movement of people, goods and services around Europe.

• AMAZING FACT •

The Low Countries have more than 5,000 miles (8,000 km) of canals, which are used for transportation and for draining the land. Because much of the region lies below sea level, water has to be pumped into canals built high above ground level. You could be standing in a field in the Low Countries and see a ship pass by above your head!

Harbor seals
Ameland
Terschelling
WEST FRISIAN ISLANDS
Vlieland
Waddenzee
Texel
Potatoes
Windmill
Natural gas
Leeuwarden
Groningen
Eurasian spoonbill
Sheep
Wheat
Clogs
Dairy cattle
Herring
Mussels
Flowers
Ijsselmeer
Alkmaar cheese market
Zuider Zee folk costume
Beef cattle
Prehistoric hunebed (burial tomb)
Cycling
Mackerel
Alkmaar
Iron and steel
THE NETHERLANDS
Diamond cutting
Barley
Natural gas
Haarlem
AMSTERDAM
Beer
Beef cattle
Dairy cattle
Tulips
Apeldoorn
Dom Cathedral tower
Pigs
Peace Palace
Poultry
Amsterdam
THE HAGUE
Utrecht
Arnhem
Chemicals
Delft pottery
Folk dancers
Rotterdam
Lek
Soccer
Rhine
Niimegen
Container ship

North Sea
Oysters
Wheat
Barley
Breda
Tilburg
's Hertogenbosch Cathedral
Maas
Rye
Eindhoven
High-tech industries
Vegetables
BAARLE-HERTOG (BELGIUM)
Chemicals
Antwerp
Dockside cranes, Antwerp port
Flax
Ostend
Tourism
Bruges
High-tech industries
Damme Canal
Ghent
Atomium building
Bicycle racing
Wheat
GERMANY
Sugar beets
FLANDERS
Iron and steel
Beer
Ghent
Iron and steel
BRUSSELS
Dairy cattle
Sugar beets
Louvain Town Hall
Crystal
Liège
Dairy cattle
Vegetables
EU former headquarters
Chocolate
Sugar beets
Wheat
Textiles
BELGIUM
Meuse
Dairy cattle
Red squirrel
Barley
FRANCE
Sambre
Fortress and town of Dinant
Red deer
Wild boars
ARDENNES
Beef cattle
Ardennes
Iron and steel
Wildcat
LUXEMBOURG
National Savings Bank
Wine
LUXEMBOURG
Esch
LOCATION
N
W
E
S
SCALE
MILES
0 10 20 30
0 10 20 30 40 50
KILOMETERS
A B C D E F G H I J
10 11 12 13 14 15 16 17

CLOGS
Worn by Dutch farmers, these traditional wooden shoes help keep feet warm and dry in damp fields. They are known locally as *klompen*.

◆ PROJECT: *Make a Paper Windmill* ◆

At one time, much of the land in the western part of the Netherlands lay under water. Windmills were used to pump and drain water from land as well as to grind grain. Windmills harness the force of the wind to produce energy. The wind turns the sails of the windmill, which are connected to a pillar. This pillar transmits the energy through a system of gears to a vertical shaft that carries the power to a water pump or mill. You can make a paper windmill and power it by blowing on it.

1. Cut a 7½- x 7½-inch (19- x 19-cm) piece of paper. Draw an X across the paper. Using a large coin or a compass, trace a circle in the center of the square.
2. Cut along the four diagonal lines up to the edge of the circle. Without folding the paper, bend every other point in to the center of the circle.
3. Stick a pushpin through the center of the circle and through all the bent-in points. Now stick the pushpin into the side of the eraser at the end of a pencil. Hold the windmill by the pencil tip and blow on it.

ALKMAAR CHEESE MARKET
Every Friday during summer in the Dutch town of Alkmaar, round balls of cheese are carried to the market on traditional wooden "sledges."

 See World Fact File pages 107–108

Western Central Europe

After World War II, Germany was divided into two countries: East Germany and West Germany. They were reunited in 1990 and Germany is now home to more than 80 million people, the largest population of any European country except Russia. Many of Germany's cities lie on rivers. The Rhine River connects the country's most important industrial region, the Ruhr Valley, to the ports of the Netherlands and the Swiss city of Basel. On its journey northward, the Rhine meanders past forests of spruce and fir, steep hillsides covered with vineyards, and cliffs crowned by medieval castles. From southern Germany, the spectacular Alps mountain range stretches across the countries of Switzerland and Austria, where it covers about two-thirds of the land. Throughout these mountains, roads and railways wind through narrow river valleys and cross steep passes. In summer, cows graze in the alpine meadows; in winter, skiers hurtle down the slopes. Switzerland is a peaceful country which hasn't been involved in a war since 1814. This has encouraged people from all over the world to deposit money in Swiss banks, and the country is now a leading financial center. In Austria, many farms and industries lie on the northeastern lowlands. This area is crossed by the Danube, Europe's second-longest river. The Danube passes through Austria's capital, Vienna—home to one-fifth of Austria's population and one of Europe's grandest cities.

AUSTRIA
Population: 7,987,000 * Capital: Vienna

GERMANY
Population: 81,338,000 * Capital: Berlin

LIECHTENSTEIN
Population: 30,700 * Capital: Vaduz

SWITZERLAND
Population: 7,085,000 * Capital: Bern

◆ Project: *Swiss Chocolate Fondue* ◆

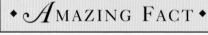

The Swiss eat a dish called fondue, which is often made from cheese. Pieces of bread are dipped in a mixture of hot melted cheese and white wine. This fondue is different—it's made with chocolate!

1. Place 8 oz (250 g) semisweet chocolate pieces into a saucepan with 1 cup (8 oz/250 ml) whipping cream.
2. Ask an adult to help you warm the ingredients gently until the chocolate has melted. Beat the mixture until it becomes glossy.
3. Let the mixture cool a little. Then spear a piece of fruit (strawberries or grapes are good) on a fork, dip it in the fondue and have a taste. Yum!

◆ Amazing Fact ◆

The country of Liechtenstein is home to only 30,700 people and is just four miles (6 km) wide. That means you could walk across it in less than two hours! The prince of Liechtenstein lives in this castle at Vaduz, the capital.

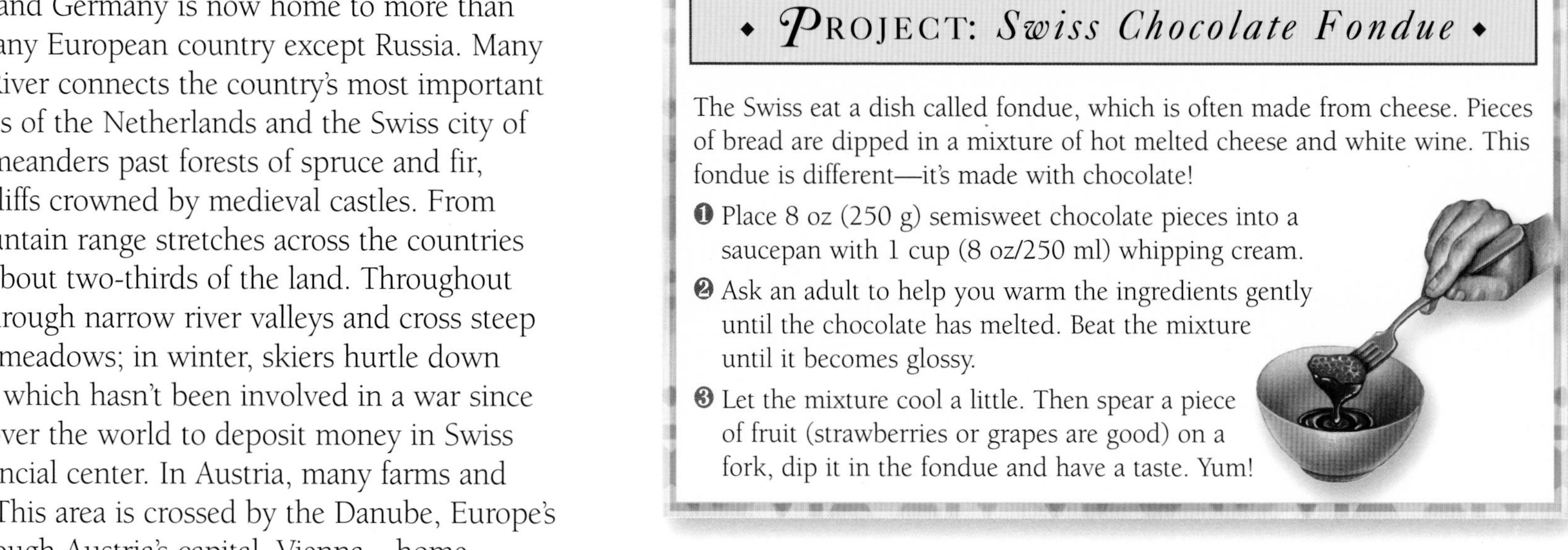
DENMARK
North Sea
Baltic Sea
THE NETHERLANDS
POLAND
Tourism
Oats
Shipbuilding
Nord-Ostsee Canal
Kiel
Cod
Herring
Vegetables
Lübeck
Rostock
High-tech industries
Hamburg
Rye
White stork
Horses
Dairy cattle
Oldenburg
Musicians of Bremen statue
Bremen
Sausages
Elbe
Potatoes
Wheat
Blackbird
Natural gas
Lüneburg heath
Sheep
Hurdy-gurdy player
Oil
Ems
Pigs
Car manufacturing
Oder
Beaver
BERLIN
Brandenburg Gate
Hannover
Weser
Textiles
Brunswick
Magdeburg
Münster
Chemicals
Timber-frame
Iron and
High-tech industries
N
W
E
S
SCALE
MILES
0
25
50
75
0
25
50
75
100
125
KILOMETERS

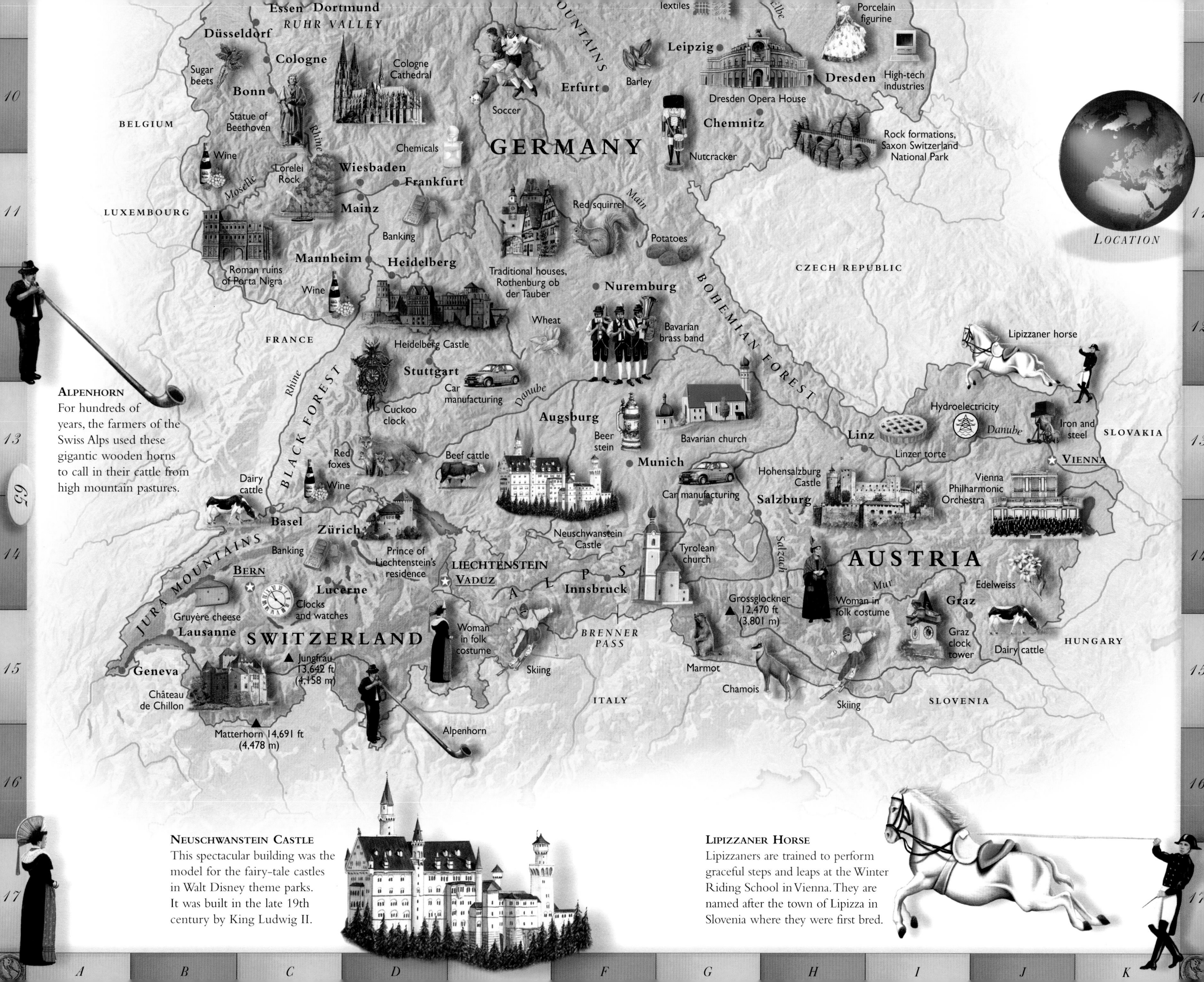
Essen
Dortmund
RUHR VALLEY
Düsseldorf
Cologne
Sugar beets
Bonn
Cologne Cathedral
Statue of Beethoven
Rhine
BELGIUM
Wine
Moselle
Lorelei Rock
Wiesbaden
Frankfurt
Chemicals
Mainz
LUXEMBOURG
Banking
Roman ruins of Porta Nigra
Mannheim
Heidelberg
Wine
Heidelberg Castle
FRANCE
Stuttgart
Car manufacturing
Cuckoo clock
BLACK FOREST
Red foxes
Wine
Dairy cattle
Basel
Zürich
Banking
Prince of Liechtenstein's residence
JURA MOUNTAINS
BERN
Lucerne
Clocks and watches
Gruyère cheese
Lausanne
SWITZERLAND
Geneva
Château de Chillon
Jungfrau 13,642 ft (4,158 m)
Matterhorn 14,691 ft (4,478 m)
Alpenhorn
Soccer
MOUNTAINS
Erfurt
Barley
GERMANY
Leipzig
Textiles
Elbe
Dresden Opera House
Chemnitz
Nutcracker
Porcelain figurine
Dresden
High-tech industries
Rock formations, Saxon Switzerland National Park
LOCATION
Red squirrel
Main
Potatoes
Traditional houses, Rothenburg ob der Tauber
Nuremburg
Wheat
Bavarian brass band
BOHEMIAN FOREST
CZECH REPUBLIC
Danube
Augsburg
Beer stein
Bavarian church
Munich
Beef cattle
Neuschwanstein Castle
LIECHTENSTEIN
VADUZ
ALPS
Innsbruck
Woman in folk costume
Skiing
BRENNER PASS
ITALY
Car manufacturing
Hohensalzburg Castle
Salzburg
Tyrolean church
Salzach
Grossglockner 12,470 ft (3,801 m)
Marmot
Chamois
Skiing
Linz
Linzer torte
Hydroelectricity
Danube
Iron and steel
Lipizzaner horse
SLOVAKIA
VIENNA
Vienna Philharmonic Orchestra
AUSTRIA
Mur
Woman in folk costume
Edelweiss
Graz
Graz clock tower
Dairy cattle
HUNGARY
SLOVENIA
10
11
12
13
14
15
16
17
A
B
C
D
E
F
G
H
I
J
K

Alpenhorn
For hundreds of years, the farmers of the Swiss Alps used these gigantic wooden horns to call in their cattle from high mountain pastures.

Neuschwanstein Castle
This spectacular building was the model for the fairy-tale castles in Walt Disney theme parks. It was built in the late 19th century by King Ludwig II.

Lipizzaner Horse
Lipizzaners are trained to perform graceful steps and leaps at the Winter Riding School in Vienna. They are named after the town of Lipizza in Slovenia where they were first bred.

Italy

Italy consists of a long, boot-shaped peninsula, the large islands of Sicily and Sardinia, and about 70 smaller islands. Within Italy lie two other countries: San Marino in the east, and the Vatican City (the world's smallest country) in the city of Rome. The Vatican City is the home of the Pope, the head of the Roman Catholic Church. Most of mainland Italy is mountainous. The Alps form a great arc around the northern border, and the Apennines stretch almost the entire length of the peninsula. Between these two mountain ranges lies the Northern Plain, a flat, fertile region drained by the Po River. This plain has Italy's richest farmland and is home to the country's most important industries, including the car factories of Turin, and Milan's fashion and design houses.

Each year, more than 50 million tourists travel to Italy to visit its ancient ruins, historic cities and museums, and to enjoy the sunny summer weather. The country's mild climate allows farmers to grow large quantities of wheat, citrus fruit, olives and grapes—Italy is the world's leading producer of olive oil and wine. Parts of Italy are regularly rocked by earthquakes, and the country has the only active volcanoes on mainland Europe. On the island of Sicily, Mount Etna has erupted at least 260 times since the first recorded eruption in 70 BC. About 60 miles (95 km) south of Sicily lie the islands of Malta. At various times in its history, Malta was ruled by the Romans, Arabs, Turks, French and British. It is now an independent republic.

ITALY
Population: 58,262,000 * Capital: Rome

MALTA
Population: 369,600 * Capital: Valletta

SAN MARINO
Population: 24,300 * Capital: San Marino

VATICAN CITY
Population: 830 * Capital: Vatican City

◆ Amazing Fact ◆

The Leaning Tower of Pisa was constructed as a bell tower between AD 1173 and 1370. Unfortunately, it was built on unstable ground, and it began to sink and tilt to one side after completion of the first three stories. Although the tower leans about 15 feet (4.5 m) out of line, it has recently been stabilized so that it will not fall over.

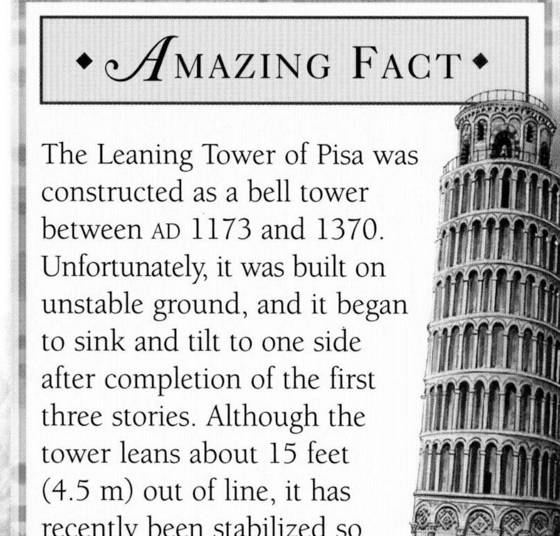

Mont Blanc 15,771 ft (4,807 m)
Matterhorn 14,691 ft (4,478 m)
Monte Rosa 15,203 ft (4,634 m)
SWITZERLAND
AUSTRIA
FRANCE
SLOVENIA
CROATIA
ALPS
DOLOMITES
APENNINES
Marmot
Skiing
Rock climbing
Bolzano
Chamois
Lake Maggiore
Lake Como
Hydroelectricity
Fashion
Milan
Car manufacturing
Violin making
Pinnacles of the Dolomites
Turin
Brescia
Parma Baptistry
Lake Garda
Dairy cattle
Verona
Wine
Rice
Milan Cathedral
Sugar beets
Venice
Corn
Trieste
Rialto Bridge
Po
Padua
Walnuts
Tourism
Genoa
Parma
Parmesan cheese
Wheat
Gulf of Venice
Ferrara
Olives
Marble
Modena
Bologna
Church of San Vitale
Fishing boat
La Spezia
Leaning Tower of Pisa
Florence Cathedral
Ravenna
Ligurian Sea
Pisa
Pasta
Sole
Rimini
Arno
Florence
SAN MARINO
San Marino
Squid
Livorno
Chianti wine
Rocca Tower, San Marino
Siena
Arezzo
Ancona
Elba
N
W
E

Colosseum
This Roman stadium was built in the first century AD and used for events such as gladiator contests. It was even flooded for mock sea battles.

Mount Vesuvius and Pompeii
In AD 79, Mount Vesuvius erupted, burying the town of Pompeii under stone and ash. The ruins were not discovered until the 18th century.

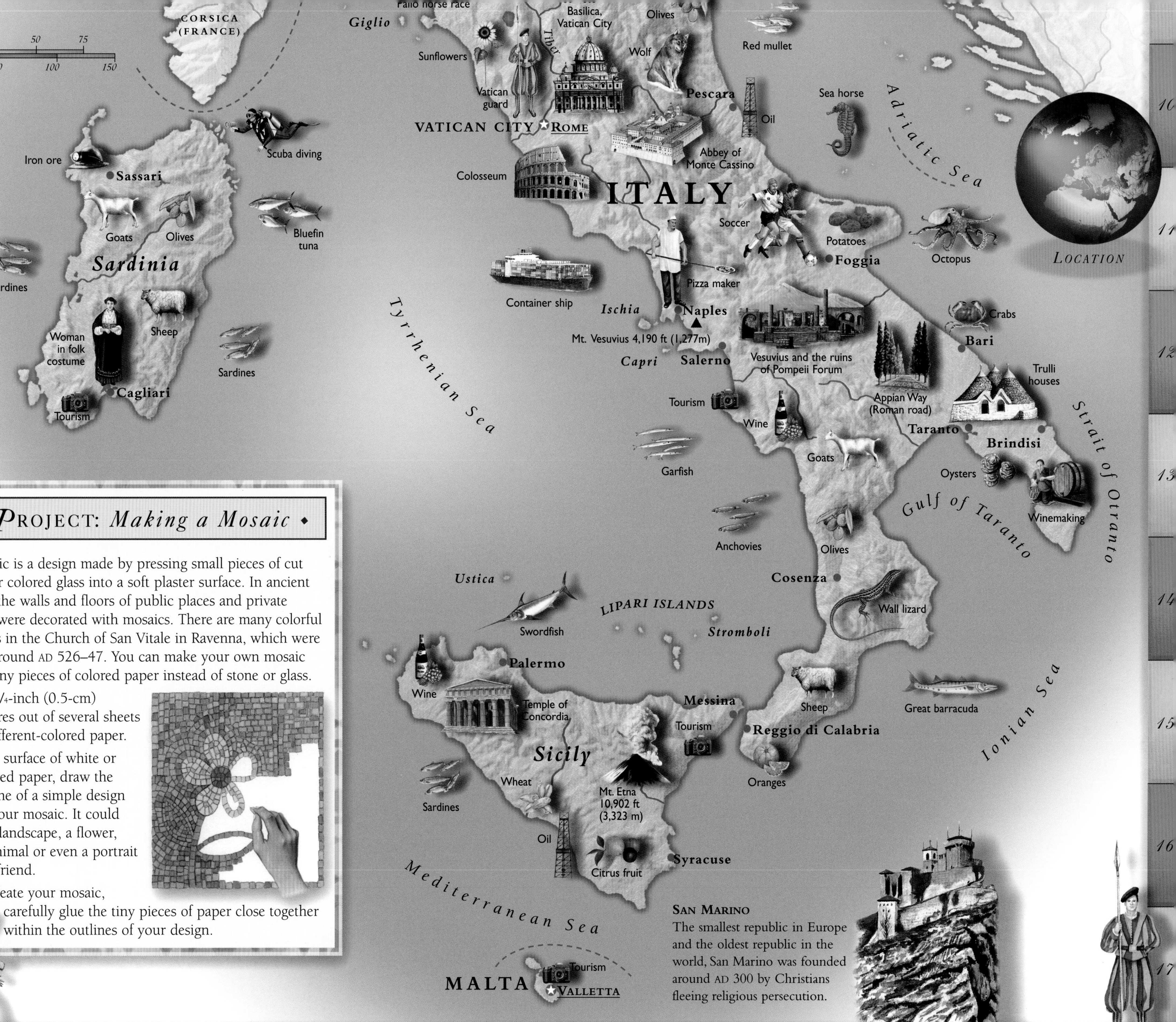
SCALE
MILES
0 25 50 75
0 50 100 150
KILOMETERS
CORSICA (FRANCE)
Giglio
Palio horse race
Sunflowers
Basilica, Vatican City
Tiber
Olives
Wolf
Red mullet
Vatican guard
VATICAN CITY
ROME
Pescara
Oil
Sea horse
Adriatic Sea
Iron ore
Scuba diving
Abbey of Monte Cassino
Colosseum
ITALY
Sassari
Goats
Olives
Bluefin tuna
Soccer
Potatoes
Foggia
Octopus
LOCATION
Sardinia
Sardines
Pizza maker
Container ship
Ischia
Naples
Crabs
Bari
Woman in folk costume
Sheep
Mt. Vesuvius 4,190 ft (1,277m)
Capri
Salerno
Vesuvius and the ruins of Pompeii Forum
Trulli houses
Sardines
Cagliari
Tourism
Tyrrhenian Sea
Tourism
Appian Way (Roman road)
Strait of Otranto
Wine
Taranto
Brindisi
Goats
Garfish
Oysters
Gulf of Taranto
Winemaking
Anchovies
Olives
Cosenza
Ustica
LIPARI ISLANDS
Wall lizard
Swordfish
Stromboli
Palermo
Wine
Temple of Concordia
Messina
Sheep
Great barracuda
Tourism
Reggio di Calabria
Ionian Sea
Sicily
Wheat
Mt. Etna 10,902 ft (3,323 m)
Oranges
Sardines
Oil
Citrus fruit
Syracuse
Mediterranean Sea
MALTA
Tourism
VALLETTA
A B C D E F G H I J K
10 11 12 13 14 15 16 17

• PROJECT: *Making a Mosaic* •

A mosaic is a design made by pressing small pieces of cut stone or colored glass into a soft plaster surface. In ancient Rome, the walls and floors of public places and private homes were decorated with mosaics. There are many colorful mosaics in the Church of San Vitale in Ravenna, which were made around AD 526–47. You can make your own mosaic using tiny pieces of colored paper instead of stone or glass.

❶ Cut ¼-inch (0.5-cm) squares out of several sheets of different-colored paper.

❷ On a surface of white or colored paper, draw the outline of a simple design for your mosaic. It could be a landscape, a flower, an animal or even a portrait of a friend.

❸ To create your mosaic, carefully glue the tiny pieces of paper close together within the outlines of your design.

SAN MARINO
The smallest republic in Europe and the oldest republic in the world, San Marino was founded around AD 300 by Christians fleeing religious persecution.

 See World Fact File page 108

Southeastern Europe

THIS REGION IS OFTEN REFERRED TO as the Balkans. It lies at the edge of Europe, close to Asia, and is home to many peoples from both continents. Throughout history, disputes between countries and ethnic groups have occurred here regularly. In 1991, the republics of Slovenia, Croatia, Bosnia and Herzegovina, and Macedonia declared their independence from Yugoslavia. This led to a war that destroyed cities, farms and industries, and left thousands of people homeless. Most of southeastern Europe is rugged and mountainous. Along the coast of Croatia, rocky slopes rise steeply from the water. Inland, forests and farms surround the peaks that spread eastward through Yugoslavia and into Romania and Bulgaria. In Bulgaria's Balkan Mountains, an area known as the Valley of the Roses produces more than two-thirds of the world's rose oil, an essential ingredient in most perfumes. Southeastern Europe's best farmland lies along the Danube River, which connects many of the region's towns to the ports of the Black Sea. In Greece, overgrazing by sheep and goats has stripped some of the land of trees and shrubs, but the warm climate allows farmers to grow olives, grapes, citrus fruit and wheat. Greece's sunny weather and scenic attractions bring tourists from all over the world. In Athens, home to one-third of Greece's population, rush-hour traffic roars past 2,000-year-old temples. On the Greek islands, clusters of white buildings cling to cliffs, and fishing boats drift across clear turquoise bays.

ALBANIA
Population: 3,414,000 * Capital: Tiranë

BOSNIA AND HERZEGOVINA
Population: 3,202,000 * Capital: Sarajevo

BULGARIA
Population: 8,775,000 * Capital: Sofia

CROATIA
Population: 4,666,000 * Capital: Zagreb

GREECE
Population: 10,648,000 * Capital: Athens

MACEDONIA
Population: 2,160,000 * Capital: Skopje

ROMANIA
Population: 23,198,000 * Capital: Bucharest

SLOVENIA
Population: 2,052,000 * Capital: Ljubljana

YUGOSLAVIA
Population: 11,102,000 * Capital: Belgrade

N
W
E
S

SCALE
MILES 0 25 50 75 100
0 50 100 150 KILOMETERS

AUSTRIA
HUNGARY
UKRAINE
MOLDOVA
SLOVENIA
LJUBLJANA
Rock Castle, Postojna
St. Stephen's Cathedral
ZAGREB
CROATIA
Drava
Rijeka
Pula
Chemicals
Beef cattle
Wild boars
Osijek
Soybeans
Potatoes
Novi Sad
Danube
Banja Luka
Bosna
Timber
BOSNIA AND HERZEGOVINA
DALMATIA
DINARIC ALPS
St. Donatus Church
Split
Tourism
Diocletian's Palace
SARAJEVO
Mostar
Iron ore
Folk dancer
White stork
BELGRADE
Parliament building
SERBIA
Farmer and barn
Textiles
Morava
YUGOSLAVIA
Niš
Gracanica Pristiaz monastery church
Timişoara
Arad
Textiles
Oradea
Oil
Iron and steel
Folk costume
Skiing
Cluj-Napoca
Timber
Chamois
ROMANIA
Mureş
Natural gas
Sibiu
TRANSYLVANIAN ALPS
Castle of Vlad Tepes
Timber
Braşov
Wine
CARPATHIAN MTS.
Moldav monastery
Siret
Prut
Iaşi
Horses
Corn
Galaţi
Ploieşti
Athenaeum
Pelican
Sturgeon
Constanţa
BUCHAREST
Iron and steel
Sheep
Craiova
Wheat
Wheat
Alexander Nevsky Cathedral
Danube
Roses
Wheat
Corn
Soccer
Tourism
Varna
BULGARIA

ITALY

Adriatic Sea

Podgorica Pristina SOFIA Shkodër Copper Corn Black kite Durrës TIRANË SKOPJE MACEDONIA Eastern Orthodox Church Vardar Mora Skiing Struma RHODOPE MTS. Mt. Musala 9,596 ft (2,925 m) Food processing Plovdiv Shipka Memorial Church Tobacco Wheat TURKEY Black Sea

ALBANIA Bitola Korçë Vlorë Inspecting carpets Iron and steel Goats Cotton Greek Orthodox monk Thessaloníki Alexandroúpolis Thásos Samothrace Lemnos LOCATION

Tourism Corfu Monastery, Meteora Mt. Olympus 9,570 ft (2,917 m) Sardines Volos GREECE NORTHERN SPORADES Aegean Sea Sailing Olives Lesbos TURKEY Bouzouki Wine Ruins of Delphi Euboea Skyros Khalkís Lignite Levkás Olives IONIAN ISLANDS Cephalonia Zákinthos Patras Parthenon ATHENS Piraeus Mackerel Chios Sámos Ándros Tinos Mykonos PELOPONNESE Tripolis Ruins of Olympia King Agamemnon's gold death mask Evzones guards CYCLADES Naxos Tourism Páros DODECANESE Thira Traditional church Windmill Rhodes Kithira Cruise ship Ionian Sea Sea of Crete Kárpathos Wine Canea Iráklion Crete Bull's head sculpture, Knossos Mediterranean Sea

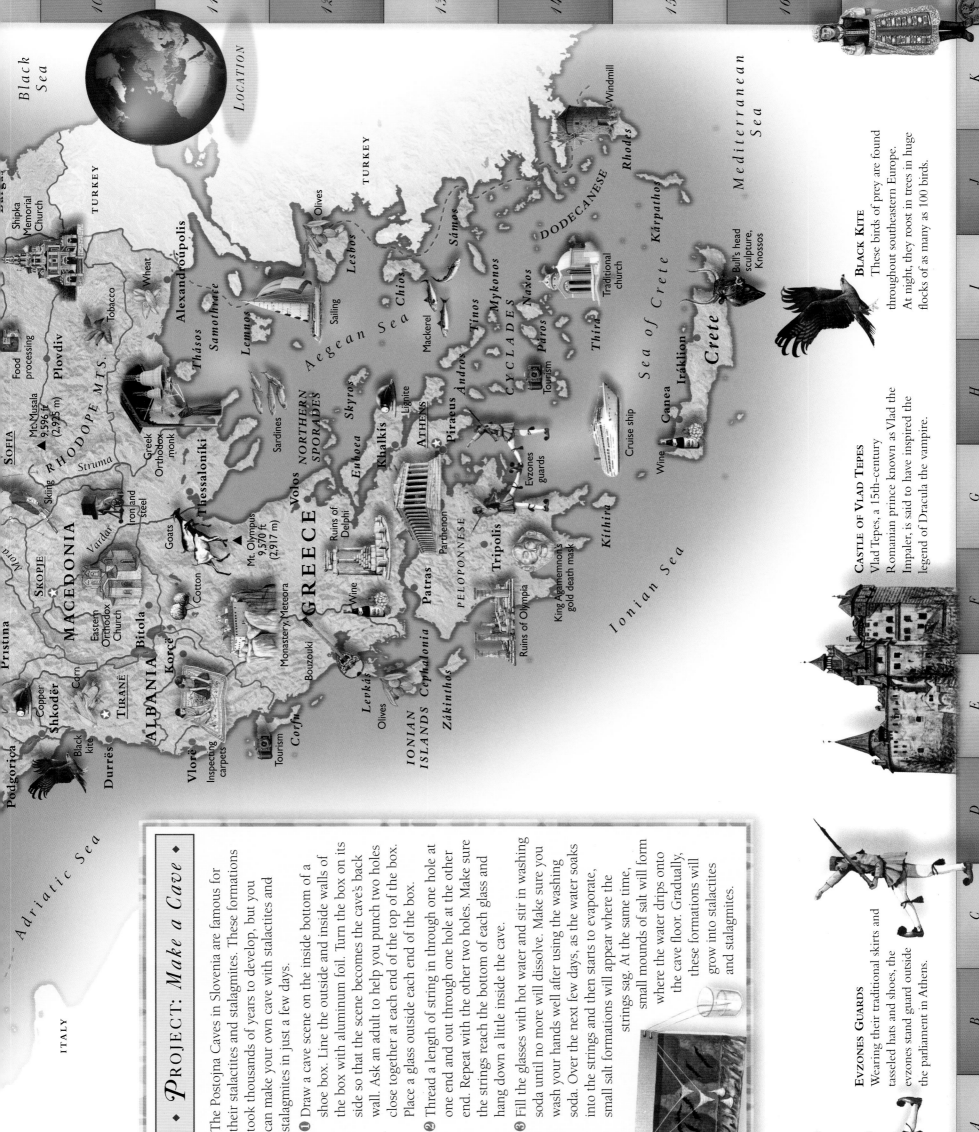

• PROJECT: *Make a Cave* •

The Postojna Caves in Slovenia are famous for their stalactites and stalagmites. These formations took thousands of years to develop, but you can make your own cave with stalactites and stalagmites in just a few days.

1. Draw a cave scene on the inside bottom of a shoe box. Line the outside and inside walls of the box with aluminum foil. Turn the box on its side so that the scene becomes the cave's back wall. Ask an adult to help you punch two holes close together at each end of the top of the box. Place a glass outside each end of the box.
2. Thread a length of string in through one hole at one end and out through one hole at the other end. Repeat with the other two holes. Make sure the strings reach the bottom of each glass and hang down a little inside the cave.
3. Fill the glasses with hot water and stir in washing soda until no more will dissolve. Make sure you wash your hands well after using the washing soda. Over the next few days, as the water soaks into the strings and then starts to evaporate, small salt formations will appear where the strings sag. At the same time, small mounds of salt will form where the water drips onto the cave floor. Gradually, these formations will grow into stalactites and stalagmites.

EVZONES GUARDS
Wearing their traditional skirts and tasseled hats and shoes, the evzones stand guard outside the parliament in Athens.

CASTLE OF VLAD TEPES
Vlad Tepes, a 15th-century Romanian prince known as Vlad the Impaler, is said to have inspired the legend of Dracula the vampire.

BLACK KITE
These birds of prey are found throughout southeastern Europe. At night, they roost in trees in huge flocks of as many as 100 birds.

A B C D E F G H I J K

10 11 12 13 14 15 16 17

Eastern Europe

In recent years, many political changes have occurred within this vast region. During 1990 and 1991, the republics of Latvia, Estonia, Lithuania, Belarus, Moldova and the Ukraine, all formerly part of the Soviet Union, became independent countries. In 1993, Czechoslovakia divided into two countries, the Czech Republic and Slovakia. Mountains line the borders of the Czech Republic and cover most of Slovakia, but elsewhere eastern Europe is generally flat. Wide grasslands cover central Hungary and most of the Ukraine. In Poland, rivers that rise in the southern mountains meander northward across a wide plain of rich farmland toward coastal swamps and sand dunes. The Baltic States of Lithuania, Latvia and Estonia are covered with meadows, marshes and more than 9,000 lakes. Around the Baltic Sea, winters can be bitterly cold, and icebreaker ships often have to clear a path between the region's ports. About two-thirds of eastern Europe's people live in cities, and many work in heavy industries such as mining, steelmaking and shipbuilding. These industries have created serious pollution problems. Acid rain has destroyed forests in Poland and the Czech Republic, and people are no longer allowed to swim in some polluted lakes in Hungary. In the Ukraine and Belarus, large areas of land can no longer be farmed because they were contaminated by radioactivity after an accident at the Chernobyl nuclear power plant near Kiev in 1986. Despite this, the Ukraine remains one of the largest producers of wheat in the world.

Look Again

- What kind of glassware is produced in the Czech Republic?
- Name a mineral that is mined in eastern Hungary.
- Ukrainians eat a soup called borscht. What is it made of?

BELARUS
Population: 10,437,000 * Capital: Minsk

CZECH REPUBLIC
Population: 10,433,000 * Capital: Prague

ESTONIA
Population: 1,625,000 * Capital: Tallinn

HUNGARY
Population: 10,319,000 * Capital: Budapest

LATVIA
Population: 2,763,000 * Capital: Riga

LITHUANIA
Population: 3,876,000 * Capital: Vilnius

MOLDOVA
Population: 4,490,000 * Capital: Chişinău

POLAND
Population: 38,792,000 * Capital: Warsaw

SLOVAKIA
Population: 5,432,000 * Capital: Bratislava

UKRAINE
Population: 51,868,000 * Capital: Kiev

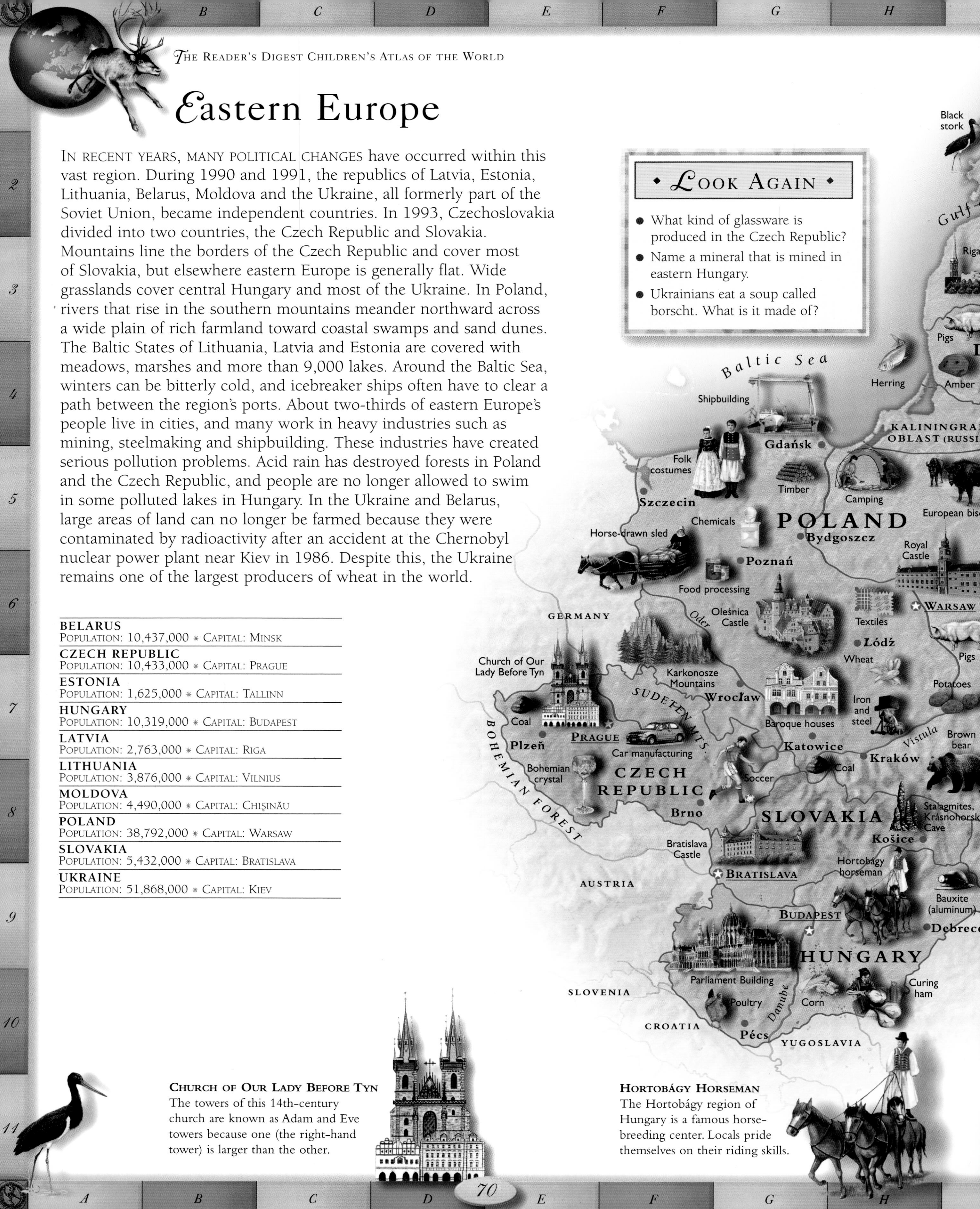

Black stork
Gulf of
Riga
Pigs
Amber
Herring
Baltic Sea
Shipbuilding
KALININGRAD OBLAST (RUSSIA)
Gdańsk
Folk costumes
Timber
Camping
European bison
Szczecin
Chemicals
POLAND
Bydgoszcz
Horse-drawn sled
Royal Castle
Poznań
Food processing
WARSAW
Oleśnica Castle
Oder
GERMANY
Textiles
Łódź
Pigs
Wheat
Church of Our Lady Before Tyn
Karkonosze Mountains
Potatoes
SUDETEN MTS.
Wrocław
Baroque houses
Iron and steel
Coal
PRAGUE
Vistula
Brown bear
Plzeň
Katowice
Car manufacturing
Kraków
BOHEMIAN FOREST
Bohemian crystal
CZECH REPUBLIC
Coal
Soccer
Brno
SLOVAKIA
Stalagmites, Krásnohorská Cave
Košice
Bratislava Castle
Hortobágy horseman
BRATISLAVA
AUSTRIA
Bauxite (aluminum)
BUDAPEST
Debrecen
HUNGARY
Parliament Building
Curing ham
SLOVENIA
Poultry
Corn
Danube
CROATIA
Pécs
YUGOSLAVIA

Church of Our Lady Before Tyn
The towers of this 14th-century church are known as Adam and Eve towers because one (the right-hand tower) is larger than the other.

Hortobágy Horseman
The Hortobágy region of Hungary is a famous horse-breeding center. Locals pride themselves on their riding skills.

◆ Project: *Painted Eggs* ◆

Symbols of rebirth and a new beginning, decorated eggs are an Easter tradition in eastern Europe. It's easy to paint an egg—the tricky part is preparing the shell. Take the raw eggs out of the refrigerator a few hours before you start. If they are too cold, they will be hard to blow.

1. Take an egg and gently prick the larger end of the shell with a pin. Chip the shell away until the hole is about 1/4-inch (0.5 cm) across.
2. Make a tiny hole in the smaller end. Put your fingers over both holes and gently shake the egg to break up the yolk. Hold the egg over a dish and blow through the small hole. The insides of the egg will slowly empty into the dish. Rinse the eggshell with water and let it dry.
3. Now you are ready to paint. Carefully thread a piece of stiff wire through the holes in the shell. Hold the egg by the wire and paint your design on it.
4. Lay the wire across a bowl so the painted egg can dry without being touched.

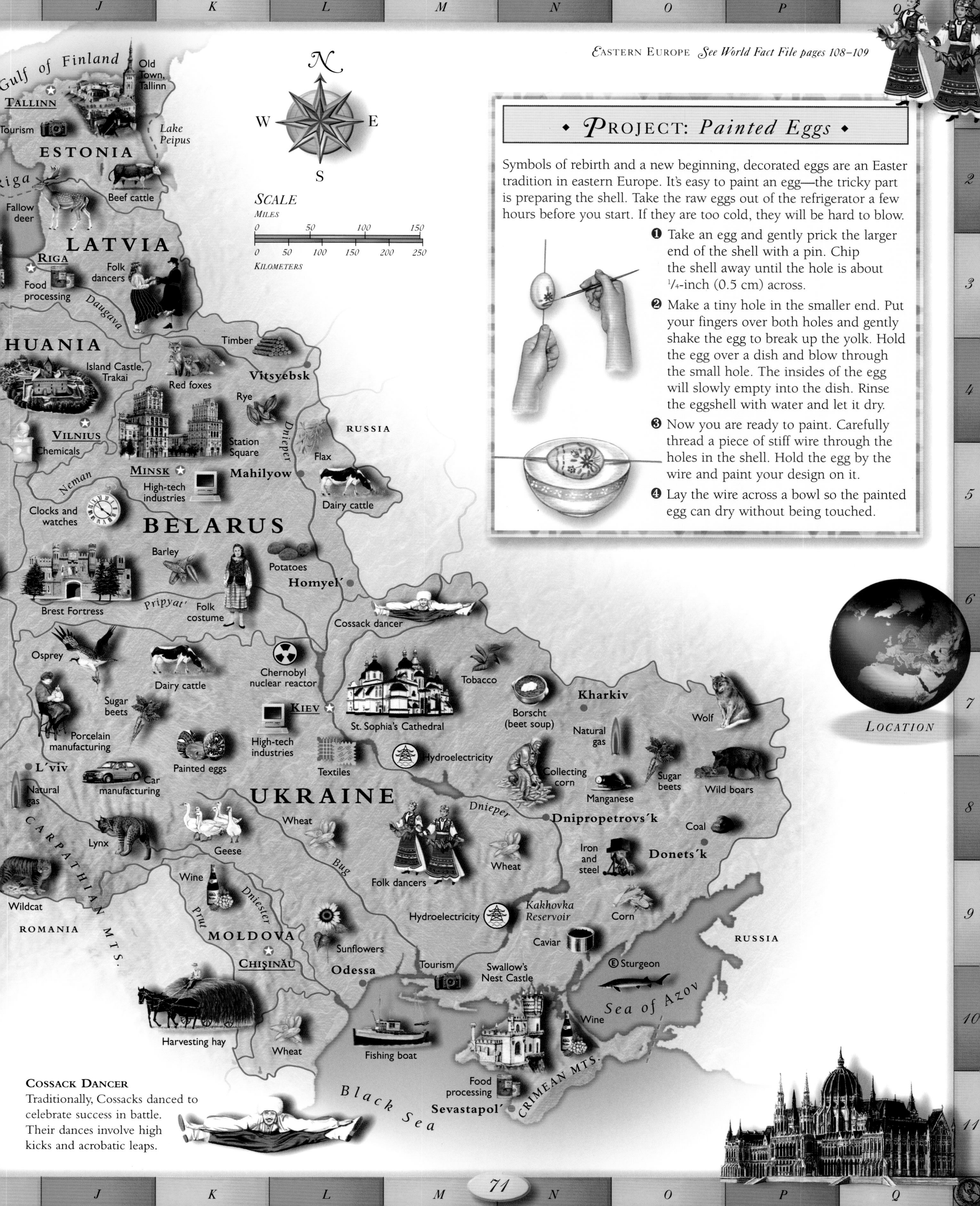
J
K
L
M
N
O
P
Q
2
3
4
5
6
7
8
9
10
11
Gulf of Finland
Old Town, Tallinn
Tallinn
Tourism
Lake Peipus
ESTONIA
Riga
Fallow deer
Beef cattle
N
W
E
S
SCALE
MILES
0
50
100
150
0
50
100
150
200
250
KILOMETERS
LATVIA
Riga
Folk dancers
Food processing
Daugava
HUANIA
Timber
Island Castle, Trakai
Red foxes
Vitsyebsk
Rye
Vilnius
Chemicals
Station Square
Dnieper
Russia
Flax
Minsk
Mahilyow
Neman
High-tech industries
Dairy cattle
Clocks and watches
BELARUS
Barley
Potatoes
Homyel'
Brest Fortress
Pripyat'
Folk costume
Cossack dancer
Osprey
Dairy cattle
Chernobyl nuclear reactor
Tobacco
Sugar beets
Kiev
St. Sophia's Cathedral
Borscht (beet soup)
Kharkiv
Wolf
Natural gas
Porcelain manufacturing
High-tech industries
Textiles
Hydroelectricity
Painted eggs
Collecting corn
Sugar beets
Wild boars
L'viv
Car manufacturing
Natural gas
Manganese
UKRAINE
Dnieper
Dnipropetrovs'k
Carpathian Mts.
Wheat
Coal
Lynx
Geese
Iron and steel
Donets'k
Wheat
Bug
Folk dancers
Wildcat
Wine
Dniester
Prut
Hydroelectricity
Kakhovka Reservoir
Corn
Romania
Moldova
Sunflowers
Caviar
Russia
Chişinău
Odessa
Tourism
Swallow's Nest Castle
Sturgeon
Sea of Azov
Harvesting hay
Wine
Wheat
Fishing boat
Food processing
Crimean Mts.
Black Sea
Sevastapol'
Location

Cossack Dancer
Traditionally, Cossacks danced to celebrate success in battle. Their dances involve high kicks and acrobatic leaps.

Northern Europe

The countries of northern Europe are known as the Nordic countries. They are sometimes called Scandinavia, but strictly speaking this name refers only to the wide peninsula occupied by Norway and Sweden. On the western side of this peninsula, fjords—spectacular, steep-sided bays formed by glaciers—and more than 150,000 islands create a maze of waterways. Inland, mountain peaks and high plateaus cover most of Norway. To the east, the marshy plains of Sweden and Finland are studded with thousands of lakes and cloaked in coniferous forests that are home to moose, brown bears and wolves. The northern half of this region has a cold climate, with long, dark, snowy winters. In the far south, the climate is more temperate and the land more fertile.

Only one-twentieth of Norway can be farmed, but more than three-quarters of Denmark is used for agriculture. There is little farmland on Iceland, a volcanic island which lies 600 miles (1,000 km) west of Norway. The island's barren interior consists mainly of volcanoes, hot springs and lava fields. Parts of Iceland are so like the surface of the moon that astronauts trained there for moon landings. Some upland areas are covered by huge sheets of ice. Vatnajökull, an ice sheet in the southeast, is larger than all the glaciers in Europe combined.

DENMARK
Population: 5,199,000 * Capital: Copenhagen

FINLAND
Population: 5,085,000 * Capital: Helsinki

ICELAND
Population: 266,000 * Capital: Reykjavík

NORWAY
Population: 4,331,000 * Capital: Oslo

SWEDEN
Population: 8,822,000 * Capital: Stockholm

Iceland
White-tailed eagle
Akureyri
Sheep
Svartifoss waterfall
Reykjavík
Vatnajökull
Strokkur geyser
Atlantic Ocean
Miles 0 50 100 150
0 100 200 Kilometers
North Cape
Cod
Hammerfest
Orca (killer whale)
North Cape monument
Barents Sea
Fishing boat
Tromsø
Reindeer
Sami (Lapp) man
Lake Inari
Sami (Lapp) man and woman
Salmon
Puffins
Lapland
Narvik
Iron ore
Lofoten Islands
Torne
Wolverine
Kemi
Elk (moose)
Herring
Bodø
Kebnekaise 6,965 ft (2,123 m)
Brown bear
Gällivare
Hydroelectricity
Timber
Arctic Circle pyramid
Rune stone
Finland
Russia
Sauna
Giant chess board
Luleå
Norwegian Sea
Skellefte
Hydroelectricity
Fjord pony
Timber
Ice hockey
Ume
Sweden
St. Lucia Day winter festival
Sailing
Oulu
Zinc
Oats
Oulujärvi
Cross-country skiing
Wolf
N E S W
Scale
Miles 0 25 50 75 100 125
0 50 100 150 200 Kilometers

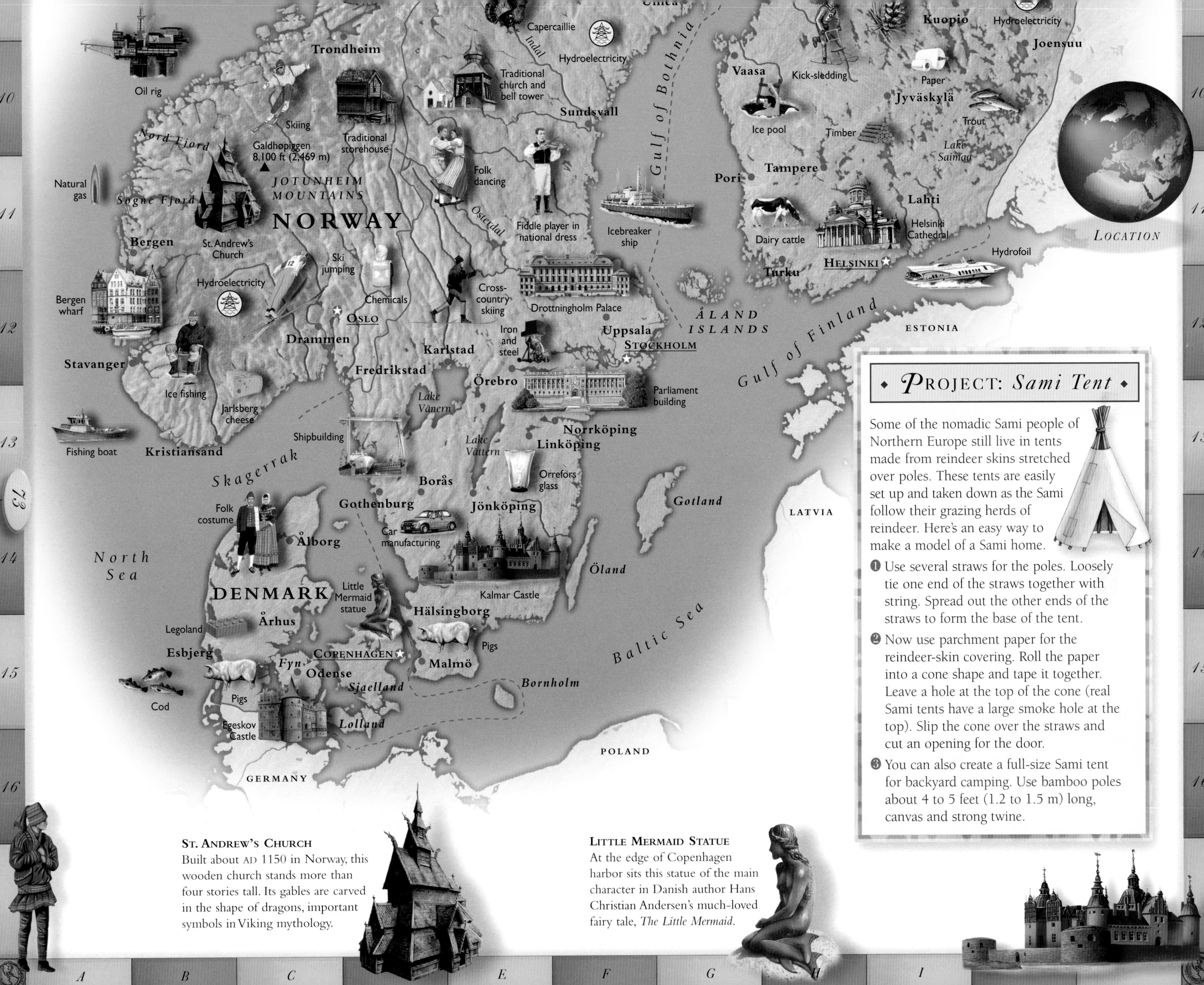
Trondheim
Oil rig
Capercaillie
Indal
Hydroelectricity
Traditional church and bell tower
Sundsvall
Gulf of Bothnia
Vaasa
Kick-sledding
Kuopio
Hydroelectricity
Joensuu
Paper
Jyväskylä
Trout
Lake Saimaa
Ice pool
Timber
Skiing
Nord Fjord
Galdhøpiggen 8,100 ft (2,469 m)
Traditional storehouse
Folk dancing
Natural gas
Sogne Fjord
JOTUNHEIM MOUNTAINS
NORWAY
Pori
Tampere
Lahti
Østerdal
Fiddle player in national dress
Icebreaker ship
Dairy cattle
Helsinki Cathedral
LOCATION
Bergen
St. Andrew's Church
Ski jumping
Hydrofoil
HELSINKI
Turku
Hydroelectricity
Bergen wharf
Chemicals
Cross-country skiing
Drottningholm Palace
OSLO
ÅLAND ISLANDS
Uppsala
ESTONIA
Drammen
Iron and steel
STOCKHOLM
Gulf of Finland
Stavanger
Karlstad
Fredrikstad
Örebro
Parliament building
Ice fishing
Lake Vänern
Jarlsberg cheese
Norrköping
Linköping
Shipbuilding
Lake Vättern
Fishing boat
Kristiansand
Skagerrak
Borås
Orrefors glass
Gotland
Folk costume
Gothenburg
Jönköping
LATVIA
Ålborg
Car manufacturing
North Sea
Öland
DENMARK
Little Mermaid statue
Kalmar Castle
Hälsingborg
Århus
Legoland
Baltic Sea
Esbjerg
COPENHAGEN
Pigs
Malmö
Fyn
Odense
Bornholm
Sjaelland
Pigs
Cod
Egeskov Castle
Lolland
POLAND
GERMANY
10
11
12
13
14
15
16
A
B
C
E
F
G
H
I

◆ PROJECT: *Sami Tent* ◆

Some of the nomadic Sami people of Northern Europe still live in tents made from reindeer skins stretched over poles. These tents are easily set up and taken down as the Sami follow their grazing herds of reindeer. Here's an easy way to make a model of a Sami home.

❶ Use several straws for the poles. Loosely tie one end of the straws together with string. Spread out the other ends of the straws to form the base of the tent.

❷ Now use parchment paper for the reindeer-skin covering. Roll the paper into a cone shape and tape it together. Leave a hole at the top of the cone (real Sami tents have a large smoke hole at the top). Slip the cone over the straws and cut an opening for the door.

❸ You can also create a full-size Sami tent for backyard camping. Use bamboo poles about 4 to 5 feet (1.2 to 1.5 m) long, canvas and strong twine.

ST. ANDREW'S CHURCH
Built about AD 1150 in Norway, this wooden church stands more than four stories tall. Its gables are carved in the shape of dragons, important symbols in Viking mythology.

LITTLE MERMAID STATUE
At the edge of Copenhagen harbor sits this statue of the main character in Danish author Hans Christian Andersen's much-loved fairy tale, *The Little Mermaid*.

Asia

The world's biggest continent, Asia stretches almost halfway around the globe and covers one-third of Earth's landmass. It has the world's tallest mountains, the world's largest lake and the world's lowest point on land. It was the birthplace of many great religions and important civilizations, and is now home to 60 percent of the people on Earth. Most Asians live in the east and south, where the climate is warm and wet and there are large areas of forest, fertile plains and hundreds of tropical islands. Deserts and barren mountain ranges dominate the southwest and center of the continent. To the north, the grasslands, or steppes, of central Asia give way to the immense coniferous forests of Russia. A belt of freezing tundra extends along the continent's north coast. Russia is the world's largest country by area, but China has the world's largest population.

Continent Facts

Regional land area: 17,139,445 sq. miles (44,391,162 sq. km), excluding European Russia
Regional population: 3,516,177,000, excluding European Russia
Independent countries: Afghanistan, Armenia, Azerbaijan, Bahrain, Bangladesh, Bhutan, Brunei, Cambodia, China, Cyprus, Georgia, India, Indonesia, Iran, Iraq, Israel, Japan, Jordan, Kazakstan, Kuwait, Kyrgyzstan, Laos, Lebanon, Malaysia, Maldives, Mongolia, Myanmar (Burma), Nepal, North Korea, Oman, Pakistan, Philippines, Qatar, Russia, Saudi Arabia, Singapore, South Korea, Sri Lanka, Syria, Taiwan, Tajikistan, Thailand, Turkey, Turkmenistan, United Arab Emirates, Uzbekistan, Vietnam, Yemen

Major Mountains and Rivers

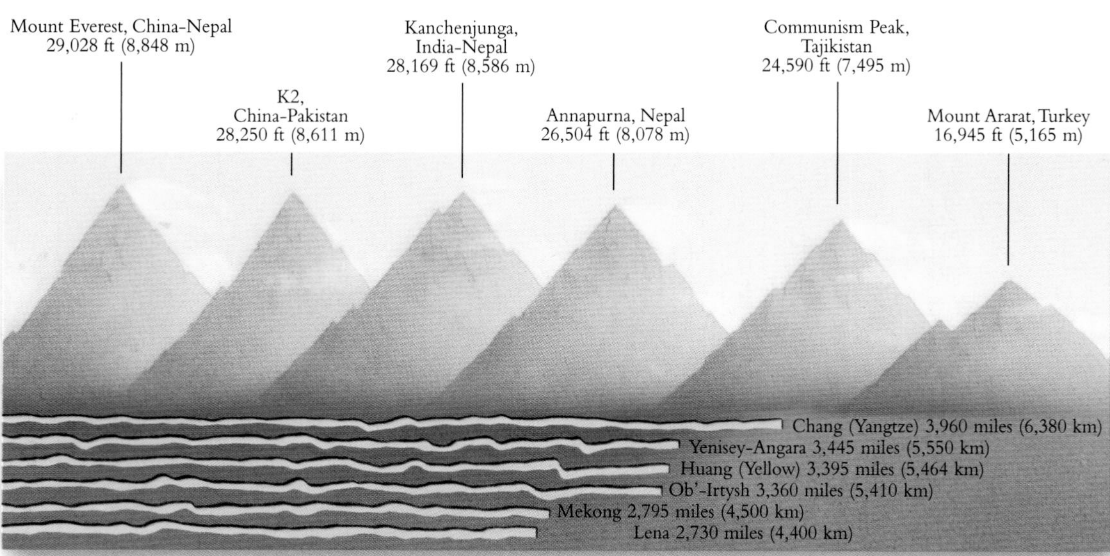
Mount Everest, China-Nepal
29,028 ft (8,848 m)
K2,
China-Pakistan
28,250 ft (8,611 m)
Kanchenjunga,
India-Nepal
28,169 ft (8,586 m)
Annapurna, Nepal
26,504 ft (8,078 m)
Communism Peak,
Tajikistan
24,590 ft (7,495 m)
Mount Ararat, Turkey
16,945 ft (5,165 m)
Chang (Yangtze) 3,960 miles (6,380 km)
Yenisey-Angara 3,445 miles (5,550 km)
Huang (Yellow) 3,395 miles (5,464 km)
Ob'-Irtysh 3,360 miles (5,410 km)
Mekong 2,795 miles (4,500 km)
Lena 2,730 miles (4,400 km)

World Records

WORLD'S HIGHEST MOUNTAIN
Mount Everest, China-Nepal, 29,028 ft (8,848 m)

WORLD'S LOWEST POINT ON LAND
Dead Sea, Israel-Jordan, 1,300 ft (400 m) below sea level

WORLD'S LARGEST LAKE BY AREA
Caspian Sea, western Asia, 143,550 sq. miles (371,800 sq. km)

WORLD'S OLDEST, DEEPEST AND LARGEST (BY VOLUME) LAKE
Lake Baikal, Russia, 25 million years old; 5,371 ft (1,637 m) deep; 5,500 cubic miles (23,000 cubic km) of water

WORLD'S LARGEST COUNTRY BY AREA
Russia, 6,592,812 sq. miles (17,075,383 sq. km)

WORLD'S LARGEST COUNTRY BY POPULATION
China, population 1,203,097,000

WORLD'S LARGEST CITY BY POPULATION
Tokyo, Japan, population 26,800,000

WORLD'S LONGEST WALL
Great Wall of China, 2,150 miles (3,460 km)

WORLD'S LONGEST RAILWAY LINE
Trans-Siberian, Russia, 5,777 miles (9,297 km)

Continent Records

LONGEST RIVER
Chang (Yangtze), 3,960 miles (6,380 km)

Political Map

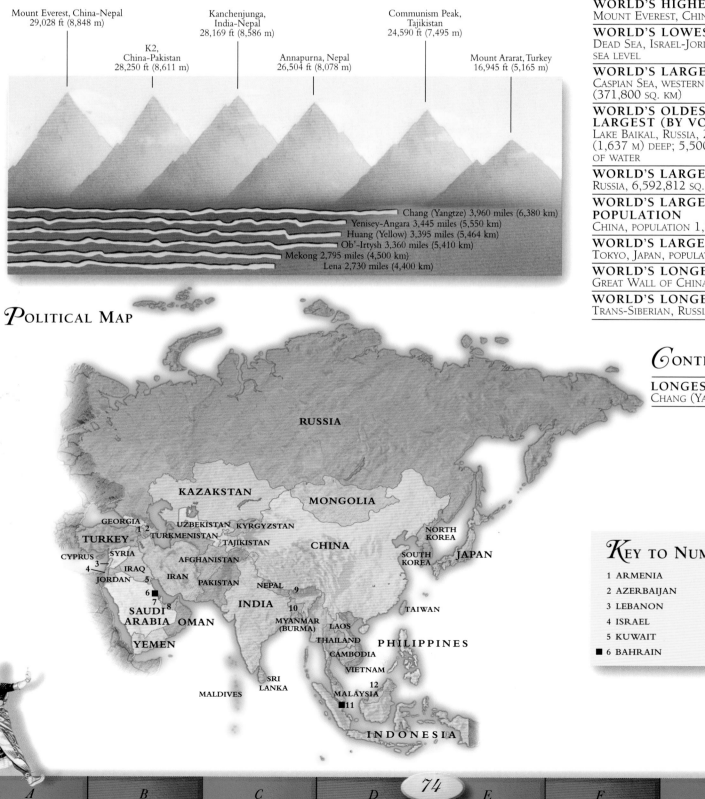

RUSSIA
KAZAKSTAN
MONGOLIA
GEORGIA
1
2
UZBEKISTAN
KYRGYZSTAN
TURKEY
TURKMENISTAN
TAJIKISTAN
CHINA
NORTH KOREA
SOUTH KOREA
JAPAN
CYPRUS
SYRIA
3
4
IRAQ
AFGHANISTAN
JORDAN
5
IRAN
PAKISTAN
NEPAL
9
6
7
8
SAUDI ARABIA
OMAN
INDIA
10
TAIWAN
MYANMAR (BURMA)
LAOS
YEMEN
THAILAND
PHILIPPINES
CAMBODIA
VIETNAM
SRI LANKA
MALDIVES
12
MALAYSIA
11
INDONESIA

Key to Numbered Countries

1 ARMENIA
2 AZERBAIJAN
3 LEBANON
4 ISRAEL
5 KUWAIT
■ 6 BAHRAIN
7 QATAR
8 UNITED ARAB EMIRATES
9 BHUTAN
10 BANGLADESH
■ 11 SINGAPORE
12 BRUNEI

AFRICA

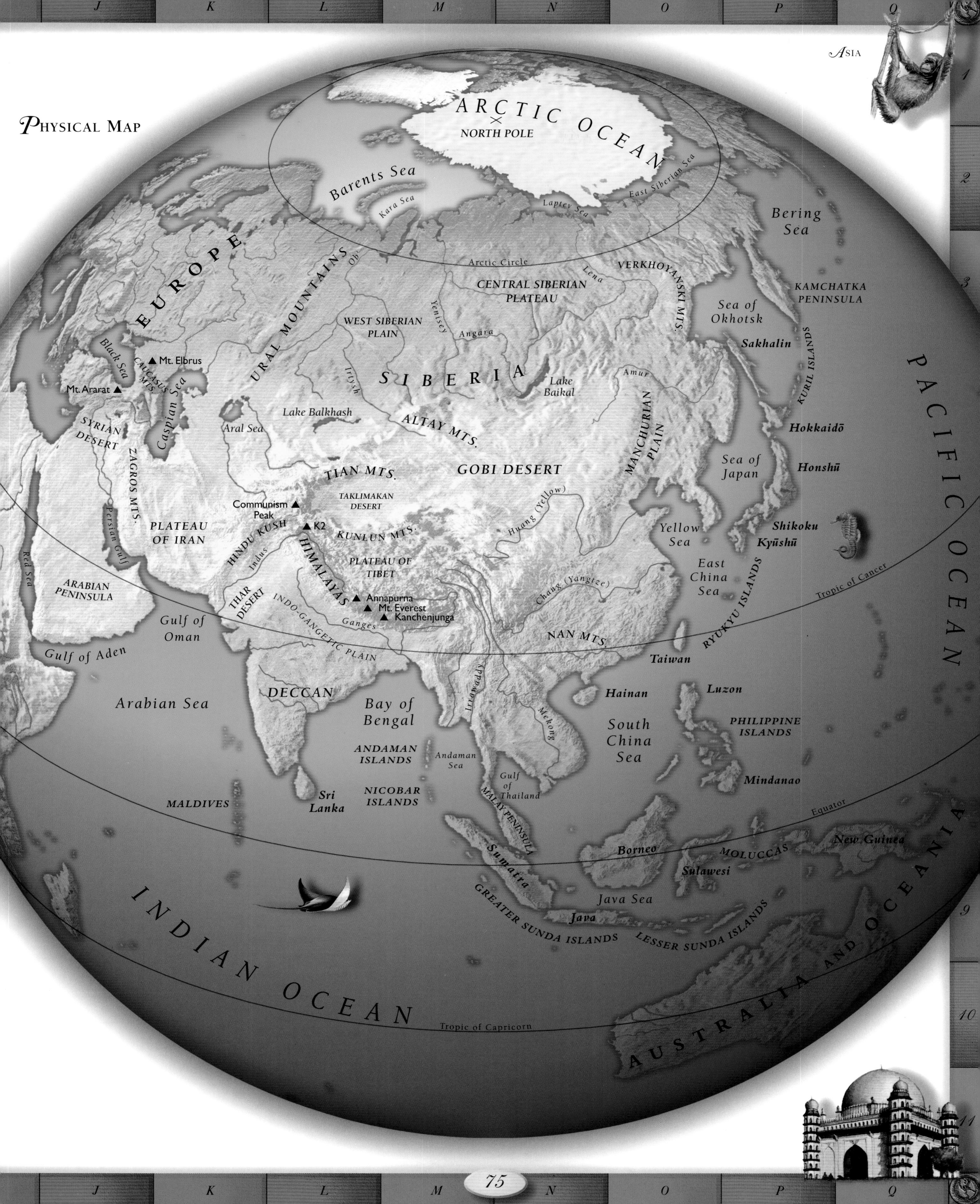

J
K
L
M
N
O
P
Q
Physical Map
ARCTIC OCEAN
NORTH POLE
Barents Sea
Kara Sea
Laptev Sea
East Siberian Sea
Bering Sea
Arctic Circle
EUROPE
URAL MOUNTAINS
Ob
Lena
VERKHOYANSKI MTS.
CENTRAL SIBERIAN PLATEAU
KAMCHATKA PENINSULA
Sea of Okhotsk
Yenisey
WEST SIBERIAN PLAIN
Angara
Sakhalin
KURIL ISLANDS
Black Sea
Mt. Elbrus
CAUCASUS MTS.
Mt. Ararat
Caspian Sea
SIBERIA
Irtysh
Lake Baikal
Amur
PACIFIC OCEAN
Aral Sea
Lake Balkhash
ALTAY MTS.
MANCHURIAN PLAIN
Hokkaidō
SYRIAN DESERT
ZAGROS MTS.
TIAN MTS.
GOBI DESERT
Sea of Japan
Honshū
Communism Peak
TAKLIMAKAN DESERT
Huang (Yellow)
Persian Gulf
PLATEAU OF IRAN
HINDU KUSH
K2
KUNLUN MTS.
Yellow Sea
Shikoku
Kyūshū
Red Sea
Indus
HIMALAYAS
PLATEAU OF TIBET
East China Sea
RYUKYU ISLANDS
ARABIAN PENINSULA
THAR DESERT
INDO-GANGETIC PLAIN
Annapurna
Mt. Everest
Kanchenjunga
Chang (Yangtze)
Tropic of Cancer
Gulf of Oman
Ganges
NAN MTS.
Gulf of Aden
Taiwan
DECCAN
Irrawaddy
Hainan
Luzon
Arabian Sea
Bay of Bengal
Mekong
South China Sea
PHILIPPINE ISLANDS
ANDAMAN ISLANDS
Andaman Sea
Gulf of Thailand
Mindanao
MALDIVES
Sri Lanka
NICOBAR ISLANDS
MALAY PENINSULA
Equator
Borneo
MOLUCCAS
New Guinea
Sumatra
Sulawesi
Java Sea
GREATER SUNDA ISLANDS
Java
LESSER SUNDA ISLANDS
INDIAN OCEAN
AUSTRALIA AND OCEANIA
Tropic of Capricorn
1
2
3
9
10
11

Russia

Russia is the largest country in the world. It covers two-thirds of Asia and one-third of Europe, and is so wide that it has eleven time zones. When the citizens of St. Petersburg are getting ready for bed, the miners and reindeer herders who live in the remote far east are already starting their next day's work. Most of Russia has a cold climate, with mild to cool summers and cold to freezing winters. In the far north, where most of the land is tundra, winter temperatures can drop to –94°F (–70°C). South of the tundra, a wide band of coniferous woodland stretches almost all the way across the country. The Ural Mountains divide Russia into two regions. West of the Urals is European Russia, which has only one-quarter of the land, but four-fifths of the population, the largest industries and the most fertile farmland. East of the Urals, in Asia, is Siberia, a vast wilderness region that is bigger than the United States and western Europe combined. In the southern part of this region near Mongolia lies Lake Baikal, the world's deepest lake, which holds one-fifth of the world's fresh water. Siberia is also rich in minerals, such as coal and oil. The Chukchi Peninsula in eastern Siberia is the most easterly point in Asia. It lies only 50 miles (82 km) from North America. Before 1991, Russia was part of an even larger country—the Soviet Union—which also included 14 present-day countries in eastern Europe and central Eurasia.

RUSSIA
Population: 149,909,000 * Capital: Moscow

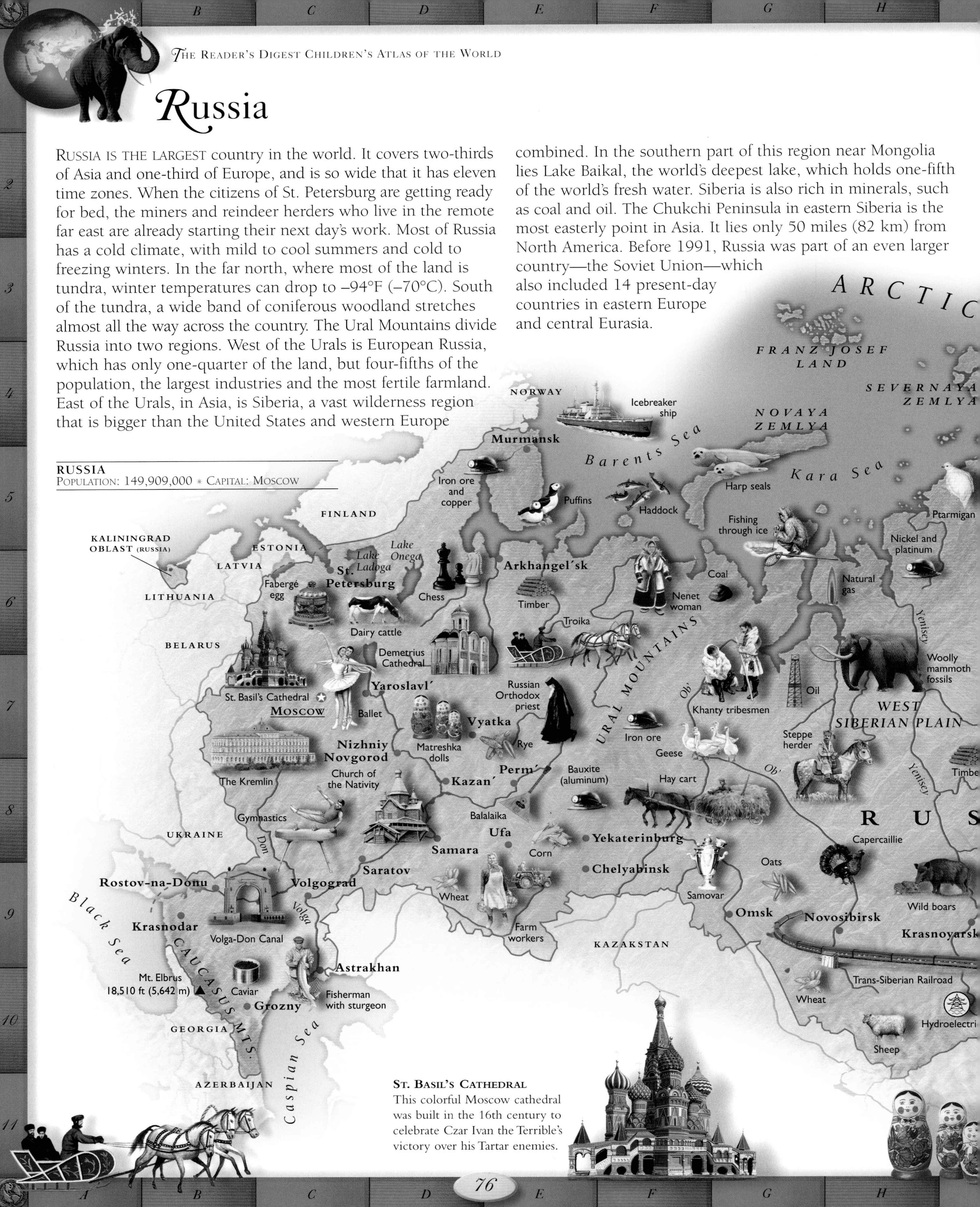
B C D E F G H
2 3 4 5 6 7 8 9 10 11
ARCTIC
FRANZ JOSEF LAND
SEVERNAYA ZEMLYA
NOVAYA ZEMLYA
NORWAY
Icebreaker ship
Murmansk
Barents Sea
Kara Sea
Harp seals
Iron ore and copper
Puffins
Haddock
Ptarmigan
FINLAND
Fishing through ice
KALININGRAD OBLAST (RUSSIA)
ESTONIA
LATVIA
Lake Ladoga
Lake Onega
St. Petersburg
Fabergé egg
Chess
Arkhangel'sk
Timber
Coal
Natural gas
Nickel and platinum
LITHUANIA
Nenet woman
Dairy cattle
Troika
BELARUS
Demetrius Cathedral
URAL MOUNTAINS
Yenisey
Woolly mammoth fossils
Ob'
Oil
St. Basil's Cathedral
MOSCOW
Ballet
Yaroslavl'
Russian Orthodox priest
Khanty tribesmen
WEST SIBERIAN PLAIN
Vyatka
Iron ore
Steppe herder
Matreshka dolls
Rye
Geese
Nizhniy Novgorod
Timber
Church of the Nativity
Perm'
Bauxite (aluminum)
Hay cart
The Kremlin
Kazan'
Gymnastics
Balalaika
RUS
UKRAINE
Don
Ufa
Yekaterinburg
Capercaillie
Samara
Corn
Saratov
Chelyabinsk
Oats
Rostov-na-Donu
Volgograd
Wheat
Samovar
Volga
Wild boars
Black Sea
Krasnodar
Omsk
Novosibirsk
Krasnoyarsk
Volga-Don Canal
Farm workers
KAZAKSTAN
CAUCASUS MTS.
Astrakhan
Trans-Siberian Railroad
Mt. Elbrus 18,510 ft (5,642 m)
Caviar
Grozny
Fisherman with sturgeon
Wheat
Hydroelectri
GEORGIA
Caspian Sea
Sheep
AZERBAIJAN

St. Basil's Cathedral
This colorful Moscow cathedral was built in the 16th century to celebrate Czar Ivan the Terrible's victory over his Tartar enemies.

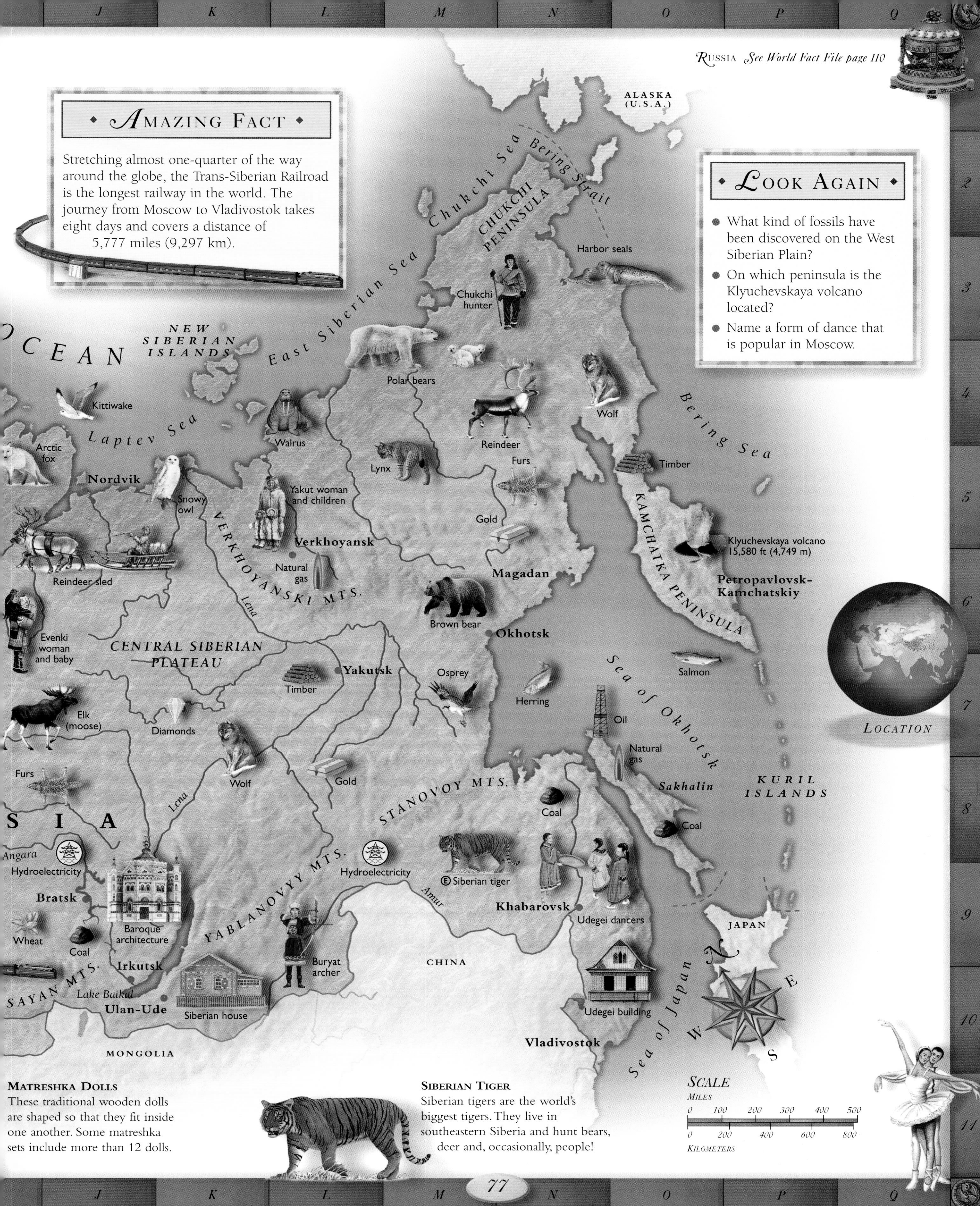
J K L M N O P Q
2
3
4
5
6
7
8
9
10
11
ALASKA (U.S.A.)
Chukchi Sea
Bering Strait
CHUKCHI PENINSULA
Harbor seals
Chukchi hunter
East Siberian Sea
NEW SIBERIAN ISLANDS
OCEAN
Polar bears
Wolf
Kittiwake
Laptev Sea
Walrus
Reindeer
Bering Sea
Arctic fox
Lynx
Furs
Timber
Nordvik
Snowy owl
Yakut woman and children
Gold
KAMCHATKA PENINSULA
Klyuchevskaya volcano 15,580 ft (4,749 m)
VERKHOYANSKI MTS.
Verkhoyansk
Natural gas
Reindeer sled
Magadan
Petropavlovsk-Kamchatskiy
Lena
Brown bear
Okhotsk
Evenki woman and baby
CENTRAL SIBERIAN PLATEAU
Yakutsk
Timber
Osprey
Salmon
Sea of Okhotsk
Herring
Elk (moose)
Diamonds
Oil
LOCATION
Natural gas
Furs
Wolf
Gold
STANOVOY MTS.
Sakhalin
KURIL ISLANDS
Coal
Coal
SIA
Lena
Angara
Hydroelectricity
Hydroelectricity
YABLANOVYY MTS.
Amur
Siberian tiger
Bratsk
Baroque architecture
Khabarovsk
Udegei dancers
JAPAN
Wheat
Coal
Irkutsk
Buryat archer
CHINA
SAYAN MTS.
Lake Baikal
Ulan-Ude
Siberian house
Udegei building
Sea of Japan
N
E
W
S
Vladivostok
MONGOLIA
SCALE
MILES
0 100 200 300 400 500
0 200 400 600 800
KILOMETERS

◆ AMAZING FACT ◆

Stretching almost one-quarter of the way around the globe, the Trans-Siberian Railroad is the longest railway in the world. The journey from Moscow to Vladivostok takes eight days and covers a distance of 5,777 miles (9,297 km).

◆ LOOK AGAIN ◆

- What kind of fossils have been discovered on the West Siberian Plain?
- On which peninsula is the Klyuchevskaya volcano located?
- Name a form of dance that is popular in Moscow.

MATRESHKA DOLLS
These traditional wooden dolls are shaped so that they fit inside one another. Some matreshka sets include more than 12 dolls.

SIBERIAN TIGER
Siberian tigers are the world's biggest tigers. They live in southeastern Siberia and hunt bears, deer and, occasionally, people!

Central Eurasia

EURASIA IS THE LANDMASS that contains Europe and Asia. Central Eurasia extends from the southeastern corner of Europe into the dry heart of Asia. Turkey forms a bridge between the two continents, which are separated by the narrow Bosporus strait. Turkey's interior is hilly and barren, but its fertile coastal regions produce tea, tobacco, and the world's largest crops of hazelnuts and raisins. South of Turkey lies the island of Cyprus, which is home to people of Turkish and Greek descent. Beyond Turkey's eastern border, the countries of Georgia, Armenia and Azerbaijan are flanked by the massive Caucasus mountains. These countries are rich in minerals: at one time, Baku, the capital of Azerbaijan, supplied half of the world's oil. Across the Caspian Sea, deserts cover most of Turkmenistan, Uzbekistan and Kazakstan. Ancient trade routes between China and Europe passed through these lands, linking cities such as Samarquand and Tashkent. In the north, the desert merges with the Kirgiz Steppe, a vast grassland; in the southeast, the Tian Mountains cover most of Kyrgyzstan and Tajikistan. Many of central Eurasia's rivers are diverted to irrigate crops. This has lowered the levels of some lakes. The Aral Sea, once the world's fourth-largest lake, has shrunk to half its former size, stranding fishing villages and boats more than 20 miles (30 km) from the shore.

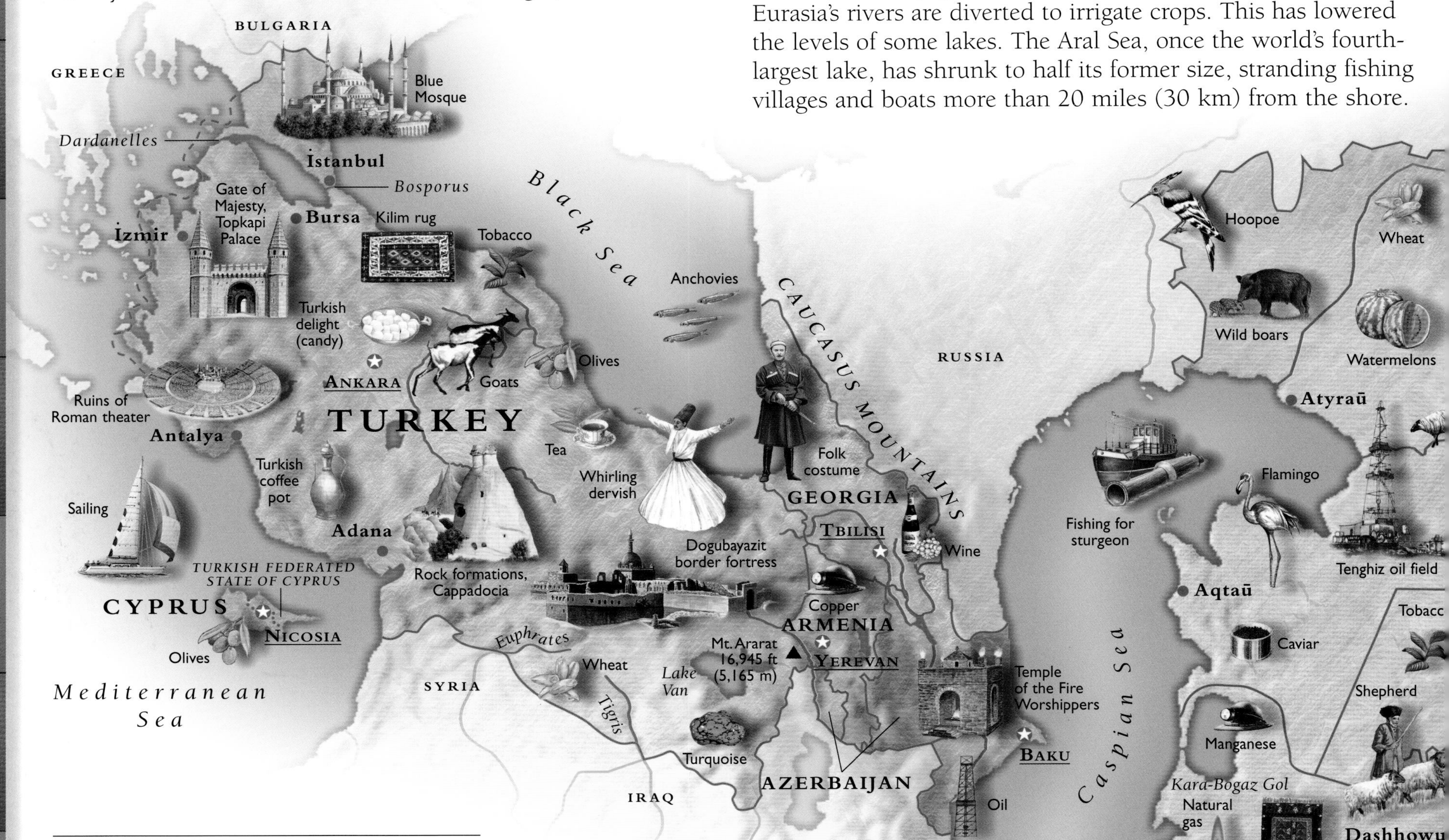

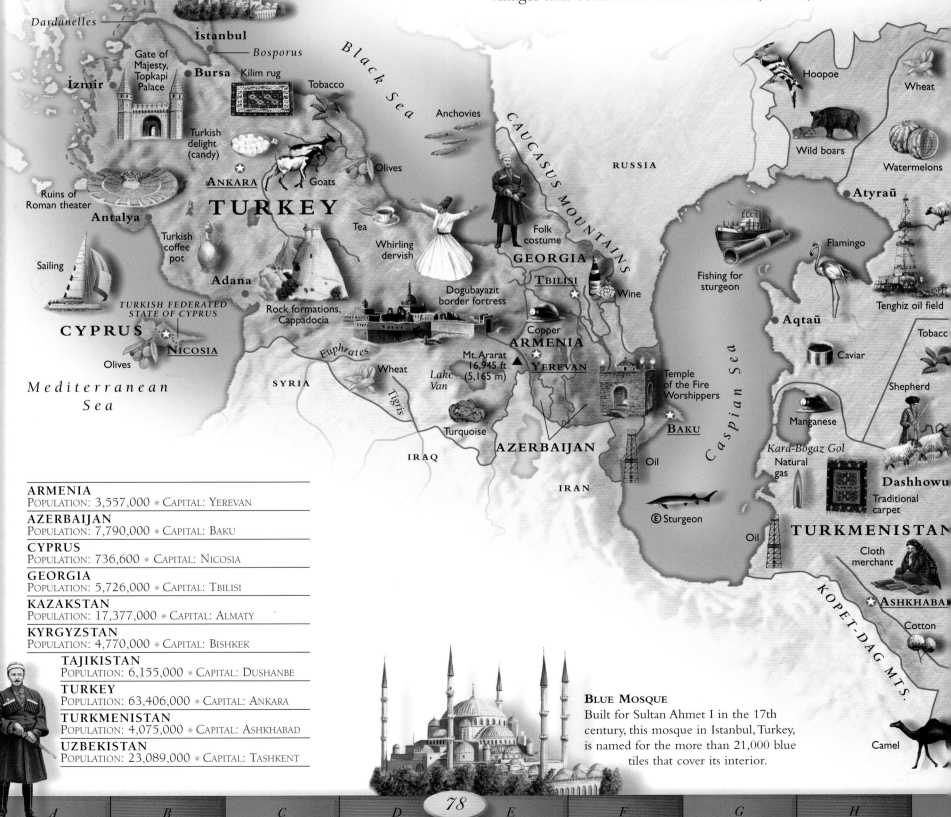

ARMENIA
POPULATION: 3,557,000 * CAPITAL: YEREVAN

AZERBAIJAN
POPULATION: 7,790,000 * CAPITAL: BAKU

CYPRUS
POPULATION: 736,600 * CAPITAL: NICOSIA

GEORGIA
POPULATION: 5,726,000 * CAPITAL: TBILISI

KAZAKSTAN
POPULATION: 17,377,000 * CAPITAL: ALMATY

KYRGYZSTAN
POPULATION: 4,770,000 * CAPITAL: BISHKEK

TAJIKISTAN
POPULATION: 6,155,000 * CAPITAL: DUSHANBE

TURKEY
POPULATION: 63,406,000 * CAPITAL: ANKARA

TURKMENISTAN
POPULATION: 4,075,000 * CAPITAL: ASHKHABAD

UZBEKISTAN
POPULATION: 23,089,000 * CAPITAL: TASHKENT

BLUE MOSQUE
Built for Sultan Ahmet I in the 17th century, this mosque in Istanbul, Turkey, is named for the more than 21,000 blue tiles that cover its interior.

 See World Fact File page 110

◆ Project: *Kilim Weaving* ◆

A kilim is a flat, woven rug traditionally made in Turkey. To make a simple kilim, you will first need to make a loom.

❶ Cut notches into the corners of a rectangular piece of cardboard. Tie a length of string to the left-hand notch and then wrap it around the cardboard, moving from left to right and leaving about ½ inch (1 cm) between strings. Tie the string off on the right-hand notch.

❷ Now weave by threading wool under and then over the strings. If you begin the first row weaving under, begin the second row weaving over, and so on. When you add a new piece of wool, tie it to the old piece. As you weave, push the rows tightly together.

❸ When the loom is full, turn it over so that it is face down and cut the two middle strings. Tie them together at the top and bottom edges of the weaving. Repeat with the rest of the strings.

❹ When all the strings have been cut and tied, remove the weaving from the loom. Trim the ends of the tied-off strings to make a fringe for your weaving.

Step 1 Step 2 Step 3

◆ Amazing Fact ◆

In Cappadocia in central Turkey, an eerie landscape of strange rock formations has been created by wind and water erosion. Early Christians made homes and churches inside caves cut into the rock. Some of these caves are still in use today.

Qostanay
Petropavl
Iron ore
Marmot
Ishim
Aktyubinsk
KIRGIZ STEPPE
Wheat
Irtysh
Sarsembek herder
Pavlodar
Bearded vulture
Yurts (nomad tents)
Barley
RUSSIA
Stranded fishing boats, Aral Sea
Textiles
Gold
Manganese
Copper
Qaraghandy
Semey
Oskemen
Hydroelectricity
KAZAKSTAN
Aral Sea
Coal
Baking bread in traditional oven
Lake Zaysan
Baykonur Cosmodrome
Lake Balkhash
White-throated kingfisher
Cotton
Saiga antelope
Spoonbill
Nukus
Folk costume
Syr Darya
Cotton
Kirgiz farmer
Street vendor selling apples
UZBEKISTAN
Chemicals
CHINA
Registan Square
Shymkent
ALMATY
Snow leopard
BISHKEK
TIAN MTS.
Bukhara
TASHKENT
KYRGYZSTAN
Samarqand
Namangan
Rice
Sheep
Cotton
Osh
Yak
Amu Dar'ya
DUSHANBE
Cotton
Karakumskiy Canal
Communism Peak 24,590 ft (7,495 m)
Musician playing longhorn
Sheep
TAJIKISTAN
Hissar fortress
AFGHANISTAN
LOCATION
N
W
E
S
SCALE
MILES
0 100 200 300
0 100 200 300 400 500
KILOMETERS

Snow Leopard
Living high in the mountains, the snow leopard needs strong paws for rock climbing and long, thick fur to keep warm.

Baykonur Cosmodrome
Formerly a Soviet Union space center, Baykonur is now leased from Kazakstan by Russia for use as its main space shuttle and rocket launching site.

The Middle East

The Middle East is a land of ancient cities and vast deserts. It is home to some of the world's oldest civilizations and was the birthplace of three of the most widespread religions—Islam, Christianity and Judaism. Though there are narrow strips of fertile land on the densely populated Mediterranean coast, along the Tigris and Euphrates rivers in Iraq, and in the highlands of northern Iran and Yemen, most of this region is hot, dry and barren. Deserts extend southward from Syria, Jordan and Israel, covering most of the Arabian Peninsula. Parts of this peninsula receive no rain for up to 10 years! Deserts also cover two-thirds of Iran. The enormous Dasht-e Kavīr salt desert in eastern Iran has almost no vegetation. Among its few inhabitants are gazelles that survive on tiny amounts of salty water. Over the centuries, the people of the Middle East have made skillful use of their limited water supplies. For thousands of years, the Tigris and Euphrates rivers have been used to water crops. Today, desalination plants on the shores of the Persian Gulf turn sea water into fresh water. The Gulf region holds half the world's reserves of oil and gas, and this has made some countries very wealthy. On average, people in the United Arab Emirates earn twice as much as people in the United States. In contrast, Yemen, which has little oil, is one of the poorest countries in the world.

BAHRAIN
Population: 575,900 * Capital: Manama

IRAN
Population: 64,625,000 * Capital: Tehran

IRAQ
Population: 20,644,000 * Capital: Baghdad

ISRAEL
Population: 5,433,000 * Capital: Jerusalem

JORDAN
Population: 4,101,000 * Capital: Amman

KUWAIT
Population: 1,817,000 * Capital: Kuwait

LEBANON
Population: 3,696,000 * Capital: Beirut

OMAN
Population: 2,125,000 * Capital: Muscat

QATAR
Population: 533,900 * Capital: Doha

SAUDI ARABIA
Population: 18,730,000 * Capital: Riyadh

SYRIA
Population: 15,452,000 * Capital: Damascus

UNITED ARAB EMIRATES
Population: 2,925,000 * Capital: Abu Dhabi

YEMEN
Population: 14,728,000 * Capital: Sanaa

Amazing Fact

The Rub' al-Khali Desert, or Empty Quarter, in southern Saudi Arabia is the biggest sand desert in the world. It is as large as France and has no towns or villages. Its only inhabitants are nomadic Bedouin people.

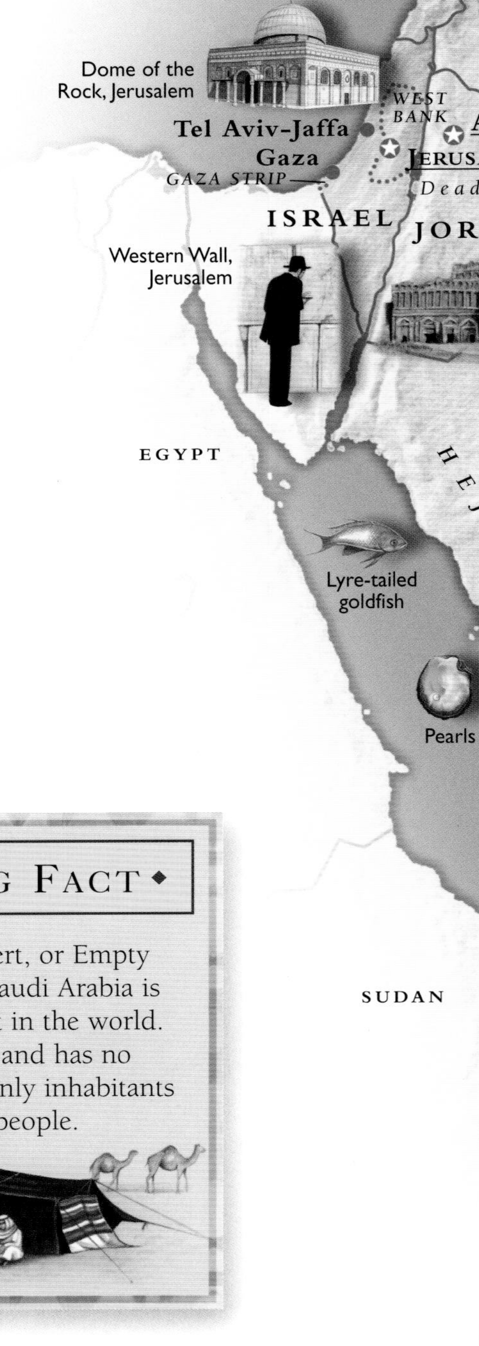
TURKEY
Aleppo
Krak des Chevaliers
Euphrates
Barle
CYPRUS
Latakia
Mediterranean Sea
LEBANON
SYRIA
SYRIAN DESERT
BEIRUT
DAMASCUS
Dome of the Rock, Jerusalem
Date palm
WEST BANK
Tel Aviv-Jaffa
AMMAN
Gaza
GAZA STRIP
JERUSALEM
Dead Sea
Scorpion
ISRAEL
JORDAN
Western Wall, Jerusalem
Royal Tombs, Petra
Lappet-faced vulture
AN NAFŪD DESERT
EGYPT
HEJAZ
Rock tombs, Madain Salah
Lyre-tailed goldfish
Date palm
Leopard gecko
Pearls
Medina
Red Sea
Veiled woman
Jeddah
Mecca
SUDAN
Barracuda
Dhow
ERITREA
Hudayd

Dome of the Rock
This Muslim temple in Jerusalem backs onto the Western Wall, a site sacred to Jews. Inside the temple is a rock that some say marks the center of the world.

Veiled Woman
Traditionally, Muslim women must keep their face and hair hidden from strangers. Many wear a long black cloak and a veil or eye-mask.

ARMENIA
AZERBAIJAN
Araks
Tobacco
Tabrīz
Caspian Sea
Barley
Rasht
Ⓔ Sturgeon
Caviar
TURKMENISTAN
Oil
Mosul
Cotton
TEHRAN
Mashhad
Friday Mosque, Samarra
Musician
Winnowing grain
DASHT-E KAVĪR (GREAT SALT DESERT)
Turquoise
ZAGROS MOUNTAINS
Royal Mosque
PLATEAU OF IRAN
BAGHDAD
Kurdish woman
Ⓔ Leopard
Tigris
Eṣfahān
Making rugs
DASHT-E LŪT
Q
AFGHANISTAN
Oil
Bedouin shepherd
IRAN
Kermān
Ziggurat (temple), Ur
Basra
Ābādān
Stone carvings, Persepolis
Oil
KUWAIT
Shīrāz
KUWAIT
Wine
PAKISTAN
Walled city of Bam
Shepherd in traditional felt coat
Camel race
Oil
Persian Gulf
Oil
Caracal
Strait of Hormuz
Eurasian griffon
BAHRAIN
Goats
Ad Dammām
MANAMA
QATAR
Water tower
Oil
Dubai
OMAN
DOHA
Gulf of Oman
Natural gas
ABU DHABI
MUSCAT
RIYADH
Zubara fort
UNITED ARAB EMIRATES
Date palm
Oil tanker
Arabian horse
Ṣūr
LOCATION
SAUDI ARABIA
(UNDEFINED BORDER)
Bedouin with falcon
Al Khuwair Mosque
Solar-powered telephone
Coconuts
Sardines
Great Mosque
N
Bedouin tent
W
E
Collecting frankincense
RUB' AL-KHALI DESERT (EMPTY QUARTER)
Arabian Sea
S
(UNDEFINED BORDER)
OMAN
Baboon
Ⓔ Arabian oryx
SCALE
MILES
0 50 100 150 200 250
0 100 200 300 400
KILOMETERS
Sand cat
Woman at well
Tiger shark
Salālah
Wheat
Apricots
YEMEN
SANAA
Al Hajrah
Chewing qat leaves
Ta'izz
Coffee
Oil
Gulf of Aden
Socotra (Yemen)
Aden
BOUTI

LOOK AGAIN

- Which animals are raced in Saudi Arabia?
- Name a gemstone that is found in northeastern Iran.
- What kind of leaf do Yemeni people enjoy chewing?

ARABIAN ORYX
This antelope may have been the origin of the myth of the unicorn. Viewed from the side, the oryx looks as though it has only one horn.

Southern Asia

SOUTHERN ASIA, OR THE Indian Subcontinent as it is also known, is separated from the rest of Asia by a series of massive mountain ranges. In the northeast, the mighty Himalayas, the highest mountains on Earth, tower over northern India and the two small kingdoms of Nepal and Bhutan. In the northwest, the dry, rugged Hindu Kush—the world's second-highest mountain range—spreads across central Afghanistan. South of these mountains, the land drops steeply to a wide, fertile plain that stretches from Pakistan to Bangladesh and covers most of northern India. Southern India consists of a large triangular plateau (the Deccan) fringed by narrow coastal plains. Just off the southeast coast lies the island of Sri Lanka.

Southern Asia has large areas of fertile land, valuable mineral reserves and expanding industries, but these resources barely support the region's huge population, and many people are very poor. One-fifth of the world's people live in southern Asia, and the population is growing rapidly. In India alone, almost 20 million babies are born each year. Four-fifths of southern Asians live in small villages, and most grow their own food. In India, Sri Lanka and Bangladesh, farmers rely on summer rains to water their crops. These rains are brought by winds known as monsoons. If too little rain falls, the crops fail. If too much rain falls, the crops, as well as buildings and people, can be washed away by devastating floods.

AFGHANISTAN
POPULATION: 21,252,000 * CAPITAL: KABUL

BANGLADESH
POPULATION: 128,095,000 * CAPITAL: DHAKA

BHUTAN
POPULATION: 1,781,000 * CAPITAL: THIMPHU

INDIA
POPULATION: 936,546,000 * CAPITAL: NEW DELHI

MALDIVES
POPULATION: 261,300 * CAPITAL: MALE

NEPAL
POPULATION: 21,561,000 * CAPITAL: KATHMANDU

PAKISTAN
POPULATION: 131,542,000 * CAPITAL: ISLAMABAD

SRI LANKA
POPULATION: 18,343,000 * CAPITAL: COLOMBO

◆ PROJECT: *Taj Mahal Tile* ◆

The Taj Mahal in India was built by Emperor Shah Jahan in memory of his beloved wife Mumtaz. Construction began in 1631, and it took 20,000 workers about 20 years to complete the building. It is covered in tiles of dazzling white marble. Each tile is carved with floral designs and inlaid with semi-precious stones. You can make your own paper Taj Mahal tile.

1. Draw floral patterns on a square of white paper.
2. Color the patterns and then use glitter, sequins, buttons or colored plastic wrap to "fashion" the jewels in the Taj Mahal's intricate designs.

UZBEKISTAN
TAJIKISTAN
TURKMENISTAN
IRAN
Nomad
Cashmere goat
KARAKORAM RANGE
K2 28,250 ft (8,611 m)
Herāt
Veiled Herāti woman
KABUL
HINDU KUSH
Shoemaker
Wheat
Natural gas
Peshawar
ISLAMABAD
Srinagar
Snow leopard
AFGHANISTAN
Qandahār
Golden Temple
CHINA
Yak
Imperial Mosque
Lahore
Amritsar
HIMALAYAS
Trekking
Bactrian camel
Tomb of Bibi Jaiwindi
Hydroelectricity
Sikhs
High-tech industries
Mt. Everest 29,028 ft (8,848 m)
Folk dancer
Annapurna 26,504 ft (8,078 m)
PAKISTAN
Indus
Thar desert woman
THAR DESERT
Delhi
NEW DELHI
NEPAL
KATHMANDU
THIMPHU
BHUTAN
Red panda
Textiles
Wheat
Hyderabad
Jaipur
Taj Mahal
Agra
Bodhnath Stupa (shrine)
Darjeeling
Tea
Mangoes
Lucknow
Brahmaputra
Shrimp
Karachi
Jodhpur
Palace of the Winds
Kanpur
Varanasi
Rice
Dancer
MYANMAR (BURMA)

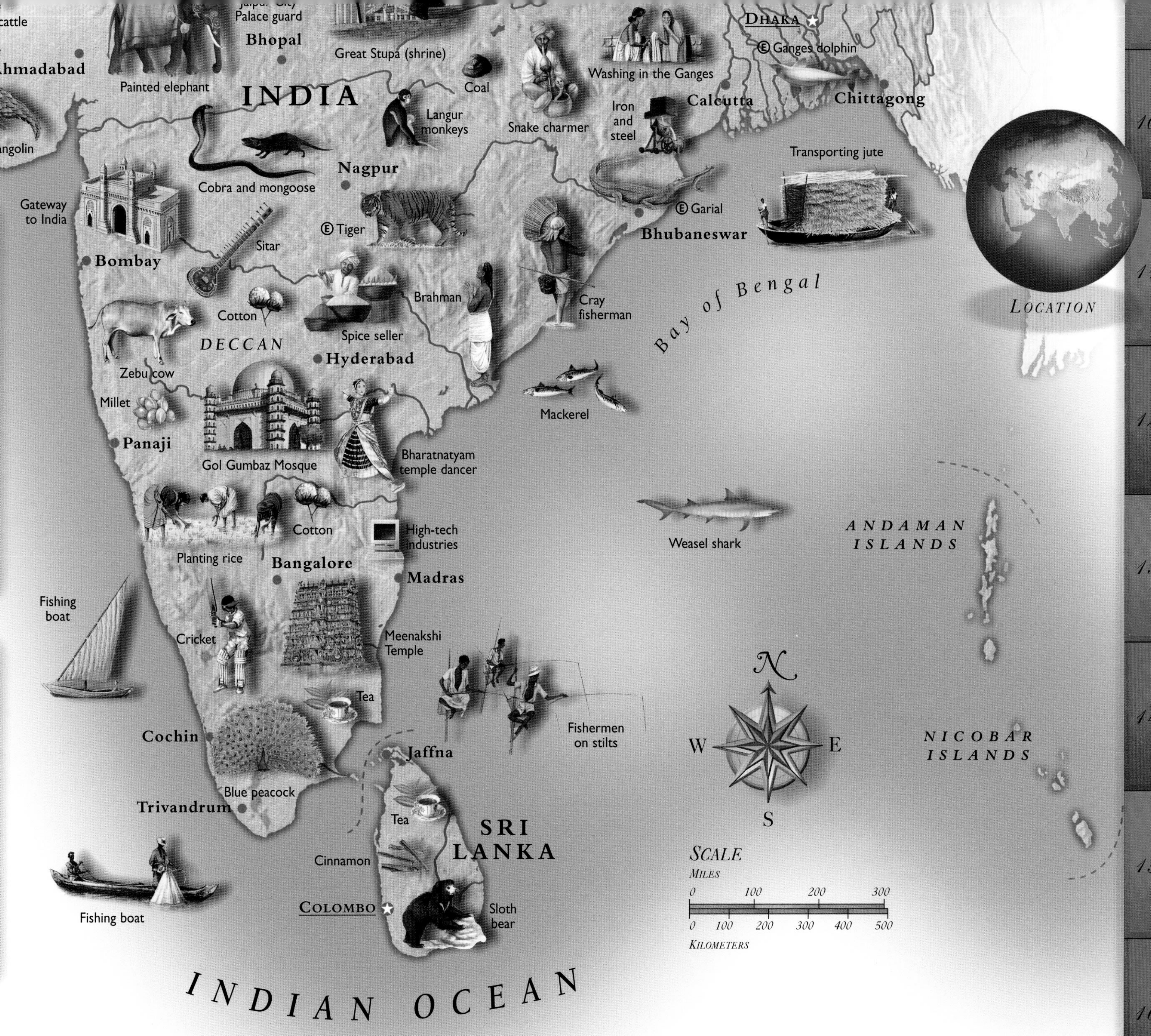

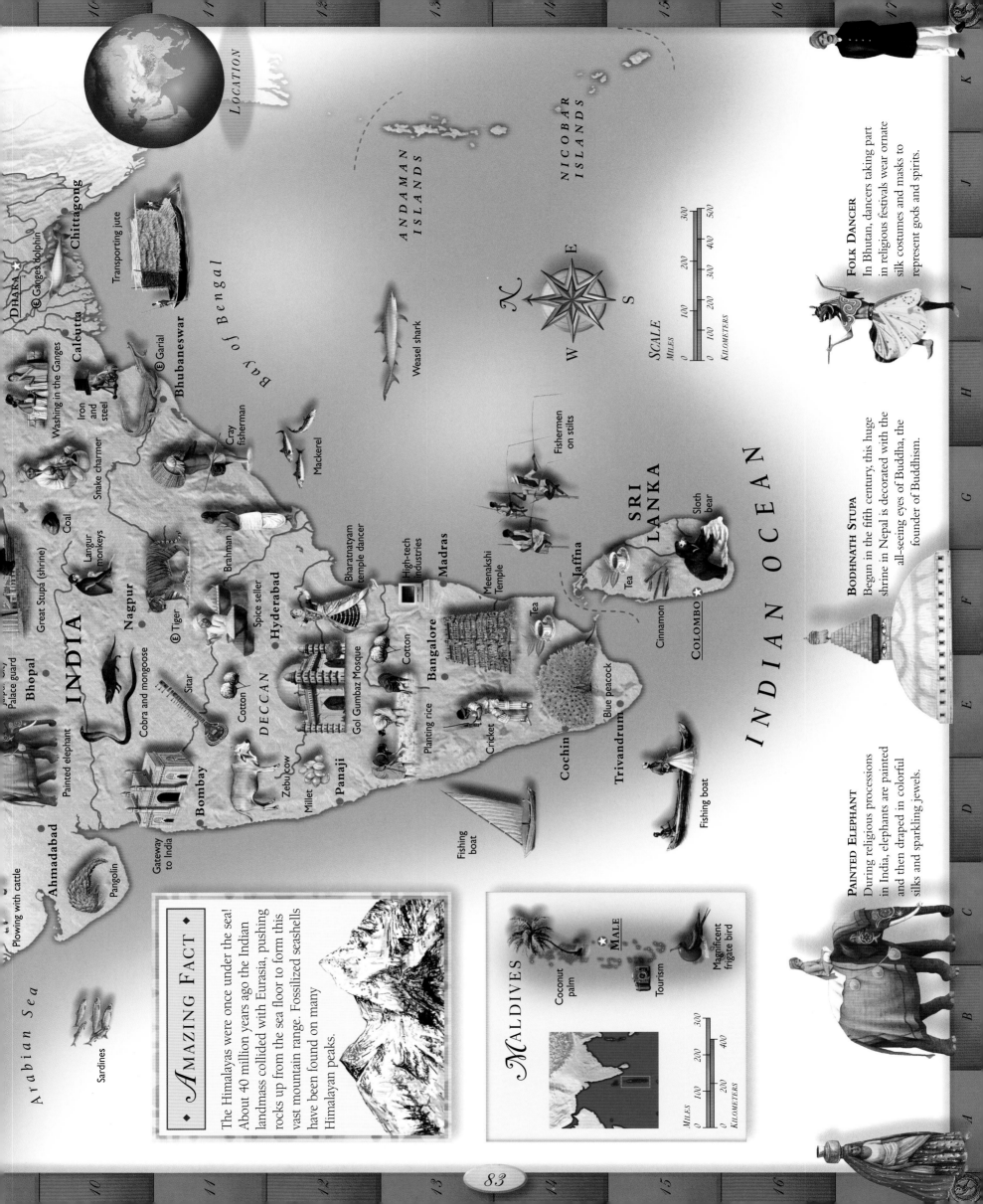

Arabian Sea
Sardines
Plowing with cattle
Ahmadabad
Pangolin
Painted elephant
Palace guard
Bhopal
INDIA
Great Stupa (shrine)
Coal
Langur monkeys
Snake charmer
Washing in the Ganges
Iron and steel
Calcutta
DHAKA
Ⓔ Ganges dolphin
Chittagong
Transporting jute
Cobra and mongoose
Nagpur
Gateway to India
Bombay
Sitar
Ⓔ Tiger
Ⓔ Garial
Bhubaneswar
Brahman
Cray fisherman
Bay of Bengal
LOCATION
Cotton
DECCAN
Spice seller
Hyderabad
Zebu cow
Millet
Panaji
Gol Gumbaz Mosque
Bharatnatyam temple dancer
Mackerel
Planting rice
Cotton
High-tech industries
Bangalore
Madras
Weasel shark
ANDAMAN ISLANDS
Fishing boat
Cricket
Meenakshi Temple
Tea
Fishermen on stilts
Cochin
Jaffna
Blue peacock
Trivandrum
Tea
SRI LANKA
Cinnamon
COLOMBO
Sloth bear
Fishing boat
N
W
E
S
NICOBAR ISLANDS
SCALE
MILES 0 100 200 300
0 100 200 300 400 500 KILOMETERS
INDIAN OCEAN

AMAZING FACT

The Himalayas were once under the sea! About 40 million years ago the Indian landmass collided with Eurasia, pushing rocks up from the sea floor to form this vast mountain range. Fossilized seashells have been found on many Himalayan peaks.

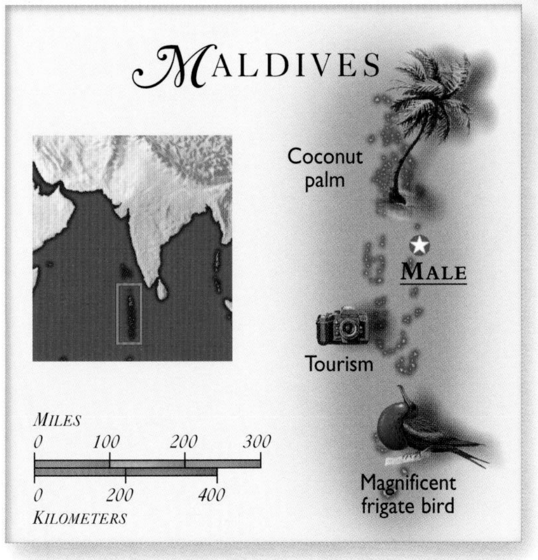

MALDIVES

Coconut palm
MALE
Tourism
Magnificent frigate bird
MILES 0 100 200 300
0 200 400 KILOMETERS

PAINTED ELEPHANT
During religious processions in India, elephants are painted and then draped in colorful silks and sparkling jewels.

BODHNATH STUPA
Begun in the fifth century, this huge shrine in Nepal is decorated with the all-seeing eyes of Buddha, the founder of Buddhism.

FOLK DANCER
In Bhutan, dancers taking part in religious festivals wear ornate silk costumes and masks to represent gods and spirits.

A B C D E F G H I J K

Southeast Asia

SOUTHEAST ASIA IS MADE UP OF a mainland peninsula and more than 20,000 islands. Throughout this hot, humid region, rugged mountains rise steeply from wide river basins and coastal plains once covered in dense rain forests. Most people live in the river valleys or near the coast, where they fish and grow food. Rice is the most important crop. On the plains, it is planted in wide, flooded fields called rice paddies. On hills and mountains, rice is grown on terraces—narrow strips of land that climb the slopes like giant staircases. In recent years, many Southeast Asians have moved from the countryside to cities in search of work. Bangkok, Ho Chi Minh City, Manila and Jakarta are now among the most crowded and fastest-growing cities in the world. Southeast Asia has many natural resources. Malaysia is the world's leading exporter of tin, Myanmar supplies most of the world's rubies, and oil has made Brunei one of the world's richest countries. Timber is the most widespread resource, and the region's rain forests supply more than three-quarters of the world's tropical hardwoods. But so many trees are being chopped down that several countries could soon run out of forest, and many animal and plant species are now endangered. Some countries restrict logging activities and have turned large areas of forest into magnificent national parks.

BRUNEI
POPULATION: 292,300 * CAPITAL: BANDAR SERI BEGAWAN

CAMBODIA
POPULATION: 10,561,000 * CAPITAL: PHNOM PENH

INDONESIA
POPULATION: 203,584,000 * CAPITAL: JAKARTA

LAOS
POPULATION: 4,837,000 * CAPITAL: VIENTIANE

MALAYSIA
POPULATION: 19,724,000 * CAPITAL: KUALA LUMPUR

MYANMAR (BURMA)
POPULATION: 45,104,000 * CAPITAL: YANGON (RANGOON)

PHILIPPINES
POPULATION: 73,266,000 * CAPITAL: MANILA

SINGAPORE
POPULATION: 2,890,000 * CAPITAL: SINGAPORE

THAILAND
POPULATION: 60,271,000 * CAPITAL: BANGKOK

VIETNAM
POPULATION: 74,393,000 * CAPITAL: HANOI

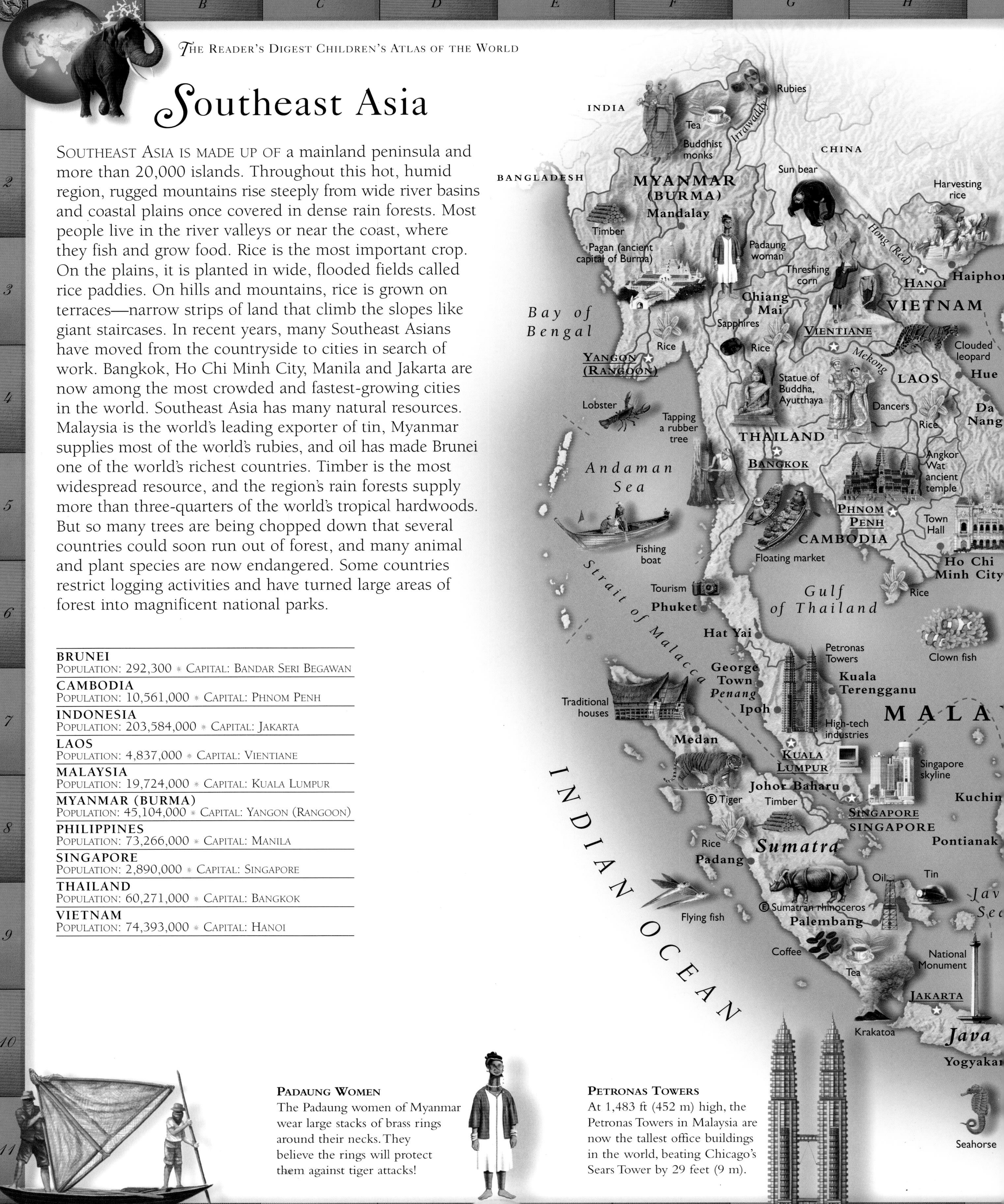
INDIA
BANGLADESH
CHINA
MYANMAR (BURMA)
Mandalay
Rubies
Tea
Buddhist monks
Irrawaddy
Sun bear
Harvesting rice
Timber
Pagan (ancient capital of Burma)
Padaung woman
Threshing corn
Hong (Red)
HANOI
Haiphong
VIETNAM
Chiang Mai
Sapphires
VIENTIANE
Bay of Bengal
Rice
YANGON (RANGOON)
Clouded leopard
Mekong
LAOS
Hue
Statue of Buddha, Ayutthaya
Dancers
Da Nang
Lobster
Tapping a rubber tree
THAILAND
BANGKOK
Angkor Wat ancient temple
Andaman Sea
PHNOM PENH
Town Hall
CAMBODIA
Fishing boat
Floating market
Ho Chi Minh City
Strait of Malacca
Tourism
Phuket
Gulf of Thailand
Hat Yai
Clown fish
Petronas Towers
George Town
Penang
Kuala Terengganu
Traditional houses
Ipoh
MALA
High-tech industries
Medan
KUALA LUMPUR
Singapore skyline
INDIAN OCEAN
Johor Baharu
Tiger
Timber
SINGAPORE
SINGAPORE
Kuching
Pontianak
Padang
Sumatra
Oil
Tin
Flying fish
Sumatran rhinoceros
Palembang
Coffee
Tea
National Monument
JAKARTA
Krakatoa
Java
Yogyakarta
Seahorse

PADAUNG WOMEN
The Padaung women of Myanmar wear large stacks of brass rings around their necks. They believe the rings will protect them against tiger attacks!

PETRONAS TOWERS
At 1,483 ft (452 m) high, the Petronas Towers in Malaysia are now the tallest office buildings in the world, beating Chicago's Sears Tower by 29 feet (9 m).

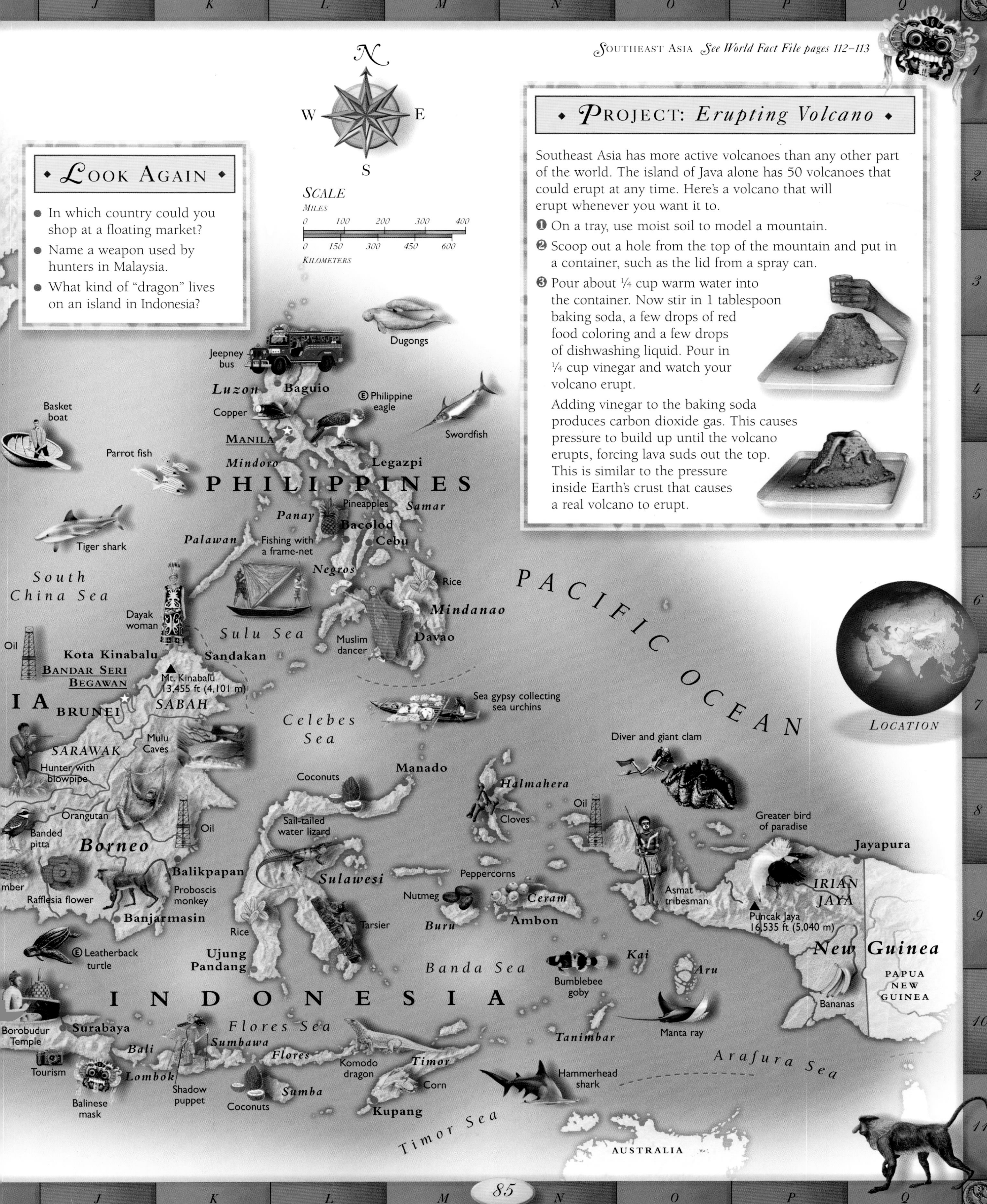
N
W
E
S
SCALE
MILES
0 100 200 300 400
0 150 300 450 600
KILOMETERS
Dugongs
Jeepney bus
Luzon
Baguio
Ⓔ Philippine eagle
Copper
Basket boat
MANILA
Swordfish
Parrot fish
Mindoro
Legazpi
PHILIPPINES
Pineapples
Samar
Panay
Bacolod
Cebu
Tiger shark
Palawan
Fishing with a frame-net
Negros
Rice
South China Sea
PACIFIC OCEAN
Mindanao
Dayak woman
Sulu Sea
Davao
Muslim dancer
Oil
Kota Kinabalu
Sandakan
BANDAR SERI BEGAWAN
Mt. Kinabalu 13,455 ft (4,101 m)
IA
BRUNEI
SABAH
Sea gypsy collecting sea urchins
LOCATION
Celebes Sea
Mulu Caves
SARAWAK
Diver and giant clam
Hunter with blowpipe
Manado
Coconuts
Halmahera
Oil
Orangutan
Sail-tailed water lizard
Cloves
Greater bird of paradise
Banded pitta
Oil
Borneo
Jayapura
Balikpapan
Peppercorns
Sulawesi
mber
Rafflesia flower
Proboscis monkey
Nutmeg
Ceram
Asmat tribesman
IRIAN JAYA
Banjarmasin
Ambon
Buru
Tarsier
Puncak Jaya 16,535 ft (5,040 m)
Rice
Ⓔ Leatherback turtle
Ujung Pandang
Kai
New Guinea
Banda Sea
Aru
PAPUA NEW GUINEA
Bumblebee goby
INDONESIA
Bananas
Borobudur Temple
Surabaya
Flores Sea
Bali
Sumbawa
Tanimbar
Manta ray
Flores
Timor
Arafura Sea
Tourism
Lombok
Komodo dragon
Hammerhead shark
Corn
Shadow puppet
Sumba
Balinese mask
Coconuts
Kupang
Timor Sea
AUSTRALIA
J K L M N O P Q
1 2 3 4 5 6 7 8 9 10 11

LOOK AGAIN

- In which country could you shop at a floating market?
- Name a weapon used by hunters in Malaysia.
- What kind of "dragon" lives on an island in Indonesia?

PROJECT: *Erupting Volcano*

Southeast Asia has more active volcanoes than any other part of the world. The island of Java alone has 50 volcanoes that could erupt at any time. Here's a volcano that will erupt whenever you want it to.

❶ On a tray, use moist soil to model a mountain.

❷ Scoop out a hole from the top of the mountain and put in a container, such as the lid from a spray can.

❸ Pour about $\frac{1}{4}$ cup warm water into the container. Now stir in 1 tablespoon baking soda, a few drops of red food coloring and a few drops of dishwashing liquid. Pour in $\frac{1}{4}$ cup vinegar and watch your volcano erupt.

Adding vinegar to the baking soda produces carbon dioxide gas. This causes pressure to build up until the volcano erupts, forcing lava suds out the top. This is similar to the pressure inside Earth's crust that causes a real volcano to erupt.

Eastern Asia

Eastern Asia includes one-quarter of the Asian mainland as well as several small islands. It is dominated by China, the third-largest (and most populous) country in the world. China is only slightly larger than the United States, but it has more than four times as many people. Eighty percent live in the eastern third of the country, where the climate is mild and wet, and most of the land is fertile. There are many large cities in eastern China, but most people live in villages where they raise pigs and chickens, and grow rice, wheat and vegetables. Western China is dry, rugged and sparsely populated. The southwestern region—Tibet—is sometimes called the "roof of the world" because it lies on the highest plateau on Earth and contains part of the tallest mountain range, the Himalayas. In the north, the barren Gobi Desert stretches into Mongolia, where many people are nomadic herders. On and around China's coast lie a number of rapidly developing countries and territories. South Korea and Taiwan have many thriving industries, including textile, car and electrical goods manufacturers. Macao, a tiny Portuguese colony on the south coast of China, is the world's most crowded place, with 57,100 people for every square mile (22,150 per sq. km). Macao will revert to Chinese rule in 1999. Neighboring Hong Kong, a former British territory which was given back to China in 1997, is the world's third-largest financial center. Its modern, high-rise office buildings tower over one of Asia's busiest harbors.

KAZAKSTAN
ALTA
Oil
Rice
Donkey cart
KYRGYZSTAN
TIAN MTS.
Ürümqi
Playing the dotar
Coal
Camel train
Kashgar
Cotton
TAJIKISTAN
TAKLIMAKAN DESERT
PAKISTAN
Apak Hoja Tomb
Cotton
ALTUN MTS.
Jade
KUNLUN MTS.
INDIA
K2 28,250 ft (8,611 m)
PLATEAU OF TIBET
Snow leopard
Milking a yak
TIBET
Tibetan monks
HIMALAYAS
NEPAL
Potala Palace
Lhasa
Xiagazê
Gyangze
Mt. Everest 29,028 ft (8,848 m)
BHUTAN

CHINA
Population: 1,203,097,000 * Capital: Beijing

MONGOLIA
Population: 2,494,000 * Capital: Ulaanbaatar

NORTH KOREA
Population: 23,487,000 * Capital: P'yŏngyang

SOUTH KOREA
Population: 45,554,000 * Capital: Seoul

TAIWAN
Population: 21,501,000 * Capital: Taipei

Amazing Fact

The Great Wall of China stretches for 2,150 miles (3,460 km) across northern China and is so large that astronauts can see it from space. It was built in the third century BC to keep out invaders from the north, and then rebuilt and expanded in the 14th century AD.

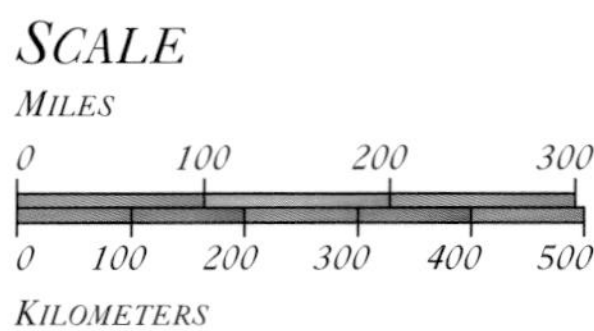
N
W
E
S

Scale
Miles 0 100 200 300
0 100 200 300 400 500 *Kilometers*

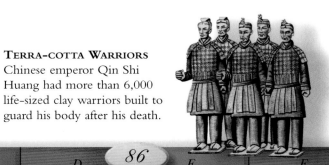

Terra-cotta Warriors
Chinese emperor Qin Shi Huang had more than 6,000 life-sized clay warriors built to guard his body after his death.

Giant Panda
There are only 1,000 giant pandas left in the wild, and they all live in bamboo forests in central China, near Chengdu.

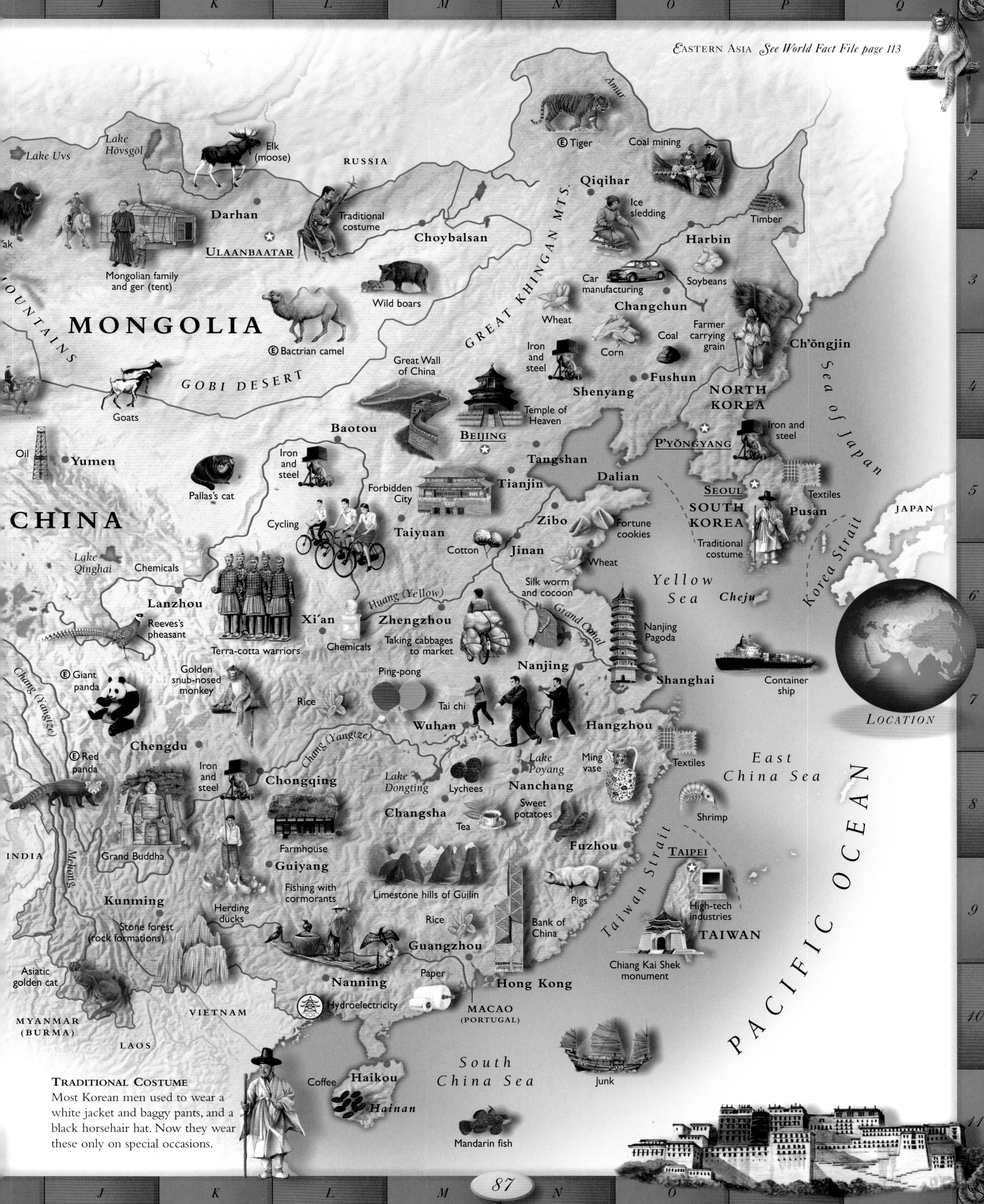
J
K
L
M
N
O
P
Q
2
3
4
5
6
7
8
9
10
11
Lake Uvs
Lake Hövsgöl
Elk (moose)
RUSSIA
Amur
Ⓔ Tiger
Coal mining
Qiqihar
Ice sledding
Timber
Darhan
Traditional costume
Choybalsan
ULAANBAATAR
Harbin
Mongolian family and ger (tent)
Wild boars
GREAT KHINGAN MTS.
Car manufacturing
Soybeans
Changchun
MONGOLIA
Ⓔ Bactrian camel
Wheat
Iron and steel
Corn
Coal
Farmer carrying grain
Ch'ŏngjin
Great Wall of China
GOBI DESERT
Fushun
Shenyang
NORTH KOREA
Goats
Temple of Heaven
BEIJING
Baotou
Iron and steel
P'YŎNGYANG
Sea of Japan
Oil
Yumen
Iron and steel
Pallas's cat
Tangshan
Dalian
Tianjin
Forbidden City
SEOUL
SOUTH KOREA
Textiles
Pusan
JAPAN
CHINA
Cycling
Taiyuan
Zibo
Fortune cookies
Cotton
Jinan
Wheat
Traditional costume
Korea Strait
Lake Qinghai
Chemicals
Silk worm and cocoon
Yellow Sea
Cheju
Lanzhou
Huang (Yellow)
Grand Canal
Xi'an
Zhengzhou
Reeves's pheasant
Nanjing Pagoda
Terra-cotta warriors
Chemicals
Taking cabbages to market
Nanjing
Container ship
Shanghai
Ⓔ Giant panda
Golden snub-nosed monkey
Ping-pong
Chang (Yangtze)
Rice
Tai chi
Wuhan
Hangzhou
LOCATION
Chengdu
Chang (Yangtze)
Ⓔ Red panda
Iron and steel
Chongqing
Lake Dongting
Lychees
Lake Poyang
Ming vase
Nanchang
Textiles
East China Sea
Changsha
Tea
Sweet potatoes
Shrimp
Grand Buddha
Farmhouse
INDIA
Mekong
Guiyang
Fuzhou
TAIPEI
Kunming
Fishing with cormorants
Limestone hills of Guilin
Pigs
Taiwan Strait
High-tech industries
PACIFIC OCEAN
Herding ducks
Stone forest (rock formations)
Rice
Bank of China
TAIWAN
Guangzhou
Asiatic golden cat
Chiang Kai Shek monument
Nanning
Paper
Hong Kong
Hydroelectricity
MACAO (PORTUGAL)
VIETNAM
MYANMAR (BURMA)
LAOS
South China Sea
Junk
Coffee
Haikou
Hainan
Mandarin fish

Traditional Costume
Most Korean men used to wear a white jacket and baggy pants, and a black horsehair hat. Now they wear these only on special occasions.

Japan See World Fact File page 113

Japan

JAPAN CONSISTS OF A long chain of 4 main islands and more than 4,000 smaller islands that lies off the east coast of the Asian mainland. The northern half of Japan has a cold temperate climate with snowy winters and mild summers. In the south the weather is more tropical, with mild winters and a summer wet season. Most of the land is mountainous, and almost two-thirds is covered in forests. Earthquakes are common, and there are many active volcanoes. Japan occupies an area smaller than the U.S. state of Montana but has 150 times as many people. Three-quarters live in cities, the largest of which are located on the large island of Honshū. Japan's capital, Tokyo, sprawls across more than 80 neighboring towns, forming the biggest urban area in the world, and is home to almost 27 million people. So many workers commute to the city center each day that railroad stations employ guards known as "pushers" to cram passengers into trains. Despite having little farmland, Japan manages to produce most of its food, including large quantities of rice. Fish is the country's most important resource, and the Japanese fishing fleet is the largest in the world. Although it has few other natural resources, Japan has become a major industrial power by importing raw materials and manufacturing high-quality goods. It is the world's top car manufacturer, has the world's foremost shipbuilding industry, and is a leading exporter of electronic goods.

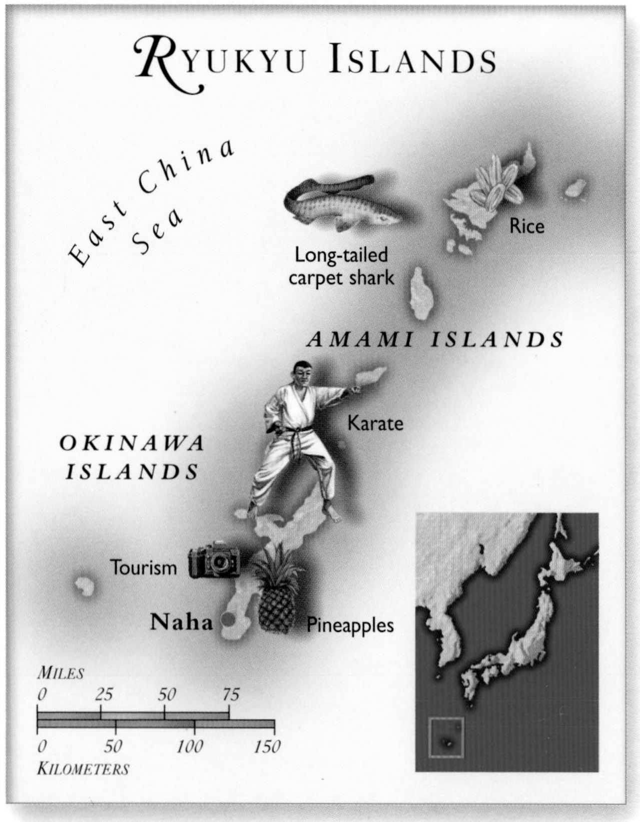

Ryukyu Islands

East China Sea
Long-tailed carpet shark
Rice
AMAMI ISLANDS
OKINAWA ISLANDS
Karate
Tourism
Naha
Pineapples
MILES 0 25 50 75
0 50 100 150 KILOMETERS

JAPAN
POPULATION: 125,506,000 ✱ CAPITAL: TOKYO

Look Again

- What kind of festival takes place in Sapporo?
- Name two kinds of shark found off the west coast of Honshū.
- Which famous mountain lies southwest of Japan's capital?

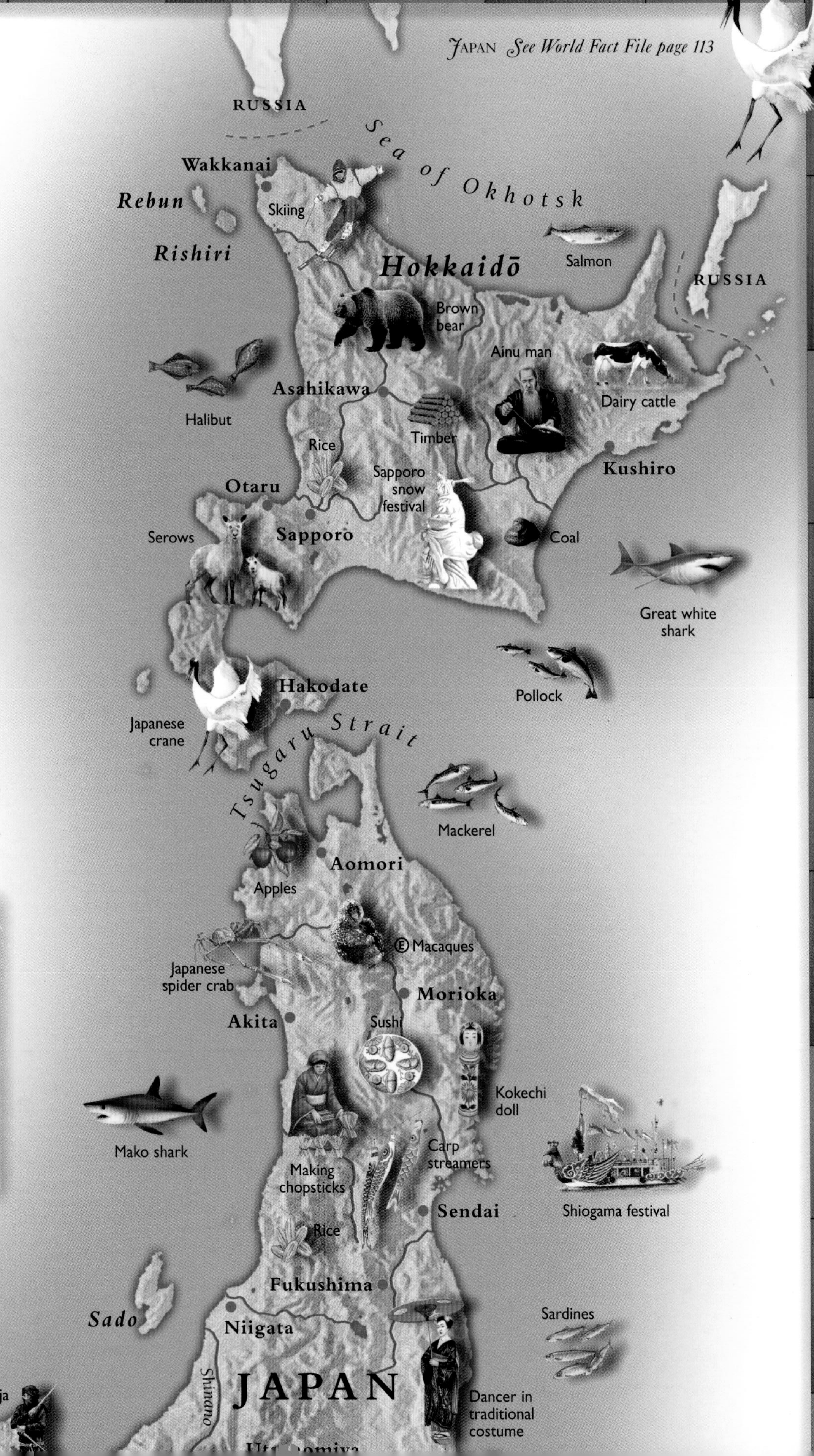

RUSSIA
Sea of Okhotsk
Wakkanai
Rebun
Rishiri
Skiing
Hokkaidō
Salmon
RUSSIA
Brown bear
Ainu man
Dairy cattle
Halibut
Asahikawa
Timber
Rice
Kushiro
Otaru
Sapporo snow festival
Serows
Sapporo
Coal
Great white shark
Pollock
Hakodate
Japanese crane
Tsugaru Strait
Mackerel
Aomori
Apples
Macaques
Japanese spider crab
Morioka
Akita
Sushi
Kokechi doll
Mako shark
Making chopsticks
Carp streamers
Shiogama festival
Sendai
Rice
Fukushima
Sardines
Sado
Niigata
Sea of Japan
Shinano
JAPAN
Ninja
Dancer in traditional costume

Swordfish
Kanazawa
Honshū
Textiles
Cherry blossom
High-tech industries
Tokyo skyline
Rice
Bullet train
Tokyo
Temple of the Golden Pavilion
Kabuki theater
Kawasaki
Yokohama
Car manufacturing
OKI ISLANDS
Squid
Geisha preparing tea
Mt. Fuji 12,388 ft (3,776 m)
Great Buddha
Nagoya
Shizuoka
Chemicals
Tea
Hamamatsu
SOUTH KOREA
Matsue
Iron and steel
Kyōto
Ōsaka
Solar-powered ship
Tiger shark
Himeji Castle
Kōbe
Shinto priest
Okayama
Wakayama
Horyuji Temple
LOCATION
Korea Strait
Hiroshima
Pearl divers
Tsushima
INLAND SEA
Tokushima
World War II monument
Mandarin oranges
Ōsaka Castle
Matsuyama
Tsushima Strait
Kitakyūshū
Torii Gate
Kōchi
Shikoku
PACIFIC OCEAN
Rice
Koto player
Fukuoka
Sumo wrestlers
Autumn harvest festival
Nagasaki
Kumamoto
Bluefin tuna
GOTŌ ISLANDS
Kyūshū
Kendo
Miyazaki
Shipbuilding
White-sided dolphin
N
E
W
S
Kagoshima
Sweet potatoes
Octopus
Traditional fishing boat
SCALE
MILES
0 25 50 75 100
0 50 100 150
KILOMETERS
ŌSUMI ISLANDS
TOKARA ISLANDS
10
11
12
13
14
15
16
B
D
E
H
I
J
K

◆ PROJECT: *Origami Penguin* ◆

Origami is the ancient Japanese art of folding paper to create decorative models. Origami models usually represent animals or people and sometimes have movable parts. In ancient Japan, origami was a highly prized art form and models often consisted of hundreds of folds. You can make your own origami model of a penguin if you follow these steps.

1. Fold a square of paper in half to make a crease. Unfold.
2. Fold the bottom corner up as shown.
3. Fold the paper in half again.
4. Fold the sides in as shown, to form the wing flaps.
5. Fold the top down to make a crease. Unfold.
6. Open the paper out and pull the tip forward.
7. Close the paper again and press the "head" flat.

Your origami penguin is finished!

KABUKI THEATER
A blend of music, drama, acrobatics and colorful costumes, kabuki first appeared in the 17th century. All the parts—even female roles—are played by men.

ŌSAKA CASTLE
Completed in AD 1584, Ōsaka Castle was the fortress of Toyotomi Hideyoshi, the general who unified feudal Japan. At the time, it was the biggest castle in Asia.

Africa

THE WORLD'S SECOND-LARGEST CONTINENT, Africa is an enormous plateau surrounded by narrow coastal plains. A thick band of tropical rain forest covers much of the center of the continent. To the north and south of this forest lie grasslands, known as savannas, and deserts. The Sahara Desert, the biggest desert in the world, spans the entire width of northern Africa, from the Atlantic Ocean to the Red Sea, and covers an area almost as large as the United States. The Kalahari and Namib deserts extend across much of the southwest. In the east, the Great Rift Valley, a series of valleys formed by cracks in Earth's crust, stretches from Syria, in Asia, to Mozambique. Africa includes 53 countries ranging from vast, mainly arid Sudan to the tiny tropical islands of the Seychelles. Arab peoples form the majority of the population in the north. The south's mainly black population is made up of hundreds of native tribes.

Major Mountains and Rivers

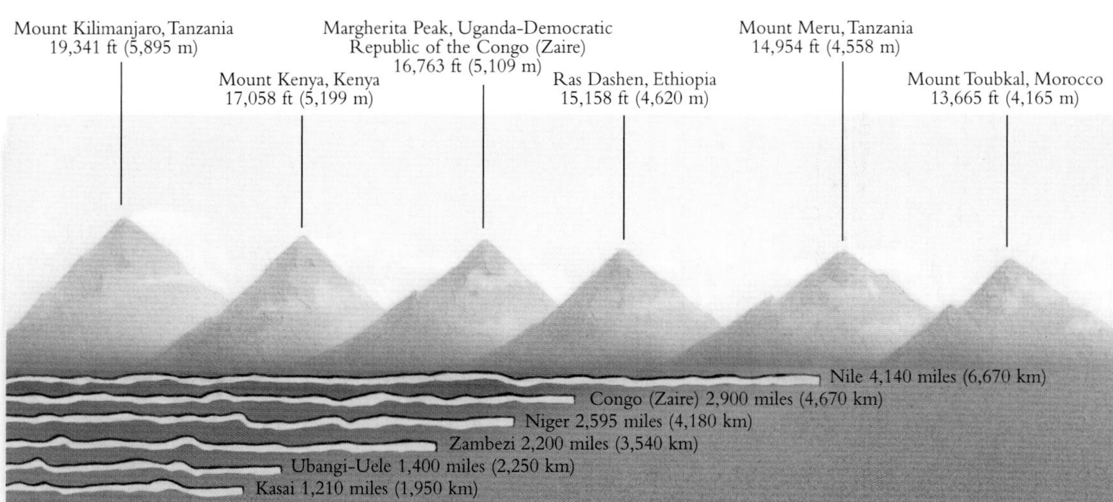
Mount Kilimanjaro, Tanzania 19,341 ft (5,895 m)
Mount Kenya, Kenya 17,058 ft (5,199 m)
Margherita Peak, Uganda-Democratic Republic of the Congo (Zaire) 16,763 ft (5,109 m)
Ras Dashen, Ethiopia 15,158 ft (4,620 m)
Mount Meru, Tanzania 14,954 ft (4,558 m)
Mount Toubkal, Morocco 13,665 ft (4,165 m)
Nile 4,140 miles (6,670 km)
Congo (Zaire) 2,900 miles (4,670 km)
Niger 2,595 miles (4,180 km)
Zambezi 2,200 miles (3,540 km)
Ubangi-Uele 1,400 miles (2,250 km)
Kasai 1,210 miles (1,950 km)

Political Map

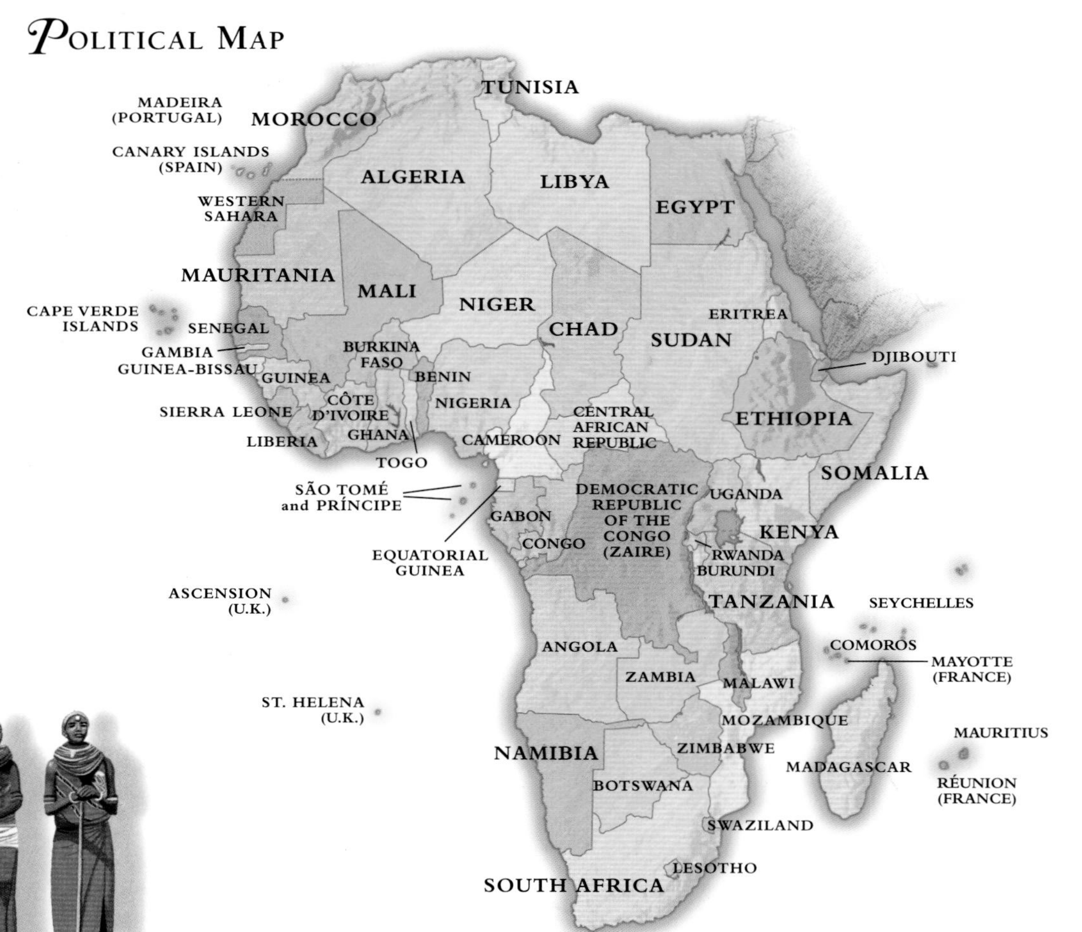
MADEIRA (PORTUGAL)
MOROCCO
TUNISIA
CANARY ISLANDS (SPAIN)
ALGERIA
LIBYA
EGYPT
WESTERN SAHARA
MAURITANIA
MALI
NIGER
CHAD
SUDAN
ERITREA
CAPE VERDE ISLANDS
SENEGAL
GAMBIA
GUINEA-BISSAU
GUINEA
BURKINA FASO
BENIN
DJIBOUTI
SIERRA LEONE
CÔTE D'IVOIRE
NIGERIA
CENTRAL AFRICAN REPUBLIC
ETHIOPIA
LIBERIA
GHANA
TOGO
CAMEROON
SOMALIA
SÃO TOMÉ and PRÍNCIPE
GABON
DEMOCRATIC REPUBLIC OF THE CONGO (ZAIRE)
UGANDA
KENYA
CONGO
EQUATORIAL GUINEA
RWANDA
BURUNDI
ASCENSION (U.K.)
TANZANIA
SEYCHELLES
ANGOLA
COMOROS
MAYOTTE (FRANCE)
ZAMBIA
MALAWI
ST. HELENA (U.K.)
MOZAMBIQUE
MAURITIUS
NAMIBIA
ZIMBABWE
MADAGASCAR
BOTSWANA
RÉUNION (FRANCE)
SWAZILAND
LESOTHO
SOUTH AFRICA

Continent Facts

Regional land area: 11,716,972 sq. miles (30,354,852 sq. km)
Regional population: 720,702,000
Independent countries: Algeria, Angola, Benin, Botswana, Burkina Faso, Burundi, Cameroon, Cape Verde Islands, Central African Republic, Chad, Comoros, Congo, Côte d'Ivoire (Ivory Coast), Democratic Republic of the Congo (Zaire), Djibouti, Egypt, Equatorial Guinea, Eritrea, Ethiopia, Gabon, Gambia, Ghana, Guinea, Guinea-Bissau, Kenya, Lesotho, Liberia, Libya, Madagascar, Malawi, Mali, Mauritania, Mauritius, Morocco, Mozambique, Namibia, Niger, Nigeria, Rwanda, São Tomé and Príncipe, Senegal, Seychelles, Sierra Leone, Somalia, South Africa, Sudan, Swaziland, Tanzania, Togo, Tunisia, Uganda, Zambia, Zimbabwe

World Records

WORLD'S LARGEST DESERT
Sahara Desert, northern Africa, 3,579,000 sq. miles (9,269,000 sq. km)

WORLD'S LONGEST RIVER
Nile River, northern Africa, 4,140 miles (6,670 km)

WORLD'S LARGEST ARTIFICIAL LAKE
Lake Volta, Ghana, 3,275 sq. miles (8,482 sq. km)

WORLD'S HIGHEST TEMPERATURE
Al-'Azīzīya, Libya, shade temperature of 136°F (58°C) recorded on September 13, 1922

Continent Records

HIGHEST MOUNTAIN
Kilimanjaro, Tanzania, 19,341 ft (5,895 m)

LOWEST POINT
Lake Assal, Djibouti, 500 ft (152 m) below sea level

LARGEST LAKE
Lake Victoria, East Africa, 26,828 sq. miles (69,485 sq. km)

LARGEST COUNTRY BY AREA
Sudan, 967,500 sq. miles (2,505,825 sq. km)

LARGEST COUNTRY BY POPULATION
Nigeria, population 101,232,000

LARGEST CITY BY POPULATION
Cairo, Egypt, population 9,700,000

◆ Amazing Fact ◆

The huge volume of water that pours over Victoria Falls, on the border between Zambia and Zimbabwe, creates a deafening roar and a cloud of spray that can be seen from more than 20 miles (32 km) away. Because of this, locals refer to the falls as "the smoke that thunders."

Physical Map

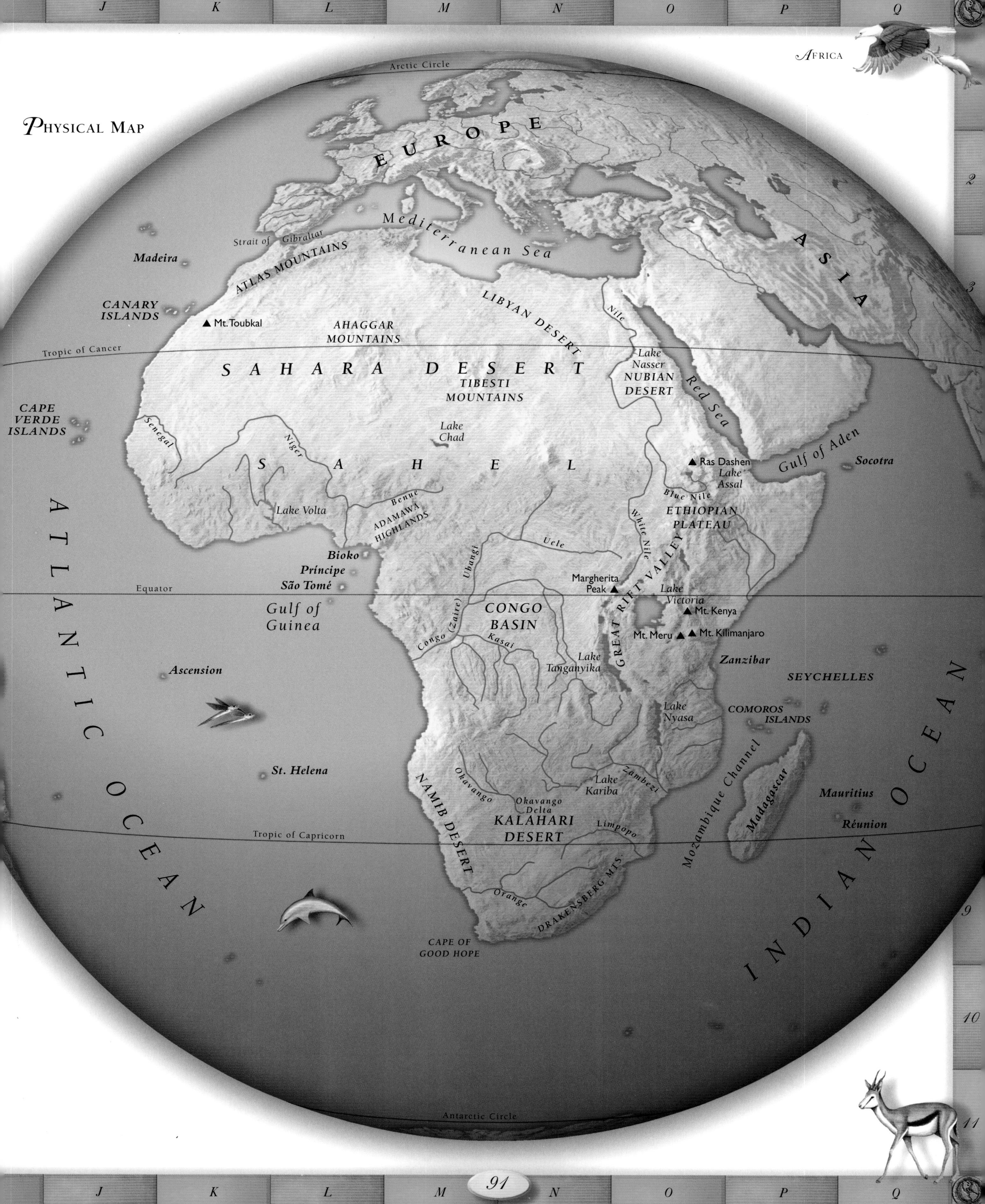

J
K
L
M
N
O
P
Q
Arctic Circle
EUROPE
ASIA
Mediterranean Sea
Strait of Gibraltar
ATLAS MOUNTAINS
Madeira
CANARY ISLANDS
Mt. Toubkal
AHAGGAR MOUNTAINS
LIBYAN DESERT
Nile
Tropic of Cancer
SAHARA DESERT
TIBESTI MOUNTAINS
Lake Nasser
NUBIAN DESERT
Red Sea
CAPE VERDE ISLANDS
Senegal
Niger
Lake Chad
SAHEL
Ras Dashen
Lake Assal
Gulf of Aden
Socotra
Blue Nile
ETHIOPIAN PLATEAU
Lake Volta
Benue
ADAMAWA HIGHLANDS
White Nile
Uele
Bioko
Príncipe
São Tomé
Ubangi
Margherita Peak
GREAT RIFT VALLEY
Equator
Lake Victoria
Mt. Kenya
Gulf of Guinea
CONGO BASIN
Congo (Zaire)
Kasai
Mt. Meru
Mt. Kilimanjaro
Lake Tanganyika
Zanzibar
Ascension
SEYCHELLES
ATLANTIC OCEAN
Lake Nyasa
COMOROS ISLANDS
St. Helena
Okavango
NAMIB DESERT
Lake Kariba
Zambezi
Mozambique Channel
Madagascar
Mauritius
Okavango Delta
KALAHARI DESERT
Limpopo
Réunion
Tropic of Capricorn
DRAKENSBERG MTS.
Orange
CAPE OF GOOD HOPE
INDIAN OCEAN
Antarctic Circle
2
3
9
10
11

Northern Africa

THE SAHARA DESERT, the largest desert in the world, covers more than half of northern Africa. On its barren, rocky plains and rolling sand dunes, the heat is fierce, water is scarce and there is little land that can be farmed. Most of the people of the Sahara are nomads, who move their camels, sheep and goats around the desert in search of water and pasture. The only usable fertile land north or east of the Sahara lies in the valleys of the Atlas Mountains and along the banks of the Nile River in Egypt. People have farmed the Nile valley for thousands of years, and it is now one of the most densely populated places on Earth. There is little farmland in Algeria and Libya, but both countries possess large oil and gas reserves which have helped them overcome serious poverty. South of the Sahara lies a wide belt of dry grasslands known as the Sahel. These grasslands suffer frequent droughts, and overfarming is turning some areas into desert. Farther south, the Sahel gives way to the tropical rain forests of central Africa. Around the Gulf of Guinea, much of the forest has been cleared to make way for farms and large plantations where cocoa beans, coffee and cotton are grown. Oil and other minerals have been discovered in a number of Gulf countries, and this has created some wealth and industries. However, only a minority of the region's huge population benefit and most people are still very poor.

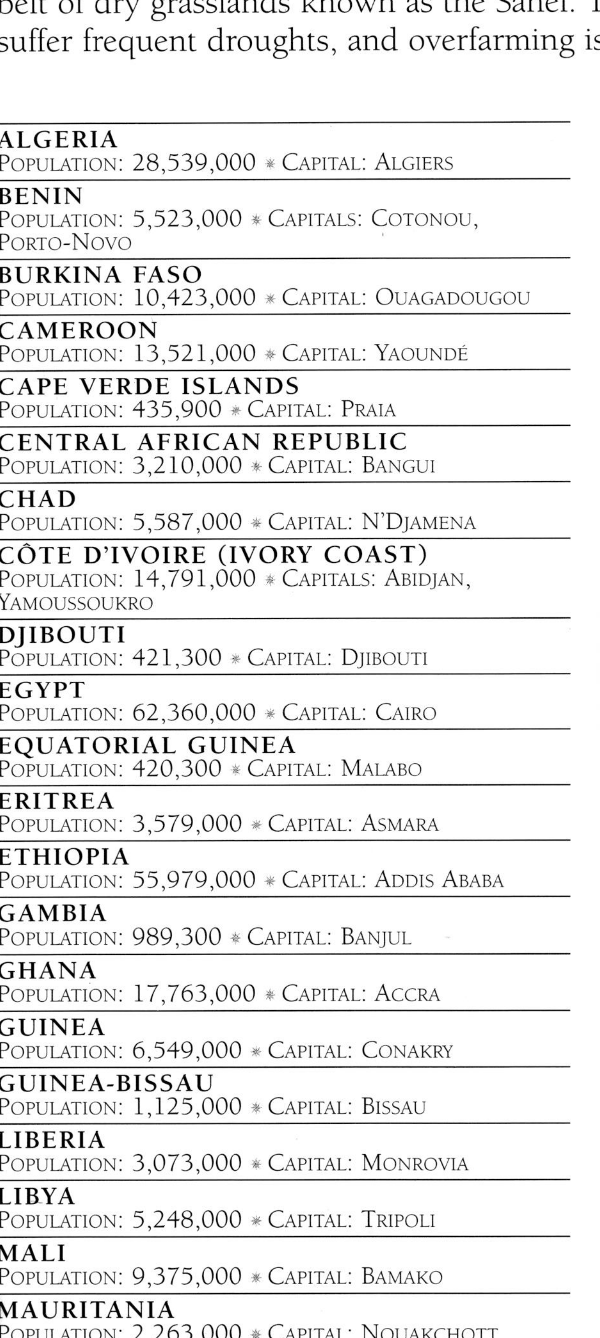
SPAIN
ALGIERS
Sardines
Tangier
Ceuta (SPAIN)
Oran
RABAT
Fès
Melilla (SPAIN)
MADEIRA (PORTUGAL)
Casablanca
Roman arch
MOROCCO
Wheat
Kouttoubia Mosque minaret
Marrakech
Mt. Toubkal 13,665 ft (4,165 m)
ATLAS MTS.
Dyeing wool for carpets
CANARY ISLANDS (SPAIN)
Sheep
El Aaiún
Tindouf
ALGERIA
WESTERN SAHARA
Nomads carrying water
Dolphin
Scorpion
Nomad with camel
Chinguetti man making tea
Tamanrasset
SAHARA
AHAGGAR MTS.
Imraguen fisherman
MAURITANIA
Woman carrying goods to market
ATLANTIC OCEAN
NOUAKCHOTT
Hippopotamus
MALI
Secretary bird
Tombouctou (Timbuktu)
Ostrich
Pounding millet
Senegal
Niger
SAHEL
DAKAR
Fishing traps
Bororro man
SENEGAL
BANJUL
Ségou
BURKINA FASO
NIAMEY
Maradi
GAMBIA
BISSAU
BAMAKO
OUAGADOUGOU
Fishing hut
GUINEA-BISSAU
GUINEA
Ivorian carrying palm wine
Cotton
Bauxite (aluminum)
BENIN
CONAKRY
Cocoa
Yams
ABUJA
Diana monkey
FREETOWN
CÔTE D'IVOIRE (IVORY COAST)
Lake Volta
TOGO
Diamonds
Bananas
SIERRA LEONE
YAMOUSSOUKRO
GHANA
NI
Cassava
COTONOU
Ibadan
MONROVIA
Coffee
LOMÉ
Lagos
LIBERIA
ABIDJAN
ACCRA
PORTO-NOVO
Bananas
Oil
Bioko
Gulf of Guinea

ALGERIA
POPULATION: 28,539,000 * CAPITAL: ALGIERS

BENIN
POPULATION: 5,523,000 * CAPITALS: COTONOU, PORTO-NOVO

BURKINA FASO
POPULATION: 10,423,000 * CAPITAL: OUAGADOUGOU

CAMEROON
POPULATION: 13,521,000 * CAPITAL: YAOUNDÉ

CAPE VERDE ISLANDS
POPULATION: 435,900 * CAPITAL: PRAIA

CENTRAL AFRICAN REPUBLIC
POPULATION: 3,210,000 * CAPITAL: BANGUI

CHAD
POPULATION: 5,587,000 * CAPITAL: N'DJAMENA

CÔTE D'IVOIRE (IVORY COAST)
POPULATION: 14,791,000 * CAPITALS: ABIDJAN, YAMOUSSOUKRO

DJIBOUTI
POPULATION: 421,300 * CAPITAL: DJIBOUTI

EGYPT
POPULATION: 62,360,000 * CAPITAL: CAIRO

EQUATORIAL GUINEA
POPULATION: 420,300 * CAPITAL: MALABO

ERITREA
POPULATION: 3,579,000 * CAPITAL: ASMARA

ETHIOPIA
POPULATION: 55,979,000 * CAPITAL: ADDIS ABABA

GAMBIA
POPULATION: 989,300 * CAPITAL: BANJUL

GHANA
POPULATION: 17,763,000 * CAPITAL: ACCRA

GUINEA
POPULATION: 6,549,000 * CAPITAL: CONAKRY

GUINEA-BISSAU
POPULATION: 1,125,000 * CAPITAL: BISSAU

LIBERIA
POPULATION: 3,073,000 * CAPITAL: MONROVIA

LIBYA
POPULATION: 5,248,000 * CAPITAL: TRIPOLI

MALI
POPULATION: 9,375,000 * CAPITAL: BAMAKO

MAURITANIA
POPULATION: 2,263,000 * CAPITAL: NOUAKCHOTT

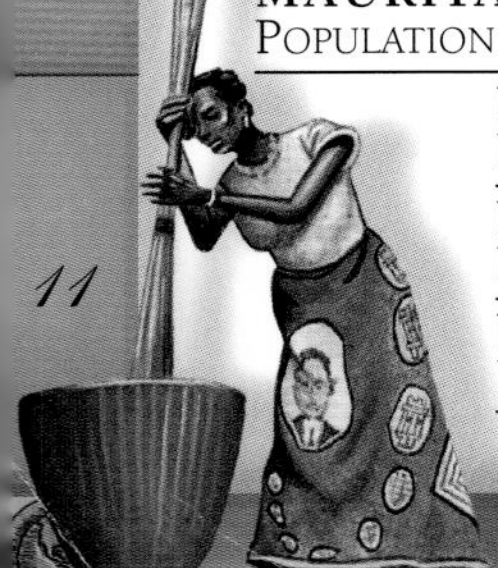

MOROCCO
POPULATION: 29,169,000 * CAPITAL: RABAT

NIGER
POPULATION: 9,280,000 * CAPITAL: NIAMEY

NIGERIA
POPULATION: 101,232,000 * CAPITAL: ABUJA

SENEGAL
POPULATION: 9,007,000 * CAPITAL: DAKAR

SIERRA LEONE
POPULATION: 4,753,000 * CAPITAL: FREETOWN

SOMALIA
POPULATION: 7,348,000 * CAPITAL: MOGADISHU

SUDAN
POPULATION: 30,120,000 * CAPITAL: KHARTOUM

TOGO
POPULATION: 4,410,000 * CAPITAL: LOMÉ

TUNISIA
POPULATION: 8,880,000 * CAPITAL: TUNIS

OSTRICH
The largest bird in the world, the ostrich, is unable to fly but can run at up to 40 miles per hour (65 kph).

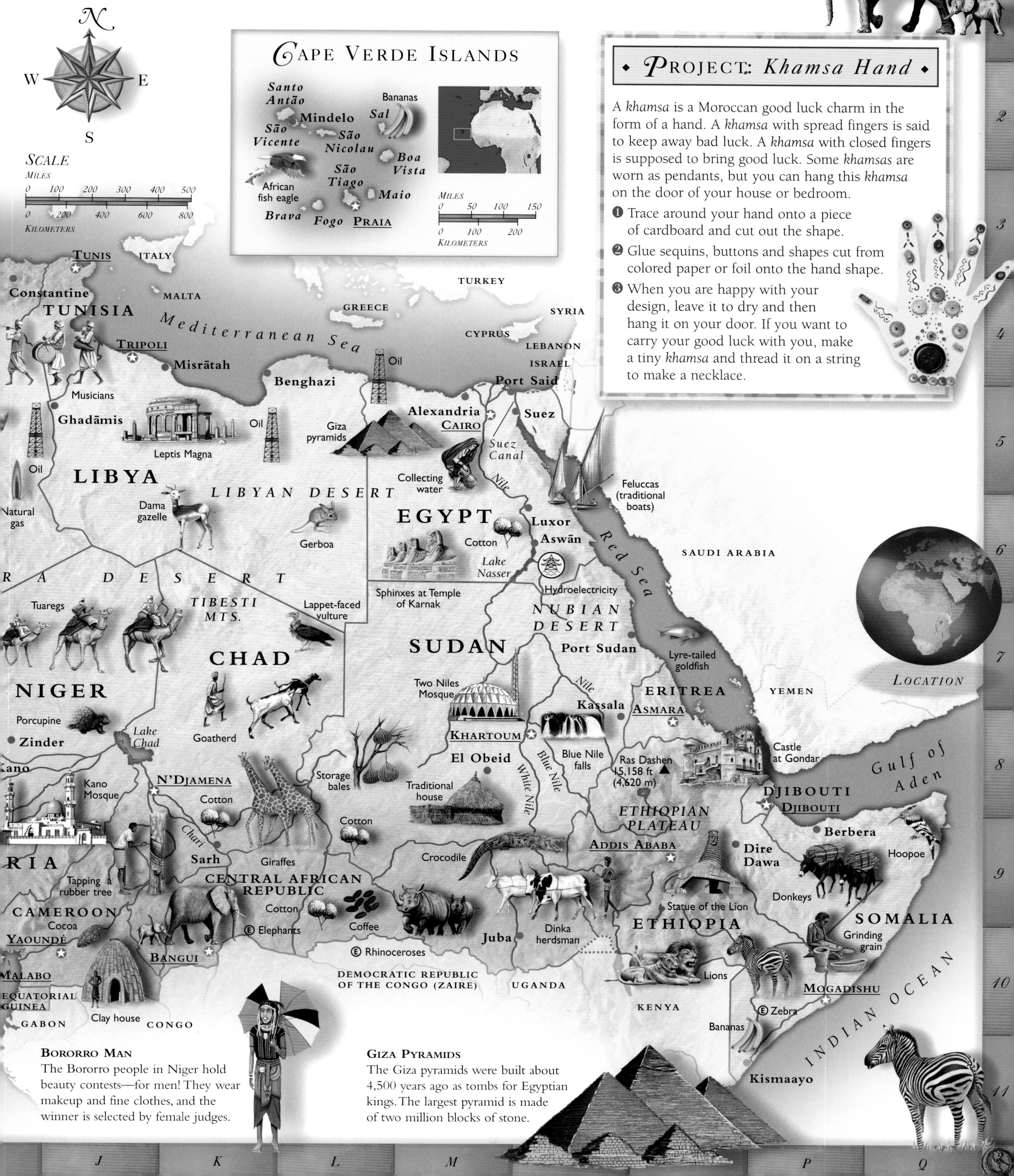

Project: Khamsa Hand

A *khamsa* is a Moroccan good luck charm in the form of a hand. A *khamsa* with spread fingers is said to keep away bad luck. A *khamsa* with closed fingers is supposed to bring good luck. Some *khamsas* are worn as pendants, but you can hang this *khamsa* on the door of your house or bedroom.

1. Trace around your hand onto a piece of cardboard and cut out the shape.
2. Glue sequins, buttons and shapes cut from colored paper or foil onto the hand shape.
3. When you are happy with your design, leave it to dry and then hang it on your door. If you want to carry your good luck with you, make a tiny *khamsa* and thread it on a string to make a necklace.

Cape Verde Islands

Santo Antão
Mindelo
São Vicente
São Nicolau
Sal
Bananas
Boa Vista
African fish eagle
São Tiago
Maio
Brava
Fogo
PRAIA
MILES 0 50 100 150
0 100 200 KILOMETERS

N W E S

SCALE
MILES 0 100 200 300 400 500
0 200 400 600 800 KILOMETERS

TUNIS
ITALY
TURKEY
Constantine
MALTA
TUNISIA
GREECE
SYRIA
Mediterranean Sea
CYPRUS
LEBANON
ISRAEL
TRIPOLI
Misrātah
Oil
Benghazi
Port Said
Musicians
Alexandria
CAIRO
Suez
Ghadāmis
Oil
Giza pyramids
Leptis Magna
Suez Canal
Oil
LIBYA
Collecting water
Nile
Feluccas (traditional boats)
LIBYAN DESERT
Natural gas
Dama gazelle
EGYPT
Luxor
Aswān
Gerboa
Cotton
Red Sea
SAUDI ARABIA
Lake Nasser
R A D E S E R T
Hydroelectricity
Sphinxes at Temple of Karnak
Tuaregs
TIBESTI MTS.
Lappet-faced vulture
NUBIAN DESERT
SUDAN
Port Sudan
Lyre-tailed goldfish
CHAD
NIGER
Nile
Two Niles Mosque
ERITREA
YEMEN
LOCATION
Kassala
ASMARA
Porcupine
Lake Chad
Goatherd
KHARTOUM
Zinder
El Obeid
Blue Nile falls
Castle at Gondar
Kano
Blue Nile
White Nile
Ras Dashen 15,158 ft (4,620 m)
Gulf of Aden
Storage bales
Traditional house
DJIBOUTI
DJIBOUTI
Kano Mosque
N'DJAMENA
Cotton
ETHIOPIAN PLATEAU
Cotton
Berbera
Chari
ADDIS ABABA
RIA
Crocodile
Dire Dawa
Hoopoe
Sarh
Giraffes
Tapping a rubber tree
CENTRAL AFRICAN REPUBLIC
Donkeys
Statue of the Lion
CAMEROON
Cotton
SOMALIA
Cocoa
Coffee
ETHIOPIA
Grinding grain
YAOUNDÉ
Elephants
Juba
Dinka herdsman
Rhinoceroses
BANGUI
Lions
MALABO
DEMOCRATIC REPUBLIC OF THE CONGO (ZAIRE)
UGANDA
MOGADISHU
EQUATORIAL GUINEA
INDIAN OCEAN
KENYA
Zebra
Clay house
GABON
CONGO
Bananas
Kismaayo

Bororro Man
The Bororro people in Niger hold beauty contests—for men! They wear makeup and fine clothes, and the winner is selected by female judges.

Giza Pyramids
The Giza pyramids were built about 4,500 years ago as tombs for Egyptian kings. The largest pyramid is made of two million blocks of stone.

Southern Africa

In the northwestern part of this region, the Congo River and its many tributaries flow through immense tropical rain forests. Crocodiles swim the waterways, and the jungles are home to chimpanzees, gorillas and tropical birds. Most of the local people live in villages near the rivers and grow their own food on small plots of cleared land. The rain forests stretch eastward across the continent toward the Great Rift Valley, a chain of dramatic, steep-sided valleys that runs down the eastern side of Africa. Within these valleys lie many deep lakes as well as a number of volcanoes, including Mount Kilimanjaro, Africa's highest mountain. On the valley floors and across the surrounding grassland plateaus, enormous herds of zebras, wildebeests and antelopes are hunted by lions, cheetahs and other predators. To protect the region's wildlife, many countries have created nature preserves, which attract tourists from all over the world. From the southern end of the Rift Valley, in Mozambique, high grasslands known as the veld spread westward toward the Kalahari and Namib deserts. In South Africa the veld is an important farming region rich in mineral resources including copper, gold and diamonds. Off the coast of Mozambique lies Madagascar, the world's fourth-largest island. Madagascar is famous for its unique wildlife, which includes many species of lemurs, unusual relatives of monkeys.

ANGOLA
Population: 10,070,000 * Capital: Luanda

BOTSWANA
Population: 1,392,000 * Capital: Gaborone

BURUNDI
Population: 6,262,000 * Capital: Bujumbura

COMOROS
Population: 549,300 * Capital: Moroni

CONGO
Population: 2,505,000 * Capital: Brazzaville

DEMOCRATIC REPUBLIC OF THE CONGO (ZAIRE)
Population: 44,061,000 * Capital: Kinshasa

GABON
Population: 1,156,000 * Capital: Libreville

KENYA
Population: 28,817,000 * Capital: Nairobi

LESOTHO
Population: 1,993,000 * Capital: Maseru

MADAGASCAR
Population: 13,862,000 * Capital: Antananarivo

MALAWI
Population: 9,808,000 * Capital: Lilongwe

MAURITIUS
Population: 1,127,000 * Capital: Port Louis

MOZAMBIQUE
Population: 18,115,000 * Capital: Maputo

NAMIBIA
Population: 1,652,000 * Capital: Windhoek

RWANDA
Population: 8,605,000 * Capital: Kigali

SÃO TOMÉ AND PRÍNCIPE
Population: 140,400 * Capital: São Tomé

SEYCHELLES
Population: 72,700 * Capital: Victoria

SOUTH AFRICA
Population: 45,095,000 * Capitals: Bloemfontein, Cape Town, Pretoria

SWAZILAND
Population: 967,000 * Capital: Mbabane

TANZANIA
Population: 28,701,000 * Capitals: Dar es Salaam, Dodoma

UGANDA
Population: 19,573,000 * Capital: Kampala

ZAMBIA
Population: 9,446,000 * Capital: Lusaka

ZIMBABWE
Population: 11,140,000 * Capital: Harare

N
W
E
S

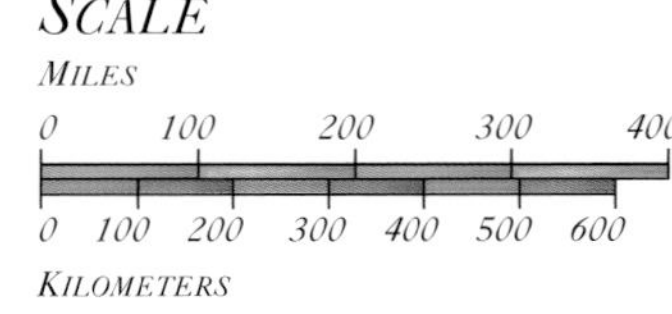
Scale
Miles
0 100 200 300 400
0 100 200 300 400 500 600
Kilometers

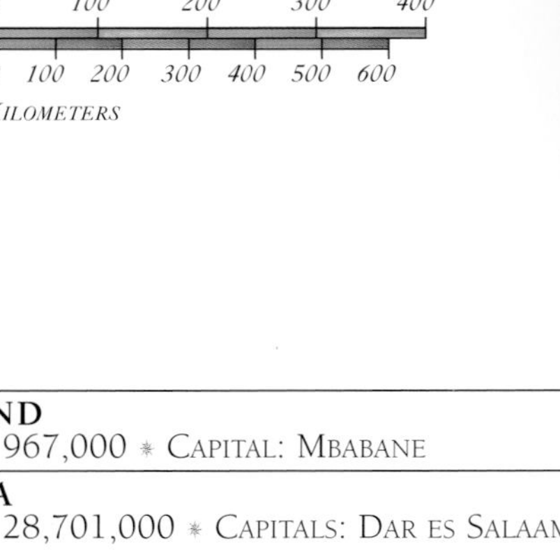

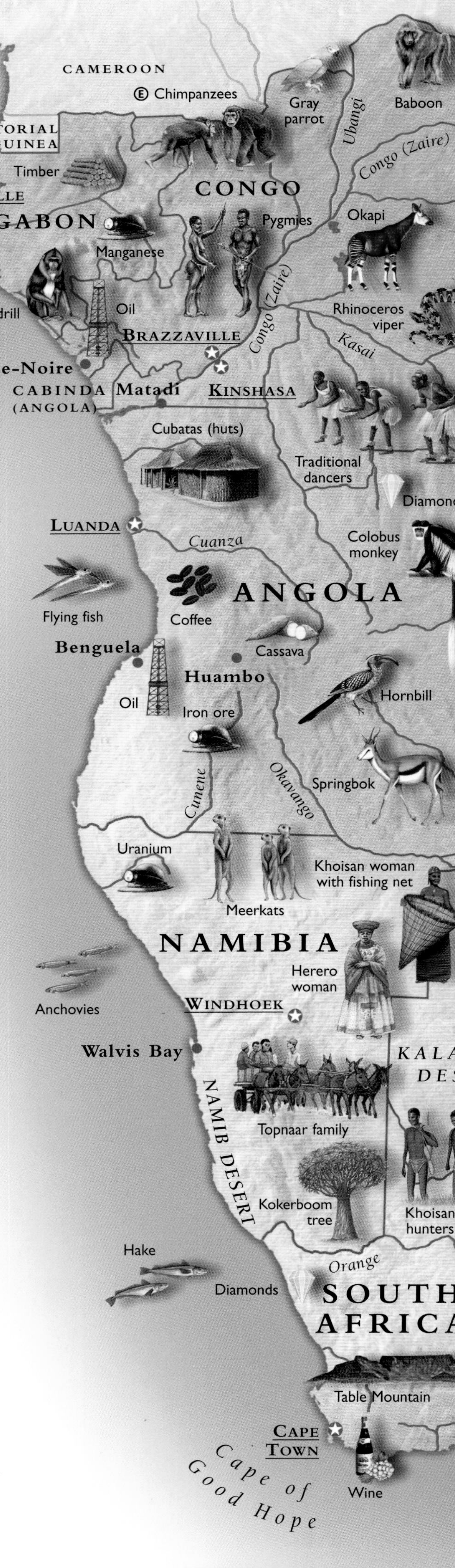
CAMEROON
Chimpanzees
Gray parrot
Baboon
Ubangi
Congo (Zaire)
SÃO TOMÉ AND PRÍNCIPE
Príncipe
São Tomé
São Tomé
EQUATORIAL GUINEA
Timber
Libreville
CONGO
GABON
Port-Gentil
Manganese
Pygmies
Okapi
Mandrill
Oil
Brazzaville
Rhinoceros viper
Kasai
Pointe-Noire
CABINDA (ANGOLA)
Matadi
Kinshasa
Cubatas (huts)
Traditional dancers
ATLANTIC OCEAN
Luanda
Cuanza
Colobus monkey
Flying fish
Coffee
ANGOLA
Benguela
Cassava
Huambo
Oil
Iron ore
Hornbill
Cunene
Okavango
Springbok
Uranium
Meerkats
Khoisan woman with fishing net
NAMIBIA
Herero woman
Anchovies
Windhoek
Walvis Bay
NAMIB DESERT
Topnaar family
Kokerboom tree
Khoisan hunters
Hake
Diamonds
Orange
Table Mountain
Cape Town
Cape of Good Hope
Wine

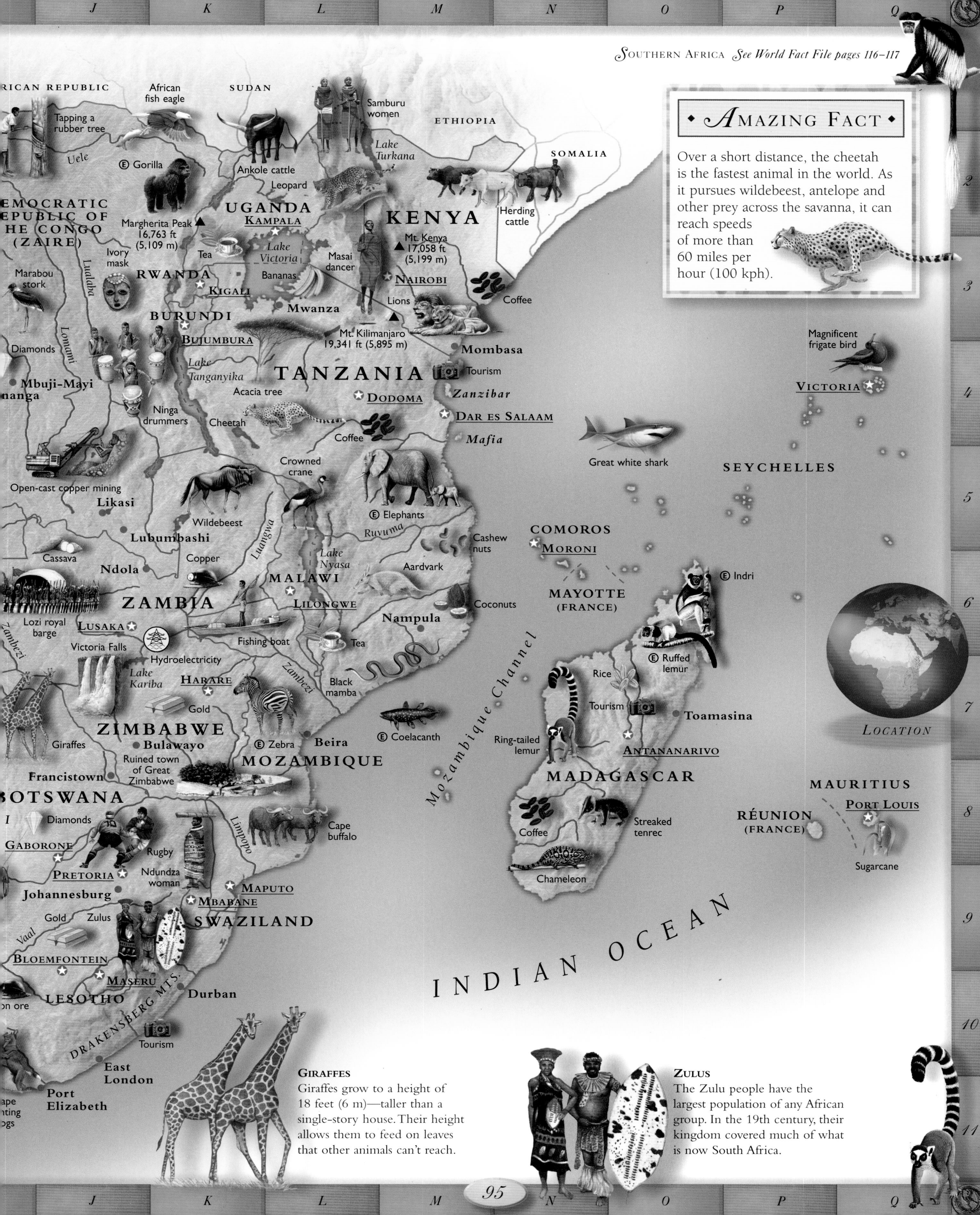
AMAZING FACT
Over a short distance, the cheetah is the fastest animal in the world. As it pursues wildebeest, antelope and other prey across the savanna, it can reach speeds of more than 60 miles per hour (100 kph).
RICAN REPUBLIC
African fish eagle
SUDAN
Samburu women
ETHIOPIA
Tapping a rubber tree
Uele
Gorilla
Ankole cattle
Lake Turkana
SOMALIA
Leopard
EMOCRATIC
EPUBLIC OF
HE CONGO
(ZAIRE)
Margherita Peak 16,763 ft (5,109 m)
UGANDA
KAMPALA
KENYA
Herding cattle
Mt. Kenya 17,058 ft (5,199 m)
Tea
Lake Victoria
Ivory mask
Lualaba
Marabou stork
RWANDA
KIGALI
Bananas
Masai dancer
NAIROBI
Coffee
Mwanza
Lions
BURUNDI
BUJUMBURA
Mt. Kilimanjaro 19,341 ft (5,895 m)
Diamonds
Lomami
Mombasa
Lake Tanganyika
TANZANIA
Tourism
Magnificent frigate bird
Mbuji-Mayi
nanga
Acacia tree
DODOMA
Zanzibar
VICTORIA
Ninga drummers
Cheetah
DAR ES SALAAM
Coffee
Mafia
Crowned crane
Great white shark
SEYCHELLES
Open-cast copper mining
Likasi
Elephants
Wildebeest
Ruvuma
Luangwa
Lubumbashi
Cashew nuts
COMOROS
MORONI
Cassava
Lake Nyasa
Ndola
Copper
Aardvark
MALAWI
Indri
ZAMBIA
LILONGWE
Coconuts
MAYOTTE (FRANCE)
Lozi royal barge
LUSAKA
Nampula
Zambezi
Fishing boat
Tea
Victoria Falls
Hydroelectricity
Ruffed lemur
Lake Kariba
HARARE
Zambezi
Black mamba
Mozambique Channel
Rice
Gold
Tourism
Toamasina
ZIMBABWE
Bulawayo
Coelacanth
LOCATION
Giraffes
Zebra
Beira
Ring-tailed lemur
ANTANANARIVO
Ruined town of Great Zimbabwe
MOZAMBIQUE
Francistown
MADAGASCAR
MAURITIUS
OTSWANA
PORT LOUIS
Diamonds
Limpopo
RÉUNION (FRANCE)
Cape buffalo
Coffee
Streaked tenrec
GABORONE
Rugby
Sugarcane
PRETORIA
Ndundza woman
Chameleon
MAPUTO
Johannesburg
MBABANE
Gold
Zulus
SWAZILAND
Vaal
INDIAN OCEAN
BLOEMFONTEIN
MASERU
LESOTHO
DRAKENSBERG MTS.
Durban
on ore
Tourism
East London
Port Elizabeth
GIRAFFES
Giraffes grow to a height of 18 feet (6 m)—taller than a single-story house. Their height allows them to feed on leaves that other animals can't reach.
ZULUS
The Zulu people have the largest population of any African group. In the 19th century, their kingdom covered much of what is now South Africa.
J K L M N O P Q
2 3 4 5 6 7 8 9 10 11

Australia and Oceania

STRETCHING FROM THE INDIAN OCEAN to the center of the Pacific Ocean, Australia and Oceania cover a vast area of the globe. But because most of this region is ocean, it has a relatively small population. Australia is by far the largest landmass. This island is so big that it is considered a continent. Oceania consists of thousands of much smaller islands that are scattered across the Pacific Ocean to the east of Australia. They are divided into three groups: Micronesia, Melanesia, and Polynesia, which includes the large islands of New Zealand. There are two main types of Pacific island: high, rugged islands that are the peaks of undersea volcanoes and submerged mountain ranges; and coral atolls—low, sandy islands formed by coral reefs growing on the tops of undersea mountains. Many of the Pacific islands are so small that they do not appear on regular maps.

Major Mountains and Rivers

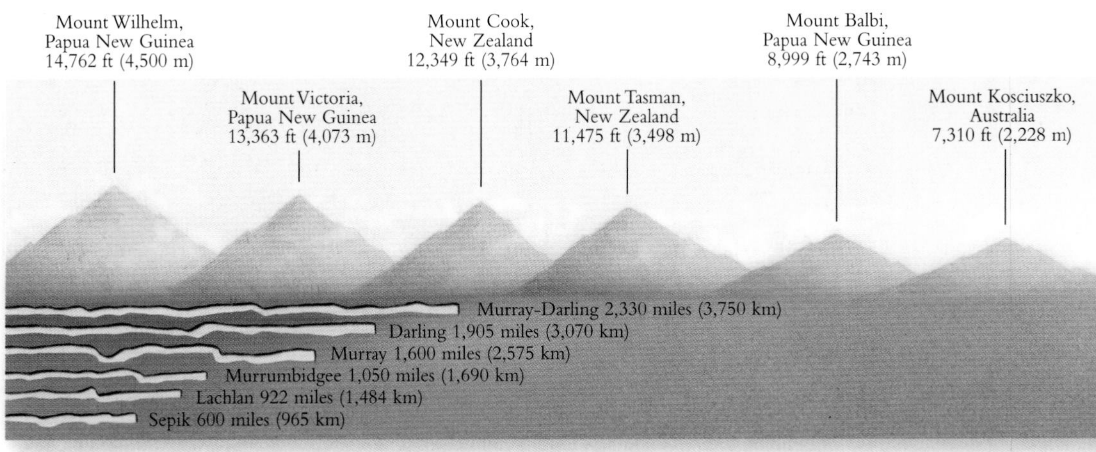
Mount Wilhelm, Papua New Guinea 14,762 ft (4,500 m)
Mount Victoria, Papua New Guinea 13,363 ft (4,073 m)
Mount Cook, New Zealand 12,349 ft (3,764 m)
Mount Tasman, New Zealand 11,475 ft (3,498 m)
Mount Balbi, Papua New Guinea 8,999 ft (2,743 m)
Mount Kosciuszko, Australia 7,310 ft (2,228 m)
Murray-Darling 2,330 miles (3,750 km)
Darling 1,905 miles (3,070 km)
Murray 1,600 miles (2,575 km)
Murrumbidgee 1,050 miles (1,690 km)
Lachlan 922 miles (1,484 km)
Sepik 600 miles (965 km)

Political Map

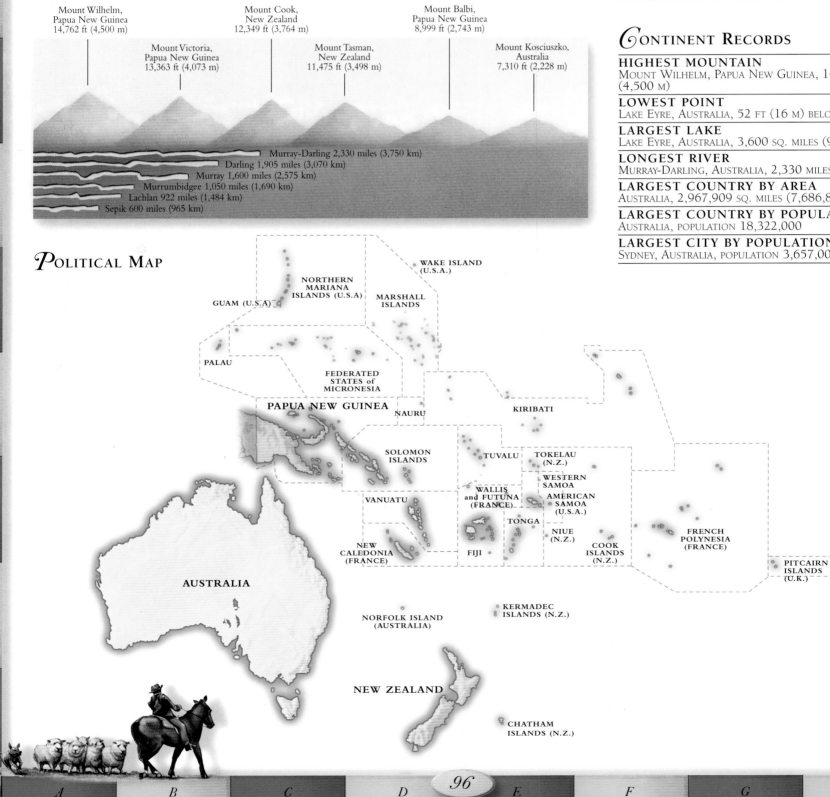

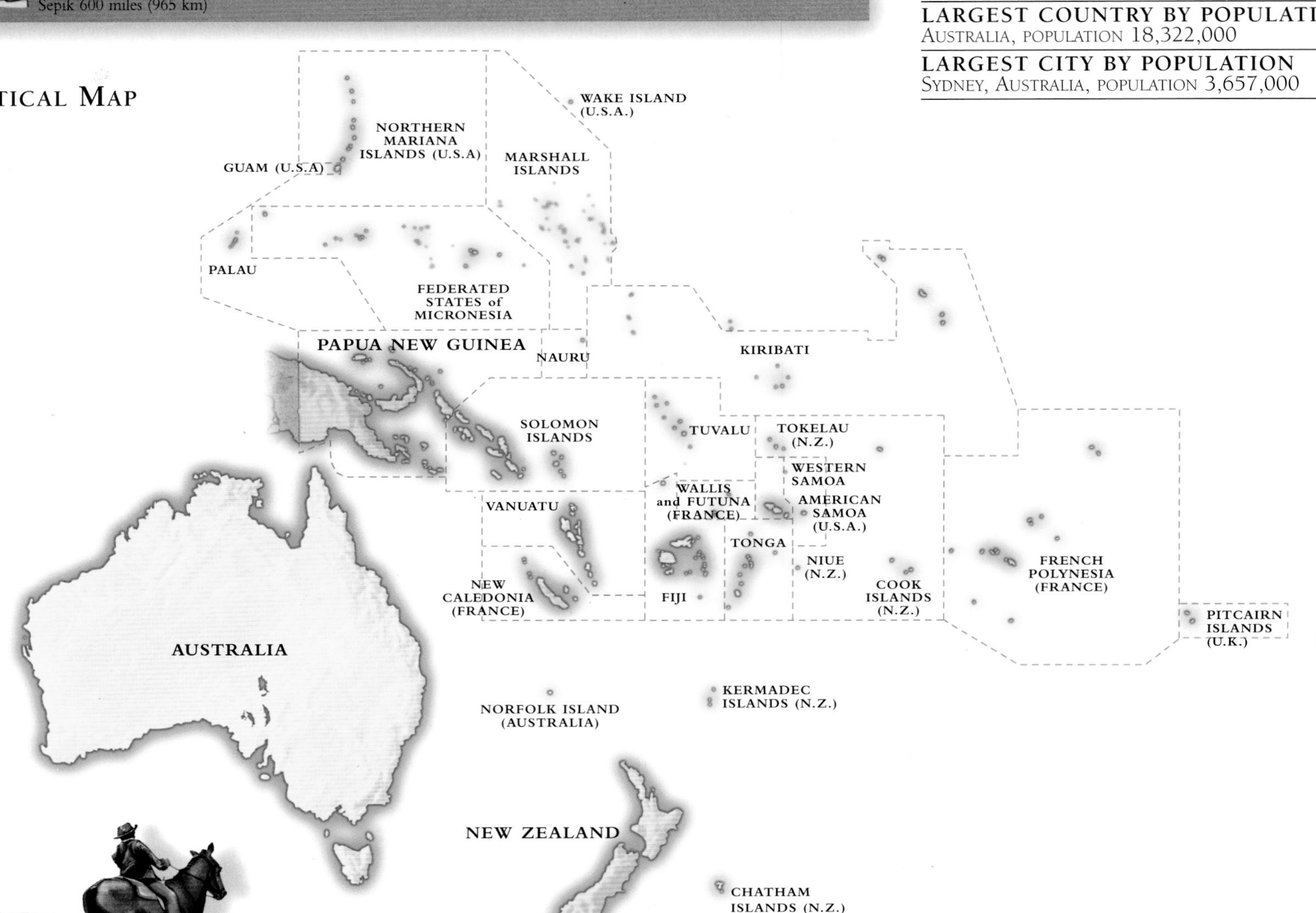
WAKE ISLAND (U.S.A.)
NORTHERN MARIANA ISLANDS (U.S.A)
GUAM (U.S.A)
MARSHALL ISLANDS
PALAU
FEDERATED STATES of MICRONESIA
PAPUA NEW GUINEA
NAURU
KIRIBATI
SOLOMON ISLANDS
TUVALU
TOKELAU (N.Z.)
WESTERN SAMOA
AMERICAN SAMOA (U.S.A.)
WALLIS and FUTUNA (FRANCE)
VANUATU
TONGA
NIUE (N.Z.)
COOK ISLANDS (N.Z.)
FRENCH POLYNESIA (FRANCE)
PITCAIRN ISLANDS (U.K.)
NEW CALEDONIA (FRANCE)
FIJI
AUSTRALIA
NORFOLK ISLAND (AUSTRALIA)
KERMADEC ISLANDS (N.Z.)
NEW ZEALAND
CHATHAM ISLANDS (N.Z.)

Continent Facts

Regional land area: 3,283,993 sq. miles (8,507,753 sq. km)
Regional population: 28,462,000
Independent countries: Australia, Federated States of Micronesia, Fiji, Kiribati, Marshall Islands, Nauru, New Zealand, Palau, Papua New Guinea, Solomon Islands, Tonga, Tuvalu, Vanuatu, Western Samoa

World Records

WORLD'S LONGEST CORAL REEF
The Great Barrier Reef, Australia, 1,260 miles (2,025 km)

WORLD'S LARGEST ROCK
Uluru (Ayers Rock), Australia, 1,143 ft (348 m) high; 1.5 miles (2.5 km) long; 1 mile (1.6 km) wide

WORLD'S LARGEST SAND ISLAND
Fraser Island, Australia, 75 miles (120 km) long

Continent Records

HIGHEST MOUNTAIN
Mount Wilhelm, Papua New Guinea, 14,762 feet (4,500 m)

LOWEST POINT
Lake Eyre, Australia, 52 ft (16 m) below sea level

LARGEST LAKE
Lake Eyre, Australia, 3,600 sq. miles (9,324 sq. km)

LONGEST RIVER
Murray-Darling, Australia, 2,330 miles (3,750 km)

LARGEST COUNTRY BY AREA
Australia, 2,967,909 sq. miles (7,686,884 sq. km)

LARGEST COUNTRY BY POPULATION
Australia, population 18,322,000

LARGEST CITY BY POPULATION
Sydney, Australia, population 3,657,000

Physical Map

J
K
L
M
N
O
P
Q
1
2
3
9
10
11
Arctic Circle
ASIA
NORTH AMERICA
PACIFIC OCEAN
Tropic of Cancer
HAWAIIAN ISLANDS
MARIANA ISLANDS
MICRONESIA
MARSHALL ISLANDS
CAROLINE ISLANDS
LINE ISLANDS
MELANESIA
Equator
GILBERT ISLANDS
Nauru
PHOENIX ISLANDS
New Guinea
Sepik
Mt. Wilhelm
New Britain
SOLOMON ISLANDS
Mt. Balbi
MARQUESAS ISLANDS
Arafura Sea
Torres Strait
Mt. Victoria
Tokelau
COOK ISLANDS
TUAMOTU ARCHIPELAGO
CAPE YORK PENINSULA
Great Barrier Reef
Tuvalu
POLYNESIA
GREAT SANDY DESERT
Coral Sea
Vanuatu
FIJI ISLANDS
SAMOA ISLANDS
SOCIETY ISLANDS
MACDONNELL RANGES
GREAT DIVIDING RANGE
New Caledonia
Tonga
PITCAIRN ISLANDS
Australia
GREAT VICTORIA DESERT
Tropic of Capricorn
Fraser Island
Lake Eyre
Darling
Norfolk Island
KERMADEC ISLANDS
Great Australian Bight
Lachlan
Murrumbidgee
Murray
Lord Howe Island
Mt. Kosciuszko
Tasman Sea
New Zealand
North Island
Tasmania
CHATHAM ISLANDS
Mt. Tasman
Mt. Cook
South Island
Stewart Island
Macquarie Island

Australia and Papua New Guinea

AUSTRALIA IS AS BIG AS the United States mainland but has a smaller population than Texas. The vast, dry interior, known as the outback, consists mainly of deserts and grasslands. It contains mineral reserves and is used for grazing huge numbers of sheep and cattle, but few people live there. Most Australians live in or near cities along the east, southeast and southwest coasts, where the climate is temperate and the land fertile. The far northeast is tropical, with areas of dense rain forest. The southeast is cooler, and mountain snowfalls are common. Most of Australia's native peoples, the Aborigines, live in towns and cities, but some still follow old traditions in the outback. Aborigines originally came to Australia more than 40,000 years ago, having crossed over from the island of New Guinea when it was still attached to Australia. Papua New Guinea, an Australian territory until 1975, is made up of several island chains and half the island of New Guinea. This main island is covered in jungle and surrounded by swampy plains. Most people live in small villages, where they grow food in gardens and raise animals. Many communities have little contact with the outside world and have retained their own traditions and languages. Papua New Guinea has over 700 languages—more than any other country in the world.

AUSTRALIA
POPULATION: 18,322,000 * CAPITAL: CANBERRA

PAPUA NEW GUINEA
POPULATION: 4,295,000 * CAPITAL: PORT MORESBY

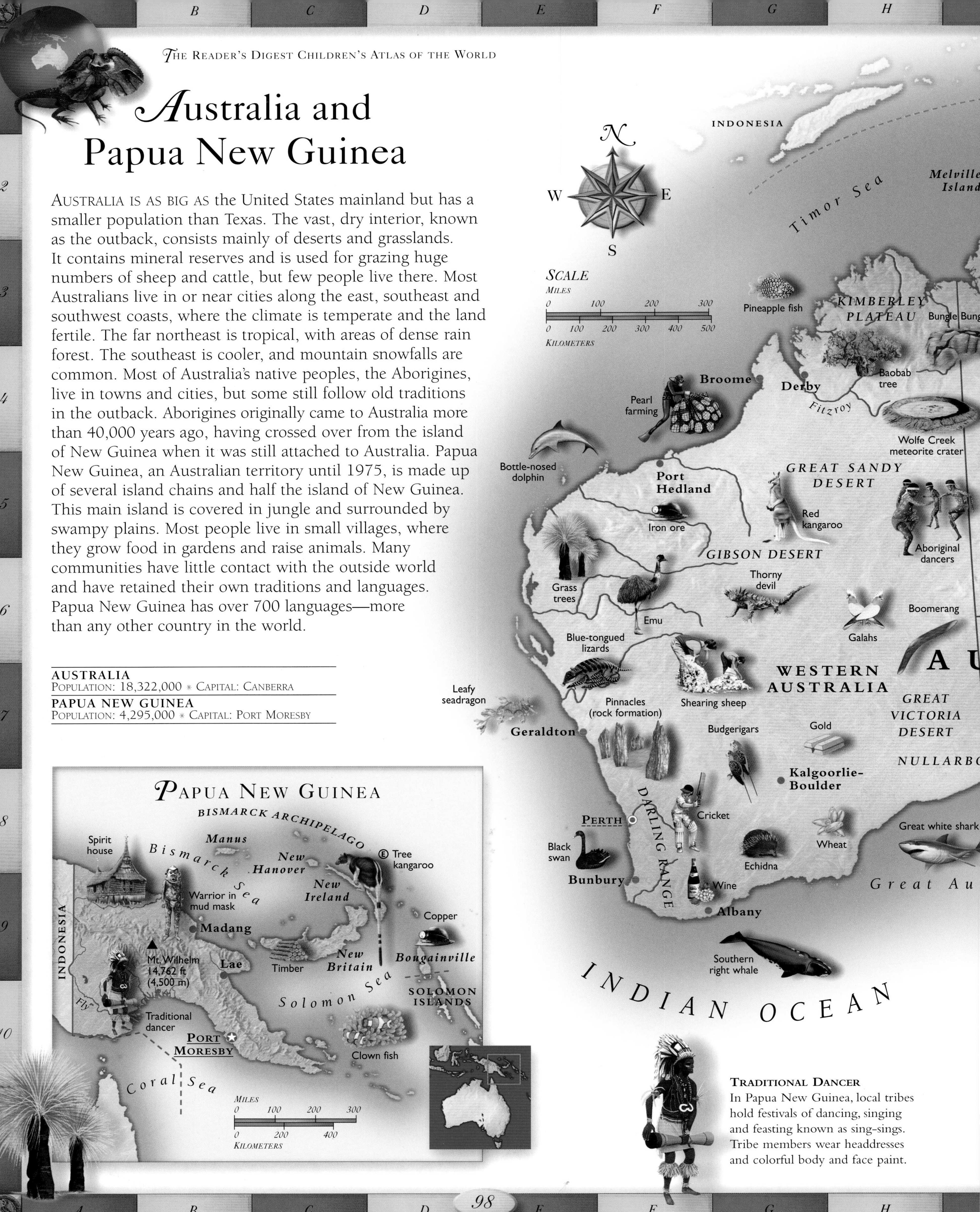

B C D E F G H
2 3 4 5 6 7 8 9 10
N
W
E
S
SCALE
MILES
0 100 200 300
0 100 200 300 400 500
KILOMETERS
INDONESIA
Timor Sea
Melville Island
KIMBERLEY PLATEAU
Pineapple fish
Bungle Bungle
Baobab tree
Broome
Derby
Fitzroy
Pearl farming
Wolfe Creek meteorite crater
Bottle-nosed dolphin
Port Hedland
GREAT SANDY DESERT
Iron ore
Red kangaroo
Aboriginal dancers
GIBSON DESERT
Thorny devil
Grass trees
Emu
Boomerang
Galahs
Blue-tongued lizards
WESTERN AUSTRALIA
A U
Leafy seadragon
Pinnacles (rock formation)
Shearing sheep
GREAT VICTORIA DESERT
Geraldton
Budgerigars
Gold
NULLARBO
Kalgoorlie-Boulder
DARLING RANGE
PERTH
Cricket
Black swan
Wheat
Great white shark
Echidna
Bunbury
Wine
Great Aus
Albany
Southern right whale
INDIAN OCEAN
PAPUA NEW GUINEA
BISMARCK ARCHIPELAGO
Spirit house
Manus
Bismarck Sea
New Hanover
Tree kangaroo
New Ireland
Warrior in mud mask
Madang
Copper
INDONESIA
Mt. Wilhelm 14,762 ft (4,500 m)
Lae
Timber
New Britain
Bougainville
Fly
Solomon Sea
SOLOMON ISLANDS
Traditional dancer
PORT MORESBY
Clown fish
Coral Sea
MILES
0 100 200 300
0 200 400
KILOMETERS
A B C D E F G H

TRADITIONAL DANCER
In Papua New Guinea, local tribes hold festivals of dancing, singing and feasting known as sing-sings. Tribe members wear headdresses and colorful body and face paint.

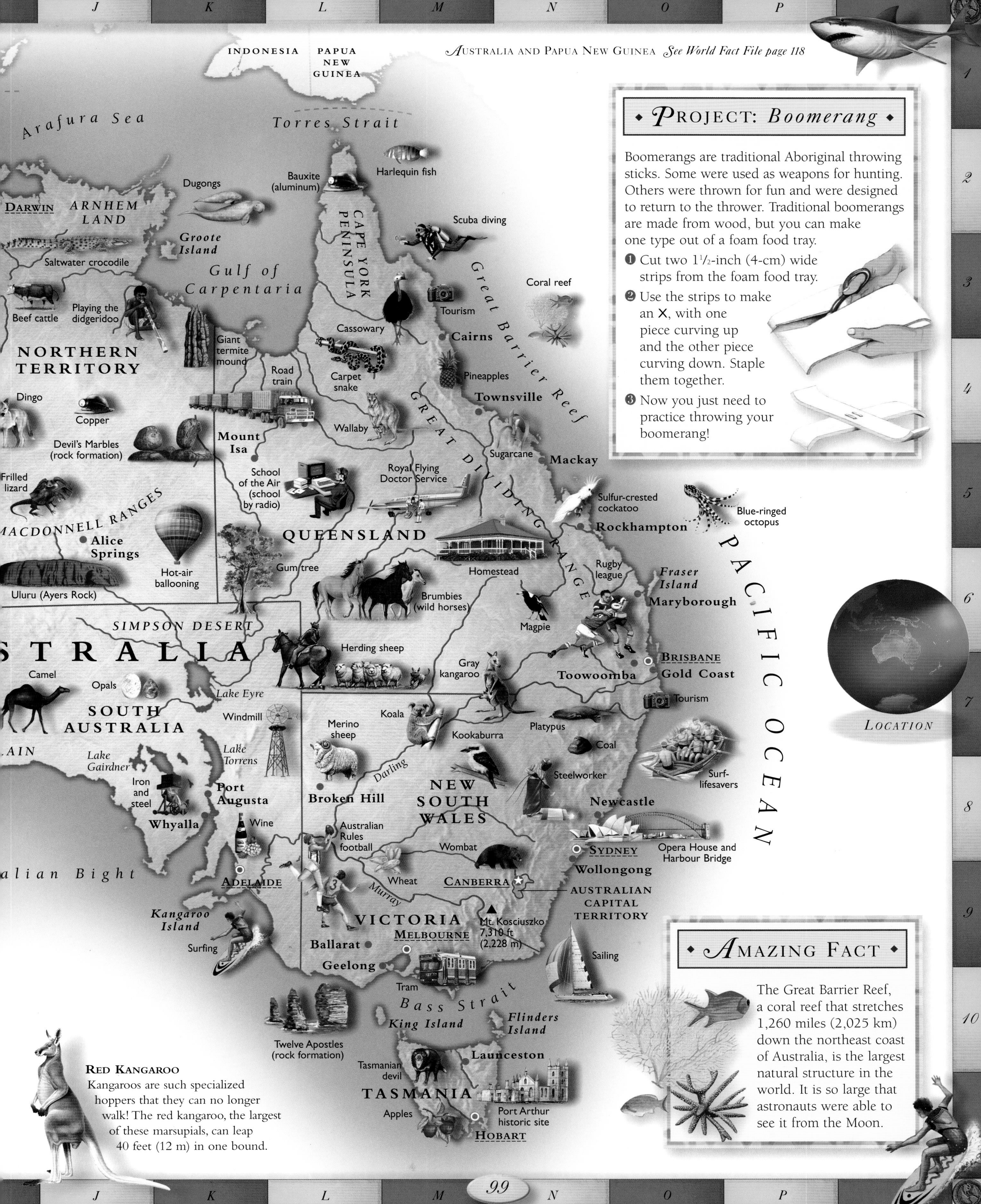
J
K
L
M
N
O
P
INDONESIA
PAPUA NEW GUINEA
Arafura Sea
Torres Strait
Bauxite (aluminum)
Harlequin fish
Dugongs
Darwin
Arnhem Land
Groote Island
Cape York Peninsula
Scuba diving
Saltwater crocodile
Gulf of Carpentaria
Great Barrier Reef
Coral reef
Beef cattle
Playing the didgeridoo
Tourism
Cassowary
Cairns
Northern Territory
Giant termite mound
Road train
Carpet snake
Pineapples
Dingo
Copper
Townsville
Great Dividing Range
Wallaby
Mount Isa
Devil's Marbles (rock formation)
Sugarcane
Mackay
Frilled lizard
School of the Air (school by radio)
Royal Flying Doctor Service
Sulfur-crested cockatoo
Blue-ringed octopus
Macdonnell Ranges
Alice Springs
Queensland
Rockhampton
Pacific Ocean
Hot-air ballooning
Gum tree
Homestead
Rugby league
Fraser Island
Maryborough
Uluru (Ayers Rock)
Brumbies (wild horses)
Magpie
Simpson Desert
Australia
Herding sheep
Brisbane
Gold Coast
Gray kangaroo
Toowoomba
Camel
Opals
Lake Eyre
Tourism
South Australia
Windmill
Koala
Merino sheep
Platypus
Kookaburra
Coal
Lake Torrens
Lake Gairdner
Darling
Steelworker
Surf-lifesavers
Iron and steel
Port Augusta
Broken Hill
New South Wales
Newcastle
Whyalla
Wine
Australian Rules football
Wombat
Opera House and Harbour Bridge
Sydney
Wollongong
Great Australian Bight
Adelaide
Wheat
Canberra
Australian Capital Territory
Murray
Kangaroo Island
Victoria
Mt. Kosciuszko 7,310 ft (2,228 m)
Melbourne
Surfing
Ballarat
Sailing
Geelong
Tram
Bass Strait
King Island
Flinders Island
Twelve Apostles (rock formation)
Launceston
Tasmanian devil
Tasmania
Apples
Port Arthur historic site
Hobart
Location
1
2
3
4
5
6
7
8
9
10

◆ Project: Boomerang ◆

Boomerangs are traditional Aboriginal throwing sticks. Some were used as weapons for hunting. Others were thrown for fun and were designed to return to the thrower. Traditional boomerangs are made from wood, but you can make one type out of a foam food tray.

1. Cut two 1½-inch (4-cm) wide strips from the foam food tray.
2. Use the strips to make an X, with one piece curving up and the other piece curving down. Staple them together.
3. Now you just need to practice throwing your boomerang!

◆ Amazing Fact ◆

The Great Barrier Reef, a coral reef that stretches 1,260 miles (2,025 km) down the northeast coast of Australia, is the largest natural structure in the world. It is so large that astronauts were able to see it from the Moon.

Red Kangaroo
Kangaroos are such specialized hoppers that they can no longer walk! The red kangaroo, the largest of these marsupials, can leap 40 feet (12 m) in one bound.

New Zealand and the Southwestern Pacific

Scattered across a vast expanse of ocean and separated from each other by great distances, the islands of the southwestern Pacific are among the most isolated places on Earth. The largest and most southerly group is New Zealand, consisting of two large islands—the North Island and the South Island—and several smaller islands. New Zealand is a modern, industrialized country. About 70 percent of the population live on the North Island, which has several active volcanoes. Lake Taupo, New Zealand's largest lake, lies in a crater that formed when a volcano exploded. The nearby volcanoes, Ruapehu and Ngauruhoe, have erupted several times in recent years. The Southern Alps form the "backbone" of the South Island. On their western side, temperate rain forests have grown up around a line of mighty glaciers that run down to the coast. More than half of New Zealand is used for growing crops and grazing animals—there are 20 sheep for every New Zealander! The country's original inhabitants, the Maori people, make up one-sixth of the population. Most other New Zealanders are descendants of British immigrants. Thousands of tropical islands lie to the north and east of New Zealand. Tourism is a growing industry in countries such as Fiji and Vanuatu. Some islands have developing towns with new businesses, but most islanders live in small villages. They fish for crabs, lobsters, turtles and tuna, and grow sweet potatoes and bananas. One of the most important export products is copra (dried coconut meat), which is used in making soap and candles.

FIJI
Population: 772,900 * Capital: Suva

NEW ZEALAND
Population: 3,407,000 * Capital: Wellington

SOLOMON ISLANDS
Population: 399,200 * Capital: Honiara

TONGA
Population: 105,600 * Capital: Nuku'alofa

VANUATU
Population: 173,600 * Capital: Port Vila

WESTERN SAMOA
Population: 209,400 * Capital: Apia

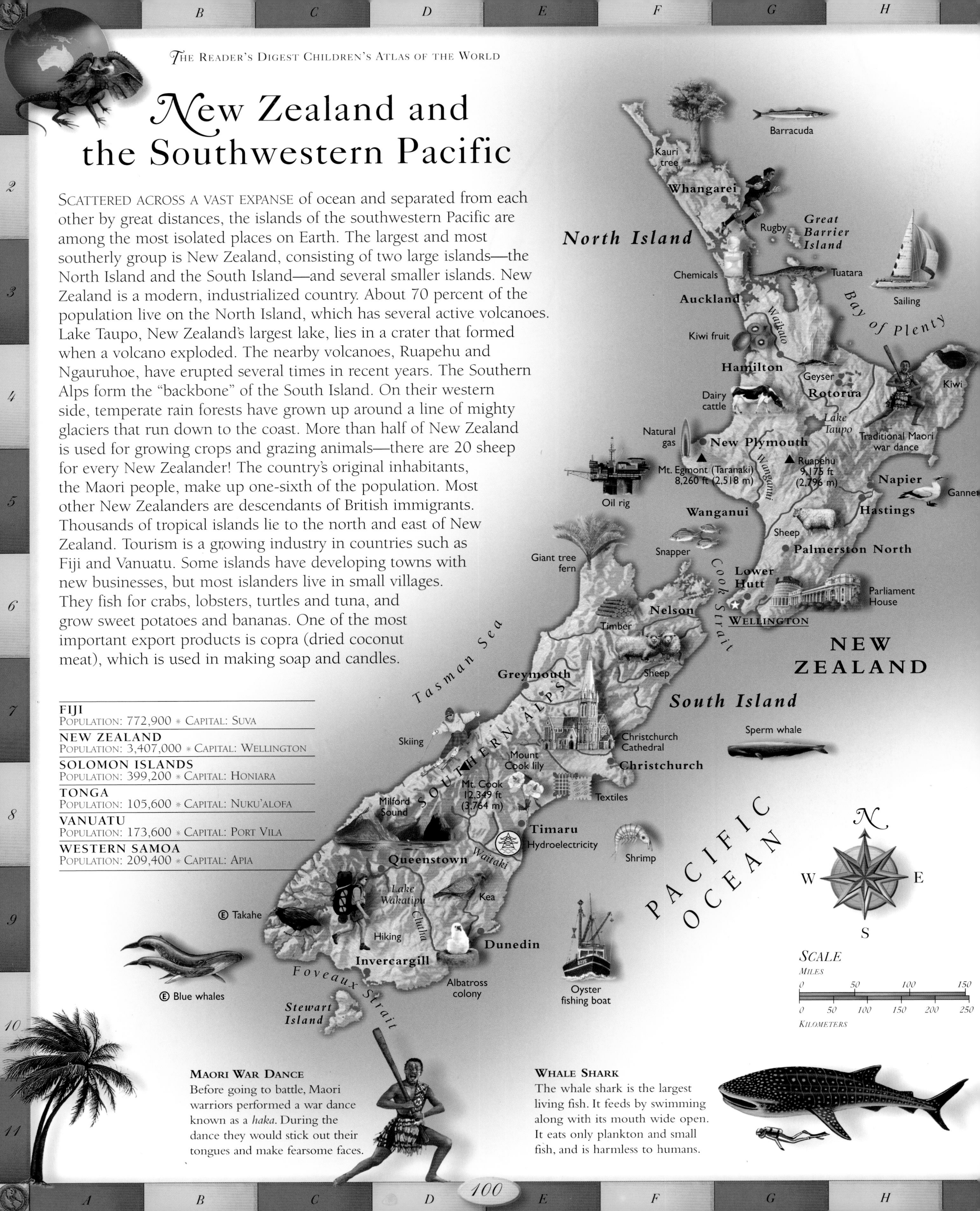

B
C
D
E
F
G
H
2
3
4
5
6
7
8
9
10
11
A
Barracuda
Kauri tree
Whangarei
North Island
Rugby
Great Barrier Island
Chemicals
Tuatara
Auckland
Sailing
Bay of Plenty
Waikato
Kiwi fruit
Hamilton
Geyser
Rotorua
Kiwi
Dairy cattle
Lake Taupo
Natural gas
New Plymouth
Traditional Maori war dance
Oil rig
Mt. Egmont (Taranaki) 8,260 ft (2,518 m)
Wanganui
Ruapehu 9,175 ft (2,796 m)
Napier
Gannet
Hastings
Wanganui
Sheep
Snapper
Palmerston North
Giant tree fern
Cook Strait
Lower Hutt
Parliament House
Nelson
Wellington
Timber
Tasman Sea
NEW ZEALAND
Sheep
Greymouth
South Island
Southern Alps
Christchurch Cathedral
Sperm whale
Skiing
Mount Cook lily
Christchurch
Mt. Cook 12,349 ft (3,764 m)
Textiles
Milford Sound
Timaru
Hydroelectricity
Shrimp
Pacific Ocean
N
W
E
S
Queenstown
Waitaki
Lake Wakatipu
Kea
Clutha
Takahe
Hiking
Dunedin
Invercargill
Scale
Miles
0 50 100 150
0 50 100 150 200 250
Kilometers
Foveaux Strait
Albatross colony
Oyster fishing boat
Blue whales
Stewart Island

Maori War Dance
Before going to battle, Maori warriors performed a war dance known as a *haka*. During the dance they would stick out their tongues and make fearsome faces.

Whale Shark
The whale shark is the largest living fish. It feeds by swimming along with its mouth wide open. It eats only plankton and small fish, and is harmless to humans.

 See World Fact File pages 118–119

Solomon Islands
House on stilts
Choiseul
Santa Isabel
Spotted cuscus
New Georgia Islands
Honiara
Malaita
Guadalcanal
Timber
San Cristóbal
Bananas
Harlequin tuskfish
Rennell
Coral Sea
Santa Cruz Islands
Miles 0 100 200
0 100 200 300 Kilometers

Samoa Islands
Western Samoa
Coconuts
Savai'i
Sala'ilua
Making tapa cloth
Apia
Upolu
Bottle-nosed dolphin
American Samoa (U.S.A.)
Pago-Pago
Preparing copra
Tutuila
Tau
Manua Islands
Manta ray
Bluefin tuna
Miles 0 25 50
0 25 50 75 Kilometers

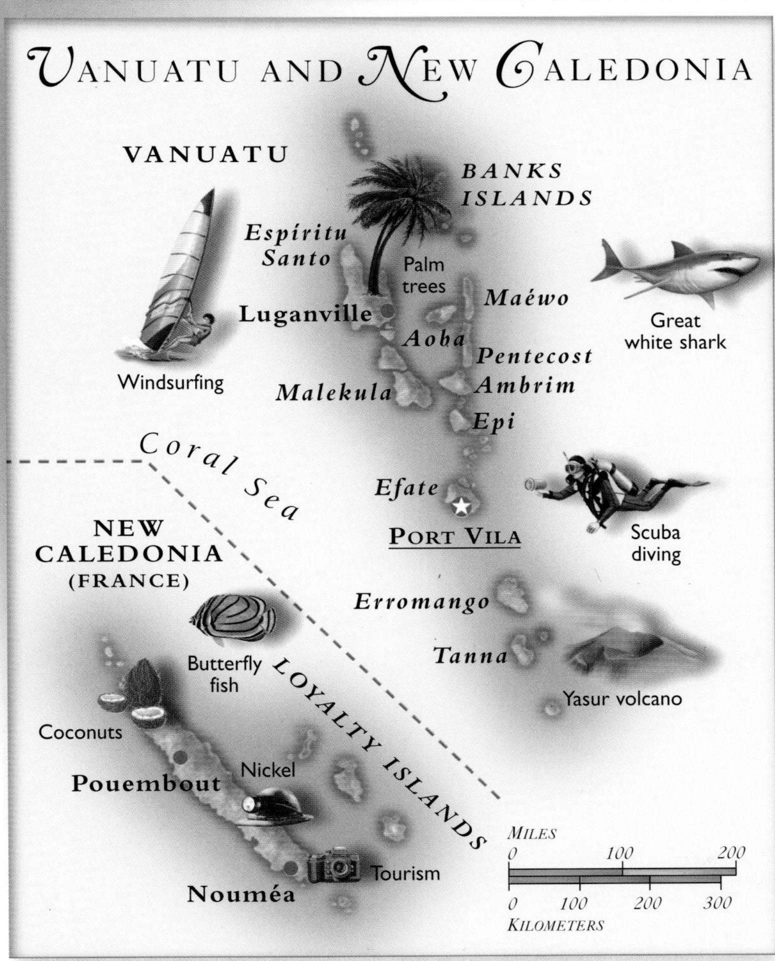
Vanuatu and New Caledonia
Vanuatu
Banks Islands
Espiritu Santo
Palm trees
Luganville
Maéwo
Aoba
Pentecost
Ambrim
Malekula
Epi
Windsurfing
Great white shark
Coral Sea
Efate
Port Vila
Scuba diving
New Caledonia (France)
Erromango
Tanna
Yasur volcano
Butterfly fish
Loyalty Islands
Coconuts
Pouembout
Nickel
Tourism
Nouméa
Miles 0 100 200
0 100 200 300 Kilometers

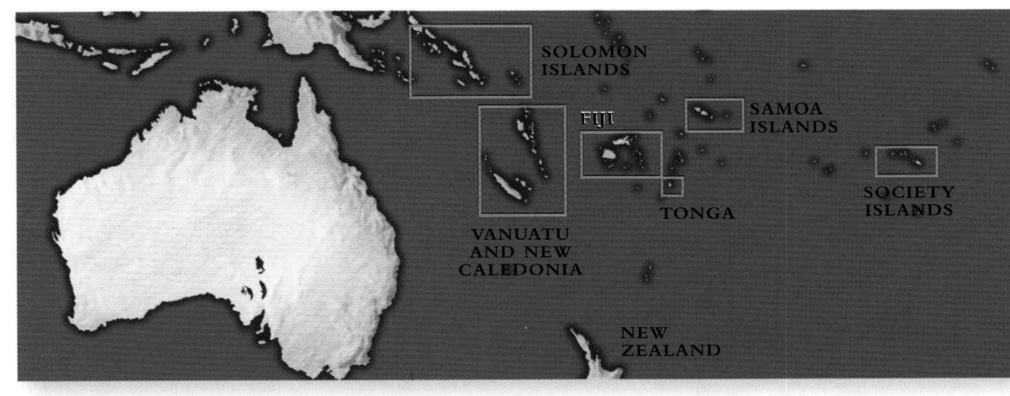
Solomon Islands
Fiji
Samoa Islands
Vanuatu and New Caledonia
Tonga
Society Islands
New Zealand

Fiji
Sugarcane
Vanua Levu
Taveuni
Koro
Tourism
Cocoa
Viti Levu
Koro Sea
Lau Group
Walking on hot coals
Suva
Gau
Lakeba
Moala
Magnificent frigate bird
Coconuts
Kandavu
Angelfish
Location
Miles 0 25 50 75
0 50 100 150 Kilometers

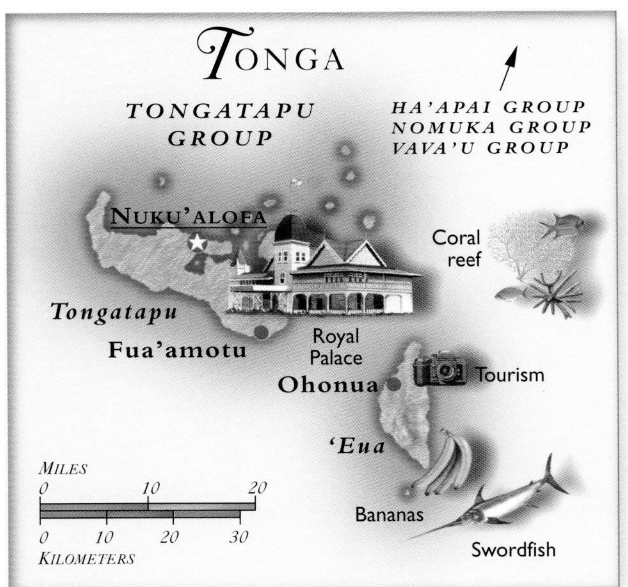
Tonga
Tongatapu Group
Ha'apai Group
Nomuka Group
Vava'u Group
Nuku'alofa
Coral reef
Tongatapu
Fua'amotu
Royal Palace
Ohonua
Tourism
'Eua
Bananas
Swordfish
Miles 0 10 20
0 10 20 30 Kilometers

Society Islands
Tupai Atoll
Bora-Bora
Lobster
French Polynesia (France)
Maupiti
Tahaa
Huahine Islands
Green turtle
Tourism
Raiatea
Outrigger boat
Leeward Islands
Pearls
Tetiaroa Atoll
Surfer in traditional dress
Windward Islands
Paopao
Papeete
Moorea
Whale shark
Palm trees
Maiao
Tahiti
Bananas
Taravao
Miles 0 25 50
0 25 50 75 Kilometers

The Polar Regions

THE REGIONS THAT SURROUND the North and South poles are the coldest and windiest parts of our planet. Both are permanently covered in snow and ice, and during winter months there is little or no daylight. Antarctica is a frozen continent surrounded by ocean. The Arctic is an area of frozen ocean surrounded by continents. In winter, the Arctic ice spreads southward, reaching North America, Europe and Asia. The northern fringes of these continents are home to native peoples who have adapted to Arctic life. They include the Saami (Lapps) of Scandinavia and the Inuit of Canada, Alaska, Greenland and Russia. A Danish territory, Greenland is the world's largest island. Most of it lies under a thick sheet of ice. Antarctica is the only continent with no permanent population. Scientists spend part of the year at research stations, but many leave Antarctica before the cold, dark winter sets in. The continent is covered by a vast ice sheet which is two miles (3 km) thick in some places. Along the coast, the ice sheet forms huge ice shelves over the ocean. Giant blocks of ice break off and float away as icebergs. Some icebergs are as large as small countries and take years to melt. There is little life in the Antarctic interior, but whales, seals and fish swim just offshore, and during the summer enormous colonies of seabirds nest along the coast and on nearby islands.

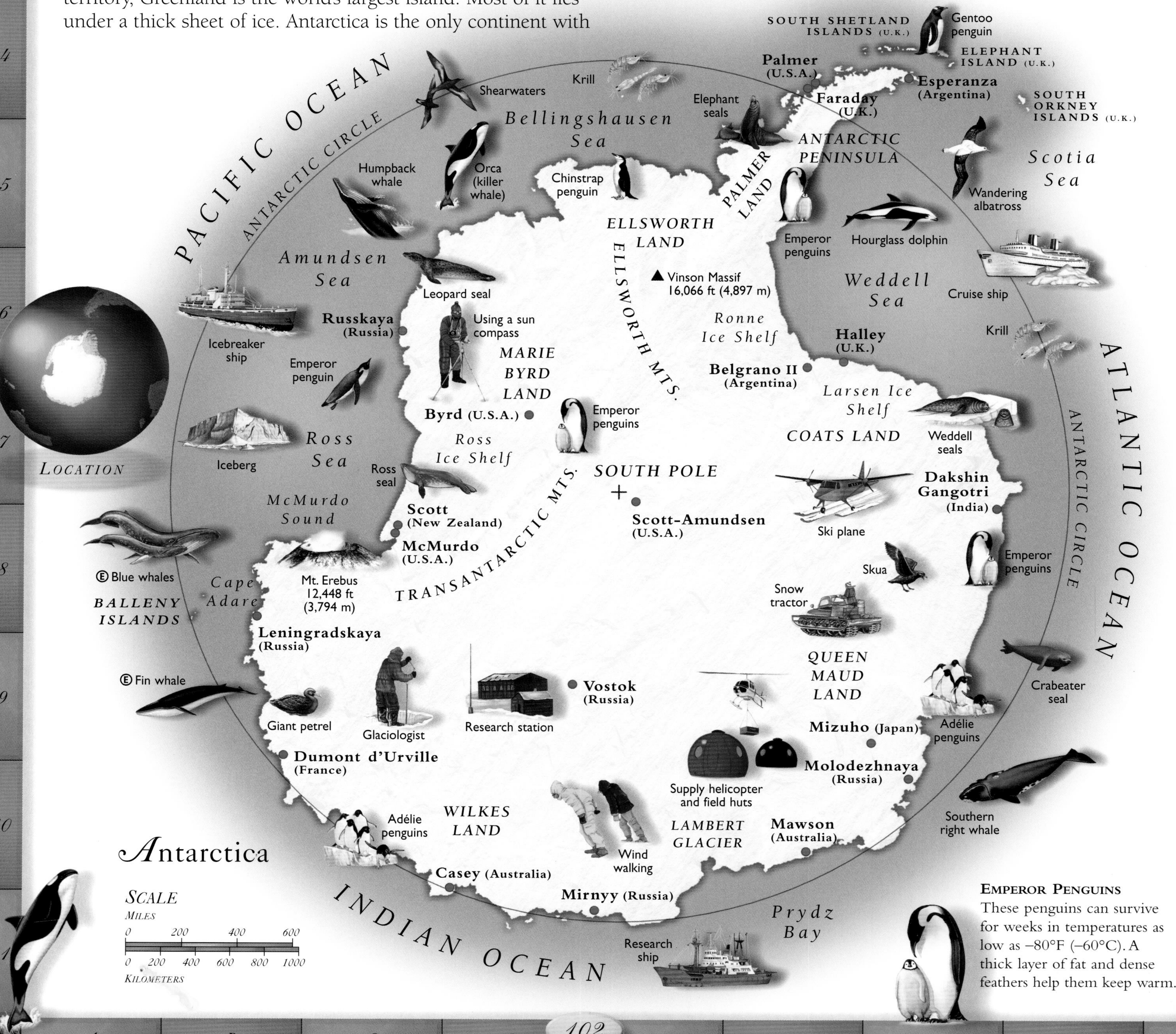
PACIFIC OCEAN
ANTARCTIC CIRCLE
Shearwaters
Krill
Bellingshausen Sea
Elephant seals
Palmer (U.S.A.)
Faraday (U.K.)
SOUTH SHETLAND ISLANDS (U.K.)
Gentoo penguin
ELEPHANT ISLAND (U.K.)
Esperanza (Argentina)
SOUTH ORKNEY ISLANDS (U.K.)
ANTARCTIC PENINSULA
PALMER LAND
Scotia Sea
Wandering albatross
Humpback whale
Orca (killer whale)
Chinstrap penguin
ELLSWORTH LAND
Emperor penguins
Hourglass dolphin
Amundsen Sea
Leopard seal
ELLSWORTH MTS.
Vinson Massif 16,066 ft (4,897 m)
Weddell Sea
Cruise ship
Icebreaker ship
Russkaya (Russia)
Using a sun compass
MARIE BYRD LAND
Ronne Ice Shelf
Halley (U.K.)
Krill
Belgrano II (Argentina)
Emperor penguin
Larsen Ice Shelf
ATLANTIC OCEAN
Byrd (U.S.A.)
Emperor penguins
Iceberg
Ross Sea
Ross Ice Shelf
COATS LAND
Weddell seals
LOCATION
Ross seal
SOUTH POLE
Dakshin Gangotri (India)
McMurdo Sound
Scott (New Zealand)
Scott-Amundsen (U.S.A.)
Ski plane
McMurdo (U.S.A.)
TRANSANTARCTIC MTS.
Emperor penguins
Blue whales
Cape Adare
Mt. Erebus 12,448 ft (3,794 m)
Skua
BALLENY ISLANDS
Snow tractor
Leningradskaya (Russia)
QUEEN MAUD LAND
Fin whale
Vostok (Russia)
Crabeater seal
Giant petrel
Glaciologist
Research station
Mizuho (Japan)
Adélie penguins
Dumont d'Urville (France)
Molodezhnaya (Russia)
Supply helicopter and field huts
Adélie penguins
WILKES LAND
Wind walking
LAMBERT GLACIER
Mawson (Australia)
Southern right whale
Antarctica
Casey (Australia)
Mirnyy (Russia)
Prydz Bay
INDIAN OCEAN
Research ship
SCALE
MILES
0 200 400 600
0 200 400 600 800 1000
KILOMETERS

Emperor Penguins
These penguins can survive for weeks in temperatures as low as –80°F (–60°C). A thick layer of fat and dense feathers help them keep warm.

The Arctic

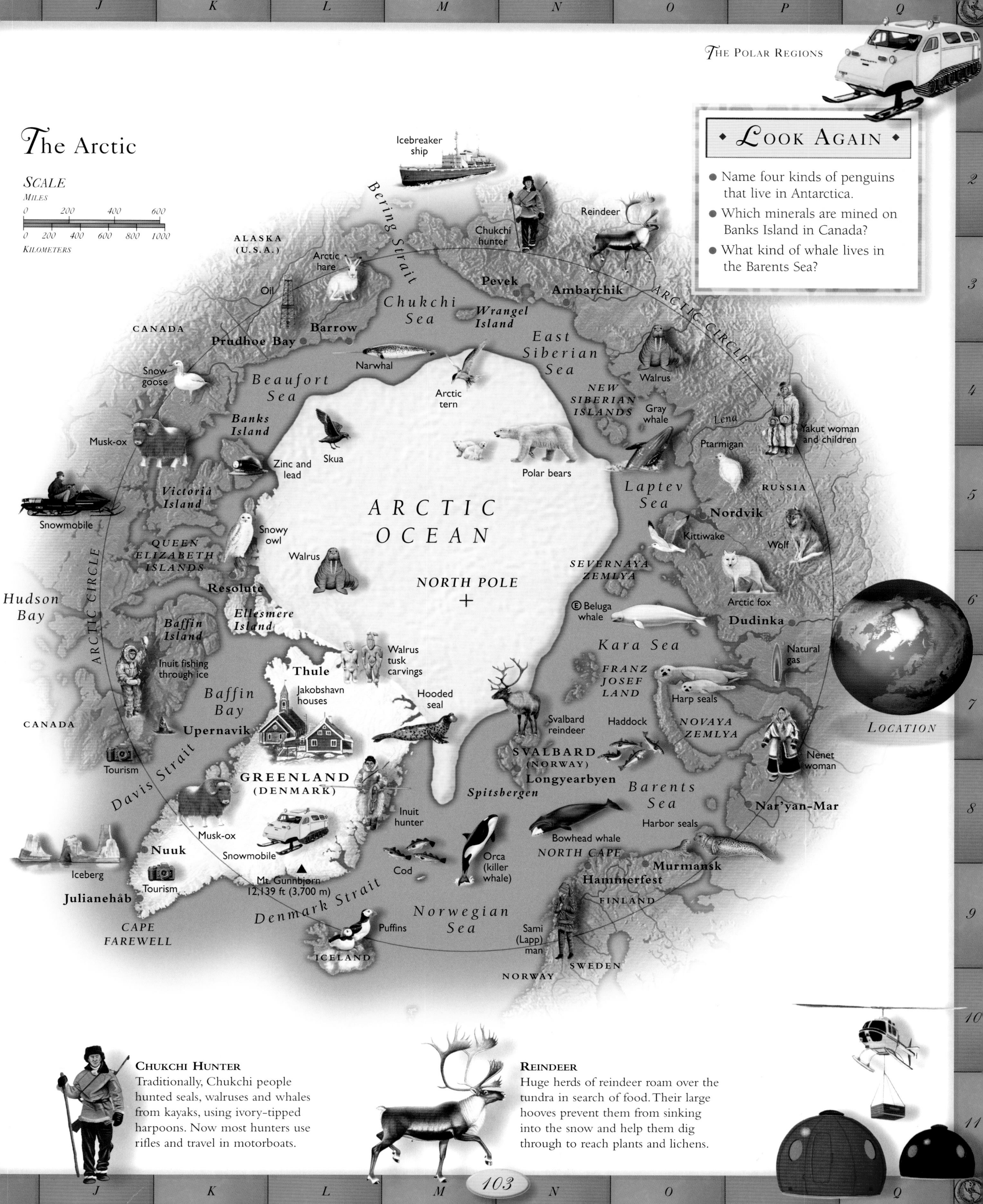
J K L M N O P Q
2 3 4 5 6 7 8 9 10 11
SCALE
MILES
0 200 400 600
0 200 400 600 800 1000
KILOMETERS
Icebreaker ship
Bering Strait
Chukchi hunter
Reindeer
ALASKA (U.S.A.)
Arctic hare
Oil
Chukchi Sea
Pevek
Ambarchik
ARCTIC CIRCLE
Wrangel Island
Barrow
CANADA
Prudhoe Bay
East Siberian Sea
Narwhal
Walrus
Snow goose
Beaufort Sea
Arctic tern
NEW SIBERIAN ISLANDS
Gray whale
Lena
Banks Island
Yakut woman and children
Musk-ox
Skua
Ptarmigan
Zinc and lead
Polar bears
Victoria Island
Laptev Sea
RUSSIA
Snowmobile
ARCTIC OCEAN
Nordvik
Snowy owl
Kittiwake
Wolf
QUEEN ELIZABETH ISLANDS
Walrus
SEVERNAYA ZEMLYA
Resolute
NORTH POLE
Hudson Bay
ARCTIC CIRCLE
Arctic fox
Ⓔ Beluga whale
Dudinka
Ellesmere Island
Baffin Island
Walrus tusk carvings
Kara Sea
Natural gas
Inuit fishing through ice
Thule
FRANZ JOSEF LAND
Baffin Bay
Jakobshavn houses
Hooded seal
Harp seals
Svalbard reindeer
Haddock
NOVAYA ZEMLYA
CANADA
Upernavik
LOCATION
Tourism
SVALBARD (NORWAY)
Nenet woman
Davis Strait
GREENLAND (DENMARK)
Longyearbyen
Spitsbergen
Barents Sea
Nar'yan-Mar
Inuit hunter
Harbor seals
Bowhead whale
Musk-ox
Nuuk
Orca (killer whale)
NORTH CAPE
Murmansk
Snowmobile
Cod
Iceberg
Hammerfest
Tourism
Mt. Gunnbjørn 12,139 ft (3,700 m)
FINLAND
Julianehåb
Denmark Strait
Norwegian Sea
CAPE FAREWELL
Puffins
Sami (Lapp) man
ICELAND
SWEDEN
NORWAY

◆ Look Again ◆

- Name four kinds of penguins that live in Antarctica.
- Which minerals are mined on Banks Island in Canada?
- What kind of whale lives in the Barents Sea?

Chukchi Hunter
Traditionally, Chukchi people hunted seals, walruses and whales from kayaks, using ivory-tipped harpoons. Now most hunters use rifles and travel in motorboats.

Reindeer
Huge herds of reindeer roam over the tundra in search of food. Their large hooves prevent them from sinking into the snow and help them dig through to reach plants and lichens.

World Fact File

NORTH AMERICA

CANADA
PRONUNCIATION: KA-nuh-duh
AREA: 3,851,809 sq. miles (9,976,185 sq. km)
POPULATION: 28,435,000
CAPITAL: Ottawa
CURRENCY: 100 cents = 1 Canadian dollar (Can$)
OFFICIAL LANGUAGES: English, French
MAIN RELIGION: Christianity 72%
EXPORTS: Newsprint, wood pulp, timber, crude petroleum, machinery, natural gas, aluminum, motor vehicles and parts, telecommunications equipment

UNITED STATES OF AMERICA
PRONUNCIATION: yoo-NEYE-tuhd STAYTS of uh-MEHR-uh-kuh
AREA: 3,619,969 sq. miles (9,375,720 sq. km)
POPULATION: 263,814,000
CAPITAL: Washington, D.C.
CURRENCY: 100 cents = 1 United States dollar (US$)
OFFICIAL LANGUAGE: English
OTHER LANGUAGE: Spanish
MAIN RELIGIONS: Christianity 86%, Judaism 2%
EXPORTS: Motor vehicles, raw materials, consumer goods, agricultural products

MEXICO
PRONUNCIATION: MEK-si-koh
AREA: 761,600 sq. miles (1,972,544 sq. km)
POPULATION: 93,986,000
CAPITAL: Mexico City
CURRENCY: 100 centavos = 1 Mexican peso (Mex$)
OFFICIAL LANGUAGE: Spanish
OTHER LANGUAGES: Regional languages
MAIN RELIGION: Christianity 95%
EXPORTS: Crude oil, oil products, coffee, silver, engines, motor vehicles, cotton, electronic goods

GUATEMALA
PRONUNCIATION: gwah-tuh-MAH-luh
AREA: 42,042 sq. miles (108,889 sq. km)
POPULATION: 10,999,000
CAPITAL: Guatemala
CURRENCY: 100 centavos = 1 Guatemalan quetzal (Q)
OFFICIAL LANGUAGE: Spanish
OTHER LANGUAGES: Quiche, Cakchiquel, Kekchi, and other regional languages
MAIN RELIGIONS: Christianity 99%, traditional Mayan religions
EXPORTS: Coffee, bananas, cotton, sugar, minerals, textiles

BELIZE
PRONUNCIATION: buh-LEEZ
AREA: 8,867 sq. miles (22,966 sq. km)
POPULATION: 214,100
CAPITAL: Belmopan
CURRENCY: 100 cents = 1 Belizean dollar (Bz$)
OFFICIAL LANGUAGE: English
OTHER LANGUAGES: Spanish, Maya, Garifuna
MAIN RELIGION: Christianity 92%
EXPORTS: Sugar, molasses, citrus fruit, bananas, clothing, fish products, timber

HONDURAS
PRONUNCIATION: hahn-DER-uhs
AREA: 43,277 sq. miles (112,087 sq. km)
POPULATION: 5,460,000
CAPITAL: Tegucigalpa
CURRENCY: 100 centavos = 1 lempira (L)
OFFICIAL LANGUAGE: Spanish
OTHER LANGUAGES: Regional languages
MAIN RELIGION: Christianity 97%
EXPORTS: Bananas, coffee, shrimp, lobsters, minerals, meat, timber

EL SALVADOR
PRONUNCIATION: el SAL-vuh-dor
AREA: 8,260 sq. miles (21,393 sq. km)
POPULATION: 5,870,000
CAPITAL: San Salvador
CURRENCY: 100 centavos = 1 Salvadoran colón (C)
OFFICIAL LANGUAGE: Spanish
OTHER LANGUAGE: Nahua
MAIN RELIGION: Christianity 92%
EXPORTS: Coffee, sugarcane, shrimp

NICARAGUA
PRONUNCIATION: ni-kuh-RAH-gwuh
AREA: 49,579 sq. miles (128,410 sq. km)
POPULATION: 4,206,000
CAPITAL: Managua
CURRENCY: 100 centavos = 1 gold cordoba (C$)
OFFICIAL LANGUAGE: Spanish
OTHER LANGUAGES: English, Indian
MAIN RELIGION: Christianity 100%
EXPORTS: Meat, coffee, cotton, sugar, bananas, seafood, gold

COSTA RICA
PRONUNCIATION: kaws-tuh REE-kuh
AREA: 19,652 sq. miles (50,899 sq. km)
POPULATION: 3,419,000
CAPITAL: San José
CURRENCY: 100 centimos = 1 Costa Rican colón (C)
OFFICIAL LANGUAGE: Spanish
OTHER LANGUAGE: English
MAIN RELIGION: Christianity 95%
EXPORTS: Coffee, bananas, sugar, textiles

PANAMA
PRONUNCIATION: PA-nuh-mah
AREA: 33,659 sq. miles (87,177 sq. km)
POPULATION: 2,681,000
CAPITAL: Panama
CURRENCY: 100 centesimos = 1 balboa (B)

PRONUNCIATION KEY

"a" sounds
a *as in* pat
ah *as in* father
ar *as in* dark
ay *as in* bay
air *as in* pair

"e" sounds
e *as in* pet
ee *as in* feet
er *as in* pert
ehr *as in* Sierra

"i" sounds
i *as in* pit
eye *as in* bite
ihr *as in* hear

"o" sounds
o *as in* pot
oh *as in* boat
aw *as in* paw
or *as in* poor
ow *as in* how
oy *as in* boy

"u" sounds
uh *as in* but *and* comma
u *as in* put *and* book
oo *as in* boot
yoo *as in* music

other sounds
th *as in* thin *and* then
sh *as in* show
zh *as in* measure
s *as in* set
ch *as in* chase
j *as in* jug
g *as in* game
ng *as in* sing

Emphasize the part of the word that is written in **BOLD CAPITAL LETTERS**

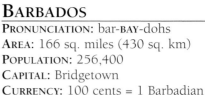

Official Language: Spanish
Other Languages: English, regional languages
Main Religion: Christianity 100%
Exports: Bananas, shrimp, sugar, coffee, clothing

The Bahamas

Pronunciation: the buh-HAH-muhz
Area: 5,386 sq. miles (13,950 sq. km)
Population: 256,600
Capital: Nassau
Currency: 100 cents = 1 Bahamian dollar (B$)
Official Language: English
Other Language: Bahamian creole
Main Religion: Christianity 95%
Exports: Pharmaceuticals, cement, rum, crayfish, refined petroleum products

Cuba

Pronunciation: KYOO-buh
Area: 42,804 sq. miles (110,862 sq. km)
Population: 10,938,000
Capital: Havana
Currency: 100 centavos = 1 Cuban peso (Cu$)
Official Language: Spanish
Main Religion: Christianity 85%
Exports: Sugar, shellfish, citrus fruit, coffee, tobacco, nickel, medical products

Jamaica

Pronunciation: juh-MAY-kuh
Area: 4,471 sq. miles (11,580 sq. km)
Population: 2,574,000
Capital: Kingston
Currency: 100 cents = 1 Jamaican dollar (J$)
Official Language: English
Other Language: Jamaican creole
Main Religion: Christianity 61%
Exports: Bauxite, sugar, bananas, rum

Haiti

Pronunciation: HAY-tee
Area: 10,714 sq. miles (27,749 sq. km)
Population: 6,540,000
Capital: Port-au-Prince
Currency: 100 centimes = 1 gourde (G)
Official Language: French
Other Language: Haitian creole
Main Religion: Christianity 96%
Exports: Clothing, coffee, sugar

Dominican Republic

Pronunciation: duh-MI-ni-kuhn ri-PUH-blik
Area: 18,657 sq. miles (48,322 sq. km)
Population: 7,511,000
Capital: Santo Domingo
Currency: 100 centavos = 1 Dominican peso (RD$)
Official Language: Spanish
Main Religion: Christianity 95%
Exports: Minerals, sugar, coffee, cocoa, gold

Antigua and Barbuda

Pronunciation: an-TEE-guh and bar-BOO-duh
Area: 171 sq. miles (443 sq. km)
Population: 65,200
Capital: St. John's
Currency: 100 cents = 1 East Caribbean dollar (EC$)
Official Language: English
Other Languages: Regional languages
Main Religions: Christianity 97%, indigenous religions 3%
Exports: Petroleum products, manufactured goods, machinery and transportation equipment, food and livestock

St. Kitts–Nevis

Pronunciation: saynt KITS - NEE-vuhs
Area: 104 sq. miles (269 sq. km)
Population: 41,000
Capital: Basseterre
Currency: 100 cents = 1 East Caribbean dollar (EC$)
Official Language: English
Main Religion: Christianity 86%
Exports: Machinery, food, beverages, electronics, tobacco

Dominica

Pronunciation: dah-muh-NEE-kuh
Area: 289 sq. miles (749 sq. km)
Population: 82,600
Capital: Roseau
Currency: 100 cents = 1 East Caribbean dollar (EC$)
Official Language: English
Other Language: French patois
Main Religion: Christianity 92%
Exports: Bananas, grapefruit, oranges, vegetables, soap, bay oil

St. Lucia

Pronunciation: saynt LOO-shuh
Area: 238 sq. miles (616 sq. km)
Population: 156,100
Capital: Castries
Currency: 100 cents = 1 East Caribbean dollar (EC$)
Official Language: English
Other Language: French patois
Main Religion: Christianity 100%
Exports: Bananas, clothing, cocoa, fruit and vegetables, coconut oil

Barbados

Pronunciation: bar-BAY-dohs
Area: 166 sq. miles (430 sq. km)
Population: 256,400
Capital: Bridgetown
Currency: 100 cents = 1 Barbadian dollar (Bds$)
Official Language: English
Other Language: Barbadian creole
Main Religion: Christianity 71%
Exports: Sugar, molasses, rum, other foods and beverages, chemicals, electrical components, clothing

St. Vincent and the Grenadines

Pronunciation: saynt VIN-suhnt and the gren-uh-DEENZ
Area: 150 sq. miles (389 sq. km)
Population: 117,300
Capital: Kingstown
Currency: 100 cents = 1 East Caribbean dollar (EC$)
Official Language: English
Other Language: French patois
Main Religion: Christianity 75%
Exports: Bananas, taro, tennis rackets

Grenada

Pronunciation: gruh-NAY-duh
Area: 133 sq. miles (344 sq. km)
Population: 94,500
Capital: St. George's
Currency: 100 cents = 1 East Caribbean dollar (EC$)
Official Language: English
Other Language: French patois
Main Religion: Christianity 85%
Exports: Bananas, cocoa, nutmeg, fruit and vegetables, clothing, mace

Trinidad and Tobago

Pronunciation: TRI-nuh-dad and tuh-BAY-goh
Area: 1,980 sq. miles (5,128 sq. km)
Population: 1,271,000
Capital: Port-of-Spain
Currency: 100 cents = 1 Trinidad and Tobago dollar (TT$)
Official Language: English
Other Languages: Hindi, French, Spanish
Main Religions: Christianity 60%, Hinduism 24%, Islam 6%
Exports: Petroleum and petroleum products, chemicals, steel products, fertilizer, sugar, cocoa, coffee, citrus fruit, flowers

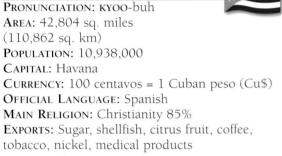

South America

Colombia
Pronunciation: kuh-LUHM-bee-uh
Area: 439,735 sq. miles (1,138,914 sq. km)
Population: 36,200,000
Capital: Bogotá
Currency: 100 centavos = 1 Colombian peso (Col$)
Official Language: Spanish
Main Religion: Christianity 95%
Exports: Petroleum, coffee, coal, bananas, flowers

Venezuela
Pronunciation: ve-nuh-ZWAY-luh
Area: 352,143 sq. miles (912,050 sq. km)
Population: 21,005,000
Capital: Caracas
Currency: 100 centimos = 1 bolivar (B)
Official Language: Spanish
Other Languages: Regional languages
Main Religion: Christianity 98%
Exports: Petroleum, bauxite and aluminum, steel, chemicals, agricultural products, manufactured goods

Guyana
Pronunciation: geye-AH-nuh
Area: 83,000 sq. miles (214,970 sq. km)
Population: 723,800
Capital: Georgetown
Currency: 100 cents = 1 Guyanese dollar (G$)
Official Language: English
Other Languages: Regional languages
Main Religions: Christianity 57%, Hinduism 33%, Islam 9%
Exports: Sugar, molasses, bauxite, rice, shrimp

Suriname
Pronunciation: SUR-uh-nah-muh
Area: 63,251 sq. miles (163,820 sq. km)
Population: 429,500
Capital: Paramaribo
Currency: 100 cents = 1 Surinamese guilder or florin (Sf)
Official Language: Dutch
Other Languages: English, Sranang Tongo, Hindustani, Javanese
Main Religions: Christianity 48%, Hinduism 27%, Islam 20%, regional religions 5%
Exports: Aluminum, shrimp, fish, rice, bananas

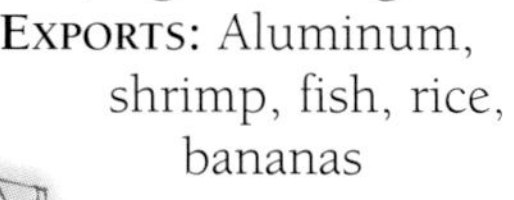

Ecuador
Pronunciation: E-kwuh-dor
Area: 109,483 sq. miles (283,561 sq. km)
Population: 10,891,000
Capital: Quito
Currency: 100 centavos = 1 sucre (S/.)
Official Language: Spanish
Other Languages: Quechua, other regional languages
Main Religion: Christianity 95%
Exports: Petroleum, bananas, shrimp, cocoa, coffee

Peru
Pronunciation: puh-ROO
Area: 496,222 sq. miles (1,285,215 sq. km)
Population: 24,087,000
Capital: Lima
Currency: 100 centavos = 1 sol (S/.)
Official Languages: Spanish, Quechua
Other Language: Aymara
Main Religion: Christianity 90%
Exports: Copper, zinc, petroleum and petroleum products, lead, refined silver, coffee, cotton

Brazil
Pronunciation: bruh-ZIL
Area: 3,284,426 sq. miles (8,506,663 sq. km)
Population: 160,737,000
Capital: Brasília
Currency: 100 centavos = 1 cruzeiro (Cr$)
Official Language: Portuguese
Other Languages: Spanish, English, French
Main Religion: Christianity 96%
Exports: Iron ore, soybean bran, bananas, orange juice, shoes, coffee, motor vehicle parts

Bolivia
Pronunciation: buh-LI-vee-uh
Area: 424,162 sq. miles (1,098,579 sq. km)
Population: 7,896,000
Capitals: La Paz (seat of government), Sucre (legal and judicial)
Currency: 100 centavos = 1 boliviano ($b)
Official Languages: Spanish, Quechua, Aymara
Main Religion: Christianity 100%
Exports: Metals, natural gas, soybeans, jewelry, timber

Chile
Pronunciation: CHI-lee
Area: 292,257 sq. miles (756,946 sq. km)
Population: 14,161,000
Capital: Santiago
Currency: 100 centavos = 1 Chilean peso (Ch$)
Official Language: Spanish
Other Languages: Regional languages
Main Religion: Christianity 99%
Exports: Copper, other metals and minerals, timber products, fish, fruit

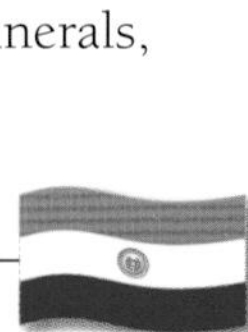

Paraguay
Pronunciation: PAR-uh-gweye
Area: 157,043 sq. miles (406,741 sq. km)
Population: 5,358,000
Capital: Asunción
Currency: 100 centimos = 1 guarani (G)
Official Language: Spanish
Other Language: Guarani
Main Religion: Christianity 97%
Exports: Cotton, soybeans, timber, vegetable oils, meat products, coffee

Argentina
Pronunciation: ar-juhn-TEE-nuh
Area: 1,072,156 sq. miles (2,776,884 sq. km)
Population: 34,293,000
Capital: Buenos Aires
Currency: 100 centavos = 1 peso argentino
Official Language: Spanish
Other Languages: English, Italian, German, French
Main Religions: Christianity 94%, Judaism 2%
Exports: Manufactured goods, meat, wheat, corn, oilseed

Uruguay
Pronunciation: OOR-uh-gweye
Area: 68,039 sq. miles (176,221 sq. km)
Population: 3,223,000
Capital: Montevideo
Currency: 100 centesimos = 1 Uruguayan peso ($Ur)
Official Language: Spanish
Main Religions: Christianity 68%, Judaism 2%
Exports: Wool, textiles, beef and other animal products, leather, rice

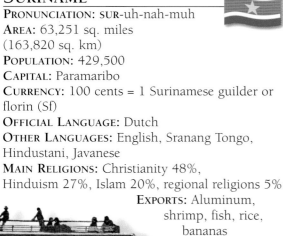

Europe

United Kingdom
Pronunciation: yoo-NEYE-tuhd KING-duhm
Area: 94,251 sq. miles (244,110 sq. km)
Population: 58,295,000
Capital: London
Currency: 100 pence = 1 British pound (£)
Official Language: English
Other Languages: Welsh, Scottish Gaelic, Irish Gaelic
Main Religions: Christianity 90%, Islam 3%, Sikh 1%, Hinduism 1%, Judaism 1%
Exports: Manufactured goods, machinery, fuels, chemicals, transportation equipment

Ireland
Pronunciation: EYER-luhnd
Area: 26,600 sq. miles (68,894 sq. km)
Population: 3,550,000
Capital: Dublin
Currency: 100 pence = 1 Irish pound (£Ir)
Official Languages: English, Irish (Gaelic)
Main Religion: Christianity 96%
Exports: Chemicals, data processing equipment, industrial machinery, livestock, animal products

Portugal
Pronunciation: POR-chi-guhl
Area: 35,383 sq. miles (91,642 sq. km)
Population: 10,562,000
Capital: Lisbon
Currency: 100 centavos = 1 Portuguese escudo (Esc)
Official Language: Portuguese
Main Religion: Christianity 98%
Exports: Clothing, shoes, machinery, cork, paper products, animal skins

Spain
Pronunciation: spayn
Area: 194,881 sq. miles (504,742 sq. km)
Population: 39,404,000
Capital: Madrid
Currency: 100 centimos = 1 peseta (PTA)
Official Language: Castilian Spanish
Other Languages: Catalan, Galician, Basque
Main Religion: Christianity 99%
Exports: Motor vehicles, manufactured goods, food, machinery

Andorra
Pronunciation: an-DOR-uh
Area: 180 sq. miles (482 sq. km)
Population: 65,800
Capital: Andorra la Vella
Currencies: 100 centimes = 1 French franc (F), 100 centimos = 1 peseta (Pta)
Official Language: Catalan
Other Languages: French, Spanish
Main Religion: Christianity 95%
Exports: Electricity, tobacco products, furniture

France
Pronunciation: frans
Area: 212,918 sq. miles (551,458 sq. km)
Population: 58,109,000
Capital: Paris
Currency: 100 centimes = 1 French franc (F)
Official Language: French
Other Languages: Occitan, German, Breton, Catalan, Arabic
Main Religions: Christianity 92%, Judaism 1%, Islam 1%
Exports: Machinery and transportation equipment, chemicals, food, agricultural products, iron and steel products, textiles, clothing

Monaco
Pronunciation: MAH-nuh-koh
Area: 0.58 sq. miles (1.5 sq. km)
Population: 31,500
Capital: Monaco
Currency: 100 centimes = 1 French franc (F)
Official Language: French
Other Languages: English, Italian, Monégasque
Main Religion: Christianity 95%
Exports: Pharmaceuticals, perfumes, clothing

The Netherlands
Pronunciation: the NE-ther-luhndz
Area: 16,033 sq. miles (41,525 sq. km)
Population: 15,453,000
Capitals: Amsterdam; The Hague (judicial)
Currency: 100 cents = 1 Netherlands guilder (Gld)
Official Language: Dutch
Main Religions: Christianity 59%, Islam 3%
Exports: Metal products, chemicals, processed food, tobacco, agricultural products

Belgium
Pronunciation: BEL-juhm
Area: 11,781 sq. miles (30,513 sq. km)
Population: 10,082,000
Capital: Brussels
Currency: 100 centimes = 1 Belgian franc (BF)
Official Languages: Dutch (Flemish), French
Other Language: German
Main Religion: Christianity 100%
Exports: Iron and steel, transportation equipment, tractors, diamonds, petroleum products

Luxembourg
Pronunciation: LUK-suhm-berg
Area: 999 sq. miles (2,587 sq. km)
Population: 404,700
Capital: Luxembourg
Currency: 100 centimes = 1 Luxembourg franc (Flux)
Official Languages: Letzeburgesh, German, French
Other Language: English
Main Religion: Christianity 99%, Judaism 1%
Exports: Steel products, chemicals, rubber products, glass, aluminum

Germany
Pronunciation: JER-muh-nee
Area: 137,735 sq. miles (356,734 sq. km)
Population: 81,338,000
Capital: Berlin
Currency: 100 pfennig = 1 deutsche mark (DM)
Official Language: German
Main Religion: Christianity 82%
Exports: Machines and machine tools, chemicals, motor vehicles, iron and steel products, agricultural products, raw materials, fuels

Switzerland
Pronunciation: SWIT-suhr-luhnd
Area: 15,941 sq. miles (41,287 sq. km)
Population: 7,085,000
Capital: Bern
Currency: 100 centimes = 1 Swiss franc (F)
Official Languages: German, French, Italian, Romansch
Main Religion: Christianity 92%
Exports: Machinery, precision instruments, metal products, food, textiles

Liechtenstein
Pronunciation: LIK-tuhn-shteyen
Area: 62 sq. miles (161 sq. km)
Population: 30,700
Capital: Vaduz
Currency: 100 centimes = 1 Swiss franc (F)
Official Language: German
Main Religion: Christianity 95%
Exports: Machinery, dental products, stamps, hardware, pottery

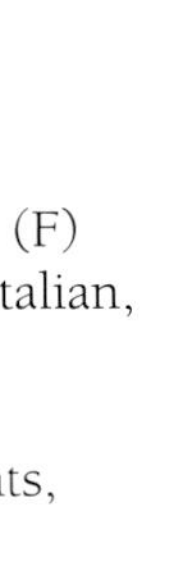

Austria

Pronunciation: aws-tree-uh
Area: 32,375 sq. miles (83,851 sq. km)
Population: 7,987,000
Capital: Vienna
Currency: 100 groschen = 1 Austrian schilling (S)
Official Language: German
Main Religion: Christianity 91%
Exports: Machinery, electrical equipment, iron and steel, lumber, textiles, paper products, chemicals

Italy

Pronunciation: it-uh-lee
Area: 116,313 sq. miles (301,251 sq. km)
Population: 58,262,000
Capital: Rome
Currency: Italian lira (L)
Official Language: Italian
Other Languages: German, French, Slovene
Main Religion: Christianity 98%
Exports: Metals, textiles, clothing, machinery, motor vehicles, transportation equipment, chemicals

San Marino

Pronunciation: san muh-ree-noh
Area: 24 sq. miles (62 sq. km)
Population: 24,300
Capital: San Marino
Currency: Italian lira (L)
Official Language: Italian
Main Religion: Christianity 95%
Exports: Building stone, lime, timber, chestnuts, wheat, wine, baked goods, animal skins, ceramics

Vatican City

Pronunciation: va-ti-kuhn city
Area: 0.17 sq. miles (0.44 sq. km)
Population: 830
Capital: Vatican City
Currency: Vatican lira (VLit)
Official Languages: Italian, Latin
Main Religion: Christianity 100%
Exports: None

Malta

Pronunciation: mawl-tuh
Area: 122 sq. miles (316 sq. km)
Population: 369,600
Capital: Valletta
Currency: 100 cents = 1 Maltese lira (Lm)
Official Languages: Maltese, English
Main Religion: Christianity 98%
Exports: Machinery and transportation equipment, clothing, shoes, printed matter

Slovenia

Pronunciation: sloh-vee-nee-uh
Area: 7,819 sq. miles (20,251 sq. km)
Population: 2,052,000
Capital: Ljubljana
Currency: 100 stotins = 1 tolar (SlT)
Official Language: Slovenian
Other Language: Serbo-Croatian
Main Religions: Christianity 96%, Islam 1%
Exports: Motor vehicles, furniture, machinery, manufactured goods, chemicals, textiles, food, raw materials

Croatia

Pronunciation: kroh-ay-shuh
Area: 21,829 sq. miles (56,537 sq. km)
Population: 4,666,000
Capital: Zagreb
Currency: 100 lipas = 1 Croatian kuna (HRK)
Official Language: Serbo-Croatian
Main Religions: Christianity 88%, Islam 1%
Exports: Machinery and transportation equipment, other manufactured goods, chemicals, food, livestock, raw materials, fuels and lubricants

Bosnia and Herzegovina

Pronunciation: bahz-nee-uh and hert-suh-goh-vee-nuh
Area: 19,904 sq. miles (51,750 sq. km)
Population: 3,202,000
Capital: Sarajevo
Currency: 100 paras = 1 dinar (D)
Official Language: Serbo-Croatian
Main Religions: Christianity 50%, Islam 40%
Exports: Timber, furniture

Yugoslavia

Pronunciation: yoo-goh-slah-vee-uh
Area: 39,449 sq. miles (102,173 sq. km)
Population: 11,102,000
Capital: Belgrade
Currency: 100 paras = 1 Yugoslav dinar (YD)
Official Language: Serbo-Croatian
Other Languages: Albanian, Hungarian
Main Religions: Christianity 70%, Islam 19%
Exports: Textiles, leather goods, machinery

Romania

Pronunciation: roh-may-nee-uh
Area: 91,699 sq. miles (237,500 sq. km)
Population: 23,198,000
Capital: Bucharest
Currency: 100 bani = 1 leu (L)
Official Language: Romanian
Other Languages: Hungarian, German
Main Religion: Christianity 82%
Exports: Metals and metal products, mineral products, textiles, electrical equipment, transportation equipment

Bulgaria

Pronunciation: buhl-gair-ee-uh
Area: 42,823 sq. miles (110,912 sq. km)
Population: 8,775,000
Capital: Sofia
Currency: 100 stotinki = 1 lev (Lv)
Official Language: Bulgarian
Main Religions: Christianity 85%, Islam 13%, Judaism 1%
Exports: Machinery, agricultural products, manufactured goods, fuels, minerals, raw materials, metals

Albania

Pronunciation: al-bay-nee-uh
Area: 11,100 sq. miles (28,749 sq. km)
Population: 3,414,000
Capital: Tiranë
Currency: 100 qindarka = 1 lek (L)
Official Language: Albanian
Other Language: Greek
Main Religions: Islam 70%, Christianity 30%
Exports: Asphalt, metals and metallic ores, electricity, crude oil, fruit and vegetables, tobacco

Macedonia

Pronunciation: ma-suh-doh-nee-uh
Area: 9,928 sq. miles (25,714 sq. km)
Population: 2,160,000
Capital: Skopje
Currency: 100 paras = 1 dinar
Official Language: Macedonian
Other Languages: Albanian, Turkish, Serbo-Croatian
Main Religions: Christianity 67%, Islam 30%
Exports: Manufactured goods, machinery and transportation equipment, raw materials, food, livestock, beverages, tobacco, chemicals

Greece

Pronunciation: grees
Area: 50,944 sq. miles (131,945 sq. km)
Population: 10,648,000
Capital: Athens
Currency: 100 lepta = 1 drachma (Dr)
Official Language: Greek
Other Languages: English, French
Main Religion: Christianity 98%
Exports: Manufactured goods, food, fuels

Estonia

Pronunciation: e-stoh-nee-uh
Area: 17,413 sq. miles (45,100 sq. km)
Population: 1,625,000
Capital: Tallinn
Currency: 100 cents = 1 Estonian kroon (EEK)
Official Language: Estonian
Other Languages: Latvian, Lithuanian, Russian
Main Religion: Christianity 100%
Exports: Textiles, food, motor vehicles, metals

Latvia

Pronunciation: LAT-vee-uh
Area: 24,595 sq. miles (63,701 sq. km)
Population: 2,763,000
Capital: Riga
Currency: 100 cents = 1 lat (Ls)
Official Language: Latvian
Other Languages: Lithuanian, Russian
Main Religion: Christianity 100%
Exports: Oil products, timber, metals, dairy products, furniture, textiles

Lithuania

Pronunciation: li-thuh-WAY-nee-uh
Area: 25,174 sq. miles (65,201 sq. km)
Population: 3,876,000
Capital: Vilnius
Currency: 100 centas = 1 litas (Lt)
Official Language: Lithuanian
Other Languages: Polish, Russian
Main Religion: Christianity 100%
Exports: Electronics, petroleum products, food, chemicals

Belarus

Pronunciation: be-luh-ROOS
Area: 80,154 sq. miles (207,599 sq. km)
Population: 10,437,000
Capital: Minsk
Currency: Belarusian rubel (BR)
Official Language: Belarusian
Other Language: Russian
Main Religion: Christianity 68%
Exports: Machinery and transportation equipment, chemicals, food

Poland

Pronunciation: POH-luhnd
Area: 120,756 sq. miles (312,758 sq. km)
Population: 38,792,000
Capital: Warsaw
Currency: 100 groszy = 1 zloty (Zl)
Official Language: Polish
Main Religion: Christianity 95%
Exports: Machinery and transportation equipment, manufactured goods, food, fuels

Czech Republic

Pronunciation: chek ri-PUH-blik
Area: 30,450 sq. miles (78,866 sq. km)
Population: 10,433,000
Capital: Prague
Currency: 100 haleru = 1 koruna (Kc)
Official Language: Czech
Other Language: Slovak
Main Religion: Christianity 47%
Exports: Manufactured goods, machinery and transportation equipment, chemicals, fuels, minerals, metals, agricultural products

Slovakia

Pronunciation: sloh-VAH-kee-uh
Area: 18,923 sq. miles (49,011 sq. km)
Population: 5,432,000
Capital: Bratislava
Currency: 100 halierov = 1 koruna (Sk)
Official Language: Slovak
Other Language: Hungarian
Main Religion: Christianity 72%
Exports: Machinery and transportation equipment, chemicals, fuels, minerals and metals, agricultural products

Ukraine

Pronunciation: yoo-KRAYN
Area: 233,089 sq. miles (603,701 sq. km)
Population: 51,868,000
Capital: Kiev
Currency: Karbovanets (Kb)
Official Language: Ukrainian
Other Languages: Russian, Romanian, Polish, Hungarian
Main Religions: Christianity 90%, Judaism 2%
Exports: Coal, electricity, metals, chemicals, machinery and transportation equipment, grain, meat

Hungary

Pronunciation: HUHNG-uh-ree
Area: 35,919 sq. miles (93,030 sq. km)
Population: 10,319,000
Capital: Budapest
Currency: 100 filler = 1 forint (Ft)
Official Language: Hungarian
Main Religion: Christianity 92%
Exports: Raw materials, machinery and transportation equipment, manufactured goods, food, agriculture, fuels, energy

Moldova

Pronunciation: mawl-DOH-vuh
Area: 13,012 sq. miles (33,701 sq. km)
Population: 4,490,000
Capital: Chişinău
Currency: Leu (L)
Official Language: Moldovian
Other Languages: Russian, Gagauz
Main Religions: Christianity 99%, Judaism 1%
Exports: Food, wine, tobacco, textiles, shoes, machinery, chemicals

Iceland

Pronunciation: EYES-luhnd
Area: 39,702 sq. miles (102,828 sq. km)
Population: 266,000
Capital: Reykjavík
Currency: 100 aurar = 1 Icelandic krona (IKr)
Official Language: Icelandic
Main Religion: Christianity 99%
Exports: Fish and fish products, animal products, minerals

Norway

Pronunciation: NOR-way
Area: 154,790 sq. miles (400,906 sq. km)
Population: 4,331,000
Capital: Oslo
Currency: 100 ore = 1 Norwegian krone (NKr)
Official Language: Norwegian
Other Languages: Lappish, Finnish
Main Religion: Christianity 91%
Exports: Petroleum and petroleum products, metals and metal products, fish and fish products, chemicals, natural gas, ships

Sweden

Pronunciation: SWEE-duhn
Area: 173,665 sq. miles (449,792 sq. km)
Population: 8,822,000
Capital: Stockholm
Currency: 100 ore = 1 Swedish krona (SKr)
Official Language: Swedish
Other Languages: Lapp, Finnish
Main Religion: Christianity 96%
Exports: Machinery, motor vehicles, paper products, pulp and wood, iron and steel products, chemicals, petroleum and petroleum products

Finland

Pronunciation: FIN-luhnd
Area: 130,128 sq. miles (337,032 sq. km)
Population: 5,085,000
Capital: Helsinki
Currency: 100 pennia = 1 markka (FmK)
Official Languages: Finnish, Swedish
Other Languages: Lapp, Russian
Main Religion: Christianity 90%
Exports: Paper and pulp, machinery, chemicals, metals, timber

Denmark

Pronunciation: DEN-mark
Area: 16,629 sq. miles (43,069 sq. km)
Population: 5,199,000
Capital: Copenhagen
Currency: 100 ore = 1 Danish krone (DKr)
Official Language: Danish
Other Languages: Faroese, Greenlandic, German
Main Religion: Christianity 93%
Exports: Meat and meat products, dairy products, transportation equipment, ships, fish, chemicals, industrial machinery

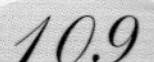

ASIA

RUSSIA
PRONUNCIATION: RUH-shuh
AREA: 6,592,812 sq. miles (17,075,383 sq. km)
POPULATION: 149,909,000
CAPITAL: Moscow
CURRENCY: 100 kopecks = 1 ruble (R)
OFFICIAL LANGUAGE: Russian
MAIN RELIGIONS: Christianity 75%, Islam, Buddhism
EXPORTS: Petroleum and petroleum products, natural gas, timber and timber products, metals, chemicals, manufactured goods

TURKEY
PRONUNCIATION: TER-kee
AREA: 301,380 sq. miles (780,574 sq. km)
POPULATION: 63,406,000
CAPITAL: Ankara
CURRENCY: 100 kurus = 1 Turkish lira (TL)
OFFICIAL LANGUAGE: Turkish
OTHER LANGUAGES: Kurdish, Arabic
MAIN RELIGION: Islam 99%
EXPORTS: Manufactured goods, food, mining products

CYPRUS
PRONUNCIATION: SEYE-pruhs
AREA: 3,572 sq. miles (9,251 sq. km)
POPULATION: 736,600
CAPITAL: Nicosia
CURRENCY: 100 cents = 1 Cypriot pound (£C); 100 kurus = 1 Turkish lira (TL)
OFFICIAL LANGUAGES: Greek, Turkish
OTHER LANGUAGE: English
MAIN RELIGIONS: Christianity 78%, Islam 18%
EXPORTS: Citrus fruit, potatoes, grapes, wine, cement, clothing, shoes

GEORGIA
PRONUNCIATION: JOR-juh
AREA: 26,911 sq. miles (69,699 sq. km)
POPULATION: 5,726,000
CAPITAL: Tbilisi
CURRENCY: Lari
OFFICIAL LANGUAGE: Georgian
OTHER LANGUAGES: Russian, Armenian, Azeri
MAIN RELIGIONS: Christianity 83%, Islam 11%
EXPORTS: Citrus fruit, tea, wine, machinery, metals, textiles, chemicals, fuel re-exports

ARMENIA
PRONUNCIATION: ar-MEE-nee-uh
AREA: 11,506 sq. miles (29,800 sq. km)
POPULATION: 3,557,000
CAPITAL: Yerevan
CURRENCY: Dram
OFFICIAL LANGUAGE: Armenian
OTHER LANGUAGE: Russian
MAIN RELIGION: Christianity 94%
EXPORTS: Gold and jewelry, aluminum, transportation equipment, electrical equipment

AZERBAIJAN
PRONUNCIATION: a-zuhr-beye-ZHAHN
AREA: 33,436 sq. miles (86,599 sq. km)
POPULATION: 7,790,000
CAPITAL: Baku
CURRENCY: 100 gopik = 1 manat
OFFICIAL LANGUAGE: Azerbaijani
OTHER LANGUAGES: Russian, Armenian
MAIN RELIGIONS: Islam 94%, Christianity 5%
EXPORTS: Oil, gas, chemicals, oil field equipment, textiles, cotton

KAZAKSTAN
PRONUNCIATION: kuh-zahk-STAHN
AREA: 1,048,300 sq. miles (2,715,097 sq. km)
POPULATION: 17,377,000
CAPITAL: Almaty
CURRENCY: Tenge
OFFICIAL LANGUAGE: Kazak
OTHER LANGUAGE: Russian
MAIN RELIGIONS: Islam 47%, Christianity 46%
EXPORTS: Oil, metals, chemicals, grain, wool, meat, coal

UZBEKISTAN
PRONUNCIATION: uz-be-ki-STAN
AREA: 173,591 sq. miles (449,601 sq. km)
POPULATION: 23,089,000
CAPITAL: Tashkent
CURRENCY: Som
OFFICIAL LANGUAGE: Uzbek
OTHER LANGUAGES: Russian, Tajik
MAIN RELIGIONS: Islam 88%, Christianity 9%
EXPORTS: Cotton, gold, natural gas, mineral fertilizer, metals, textiles, food

TURKMENISTAN
PRONUNCIATION: terk-me-nuh-STAN
AREA: 188,455 sq. miles (488,098 sq. km)
POPULATION: 4,075,000
CAPITAL: Ashkhabad
CURRENCY: Manat
OFFICIAL LANGUAGE: Turkmen
OTHER LANGUAGES: Russian, Uzbek
MAIN RELIGIONS: Islam 87%, Christianity 11%
EXPORTS: Natural gas, cotton, petroleum products, electricity, textiles, carpets

KYRGYZSTAN
PRONUNCIATION: kihr-gi-STAN
AREA: 76,641 sq. miles (198,500 sq. km)
POPULATION: 4,770,000
CAPITAL: Bishkek
CURRENCY: Som
OFFICIAL LANGUAGE: Kyrgyz
OTHER LANGUAGE: Russian
MAIN RELIGION: Islam 70%
EXPORTS: Wool, chemicals, cotton, metals, shoes, machinery, tobacco

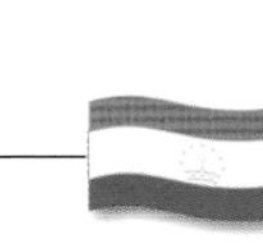

TAJIKISTAN
PRONUNCIATION: tah-ji-ki-STAN
AREA: 55,251 sq. miles (143,100 sq. km)
POPULATION: 6,155,000
CAPITAL: Dushanbe
CURRENCY: 100 kopeks = 1 Tajik ruble (TR)
OFFICIAL LANGUAGE: Tajik
OTHER LANGUAGE: Russian
MAIN RELIGION: Islam 85%
EXPORTS: Cotton, aluminum, fruit and vegetables, textiles

SYRIA
PRONUNCIATION: SIHR-ee-uh
AREA: 71,498 sq. miles (185,180 sq. km)
POPULATION: 15,452,000
CAPITAL: Damascus
CURRENCY: 100 piastres = 1 Syrian pound (£S)
OFFICIAL LANGUAGE: Arabic
OTHER LANGUAGES: Kurdish, Armenian, Aramaic, Circassian, French
MAIN RELIGIONS: Islam 90%, Christianity 10%
EXPORTS: Petroleum, textiles, cotton, fruit and vegetables, wheat, barley, chickens

IRAQ

PRONUNCIATION: i-RAHK
AREA: 168,927 sq. miles (437,521 sq. km)
POPULATION: 20,644,000
CAPITAL: Baghdad
CURRENCY: 1,000 fils = 1 Iraqi dinar (ID)
OFFICIAL LANGUAGES: Arabic, Kurdish (in Kurdish regions)
OTHER LANGUAGES: Assyrian, Armenian
MAIN RELIGIONS: Islam 97%, Christianity 3%
EXPORTS: Crude oil and refined products, fertilizer, sulfur

IRAN

PRONUNCIATION: i-RAHN
AREA: 635,932 sq. miles (1,647,064 sq. km)
POPULATION: 64,625,000
CAPITAL: Tehran
CURRENCY: 100 dinars = 1 rial (R)
OFFICIAL LANGUAGE: Farsi (Persian)
OTHER LANGUAGES: Turkic, Kurdish
MAIN RELIGION: Islam 99%
EXPORTS: Petroleum, carpets, fruit, nuts, animal skins

LEBANON

PRONUNCIATION: LE-buh-nuhn
AREA: 3,949 sq. miles (10,228 sq. km)
POPULATION: 3,696,000
CAPITAL: Beirut
CURRENCY: 100 piastres = 1 Lebanese pound (£L)
OFFICIAL LANGUAGES: Arabic, French
OTHER LANGUAGES: Armenian, English
MAIN RELIGIONS: Islam 70%, Christianity 30%
EXPORTS: Agricultural products, chemicals, textiles, metals, jewelry

ISRAEL

PRONUNCIATION: IZ-ray-uhl
AREA: 7,992 sq. miles (20,699 sq. km)
POPULATION: 5,433,000
CAPITAL: Jerusalem
CURRENCY: 100 new agorot = 1 Israeli shekel (IS)
OFFICIAL LANGUAGE: Hebrew, Arabic
OTHER LANGUAGES: English
MAIN RELIGIONS: Judaism 82%, Islam 14%, Christianity 2%
EXPORTS: Machinery, cut diamonds, chemicals, textiles, agricultural products, metals

JORDAN

PRONUNCIATION: JOR-duhn
AREA: 34,575 sq. miles (89,549 sq. km)
POPULATION: 4,101,000
CAPITAL: Amman
CURRENCY: 1,000 fils = 1 Jordanian dinar (JD)
OFFICIAL LANGUAGE: Arabic
OTHER LANGUAGE: English
MAIN RELIGIONS: Islam 92%, Christianity 8%
EXPORTS: Phosphates, fertilizer, potash, agricultural products, manufactured goods

SAUDI ARABIA

PRONUNCIATION: SOW-dee uh-RAY-bee-uh
AREA: 865,000 sq. miles (2,240,350 sq. km)
POPULATION: 18,730,000
CAPITAL: Riyadh
CURRENCY: 100 halalas = 1 Saudi riyal (SR)
OFFICIAL LANGUAGE: Arabic
MAIN RELIGION: Islam 100%
EXPORTS: Petroleum and petroleum products

KUWAIT

PRONUNCIATION: koo-WAYT
AREA: 6,880 sq. miles (17,819 sq. km)
POPULATION: 1,817,000
CAPITAL: Kuwait
CURRENCY: 1,000 fils = 1 Kuwaiti dinar (KD)
OFFICIAL LANGUAGE: Arabic
OTHER LANGUAGE: English
MAIN RELIGIONS: Islam 85%, Christianity 8%, Hinduism and Parsi 2%
EXPORTS: Oil

BAHRAIN

PRONUNCIATION: bah-RAYN
AREA: 255 sq. miles (661 sq. km)
POPULATION: 575,900
CAPITAL: Manama
CURRENCY: 1,000 fils = 1 Bahraini dinar (BD)
OFFICIAL LANGUAGE: Arabic
OTHER LANGUAGES: English, Farsi, Urdu
MAIN RELIGION: Islam 100%
EXPORTS: Petroleum and petroleum products, aluminum

QATAR

PRONUNCIATION: KAH-tuhr
AREA: 4,400 sq. miles (11,395 sq. km)
POPULATION: 533,900
CAPITAL: Doha
CURRENCY: 100 dirhams = 1 Qatari riyal (QR)
OFFICIAL LANGUAGE: Arabic
OTHER LANGUAGE: English
MAIN RELIGION: Islam 95%
EXPORTS: Petroleum products, steel, fertilizer

UNITED ARAB EMIRATES

PRONUNCIATION: yoo-NEYE-tuhd A-ruhb EM-uh-ruhts
AREA: 30,000 sq. miles (77,701 sq. km)
POPULATION: 2,925,000
CAPITAL: Abu Dhabi
CURRENCY: 100 fils = 1 Emirian dirham (Dh)
OFFICIAL LANGUAGE: Arabic
OTHER LANGUAGES: Persian, English, Hindi, Urdu
MAIN RELIGION: Islam 96%
EXPORTS: Crude oil, natural gas, dried fish, dates

OMAN

PRONUNCIATION: oh-MAHN
AREA: 82,000 sq. miles (212,380 sq. km)
POPULATION: 2,125,000
CAPITAL: Muscat
CURRENCY: 1,000 baiza = 1 Omani rial (RO)
OFFICIAL LANGUAGE: Arabic
OTHER LANGUAGES: English, Baluchi, Urdu, Indian languages
MAIN RELIGIONS: Islam 86%, Hinduism 13%
EXPORTS: Petroleum, fish, copper, textiles

YEMEN

PRONUNCIATION: YE-muhn
AREA: 203,849 sq. miles (527,969 sq. km)
POPULATION: 14,728,000
CAPITAL: Sanaa
CURRENCY: 100 fils = 1 rial
OFFICIAL LANGUAGE: Arabic
MAIN RELIGION: Islam 99%
EXPORTS: Crude oil, cotton, coffee, animal skins, vegetables, dried and salted fish

Afghanistan

Pronunciation: af-GA-nuh-stan
Area: 250,775 sq. miles (649,507 sq. km)
Population: 21,252,000
Capital: Kabul
Currency: 100 puls = 1 afghani (AF)
Official Languages: Afghan, Persian, Pashto
Other Languages: Uzbek, Turkmen
Main Religions: Islam 99%, Hinduism and Judaism 1%
Exports: Fruit, nuts, handwoven carpets, wool, cotton, animal skins, precious and semiprecious gemstones

Pakistan

Pronunciation: pa-ki-STAN
Area: 310,403 sq. miles (803,944 sq. km)
Population: 131,542,000
Capital: Islamabad
Currency: 100 paisa = 1 Pakistani rupee (PRe)
Official Languages: Urdu, English
Other Languages: Punjabi, Sindhi, Pashto, Baluchi
Main Religion: Islam 97%
Exports: Cotton, textiles, clothing, rice, leather, carpets

India

Pronunciation: IN-dee-uh
Area: 1,195,063 sq. miles (3,095,472 sq. km)
Population: 936,546,000
Capital: New Delhi
Currency: 100 paise = 1 Indian rupee (Re)
Official Languages: Hindi, English
Other Languages: Hindustani, Bengali, Telugu, Marathi, Tamil, Urdu, Gujarati, Malayalam, Kannada, Oriya, Punjabi, Assamese, Kashmiri, Rajasthani, Sindhi, Sanskrit
Main Religions: Hinduism 80%, Islam 14%, Christianity 3%
Exports: Clothing, gemstones and jewelry, engineering equipment, chemicals, leather goods, cotton yarn, fabric

Nepal

Pronunciation: nuh-PAHL
Area: 54,362 sq. miles (140,798 sq. km)
Population: 21,561,000
Capital: Kathmandu
Currency: 100 paisa = 1 Nepalese rupee (NR)
Official Language: Nepali
Main Religions: Hinduism 90%, Buddhism 5%, Islam 3%
Exports: Carpets, clothing, leather goods, jute goods, grain

Bhutan

Pronunciation: boo-TAHN
Area: 16,000 sq. miles (41,440 sq. km)
Population: 1,781,000
Capital: Thimphu
Currency: 100 chetrums = 1 ngultrum (Nu); Indian currency is also legal tender
Official Language: Dzongkha
Other Languages: Tibetan and Nepali
Main Religions: Buddhism 75%, Hinduism 25%
Exports: Timber, handicrafts, cement, fruit, electricity, gemstones, spices

Bangladesh

Pronunciation: bahng-gluh-DESH
Area: 55,126 sq. miles (142,776 sq. km)
Population: 128,095,000
Capital: Dhaka
Currency: 100 paisa = 1 taka (Tk)
Official Language: Bengali
Other Language: English
Main Religions: Islam 83%, Hinduism 16%, Buddhism and Christianity 1%
Exports: Garments, jute and jute goods, leather, shrimp

Maldives

Pronunciation: MAWL-deevz
Area: 115 sq. miles (298 sq. km)
Population: 261,300
Capital: Male
Currency: 100 laari = 1 rufiyaa (Rf)
Official Language: Divehi (Maldivian)
Other Language: English
Main Religion: Islam 100%
Exports: Fish, clothing

Sri Lanka

Pronunciation: sree LAHNG-kuh
Area: 25,332 sq. miles (65,610 sq. km)
Population: 18,343,000
Capital: Colombo
Currency: 100 cents = 1 Sri Lankan rupee (SLRe)
Official Languages: Sinhala, Tamil
Other Language: English

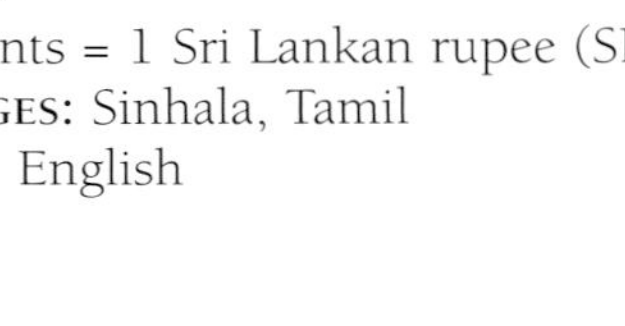

Main Religions: Buddhism 69%, Hinduism 15%, Christianity 8%, Islam 8%
Exports: Textiles, tea, diamonds and other precious gemstones, petroleum products, rubber products, agricultural products, marine products

Myanmar (Burma)

Pronunciation: MYAHN-mar (BER-muh)
Area: 261,789 sq. miles (678,034 sq. km)
Population: 45,104,000
Capital: Yangon (Rangoon)
Currency: 100 pyas = 1 kyat (K)
Official Language: Burmese
Main Religions: Buddhism 89%, Christianity 4%, Islam 4%
Exports: Pulses and beans, rice, timber

Laos

Pronunciation: lows
Area: 91,428 sq. miles (236,799 sq. km)
Population: 4,837,000
Capital: Vientiane
Currency: 100 at = 1 kip (K)
Official Language: Lao
Other Languages: French, English
Main Religions: Buddhism 60%, animism 34%, Christianity 2%
Exports: Electricity, timber products, coffee, tin, textiles

Vietnam

Pronunciation: vee-et-NAHM
Area: 130,468 sq. miles (337,912 sq. km)
Population: 74,393,000
Capital: Hanoi
Currency: 100 xu = 1 dong (D)
Official Language: Vietnamese
Other Languages: French, Chinese, English, Khmer, tribal languages
Main Religions: Buddhism 55%, Christianity 7%, Taoism, indigenous religions, Islam
Exports: Petroleum, rice, agricultural products, marine products, coffee

Thailand

Pronunciation: TEYE-land
Area: 198,455 sq. miles (513,998 sq. km)
Population: 60,271,000
Capital: Bangkok
Currency: 100 satang = 1 baht (B)
Official Language: Thai
Other Languages: English, Chinese, Malay
Main Religions: Buddhism 95%, Islam 4%
Exports: Machinery, manufactured goods, agricultural products, fish

Cambodia

Pronunciation: kam-BOH-dee-uh
Area: 69,898 sq. miles (181,036 sq. km)
Population: 10,561,000
Capital: Phnom Penh
Currency: 100 sen = 1 riel (CR)
Official Language: Khmer
Other Language: French
Main Religions: Buddhism 95%, Islam 2%
Exports: Timber, rubber, soybeans, sesame

Malaysia

Pronunciation: muh-LAY-zhuh
Area: 128,727 sq. miles (333,403 sq. km)
Population: 19,724,000
Capital: Kuala Lumpur
Currency: 100 sen = 1 ringgit (M$)
Official Language: Malay
Other Languages: English, Mandarin, Tamil, Hakka, regional languages
Main Religions: Islam 53%, Buddhism 17%, Confucianism 12%, Christianity 9%, Hinduism 7%
Exports: Electronic equipment, petroleum and petroleum products, palm oil, timber and timber products, rubber, textiles

Philippines

Pronunciation: FI-luh-peenz
Area: 115,651 sq. miles (299,536 sq. km)
Population: 73,266,000
Capital: Manila
Currency: 100 centavos = 1 Philippine peso (P)
Official Languages: Pilipino, English
Other Languages: Regional languages
Main Religions: Christianity 92%, Islam 5%, Buddhism 3%
Exports: Electronics, textiles, coconut products, copper, fish

Singapore

Pronunciation: SING-uh-por
Area: 225 sq. miles (583 sq. km)
Population: 2,890,000
Capital: Singapore
Currency: 100 cents = 1 Singapore dollar (S$)
Official Languages: Chinese, Malay, Tamil, English
Main Religions: Buddhism 28%, Islam 15%, Christianity 13%, Taoism 13%, Hinduism 5%
Exports: Computer equipment, rubber and rubber products, petroleum products, telecommunications equipment

Brunei

Pronunciation: broo-NEYE
Area: 2,226 sq. miles (5,765 sq. km)
Population: 292,300
Capital: Bandar Seri Begawan
Currency: 100 cents = 1 Bruneian dollar (B$)
Official Language: Malay
Other Languages: English, Chinese
Main Religions: Islam 63%, Buddhist 14%, Christianity 8%, indigenous religions
Exports: Crude oil, liquefied natural gas, petroleum products

Indonesia

Pronunciation: in-duh-NEE-zhuh
Area: 779,675 sq. miles (2,019,358 sq. km)
Population: 203,584,000
Capital: Jakarta
Currency: 100 sen = 1 Indonesian rupiah (Rp)
Official Language: Bahasa Indonesia
Other Languages: English, Dutch, Javanese, regional languages
Main Religions: Islam 87%, Christianity 9%, Hinduism 2%, Buddhism 1%
Exports: Manufactured goods, fuels, food, raw materials

China

Pronunciation: CHEYE-nuh
Area: 3,700,000 sq. miles (9,583,000 sq. km)
Population: 1,203,097,000
Capital: Beijing
Currency: 10 jiao = 1 yuan (Y)
Official Language: Mandarin
Other Languages: Cantonese, Shanghainese, Fuzhou, Hokkien-Taiwanese
Main Religions: Daoism (Taoism) 20%, Buddhism 6%
Exports: Textiles, clothing, shoes, toys, machinery, weapons

Mongolia

Pronunciation: mahn-GOHL-yuh
Area: 604,247 sq. miles (1,565,000 sq. km)
Population: 2,494,000
Capital: Ulaanbaatar
Currency: 100 mongos = 1 tugrik (Tug)
Official Language: Khalkha Mongol
Other Languages: Turkic, Russian, Chinese
Main Religions: Buddhism 95%, Islam 4%
Exports: Copper, livestock, animal products, cashmere, wool, animal skins, metals

North Korea

Pronunciation: north kuh-REE-uh
Area: 46,609 sq. miles (120,717 sq. km)
Population: 23,487,000
Capital: P'yŏngyang
Currency: 100 chon = 1 North Korean won (NKW)
Official Language: Korean
Main Religions: Chondogya 14%, Buddhism 2%, Christianity 1%
Exports: Minerals, metal products, agricultural and fishery products, manufactured goods

South Korea

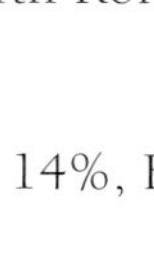

Pronunciation: sowth kuh-REE-uh
Area: 38,022 sq. miles (98,477 sq. km)
Population: 45,554,000
Capital: Seoul
Currency: 100 chon = 1 South Korean won (W)
Official Language: Korean
Other Language: English
Main Religions: Christianity 49%, Buddhism 47%, Confucianism 3%
Exports: Electronic and electrical equipment, machinery, steel, motor vehicles, ships, textiles, clothing, shoes, fish

Taiwan

Pronunciation: TEYE-WAHN
Area: 13,887 sq. miles (35,967 sq. km)
Population: 21,501,000
Capital: Taipei
Currency: 100 cents = 1 New Taiwan dollar (NT$)
Official Language: Mandarin
Other Languages: Fukien, Hakka
Main Religions: Buddhism 43%, Daoism (Taoism) 21%, Christianity 7%, Confucianism
Exports: Electrical machinery, electronic goods, textiles, shoes, food, timber products

Japan

Pronunciation: juh-PAN
Area: 143,619 sq. miles (371,973 sq. km)
Population: 125,506,000
Capital: Tokyo
Currency: 100 sen = 1 yen (¥)
Official Language: Japanese
Main Religions: Shinto and Buddhism 84%
Exports: Machinery, motor vehicles, consumer electronics

Africa

Morocco

Pronunciation: muh-**rah**-koh
Area: 172,413 sq. miles (446,550 sq. km)
Population: 29,169,000
Capital: Rabat
Currency: 100 centimes = 1 Moroccan dirham (DH)
Official Language: Arabic
Other Languages: Berber, French
Main Religions: Islam 99%, Christianity 1%
Exports: Food, beverages, consumer goods, phosphates

Algeria

Pronunciation: al-**jihr**-ee-uh
Area: 918,497 sq. miles (2,378,907 sq. km)
Population: 28,539,000
Capital: Algiers
Currency: 100 centimes = 1 Algerian dinar (DA)
Official Language: Arabic
Other Languages: French, Berber
Main Religions: Islam 99%, Christianity and Judaism 1%
Exports: Petroleum, natural gas

Tunisia

Pronunciation: too-**nee**-zhuh
Area: 63,378 sq. miles (164,149 sq. km)
Population: 8,880,000
Capital: Tunis
Currency: 1,000 millimes = 1 Tunisian dinar (TD)
Official Language: Arabic
Other Languages: French, Berber
Main Religions: Islam 98%, Christianity 1%, Judaism 1%
Exports: Agricultural products, chemicals

Libya

Pronunciation: **li**-bee-uh
Area: 679,360 sq. miles (1,759,540 sq. km)
Population: 5,248,000
Capital: Tripoli

Currency: 1,000 dirhams = 1 Libyan dinar (LD)
Official Language: Arabic
Other Languages: Italian, English
Main Religion: Islam 97%
Exports: Crude oil, refined petroleum products, natural gas

Cape Verde Islands

Pronunciation: kayp **vaird** islands
Area: 1,557 sq. miles (4,033 sq. km)
Population: 435,900
Capital: Praia
Currency: 100 centavos = 1 Cape Verdean escudo (CVEsc)
Official Language: Portuguese
Other Language: Cape Verde creole
Main Religion: Christianity 97%
Exports: Fish, bananas, animal skins

Egypt

Pronunciation: **ee**-juhpt
Area: 386,900 sq. miles (1,002,071 sq. km)
Population: 62,360,000
Capital: Cairo
Currency: 100 piasters = 1 Egyptian pound (£E)
Official Language: Arabic
Other Languages: English, French
Main Religions: Islam 94%, Christianity 6%
Exports: Crude oil and petroleum products, cotton, textiles, metal products, chemicals

Mauritania

Pronunciation: maw-ruh-**tay**-nee-uh
Area: 397,955 sq. miles (1,030,807 sq. km)
Population: 2,263,000
Capital: Nouakchott
Currency: 5 khoums = 1 ouguiya (UM)
Official Languages: Hasaniya Arabic, Wolof
Other Languages: French, Pular, Soninke
Main Religion: Islam 100%
Exports: Iron ore, fish, fish products

Mali

Pronunciation: **mah**-lee
Area: 478,652 sq. miles (1,239,709 sq. km)
Population: 9,375,000
Capital: Bamako
Currency: 100 centimes = 1 CFA franc (CFAF)
Official Language: French
Other Languages: Regional languages
Main Religions: Islam 90%, indigenous religions 9%, Christianity 1%
Exports: Cotton, livestock, gold

Burkina Faso

Pronunciation: ber-**kee**-nuh **fah**-soh
Area: 105,869 sq. miles (274,201 sq. km)
Population: 10,423,000
Capital: Ouagadougou
Currency: 100 centimes = 1 CFA franc (CFAF)
Official Language: French
Other Languages: Tribal languages
Main Religions: Islam 50%, indigenous religions 40%, Christianity 10%
Exports: Cotton, gold, animal products

Niger

Pronunciation: **neye**-juhr
Area: 459,073 sq. miles (1,188,999 sq. km)
Population: 9,280,000
Capital: Niamey
Currency: 100 centimes = 1 CFA franc (CFAF)
Official Language: French
Other Languages: Hausa, Djerma
Main Religions: Islam 80%, indigenous religions 14%, Christianity 1%
Exports: Uranium ore, livestock, cowpeas, onions

Chad

Pronunciation: chad
Area: 495,752 sq. miles (1,283,998 sq. km)
Population: 5,587,000
Capital: N'Djamena
Currency: 100 centimes = 1 CFA franc (CFAF)
Official Languages: French, Arabic
Other Languages: Sara, Sango
Main Religions: Islam 50%, Christianity 25%, indigenous religions and animism 25%
Exports: Cotton, cattle, textiles, fish

Sudan

Pronunciation: soo-**dan**
Area: 967,500 sq. miles (2,505,825 sq. km)
Population: 30,120,000
Capital: Khartoum
Currency: 100 piastres = 1 Sudanese pound (£S)
Official Language: Arabic
Other Languages: Nubian, Ta Bedawie, Nilotic, Nilo-Hamitic, regional languages, English
Main Religions: Islam 70%, indigenous religions 25%, Christianity 5%
Exports: Gum, livestock, cotton, sesame, peanuts

Eritrea

Pronunciation: ehr-uh-**tree**-uh
Area: 45,405 sq. miles (117,599 sq. km)
Population: 3,579,000
Capital: Asmara
Currency: 100 cents = 1 birr (Br)
Official Languages: Arabic, Tigrinya, Tigre
Other Languages: African languages
Main Religions: Islam 50%, Christianity 50%
Exports: Salt, animal skins, oilseed

Ethiopia

Pronunciation: ee-thee-OH-pee-uh
Area: 471,775 sq. miles (1,221,897 sq. km)
Population: 55,979,000
Capital: Addis Ababa
Currency: 100 cents = 1 birr (Br)
Official Language: Amharic
Other Languages: African languages, Arabic, English
Main Religions: Islam 50%, Christianity 40%, animism 10%
Exports: Coffee, leather products, gold

Djibouti

Pronunciation: ji-BOO-tee
Area: 8,880 sq. miles (22,999 sq. km)
Population: 421,300
Capital: Djibouti
Currency: 100 centimes = 1 Djiboutian franc (DF)
Official Languages: French, Arabic
Other Languages: Somali, Afar
Main Religions: Islam 94%, Christianity 6%
Exports: Animal skins, coffee

Somalia

Pronunciation: soh-MAH-lee-uh
Area: 246,154 sq. miles (637,539 sq. km)
Population: 7,348,000
Capital: Mogadishu
Currency: 100 cents = 1 Somali shilling (So.Sh.)
Official Language: Somali
Other Languages: Arabic, Italian, English
Main Religion: Islam 99%
Exports: Bananas, livestock, fish, animal skins

Senegal

Pronunciation: sen-i-GAWL
Area: 76,124 sq. miles (197,161 sq. km)
Population: 9,007,000
Capital: Dakar
Currency: 100 centimes = 1 CFA franc (CFAF)
Official Language: French
Other Languages: Regional languages
Main Religions: Islam 92%, indigenous religions 6%, Christianity 2%
Exports: Fish, peanuts, petroleum products, phosphates, cotton

Gambia

Pronunciation: GAM-bee-uh
Area: 4,003 sq. miles (10,368 sq. km)
Population: 989,300
Capital: Banjul
Currency: 100 bututs = 1 dalasi (D)
Official Language: English
Other Languages: African languages
Main Religions: Islam 90%, Christianity 9%, indigenous religions 1%
Exports: Peanuts, fish, palm kernels

Guinea-Bissau

Pronunciation: gi-nee-bi-SOW
Area: 13,948 sq. miles (36,125 sq. km)
Population: 1,125,000
Capital: Bissau
Currency: 100 centavos = 1 Guinea-Bissauan peso (PG)
Official Language: Portuguese
Other Languages: Criolo, African languages
Main Religions: Indigenous religions 65%, Islam 30%, Christianity 5%
Exports: Cashews, fish, peanuts, palm kernels

Guinea

Pronunciation: GI-nee
Area: 94,925 sq. miles (245,856 sq. km)
Population: 6,549,000
Capital: Conakry
Currency: 100 centimes = 1 Guinean franc (FG)
Official Language: French
Other Languages: Tribal languages
Main Religions: Islam 85%, Christianity 8%, indigenous religions 7%
Exports: Bauxite, alumina, diamonds, gold, coffee, pineapples, bananas, palm kernels

Sierra Leone

Pronunciation: see-EHR-uh lee-OHN
Area: 27,699 sq. miles (71,740 sq. km)
Population: 4,753,000
Capital: Freetown
Currency: 100 cents = 1 leone (Le)
Official Language: English
Other Languages: Mende, Temne, Krio
Main Religions: Islam 60%, indigenous religions 30%, Christianity 10%
Exports: Diamonds and other minerals, coffee, cocoa, fish

Liberia

Pronunciation: leye-BIHR-ee-uh
Area: 43,000 sq. miles (111,370 sq. km)
Population: 3,073,000
Capital: Monrovia
Currency: 100 cents = 1 Liberian dollar (L$)
Official Language: English
Other Languages: Niger-Congo languages
Main Religions: Indigenous religions 70%, Islam 20%, Christianity 10%
Exports: Iron ore, rubber, timber, coffee

Côte d'Ivoire (Ivory Coast)

Pronunciation: koht dee-VWAR
Area: 124,503 sq. miles (322,463 sq. km)
Population: 14,791,000
Capitals: Abidjan (seat of government), Yamoussoukro (official)
Currency: 100 centimes = 1 CFA franc (CFAF)
Official Language: French
Other Languages: Regional languages
Main Religions: Islam 60%, indigenous religions 25%, Christianity 12%
Exports: Cocoa, coffee, timber, petroleum, cotton, bananas, pineapples, palm oil

Ghana

Pronunciation: GAH-nuh
Area: 92,100 sq. miles (238,539 sq. km)
Population: 17,763,000
Capital: Accra
Currency: 100 pesewas = 1 cedi (₵)
Official Language: English
Other Languages: African languages
Main Religions: Indigenous religions 38%, Islam 30%, Christianity 24%
Exports: Cocoa, gold, timber, tuna, bauxite, aluminum

Togo

Pronunciation: TOH-goh
Area: 21,853 sq. miles (56,599 sq. km)
Population: 4,410,000
Capital: Lomé
Currency: 100 centimes = 1 CFA franc (CFAF)
Official Language: French
Other Languages: Regional languages
Main Religions: Indigenous religions 70%, Christianity 20%, Islam 10%
Exports: Phosphates, cotton, cocoa, coffee

Benin

Pronunciation: buh-NEEN
Area: 43,483 sq. miles (112,621 sq. km)
Population: 5,523,000
Capitals: Cotonou (de facto), Porto-Novo (legal)
Currency: 100 centimes = 1 CFA franc (CFAF)
Official Language: French
Other Languages: Fon, Yoruba, regional languages
Main Religions: Indigenous religions 70%, Islam 15%, Christianity 15%
Exports: Cotton, crude oil, palm products, cocoa

Nigeria

Pronunciation: neye-JIHR-ee-uh
Area: 356,669 sq. miles (923,773 sq. km)
Population: 101,232,000
Capital: Abuja
Currency: 100 kobo = 1 naira (₦)
Official Language: English
Other Languages: Regional languages
Main Religions: Islam 50%, Christianity 40%, indigenous religions 10%
Exports: Oil, cocoa, rubber

Cameroon

Pronunciation: ka-muh-ROON
Area: 183,591 sq. miles (475,501 sq. km)
Population: 13,521,000
Capital: Yaoundé
Currency: 100 centimes = 1 CFA franc (CFAF)
Official Languages: English, French
Other Languages: African languages
Main Religions: Indigenous religions 51%, Christianity 33%, Islam 16%
Exports: Petroleum products, timber, cocoa beans, aluminum, coffee, cotton

Equatorial Guinea

Pronunciation: e-kwuh-TOR-ee-uhl GI-nee
Area: 10,825 sq. miles (28,037 sq. km)
Population: 420,300
Capital: Malabo
Currency: 100 centimes = 1 CFA franc (CFAF)
Official Language: Spanish
Other Languages: Pidgin English, regional languages
Main Religion: Christianity 85%
Exports: Coffee, timber, cocoa

Central African Republic

Pronunciation: SEN-truhl AF-ri-kuhn ri-PUH-blik
Area: 240,376 sq. miles (622,374 sq. km)
Population: 3,210,000
Capital: Bangui
Currency: 100 centimes = 1 CFA franc (CFAF)
Official Language: French
Other Languages: Sangho, Arabic, Hunsa, Swahili
Main Religions: Christianity 50%, indigenous religions 24%, Islam 15%
Exports: Diamonds, timber, cotton, coffee, tobacco

São Tomé and Príncipe

Pronunciation: sow tuh-MAY and PRIN-suh-pee
Area: 372 sq. miles (963 sq. km)
Population: 140,400
Capital: São Tomé
Currency: 100 centimos = 1 dobra (Db)
Official Language: Portuguese
Main Religion: Christianity 100%
Exports: Cocoa, copra, coffee, palm oil

Gabon

Pronunciation: ga-BOHN
Area: 102,317 sq. miles (265,001 sq. km)
Population: 1,156,000
Capital: Libreville
Currency: 100 centimes = 1 CFA franc (CFAF)
Official Language: French
Other Languages: African languages
Main Religions: Christianity 60%, animism 40%, Islam 1%
Exports: Crude oil, timber, manganese, uranium

Congo

Pronunciation: KAHN-goh
Area: 132,047 sq. miles (342,002 sq. km)
Population: 2,505,000
Capital: Brazzaville
Currency: 100 centimes = 1 CFA franc (CFAF)
Official Language: French
Other Languages: African languages
Main Religions: Christianity 50%, animism 48%, Islam 2%
Exports: Crude oil, timber, sugar, cocoa, coffee, diamonds

Democratic Republic of the Congo (Zaire)

Pronunciation: de-muh-KRA-tik ri-PUH-blik of the KAHN-goh
Area: 905,356 sq. miles (2,344,872 sq. km)
Population: 44,061,000
Capital: Kinshasa
Currency: 100 makuta = 1 new zaire (NZ)
Official Language: French
Other Languages: Lingala, Swahili, Kingwana, Kikongo, Tshiluba
Main Religions: Christianity 70%, Kimbanguism 10%, Islam 10%
Exports: Copper, coffee, diamonds, crude oil

Uganda

Pronunciation: yoo-GAN-duh
Area: 91,134 sq. miles (236,037 sq. km)
Population: 19,573,000
Capital: Kampala
Currency: 100 cents = 1 Ugandan shilling (USh)
Official Language: English
Other Languages: Luganda, Swahili, Bantu and other regional languages
Main Religions: Christianity 66%, indigenous religions 18%, Islam 16%
Exports: Coffee, cotton, tea

Kenya

Pronunciation: KEN-yuh
Area: 224,960 sq. miles (582,646 sq. km)
Population: 28,817,000
Capital: Nairobi
Currency: 100 cents = 1 Kenyan shilling (KSh)
Official Languages: English, Swahili
Other Languages: Indigenous languages
Main Religions: Christianity 66%, indigenous religions 26%
Exports: Tea, coffee, petroleum products

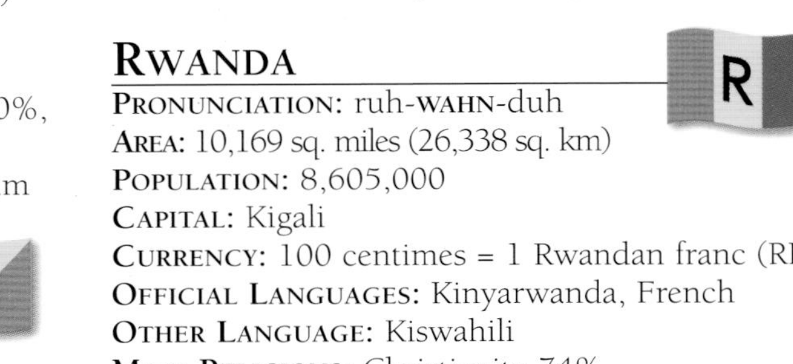

Rwanda

Pronunciation: ruh-WAHN-duh
Area: 10,169 sq. miles (26,338 sq. km)
Population: 8,605,000
Capital: Kigali
Currency: 100 centimes = 1 Rwandan franc (RF)
Official Languages: Kinyarwanda, French
Other Language: Kiswahili
Main Religions: Christianity 74%, indigenous religions 25%, Islam 1%
Exports: Coffee, tea, minerals

Burundi

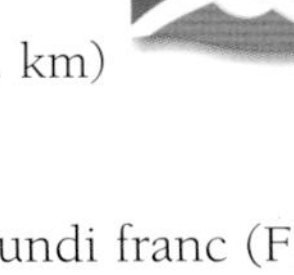

Pronunciation: boo-RUN-dee
Area: 10,759 sq. miles (27,866 sq. km)
Population: 6,262,000
Capital: Bujumbura
Currency: 100 centimes = 1 Burundi franc (FBu)
Official Languages: Kirundi, French
Other Language: Swahili
Main Religions: Christianity 67%, indigenous religions 32%, Islam 1%
Exports: Coffee, tea, cotton, animal skins

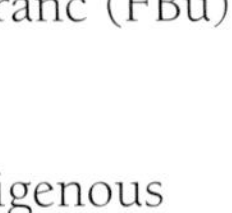

Tanzania

Pronunciation: tan-zuh-NEE-uh
Area: 364,900 sq. miles (945,091 sq. km)
Population: 28,701,000
Capitals: Dar es Salaam (seat of government), Dodoma (official)

Currency: 100 cents = 1 Tanzanian shilling (TSh)
Official Languages: Swahili, English
Main Religions: Christianity 45%, Islam 35%, indigenous religions 20%
Exports: Coffee, cotton, tobacco, tea, cashew nuts, sisal (fiber)

Angola

Pronunciation: ang-GOH-luh
Area: 481,351 sq. miles (1,246,699 sq. km)
Population: 10,070,000
Capital: Luanda
Currency: 100 lwei = 1 kwanza (Kz)
Official Language: Portuguese
Other Languages: Bantu and other African languages
Main Religions: Christianity 53%, indigenous religions 47%
Exports: Oil, diamonds, refined petroleum products, gas, coffee, sisal (fiber), fish and fish products, timber, cotton

Zambia

Pronunciation: ZAM-bee-uh
Area: 290,585 sq. miles (752,615 sq. km)
Population: 9,446,000
Capital: Lusaka
Currency: 100 ngwee = 1 Zambian kwacha (ZK)
Official Language: English
Other Languages: Regional languages
Main Religions: Christianity 75%, indigenous religions 23%, Islam and Hinduism 1%
Exports: Copper, zinc, cobalt, lead, tobacco

Zimbabwe

Pronunciation: zim-BAH-bway
Area: 150,820 sq. miles (390,624 sq. km)
Population: 11,140,000
Capital: Harare
Currency: 100 cents = 1 Zimbabwean dollar (Z$)
Official Language: English
Other Languages: Regional languages
Main Religions: Syncretic (part Christianity, part indigenous religions) 50%, Christianity 25%, indigenous religions 24%
Exports: Tobacco, manufactured goods, gold, textiles

Malawi

Pronunciation: muh-LAH-wee
Area: 45,747 sq. miles (118,485 sq. km)
Population: 9,808,000
Capital: Lilongwe
Currency: 100 tambala = 1 Malawian kwacha (MK)
Official Languages: English, Chichewa
Other Languages: Regional languages
Main Religions: Christianity 75%, Islam 20%, indigenous religions 5%
Exports: Tobacco, tea, sugar, coffee, peanuts, timber products

Mozambique

Pronunciation: moh-zahm-BEEK
Area: 297,846 sq. miles (771,421 sq. km)
Population: 18,115,000
Capital: Maputo
Currency: 100 centavos = 1 metical (Mt)
Official Language: Portuguese
Other Languages: Regional languages
Main Religions: Indigenous religions 60%, Christianity 30%, Islam 10%
Exports: Shrimp, cashews, cotton, sugar, copra, citrus fruit

Namibia

Pronunciation: nuh-MI-bee-uh
Area: 318,321 sq. miles (824,451 sq. km)
Population: 1,652,000
Capital: Windhoek
Currency: 100 cents = 1 South African rand (R)
Official Language: English
Other Languages: Afrikaans, German, regional languages
Main Religion: Christianity 90%
Exports: Diamonds, copper, gold, zinc, lead, uranium, cattle, processed fish

Botswana

Pronunciation: bawt-SWAH-nuh
Area: 219,916 sq. miles (569,582 sq. km)
Population: 1,392,000
Capital: Gaborone
Currency: 100 thebe = 1 pula (P)
Official Language: English
Other Language: Setswana
Main Religions: Indigenous religions 50%, Christianity 50%
Exports: Diamonds, copper and nickel, meat

South Africa

Pronunciation: sowth AF-ri-kuh
Area: 471,445 sq. miles (1,221,043 sq. km)
Population: 45,095,000
Capitals: Bloemfontein (judicial), Cape Town (legislative), Pretoria (administrative)
Currency: 100 cents = 1 rand (R)
Official Languages: Afrikaans, English, Xhosa, Zulu and other regional languages
Main Religions: Christianity 67%, Hinduism, Islam
Exports: Gold, diamonds and other minerals and metals, food, chemicals

Swaziland

Pronunciation: SWAH-zee-land
Area: 6,705 sq. miles (17,366 sq. km)
Population: 967,000
Capital: Mbabane
Currency: 100 cents = 1 lilangeni (E)
Official Languages: English, Swazi
Main Religions: Christianity 60%, indigenous religions 40%
Exports: Sugar, wood pulp, cotton, asbestos

Lesotho

Pronunciation: luh-SOH-toh
Area: 11,716 sq. miles (30,344 sq. km)
Population: 1,993,000
Capital: Maseru
Currency: 100 licente = 1 loti (L)
Official Languages: English, Sesotho
Other Languages: Zulu, Xhosa
Main Religions: Christianity 80%, indigenous religions 20%
Exports: Wool, mohair, wheat, cattle, peas, beans, corn, animal skins, baskets

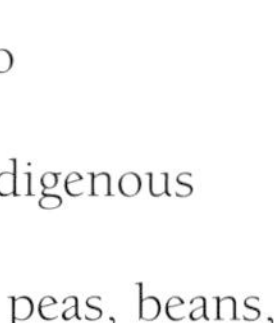

Comoros

Pronunciation: KAH-muh-rohz
Area: 719 sq. miles (1,862 sq. km)
Population: 549,300
Capital: Moroni
Currency: 100 centimes = 1 Comoran franc (CF)
Official Languages: Arabic, French
Other Language: Comoran
Main Religions: Islam 86%, Christianity 14%
Exports: Vanilla, cloves, perfume oil, copra

Madagascar

Pronunciation: ma-duh-GAS-kuhr
Area: 226,657 sq. miles (587,042 sq. km)
Population: 13,862,000
Capital: Antananarivo
Currency: 100 centimes = 1 Malagasy franc (FMG)
Official Languages: French, Malagasy
Main Religions: Indigenous religions 52%, Christianity 41%, Islam 7%
Exports: Coffee, vanilla, cloves, shellfish, sugar, petroleum products

Seychelles

Pronunciation: say-SHELZ
Area: 107 sq. miles (277 sq. km)
Population: 72,700
Capital: Victoria
Currency: 100 cents = 1 Seychelles rupee (SR)
Official Languages: English, French
Other Language: Seychelles creole
Main Religion: Christianity 98%
Exports: Fish, cinnamon, copra, petroleum products

Mauritius

Pronunciation: maw-RI-shuhs
Area: 720 sq. miles (1,865 sq. km)
Population: 1,127,000
Capital: Port Louis
Currency: 100 cents = 1 Mauritian rupee (MauR)
Official Language: English
Other Languages: Mauritian creole, French, Hindi, Urdu, Hakka, Bojpoori
Main Religions: Hinduism 52%, Christianity 26%, Islam 17%
Exports: Textiles, sugar, light manufactured goods

AUSTRALIA AND OCEANIA

AUSTRALIA

PRONUNCIATION: aw-STRAYL-yuh
AREA: 2,967,909 sq. miles (7,686,884 sq. km)
POPULATION: 18,322,000
CAPITAL: Canberra
CURRENCY: 100 cents = 1 Australian dollar ($A)
OFFICIAL LANGUAGE: English
OTHER LANGUAGES: Aboriginal languages
MAIN RELIGION: Christianity 76%
EXPORTS: Coal, gold, meat, wool, wheat, machinery and transportation equipment

PAPUA NEW GUINEA

PRONUNCIATION: PA-pyoo-uh noo GI-nee
AREA: 178,260 sq. miles (461,693 sq. km)
POPULATION: 4,295,000
CAPITAL: Port Moresby
CURRENCY: 100 toea = 1 kina (K)
OFFICIAL LANGUAGES: English, pidgin English, Motu
OTHER LANGUAGES: Regional languages
MAIN RELIGIONS: Christianity 66%, indigenous religions 34%
EXPORTS: Gold, copper ore, oil, lumber, palm oil, coffee, cocoa, lobster

NEW ZEALAND

PRONUNCIATION: noo ZEE-luhnd
AREA: 103,736 sq. miles (268,676 sq. km)
POPULATION: 3,407,000
CAPITAL: Wellington
CURRENCY: 100 cents = 1 New Zealand dollar (NZ$)
OFFICIAL LANGUAGE: English
OTHER LANGUAGE: Maori
MAIN RELIGION: Christianity 67%
EXPORTS: Wool, lamb, mutton, beef, fish, cheese, chemicals, forestry products, fruit and vegetables, manufactured goods

SOLOMON ISLANDS

PRONUNCIATION: SAH-luh-muhn islands
AREA: 11,500 sq. miles (29,785 sq. km)
POPULATION: 399,200
CAPITAL: Honiara
CURRENCY: 100 cents = 1 Solomon Islands dollar (SI$)
OFFICIAL LANGUAGE: English
OTHER LANGUAGE: Melanesian pidgin
MAIN RELIGIONS: Christianity 96%, indigenous religions 4%
EXPORTS: Fish, timber, palm oil, cocoa, copra

WESTERN SAMOA

PRONUNCIATION: WEST-ern suh-MOH-uh
AREA: 1,100 sq. miles (2,850 sq. km)
POPULATION: 209,400
CAPITAL: Apia
CURRENCY: 100 sene = 1 tala (WS$)
OFFICIAL LANGUAGES: Samoan (Polynesian), English
MAIN RELIGION: Christianity 99%
EXPORTS: Coconut oil and cream, taro, copra, cocoa

VANUATU

PRONUNCIATION: van-wah-TOO
AREA: 5,700 sq. miles (14,763 sq. km)
POPULATION: 173,600
CAPITAL: Port Vila
CURRENCY: 100 centimes = 1 vatu (VT)
OFFICIAL LANGUAGES: English, French
OTHER LANGUAGE: Bislama
MAIN RELIGIONS: Christianity 77%, indigenous religions 8%
EXPORTS: Copra, beef, cocoa, timber, coffee

FIJI

PRONUNCIATION: FEE-jee
AREA: 7,055 sq. miles (18,272 sq. km)
POPULATION: 772,900
CAPITAL: Suva
CURRENCY: 100 cents = 1 Fijian dollar (F$)
OFFICIAL LANGUAGE: English
OTHER LANGUAGES: Fijian, Hindustani
MAIN RELIGIONS: Christianity 52%, Hinduism 38%, Islam 8%
EXPORTS: Sugar, clothing, gold, processed fish, timber

TONGA

PRONUNCIATION: TAHNG-guh
AREA: 270 sq. miles (699 sq. km)
POPULATION: 105,600
CAPITAL: Nuku'alofa
CURRENCY: 100 seniti = 1 pa'anga (T$)
OFFICIAL LANGUAGES: Tongan, English
MAIN RELIGION: Christianity 70%
EXPORTS: Squash, vanilla, fish, root crops, coconut oil

KIRIBATI

PRONUNCIATION: kihr-uh-BAH-tee
AREA: 277 sq. miles (717 sq. km)
POPULATION: 79,400
CAPITAL: Tarawa
CURRENCY: 100 cents = 1 Australian dollar ($A)
OFFICIAL LANGUAGE: English
OTHER LANGUAGE: Gilbertese
MAIN RELIGION: Christianity 94%
EXPORTS: Copra, seaweed, fish

MARSHALL ISLANDS

PRONUNCIATION: MAR-shuhl islands
AREA: 70 sq. miles (181 sq. km)
POPULATION: 56,200
CAPITAL: Majuro
CURRENCY: 100 cents = 1 United States dollar (US$)
OFFICIAL LANGUAGE: English
OTHER LANGUAGES: Marshallese, Japanese
MAIN RELIGION: Christianity 98%
EXPORTS: Coconut oil, fish, livestock, coffee

FEDERATED STATES OF MICRONESIA

PRONUNCIATION: FE-der-ayt-ed STAYTS of meye-kruh-NEE-zhuh
AREA: 266 sq. miles (689 sq. km)
POPULATION: 123,000
CAPITAL: Palikir
CURRENCY: 100 cents = 1 United States dollar (US$)
OFFICIAL LANGUAGE: English
OTHER LANGUAGES: Regional languages
MAIN RELIGION: Christianity 97%
EXPORTS: Fish, copra, bananas, black pepper

NAURU

PRONUNCIATION: nah-OO-roo
AREA: 8.5 sq. miles (22 sq. km)
POPULATION: 10,150
CAPITAL: None. Government offices in Yaren district
CURRENCY: 100 cents = 1 Australian dollar ($A)
OFFICIAL LANGUAGE: Nauruan
OTHER LANGUAGE: English
MAIN RELIGION: Christianity 100%
EXPORT: Phosphates

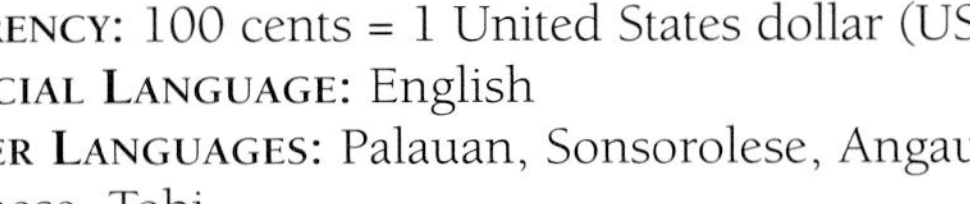

PALAU

PRONUNCIATION: puh-LOW
AREA: 191 sq. miles (495 sq. km)
POPULATION: 16,700
CAPITAL: Koror
CURRENCY: 100 cents = 1 United States dollar (US$)
OFFICIAL LANGUAGE: English
OTHER LANGUAGES: Palauan, Sonsorolese, Angaur, Japanese, Tobi
MAIN RELIGIONS: Christianity 67%, Modekngei religion 33%
EXPORTS: Shellfish, tuna, copra, handicrafts

TUVALU

PRONUNCIATION: too-VAH-loo
AREA: 9 sq. miles (23 sq. km)
POPULATION: 10,000
CAPITAL: Funafuti Island
CURRENCY: 100 cents = 1 Tuvaluan dollar ($T) or 1 Australian dollar ($A)
OFFICIAL LANGUAGES: Tuvaluan, English
MAIN RELIGION: Christianity 97%
EXPORTS: Copra

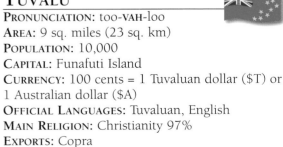

Territories and Dependencies

The countries listed below govern land outside their national borders. These areas of land are known as territories or dependencies. Some territories are governed directly by the country to which they belong. Others receive only protection and financial assistance, and have their own governments and laws.

United States of America

American Samoa: South Pacific Ocean; 76 sq. miles (197 sq. km); population 57,400
Guam: Western Pacific Ocean; 209 sq. miles (541 sq. km); population 153,400
Midway: Central Pacific Ocean; 2 sq. miles (5 sq. km); no permanent population
Northern Mariana Islands: North Pacific Ocean; 184 sq. miles (477 sq. km); population 51,000
Puerto Rico: Caribbean Sea; 70 sq. miles (113 sq. km); population 3,813,000
Virgin Islands of the United States: Caribbean Sea; 133 sq. miles (345 sq. km); population 97,250
Wake Island: North Pacific Ocean; 3 sq. miles (7.7 sq. km); population 300

United Kingdom

Anguilla: Caribbean Sea; 35 sq. miles (91 sq. km); population 7,100
Bermuda: North Atlantic Ocean; 20 sq. miles (52 sq. km); population 61,700
British Indian Ocean Territory: Indian Ocean; 23 sq. miles (60 sq. km); no permanent population
British Virgin Islands: Caribbean Sea; 59 sq. miles (153 sq. km); population 13,000
Cayman Islands: Caribbean Sea; 118 sq. miles (306 sq. km); population 33,200
Falkland Islands and Dependencies (South Georgia and South Sandwich Islands): South Atlantic Ocean; 6,270 sq. miles (16,240 sq. km); population 2,350
Gibraltar: Southern Spain; 2.25 sq. miles (6 sq. km); population 31,900
Guernsey: English Channel; 30 sq. miles (78 sq. km); population 64,400
Isle of Man: Irish Sea; 221 sq. miles (572 sq. km); population 72,800
Jersey: English Channel; 45 sq. miles (116 sq. km); population 86,700
Montserrat: Caribbean Sea; 40 sq. miles (104 sq. km); population 12,700
Pitcairn Islands: South Pacific Ocean; 18 sq. miles (47 sq. km); population 60
St. Helena and Dependencies (Ascension Island and Tristan da Cunha): South Atlantic Ocean; 119 sq. miles (308 sq. km); population 6,770
Turks and Caicos Islands: Caribbean Sea; 166 sq. miles (430 sq. km); population 13,900

Portugal

Macao: South coast of China; 6 sq. miles (16 sq. km); population 490,900

France

French Guiana: Northern South America; 35,126 sq. miles (90,976 sq. km); population 145,300
French Polynesia: South Pacific Ocean; 1,261 sq. miles (3,266 sq. km); population 220,000
Guadeloupe: Caribbean Sea; 582 sq. miles (1,507 sq. km); population 408,800
Martinique: Caribbean Sea; 425 sq. miles (1,101 sq. km); population 394,800
Mayotte: Mozambique Channel, Africa; 144 sq. miles (373 sq. km); population 97,100
New Caledonia: South Pacific Ocean; 7,367 sq. miles (19,081 sq. km); population 184,600
Réunion: Indian Ocean; 969 sq. miles (2,510 sq. km); population 666,000
St-Pierre and Miquelon: North Atlantic Ocean; 93 sq. miles (241 sq. km); population 6,760
Wallis and Futuna Islands: South Pacific Ocean; 106 sq. miles (275 sq. km); population 14,500

The Netherlands

Aruba: Caribbean Sea; 69 sq. miles (179 sq. km); population 66,000
Netherlands Antilles: Caribbean Sea; 371 sq. miles (961 sq. km); population 203,500

Norway

Jan Mayen Island: North Atlantic Ocean; 144 sq. miles (373 sq. km); no permanent population
Svalbard: Arctic Ocean; 23,958 sq. miles (62,052 sq. km); population 2,910

Denmark

Faeroe Islands: North Atlantic Ocean; 540 sq. miles (1,399 sq. km); population 48,500
Greenland: North Atlantic Ocean; 840,000 sq. miles (2,175,000 sq. km); population 57,700

Australia

Christmas Island: Indian Ocean; 52 sq. miles (135 sq. km); population 890
Cocos (Keeling) Islands: Indian Ocean; 9 sq. miles (23 sq. km); population 600
Heard and McDonald Islands: Indian Ocean; 113 sq. miles (293 sq. km); no permanent population
Norfolk Island: South Pacific Ocean; 13 sq. miles (34 sq. km); population 2,760

New Zealand

Cook Islands: South Pacific Ocean; 92 sq. miles (238 sq. km); population 19,300
Niue: South Pacific Ocean; 100 sq. miles (259 sq. km); population 1,840
Tokelau: South Pacific Ocean; 4 sq. miles (10 sq. km); population 1,500

Disputed Territories

Gaza Strip (Palestine): Middle East; disputed by Israel and Palestine, Palestinian interim self-government; 146 sq. miles (378 sq. km); population 813,300
Kashmir: Southern Asia; disputed by India and Pakistan; 53,665 sq. miles (138,992 sq. km); population 7,718,700
Turkish Federated State of Cyprus: Mediterranean Sea; disputed by Turkey and Cyprus; 1,322 sq. miles (3,424 sq. km); population 135,400
West Bank (Palestine): Middle East; disputed by Israel and Palestine, Palestinian interim self-government; 2,100 sq. miles (5,640 sq. km); population 1,320,000
Western Sahara: Northwestern Africa; disputed by Morocco and separatist movement; 102,703 sq. miles (266,001 sq. km); population 217,250

Glossary

acid rain ~ Rain that has combined with pollution in the atmosphere to form an acid. Acid rain can kill plants and damage buildings.
adaptation ~ A change that occurs in a plant's structure or in an animal's body or behavior to allow it to cope better with its environment.
agriculture ~ The use of the land to grow crops and raise animals. Agriculture is another word for farming.
altitude ~ The height of a place or object above sea level.
ancestor ~ A member of a person's family who lived a long time ago.
Antarctic Circle ~ A line of latitude at 66.5° south which marks the boundary of Earth's southern polar region. South of this line there is continuous daylight in midsummer and continuous darkness in midwinter.
archipelago ~ A large group of islands.
Arctic Circle ~ A line of latitude at 66.5° north that marks the boundary of Earth's northern polar region. North of this line there is continuous daylight in midsummer and continuous darkness in midwinter.
arid ~ Having low rainfall and, as a result, little vegetation. Very arid areas are called deserts.
atoll ~ A low, ring-shaped, sandy island enclosing a lagoon. An atoll is usually formed by the growth of a coral reef on top of an undersea mountain.
axis ~ An imaginary line through the center of Earth around which the planet is constantly rotating.

■

basin ~ 1. A wide, bowl-shaped depression in the landscape. 2. An area of land that is drained by a river and its tributaries.
bay ~ A body of water partly enclosed by land.
bight ~ A recess in a stretch of coastline which forms a large bay.
border ~ A line that separates one country from another.

■

canal ~ An artificial waterway, normally created by digging a large ditch to carry water to an irrigation area or to create a transportation route for shipping.
canyon ~ A deep, steep-sided valley formed by a river.
cape ~ A piece of land that juts out into a lake or sea.
capital ~ The city where a state or country's government is located. Sometimes a country has more than one capital because parts of its government are located in different cities.
cartographer ~ A person who makes maps. The science of making maps is known as cartography.
channel ~ A narrow stretch of water between two landmasses.
climate ~ The pattern of weather that occurs in a place over an extended period of time. Earth can be divided into a number of climate zones.
compass ~ 1. A device that contains a magnetic needle which indicates the direction of north. 2. An arrow or similar icon that indicates the direction of north on a map.
coniferous ~ Coniferous trees are evergreen trees that produce seeds inside cones and usually have thin, needle-shaped or scaly leaves.
continent ~ One of Earth's seven major landmasses: Europe, Asia, Africa, North America, South America, Australia and Antarctica.
coral ~ A hard, rocky material formed by the skeletons of tiny creatures called coral polyps.
crop ~ A plant that is grown in large quantities by farmers. Crops include foods such as cereals and vegetables as well as other plants such as cotton and tobacco.
crust ~ The hard, thin rocky layer that covers the surface of Earth. The crust is broken into segments called plates.
culture ~ The shared traditions and way of life of a people.
currency ~ The kind of money used in a country.

■

dam ~ A wall-like barrier built to hold back the water of a river and create an artificial lake called a reservoir.
deciduous ~ Deciduous trees shed their leaves every year, usually in fall. The tree remains bare during winter but grows new leaves in spring.
deforestation ~ The cutting down of forest trees for timber, or to clear land for farming or building.
delta ~ A fan-shaped area of land formed by silt deposited by rivers where they empty into the sea.
dependency ~ A region or landmass governed by another country.
descendants ~ The offspring of a person, including his or her children, children's children, and so on.
desert ~ A dry area with low rainfall and sparse vegetation that is adapted to withstand drought.

■

earthquake ~ A shaking of the ground caused by the sudden movement of part of Earth's crust.
ecosystem ~ A community of plants and animals and the environment to which they are adapted.
endangered ~ An animal or plant species that is in danger of becoming extinct.
environment ~ The natural surroundings of a community of plants and animals, particularly the shape of the land, the climate and the soil.
equator ~ An imaginary line that circles the globe midway between the North and South poles. The equator divides the world into the Northern and Southern hemispheres.
ethnic group ~ A group of people sharing the same origin, language, nationality and lifestyle.
evergreen ~ An evergreen tree is a tree that does not shed its leaves in winter.
evolution ~ A process of gradual change, especially in living things.
exports ~ Goods that are sold to other countries.
extinct ~ An extinct species of animal or plant is one that no longer exists because all the individual animals or plants died.

■

federation ~ A union, by mutual agreement, of states or territories to form one country.
fertile ~ Fertile land is land with good soil. Plants grow well in fertile land if there is good rainfall or irrigation.
fjord ~ A deep, steep-sided valley gouged out by a glacier and later flooded by the sea to form a narrow inlet.
forestry ~ The science of making use of and managing forest resources.
fossil ~ The remains or traces of a prehistoric plant or animal, normally found between layers of rock.
fossil fuel ~ Fuel found deep underground which formed from the decayed remains of prehistoric plants and animals. The most common fossil fuels are coal, oil and natural gas.

■

gazetteer ~ An index of place names.
geyser ~ A spring that boils and emits hot water and steam.
glacier ~ A large mass of ice that moves slowly down the side of a mountain or along a valley, and is constantly replenished by snowfall at the top of the mountain.
gorge ~ A deep, steep-sided, rocky valley.
grassland ~ A large area of land covered with grass plants.
Greenwich meridian ~ An imaginary line that extends from the North Pole to the South Pole through Greenwich, England, and that marks 0° longitude.
gulf ~ A large bay.

■

hemisphere ~ One half of the world. Earth is divided into Northern and Southern hemispheres by the equator, and into Eastern and Western hemispheres by the Greenwich meridian (0°) and 180° line.
high-tech industries ~ Industries that produce electronic goods such as computers.
hydroelectricity ~ Electricity produced using the power of running water.

■

iceberg ~ A large block of ice floating in the sea. Icebergs break off the ends of glaciers and ice sheets. The part of an iceberg under the surface of the sea is usually eight times as large as the part above the surface.
ice cap ~ A sheet of ice and snow that covers an area permanently. Ice caps are found in polar regions and on some high mountaintops.

immigrant ~ A person who has come from one country to live in another.
independent ~ Not governed by another country.
inlet ~ A narrow bay.
irrigation ~ The process of providing water to farmland by artificial means, such as pumping water from rivers, lakes and dams, or diverting water through channels and pipes.
island ~ An area of land surrounded by water.

■

kingdom ~ A country whose ruler or head of state is a king or queen.

■

lagoon ~ 1. A shallow area of salt water separated from the sea by a strip of land. 2. Inland bodies of water that were previously part of a river.
landmass ~ A large area of land not covered by water.
latitude ~ Distance north or south of the equator measured in degrees.
livestock ~ Animals, such as cattle or sheep, raised by farmers.
longitude ~ Distance east or west of the Greenwich meridian measured in degrees.

■

marsh ~ An area of wet land containing plants adapted to growth in water. Also called a swamp or wetland.
manufacturing ~ The making of useful products from raw materials.
migration ~ Movement of people or animals to another country or region. Many animals migrate to find food or avoid severe weather.
mineral ~ A substance occurring naturally in Earth's crust that is neither plant nor animal. Well-known minerals include chalk, clay and many metals.

■

native people ~ The original human inhabitants of a region or country.
nomad ~ A person who does not live in one place but continually moves around. Nomads often move in search of food and water for themselves and their animals.
North Pole ~ see pole

■

oasis ~ A patch of land in a desert where there is water and more vegetation than elsewhere.

■

peninsula ~ A long strip of land that extends outward from a larger landmass and is almost surrounded by water.
plain ~ An area of flat or rolling land with shallow river valleys.
plantation ~ A piece of land where a particular tree crop is grown. Such crops include forest trees, rubber and coconut palms.
plate ~ One of the segments of Earth's crust.
plateau ~ An area of flat or rolling land with deep river valleys, gorges and canyons.
pole ~ The points on Earth's surface representing the ends of the planet's axis, around which it is constantly rotating. The North Pole is Earth's most northern point. The South Pole is the most southern point. The regions around the poles are known as the polar regions.
population ~ 1. The people who live in a place. 2. The total number of people living in a place.
populous ~ A populous country is a country with a large population.
principality ~ A country whose ruler or head of state is a prince or princess.

■

radioactive ~ Radioactive materials emit high-energy particles in the form of invisible rays. Some natural substances, such as uranium, are radioactive.
rain forest ~ A type of dense forest that grows in regions of high rainfall.
range ~ 1. A chain of mountains. 2. An area of open grassland where animals graze.
raw materials ~ Natural substances which can be turned into useful products. Examples include timber, coal and coffee beans. Raw materials are also known as resources.
reef ~ A ridge of rock, sand or coral lying just below the surface of the sea.
republic ~ A country led by an elected representative called a president.
reservoir ~ An artificial lake, usually created by building a dam across a river.
resources ~ Substances or materials that occur naturally in a place and are of value to the area's inhabitants. Resources that can never be used up, such as water and waves, are called renewable resources. Resources that will eventually be used up, such as coal and other minerals, are known as nonrenewable resources.
river basin ~ An area of land drained by a river and its tributaries.
rural ~ Relating to the countryside. Rural industry means industry located in country areas.

■

savanna ~ A type of grassland with scattered trees. Most savannas occur in tropical areas that have a distinct summer wet season.
scale ~ An indication on a map of how distances on the map relate to actual distances.
scrub ~ An area of land covered with shrubs and low trees.
sea level ~ The average height of the surface of the sea, which is used as a base point for measuring altitude.
South Pole ~ see pole
species ~ Animals or plants of the same type.
steppe ~ A type of dry grassland that covers parts of eastern Europe and central Asia.
strait ~ A narrow strip of water that connects two larger bodies of water.
swamp ~ An area of wet land containing plants adapted to growth in water. Also called a marsh or wetland.

■

technology ~ The use of scientific knowledge to carry out certain tasks or solve certain problems. Using machines in industry is an example of technology.
temperate ~ Neither hot nor cold. Most of Earth's temperate regions are located between the tropics and the polar regions.
territory ~ 1. A large area of land. 2. All the land and sea governed by a country or state. 3. A region or landmass governed by a country that is located in another part of the world.
textiles ~ Woven or knitted fabrics.
time zone ~ A region in which everyone uses the same time. The world is divided into 24 time zones. The time in each zone is usually one hour earlier than the zone to its east.
trade ~ The buying and selling of goods.
tributary ~ A stream or river that flows into a larger stream or river.
Tropic of Cancer/Capricorn ~ see tropics
tropics ~ 1. The hot, wet regions of Earth that lie near the equator. 2. Either of two lines of latitude: the Tropic of Cancer at 23.5° north and the Tropic of Capricorn at 23.5° south. Because Earth is tilted at an angle of 23.5°, these lines mark the point at which the Sun is directly overhead in summer.
tundra ~ A cold, barren area where much of the soil is frozen and the vegetation consists of only mosses, lichens and other small plants adapted to withstanding intense cold. Tundra is found near the Arctic Circle and on mountaintops.

■

urban ~ Relating to cities. A country's urban population is the number of people that live in its cities.

■

valley ~ A long, narrow depression in the land along which a river usually flows.
vegetation ~ The community of plants that is characteristic of a particular region.
volcano ~ A mountain that has been built up from molten rock erupting through a hole in Earth's crust.

■

wetland ~ An area of wet land containing plants adapted to growth in water. Also called a swamp or marsh.
woodland ~ An area of land covered with widely spaced trees and shrubs.

Index and Gazetteer

D

E

F

G

M

N

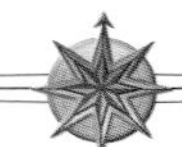

Acknowledgments

Weldon Owen would like to thank the following people for their assistance in the production of this book:
Helen Bateman, Anthony Burton, Alastair Campbell, Jo Collard, Melanie Corfield, Simon Corfield, Sharon Dalgleish, Libby Frederico, Kathy Gammon, Kathy Gerrard, Janine Googan, Greg Hassall, Lynn Humphries, Chris Jackson, Megan Johnston, Ralph Kelly, Jennifer Le Gras, Rosemary McDonald, Kylie Mulquin, Nicholas Rowland, Rachel Smith, Julie Stanton, Dawn Titmus, Greg Tobin, Wendy van Buuren, Michael Wyatt

Cartographic sources: U.S. Central Intelligence Agency; International Boundaries Research Unit, Durham University, United Kingdom; U.S. Geographer General

Photographic credits: 14 bottom left, **David Weintraub**/The Photo Library—Sydney; 14 bottom center, **Stephen Wilkes**/The Image Bank; 14 bottom right, **Mats Wibe Lund**/Icelandic Photo; 15 center far right, **David Hardy**/SPL/The Photo Library—Sydney; 15 bottom left, **Francois Gohier**/Ardea London; 15 bottom center, **B. McDairmant**/Ardea London; 15 bottom right, **International Photo Library**; 16 top far right, **Robert Harding** Picture Library; 16 bottom, **David W. Hamilton**/The Image Bank; 17 top left, **Jeffrey C. Drewitz**/The Photo Library—Sydney; 17 top center left, **Sobel/Klonsky**/The Image Bank; 17 top center, **Horizon International**; 17 top center right, **Staffan Widstrand**/Bruce Coleman Limited; 17 top right, **Christer Fredriksson**/Bruce Coleman Limited; 19 top center, **Alain Compost**/Bruce Coleman Limited; 27 top, **Horizon International**; 27 center, **Shone/Gamma/Picturemedia**; 27 bottom, **Witt/Sipa Press**/The Photo Library—Sydney

The
Polar Regions
102
Northern
Europe
72
Northern
Europe
72
The United
Kingdom and the
Republic of Ireland
56
The Low
Countries
62
Western Central Europe
64
France
60
Spain and Portugal
58
Italy
Western Canada
and Alaska
34
Eastern Canada
36
Central
United
States
42
Western
United States
44
38
Northeastern
United States
Southern
United States
40
Mexico,
Central America
and the Caribbean
46
Northern
Africa
92
Northern
South America
50
Southern
South America
52